A Kodansha Comics Trade Paperback Original
Golosseum 2 copyright © 2016 Yasushi Baba
English translation copyright © 2018 Yasushi Baba

Published in the United States by Kodansha Comics, an imprint of Kodansha USA Publishing, LLC, New York.

Publication rights for this English edition arranged through Kodansha Ltd, Tokyo.

ISBN 978-1-63236-696-2

Original cover design by Takashi Shimoyama (Red Rooster)

Printed in the United States of America.

www.kodanshacomics.com

9 8 7 6 5 4 3 2 1
Translation: Kevin Gifford
Lettering: Evan Hayden
Editing: Ajani Oloye
Kodansha Comics edition cover design by Phil Balsman

KC KODANSHA COMICS

The award-winning manga about what happens inside you!

"Far more entertaining than it ought to be... what kid doesn't want to think that every time they sneeze a torpedo shoots out their nose?"
–Anime News Network

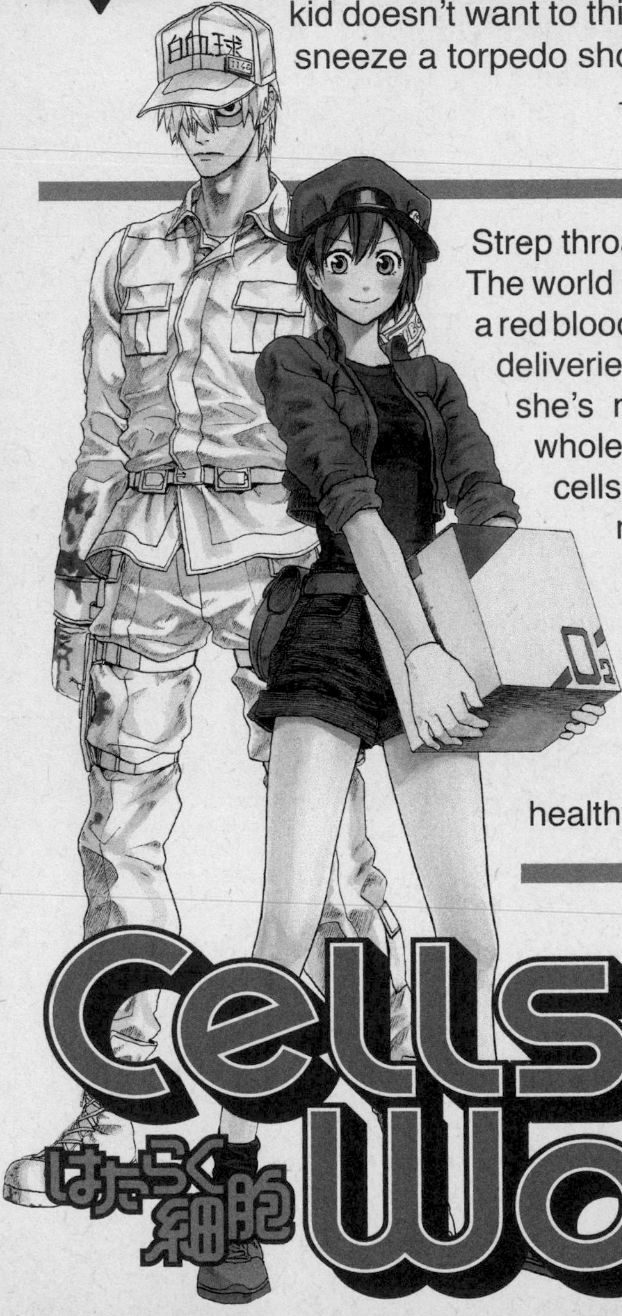

Strep throat! Hay fever! Influenza! The world is a dangerous place for a red blood cell just trying to get her deliveries finished. Fortunately, she's not alone...she's got a whole human body's worth of cells ready to help out! The mysterious white blood cells, the buff and brash killer T cells, even the cute little platelets—everyone's got to come together if they want to keep you healthy!

Cells at Work!

はたらく細胞

By Akane Shimizu

HAPPINESS

—ハピネス—

By Shuzo Oshimi

From the creator of *The Flowers of Evil*

Nothing interesting is happening in Makoto Ozaki's first year of high school. His life is a series of quiet humiliations: low-grade bullies, unreliable friends, and the constant frustration of his adolescent lust. But one night, a pale, thin girl knocks him to the ground in an alley and offers him a choice. Now everything is different. Daylight is searingly bright. Food tastes awful. And worse than anything is the terrible, consuming thirst...

Praise for Shuzo Oshimi's *The Flowers of Evil*

"A shockingly readable story that vividly—one might even say queasily—evokes the fear and confusion of discovering one's own sexuality. Recommended." —The Manga Critic

"A page-turning tale of sordid middle school blackmail." —Otaku USA Magazine

"A stunning new horror manga." —Third Eye Comics

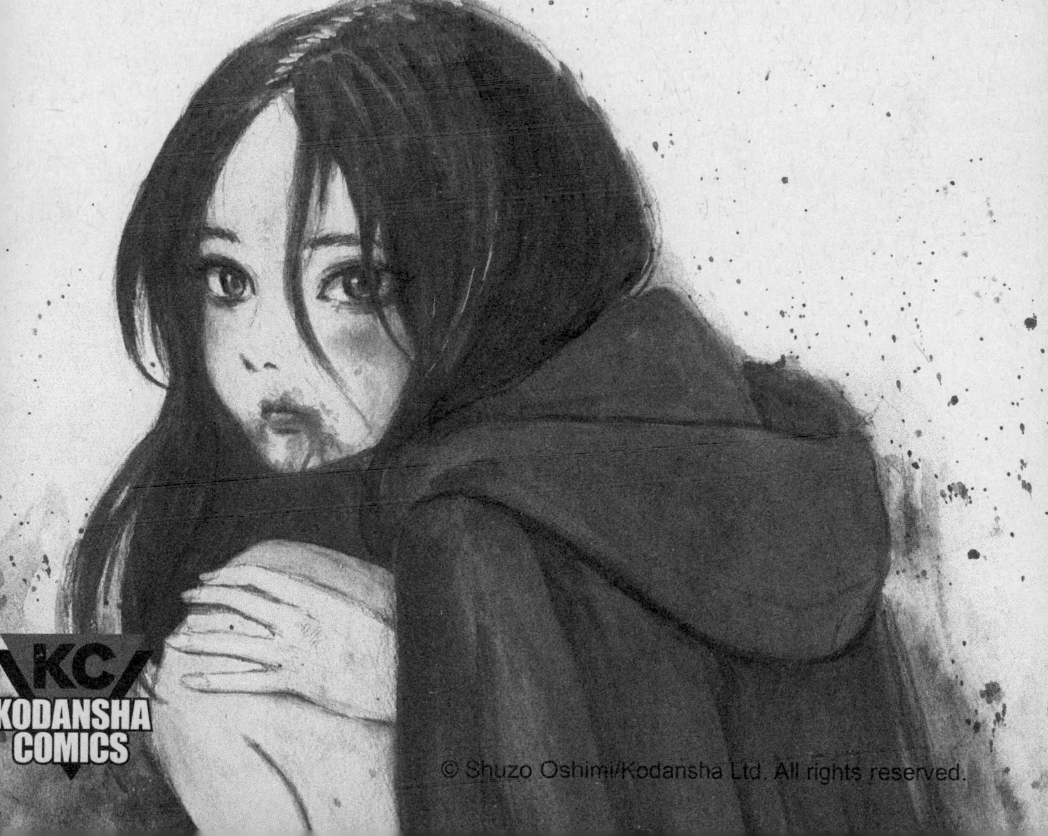

KC KODANSHA COMICS

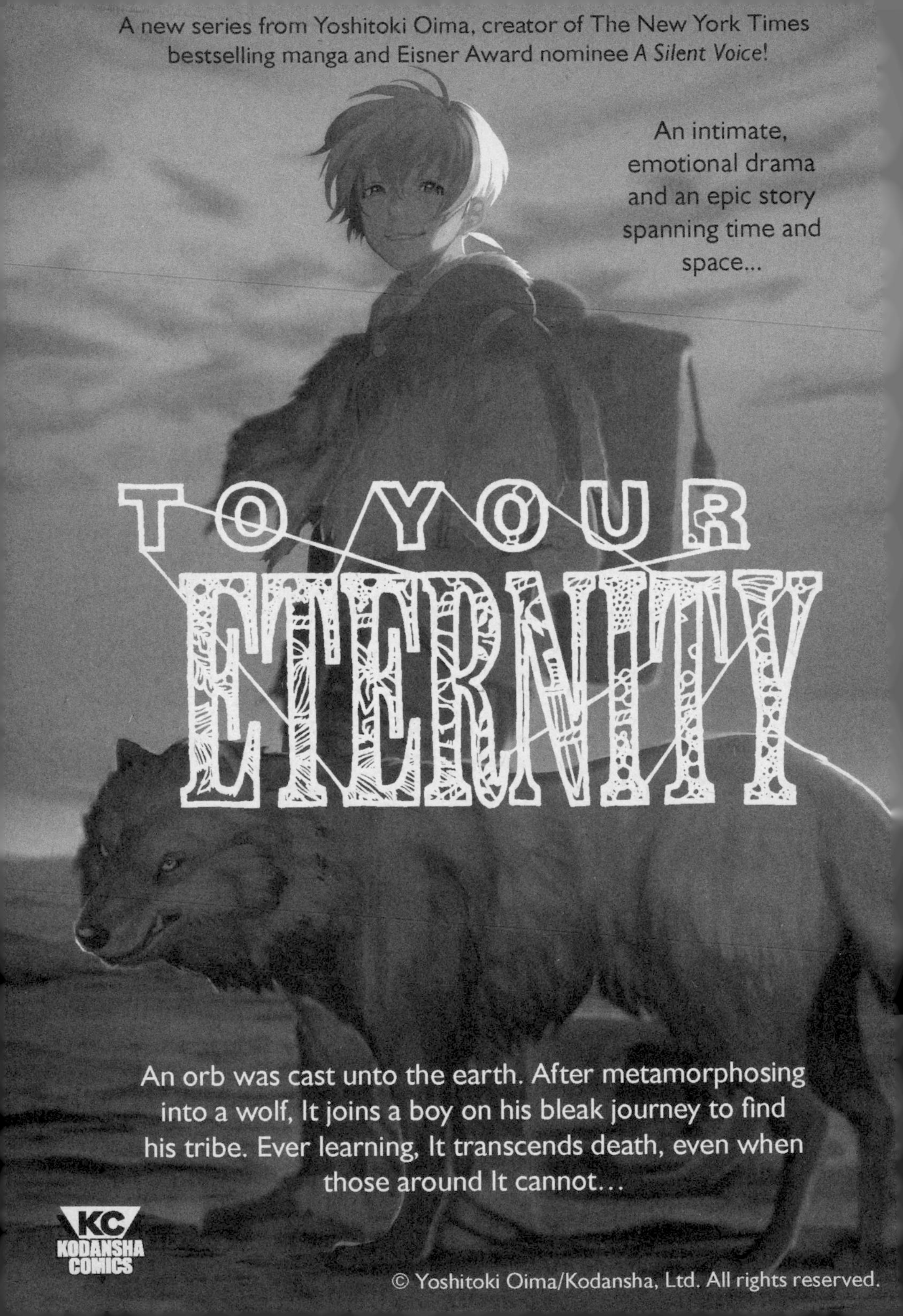
A new series from Yoshitoki Oima, creator of The New York Times bestselling manga and Eisner Award nominee A Silent Voice!
An intimate, emotional drama and an epic story spanning time and space...
TO YOUR ETERNITY
An orb was cast unto the earth. After metamorphosing into a wolf, It joins a boy on his bleak journey to find his tribe. Ever learning, It transcends death, even when those around It cannot...
KC KODANSHA COMICS
© Yoshitoki Oima/Kodansha, Ltd. All rights reserved.

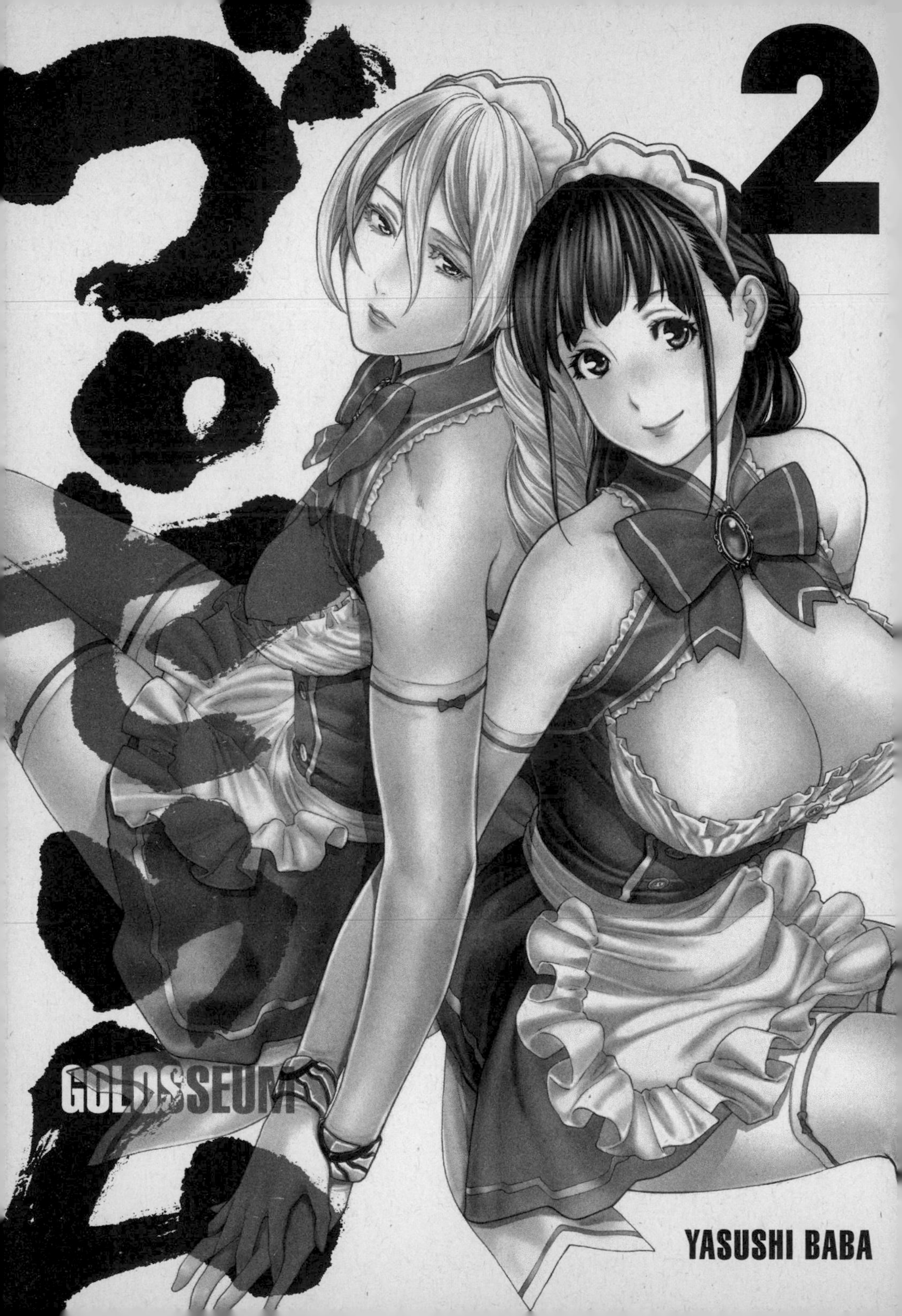
2
GOLOSSEUM
YASUSHI BABA

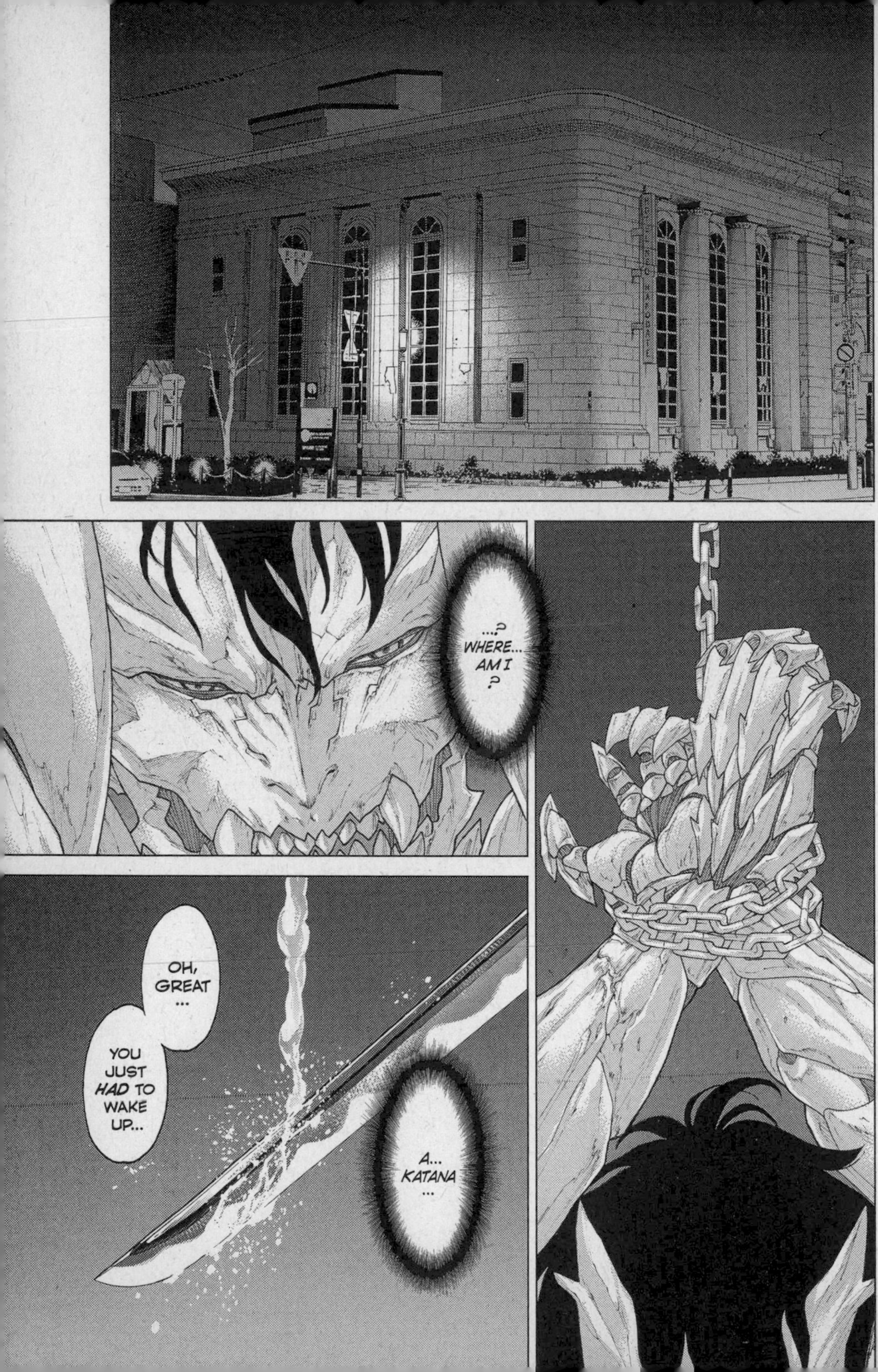
...? WHERE... AM I ?
A... KATANA ...
OH, GREAT ...
YOU JUST *HAD* TO WAKE UP...

CHAPTER 5
HAKODATE STARGATE

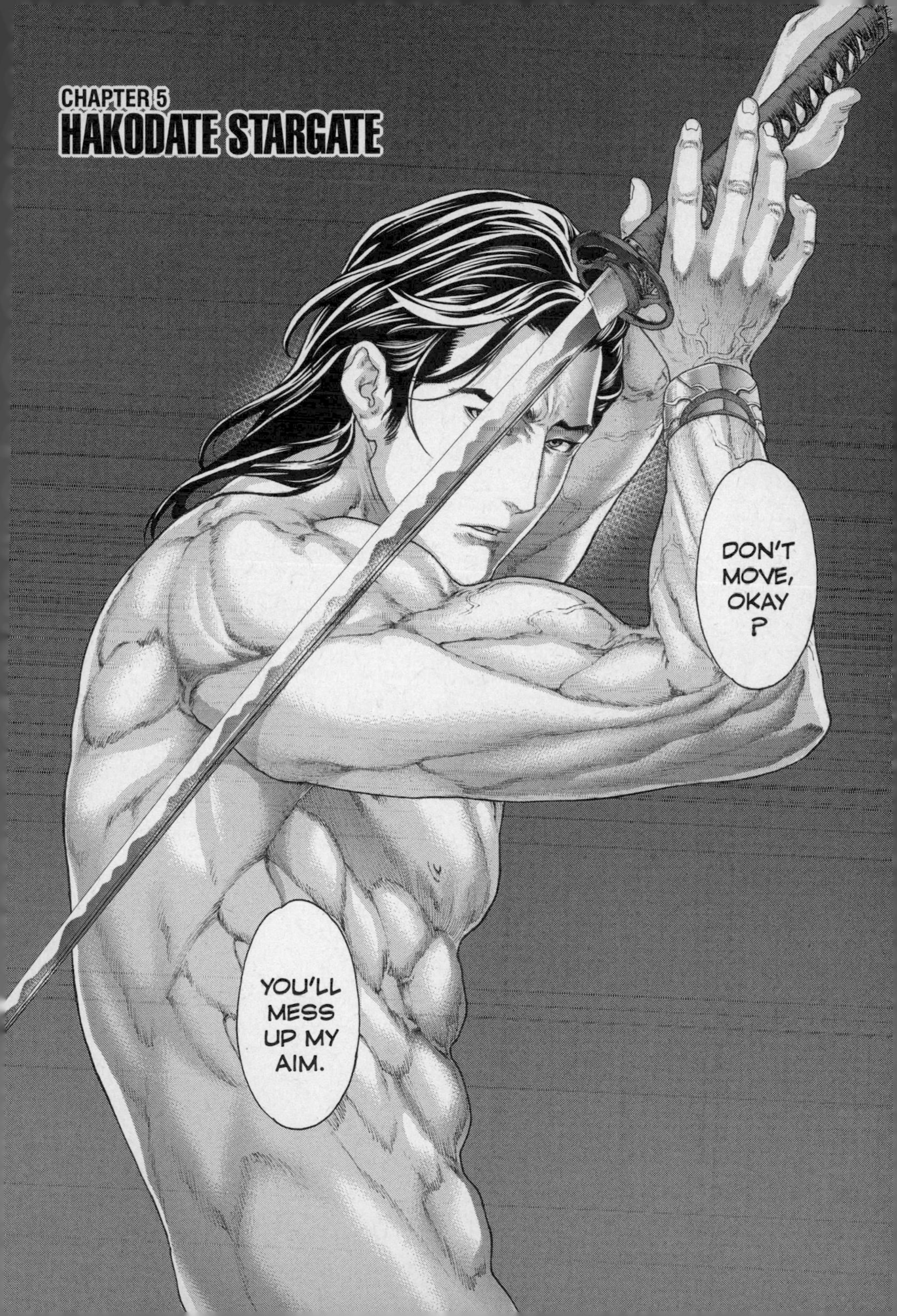
DON'T MOVE, OKAY?
YOU'LL MESS UP MY AIM.

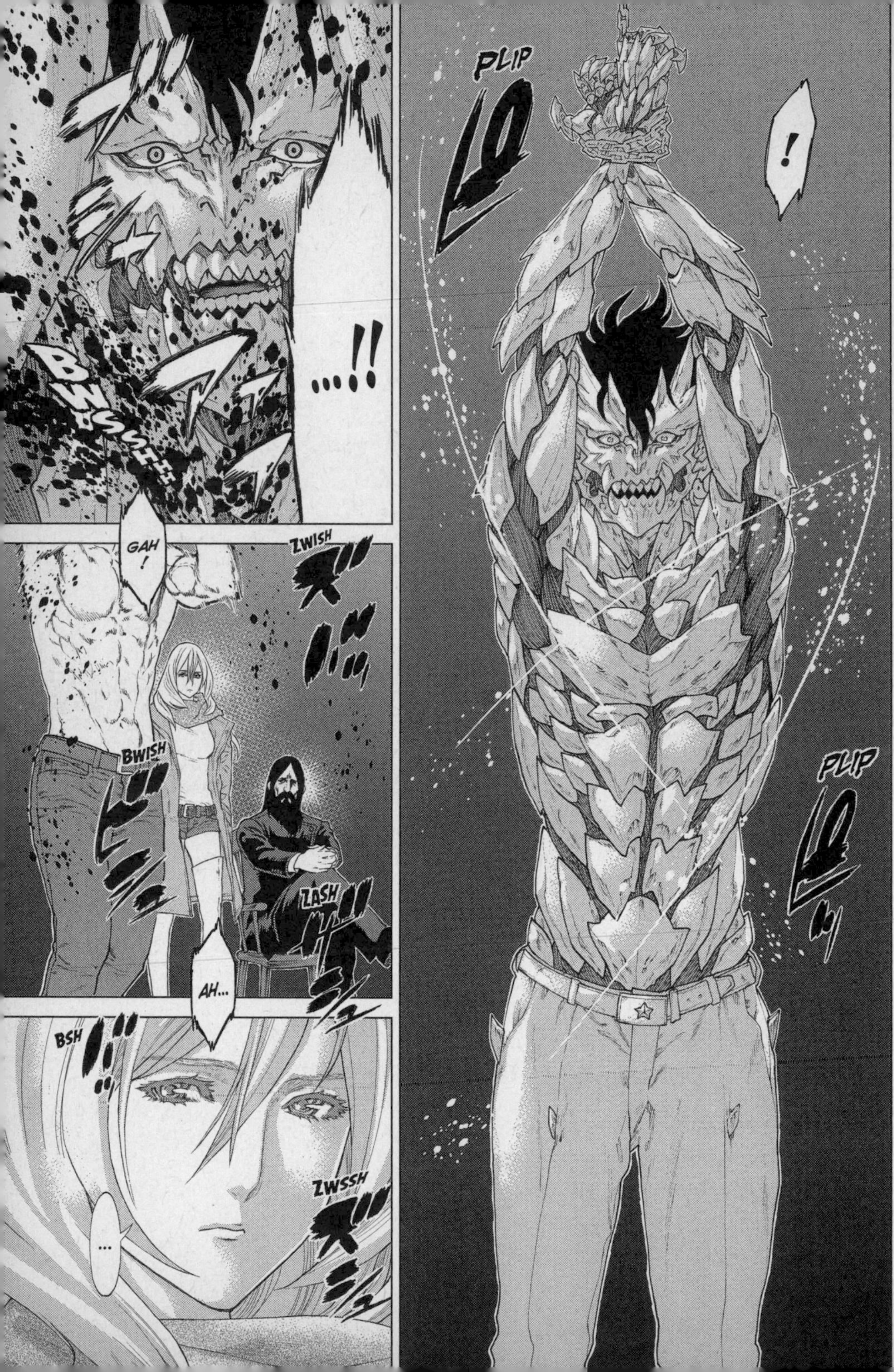
!
PLIP
PLIP
...!!
BWSSHHH
GAH!
ZWISH
BWISH
ZASH
AH...
BSH
ZWSSH
...

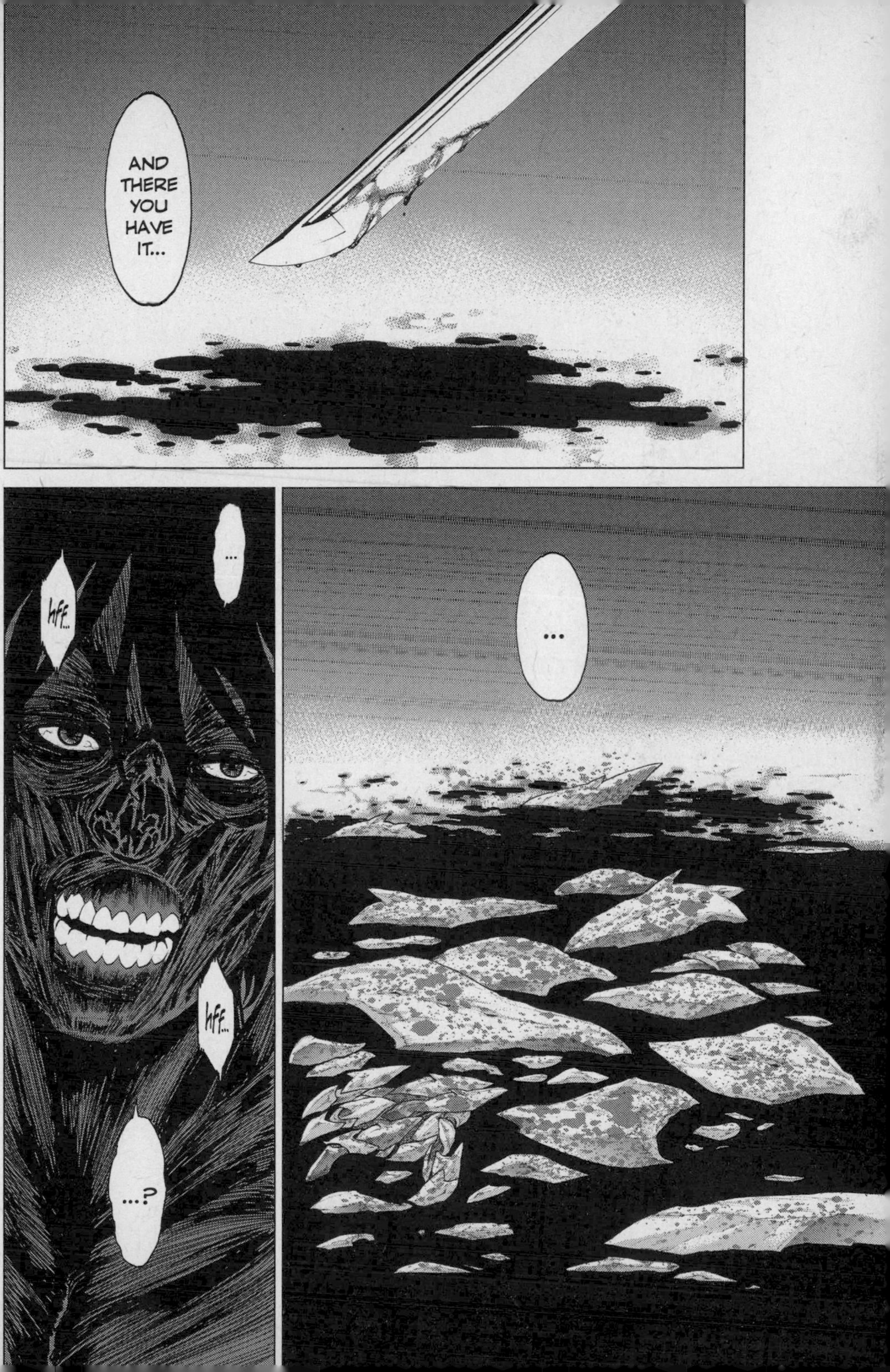
AND THERE YOU HAVE IT...
...
...
hff...
hff...
...?

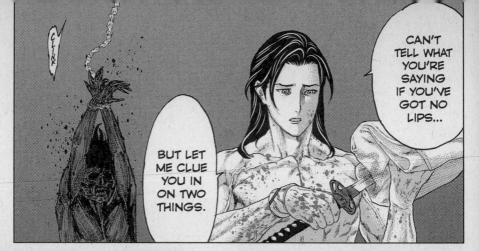

CAN'T TELL WHAT YOU'RE SAYING IF YOU'VE GOT NO LIPS...
CLINK
BUT LET ME CLUE YOU IN ON TWO THINGS.
ONE ...
YOUR PEACE-MAKER IS RIGHT HERE.
IT'S SET UP SO YOU CAN'T TAKE IT OFF WHILE YOU'RE STILL ALIVE, SO...
...WE HAD YOU DIE FOR US.
STOPPED YOUR HEART FOR A FEW MINUTES.
PUT IT BACK ON.
snag
HURRY UP, BEFORE HE DIES.

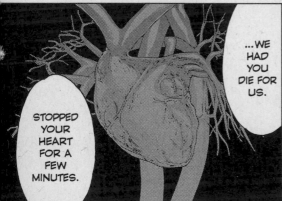

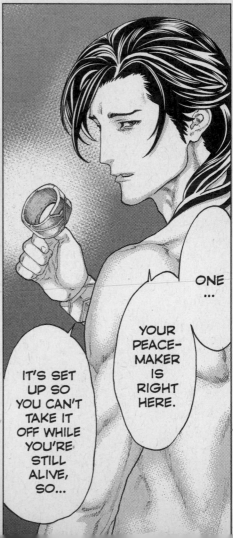

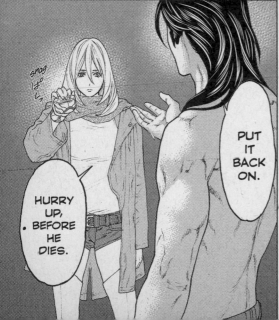

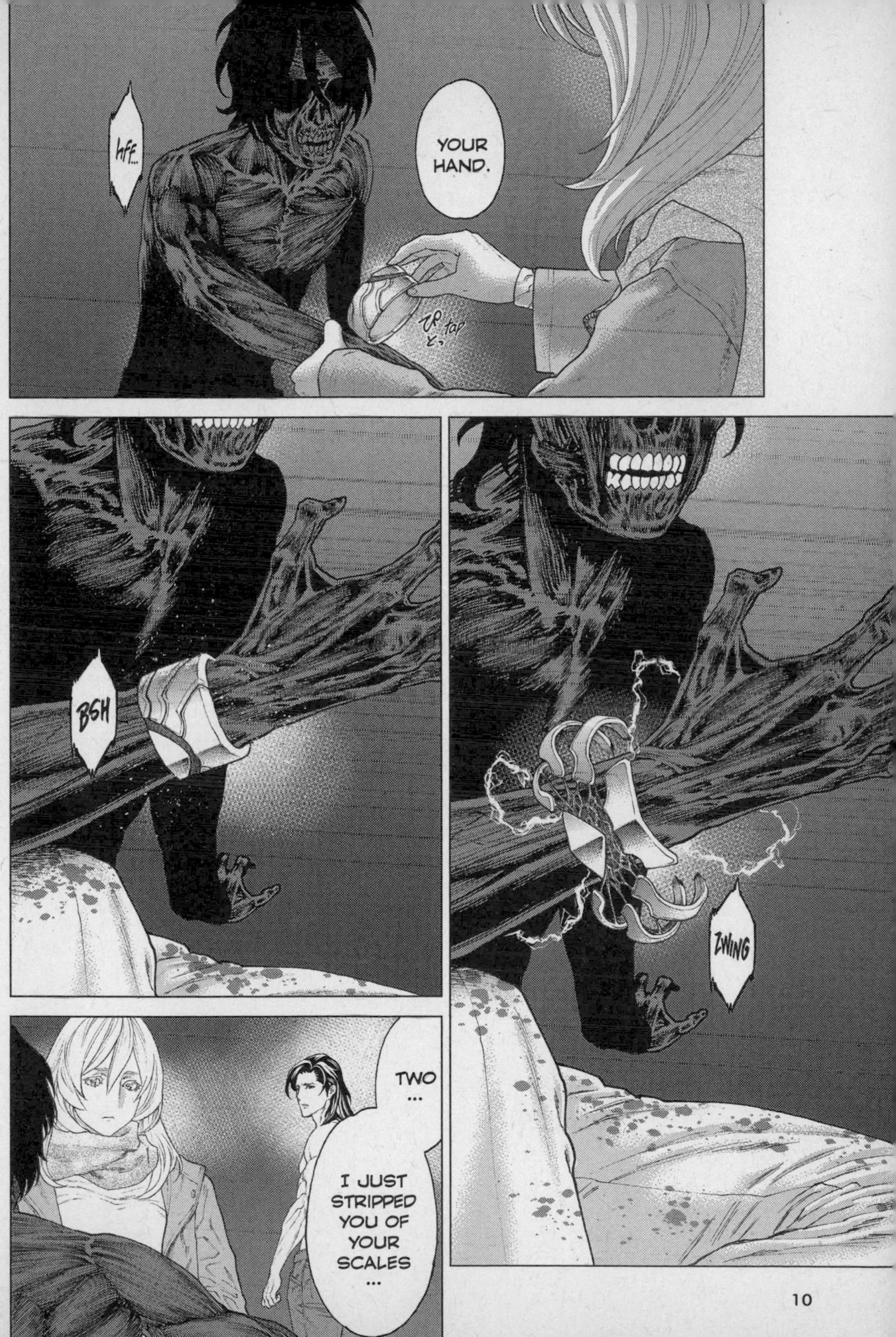
YOUR HAND.
hff...
tap
ZWING
BSH
TWO ...
I JUST STRIPPED YOU OF YOUR SCALES ...

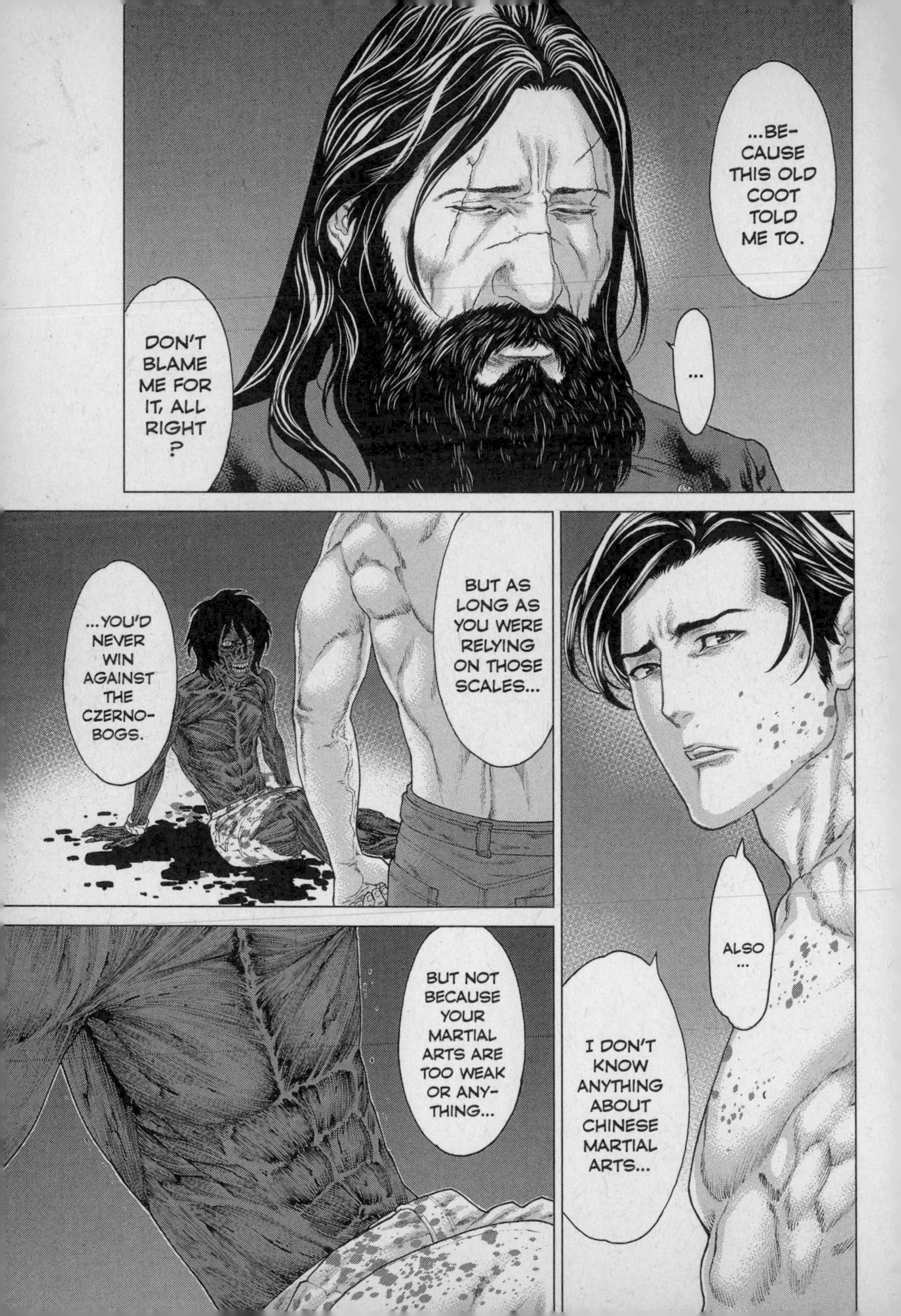
...BE-CAUSE THIS OLD COOT TOLD ME TO.
...
DON'T BLAME ME FOR IT, ALL RIGHT?
ALSO...
I DON'T KNOW ANYTHING ABOUT CHINESE MARTIAL ARTS...
BUT AS LONG AS YOU WERE RELYING ON THOSE SCALES...
...YOU'D NEVER WIN AGAINST THE CZERNO-BOGS.
BUT NOT BECAUSE YOUR MARTIAL ARTS ARE TOO WEAK OR ANY-THING...

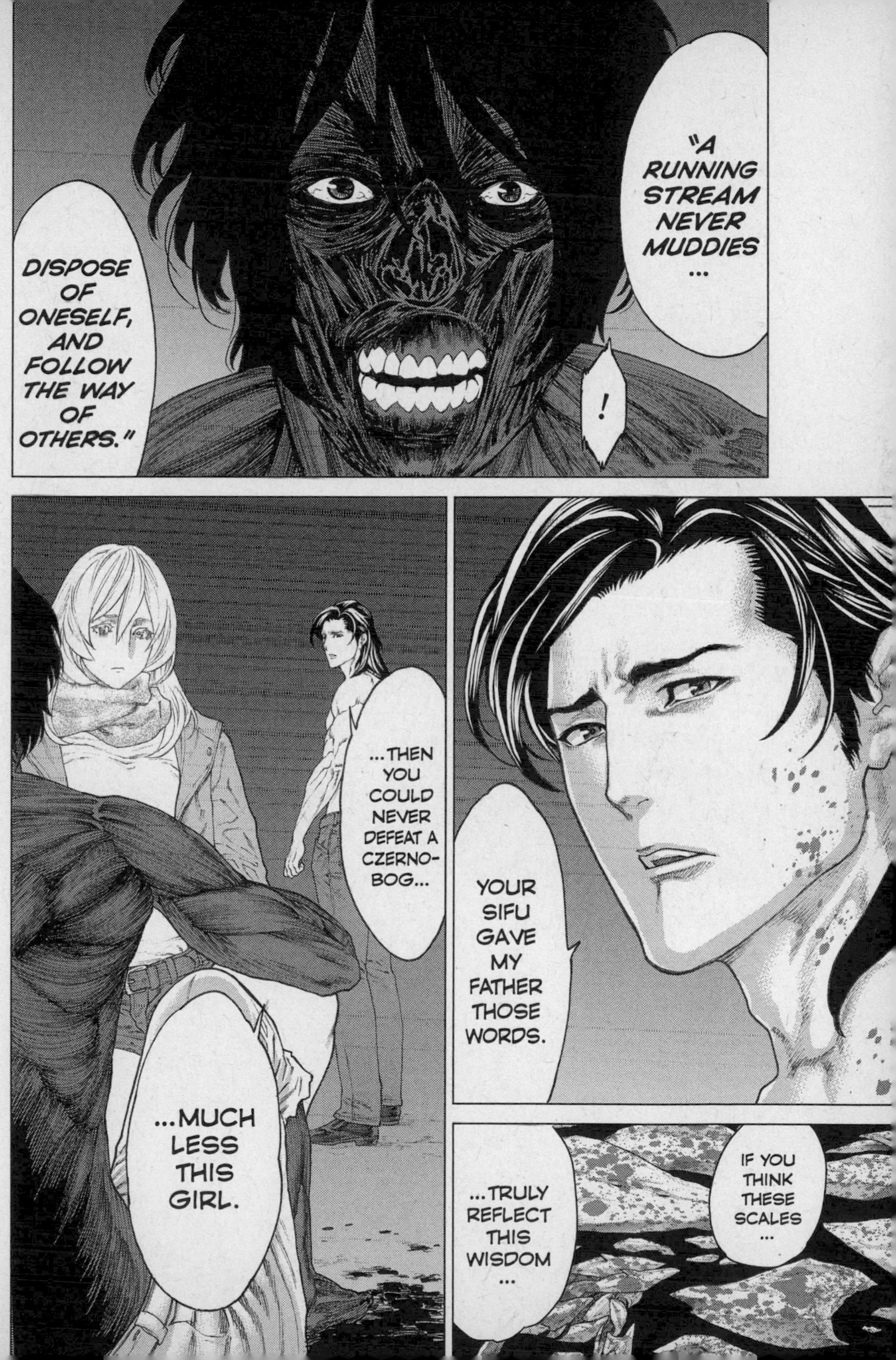
"A RUNNING STREAM NEVER MUDDIES ...
!
DISPOSE OF ONESELF, AND FOLLOW THE WAY OF OTHERS."
YOUR SIFU GAVE MY FATHER THOSE WORDS.
IF YOU THINK THESE SCALES ...
...TRULY REFLECT THIS WISDOM ...
...THEN YOU COULD NEVER DEFEAT A CZERNO-BOG...
...MUCH LESS THIS GIRL.

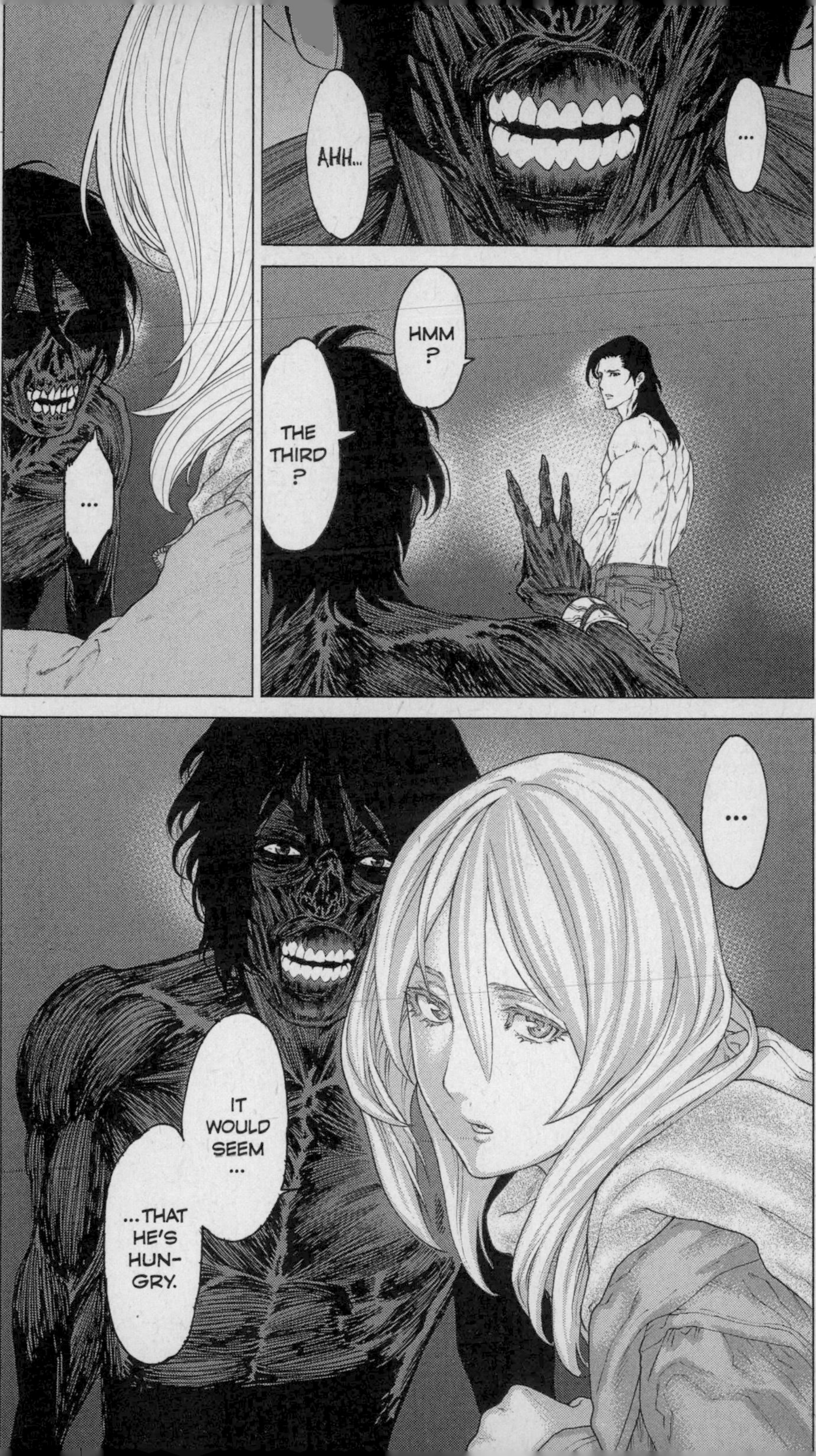
...
AHH...
HMM?
THE THIRD?
...
...
IT WOULD SEEM ...
...THAT HE'S HUN-GRY.

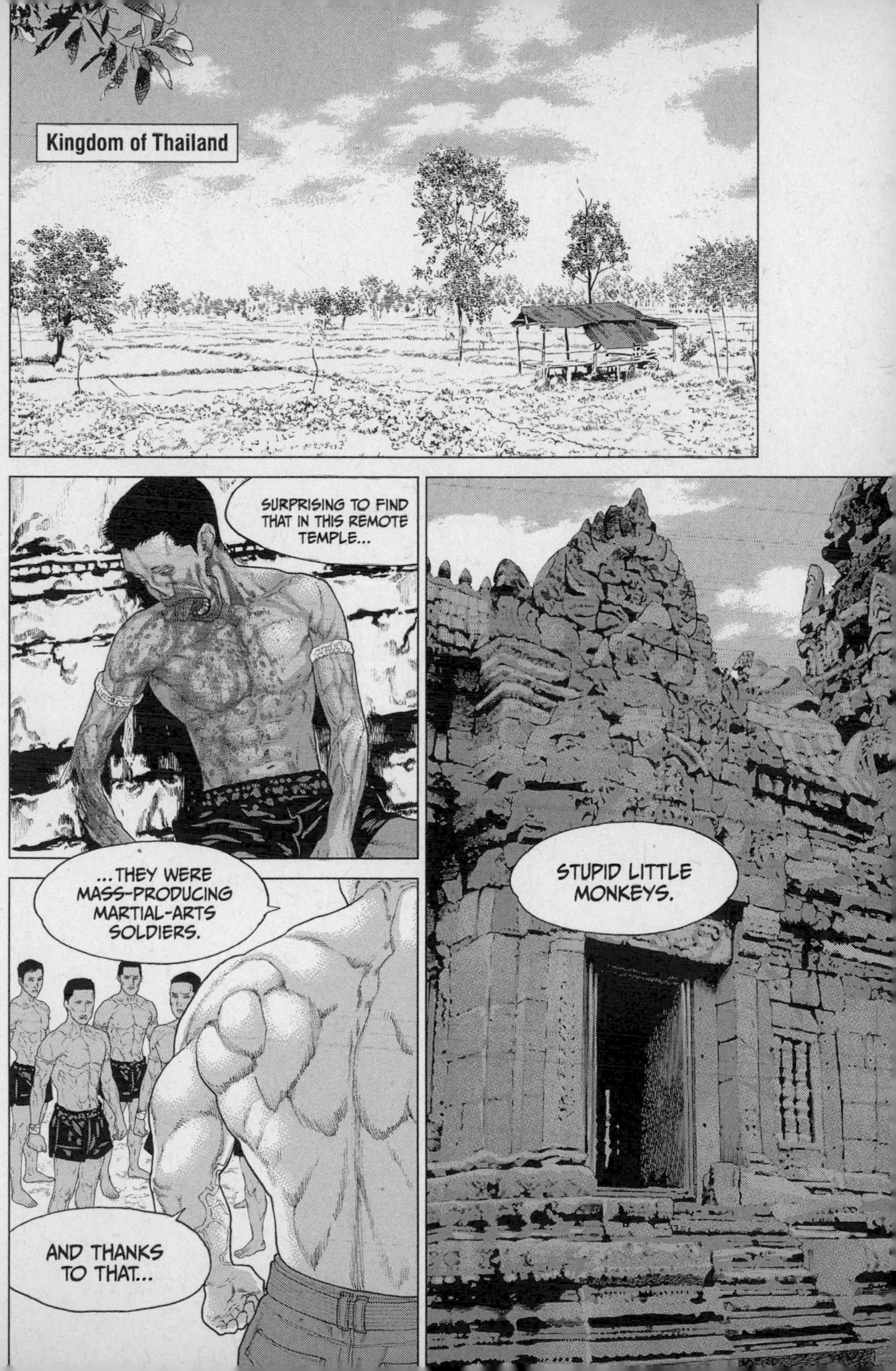
Kingdom of Thailand
STUPID LITTLE MONKEYS.
SURPRISING TO FIND THAT IN THIS REMOTE TEMPLE...
...THEY WERE MASS-PRODUCING MARTIAL-ARTS SOLDIERS.
AND THANKS TO THAT...

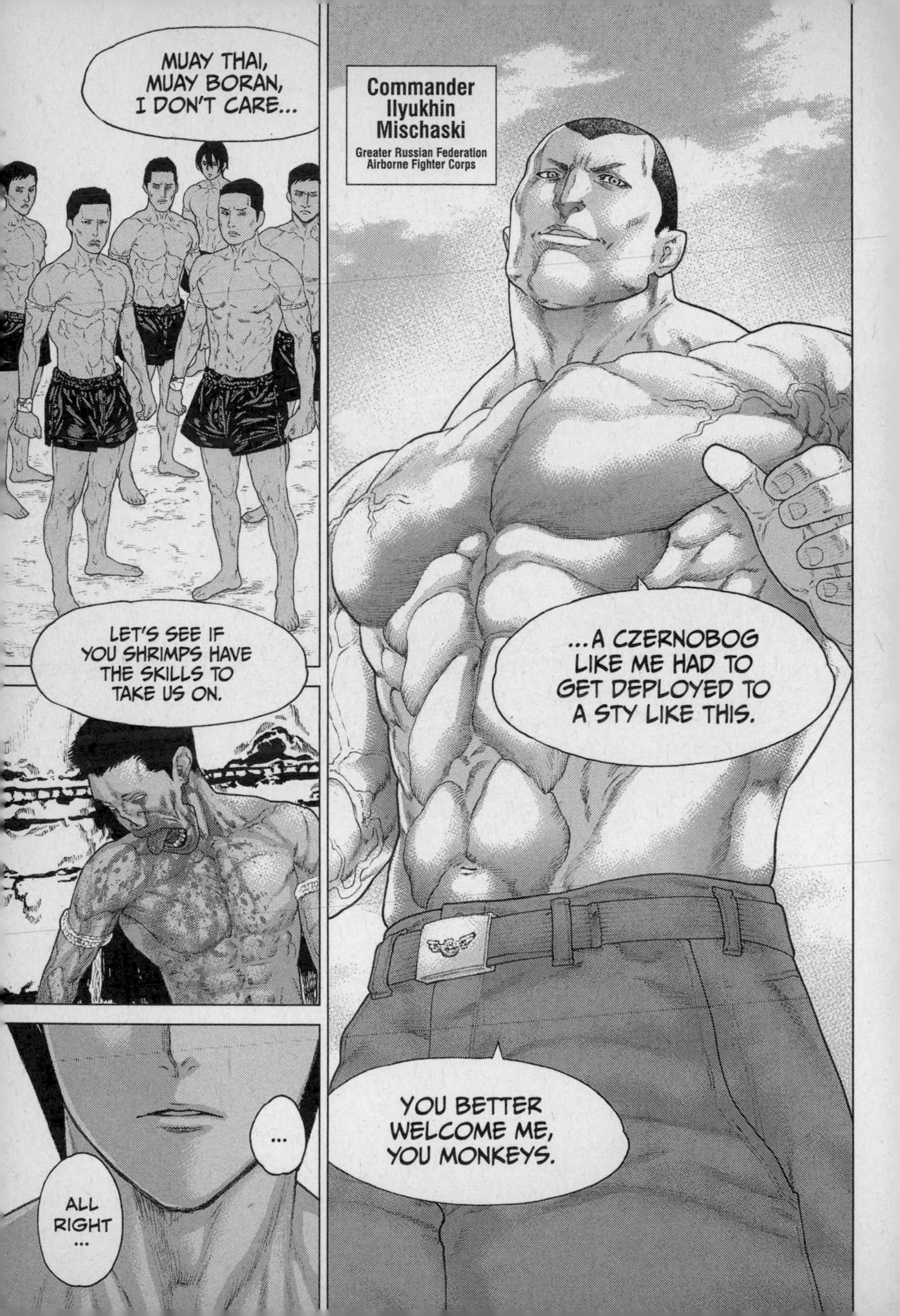
Commander Ilyukhin Mischaski
Greater Russian Federation Airborne Fighter Corps
...A CZERNOBOG LIKE ME HAD TO GET DEPLOYED TO A STY LIKE THIS.
YOU BETTER WELCOME ME, YOU MONKEYS.
MUAY THAI, MUAY BORAN, I DON'T CARE...
LET'S SEE IF YOU SHRIMPS HAVE THE SKILLS TO TAKE US ON.
...
ALL RIGHT ...

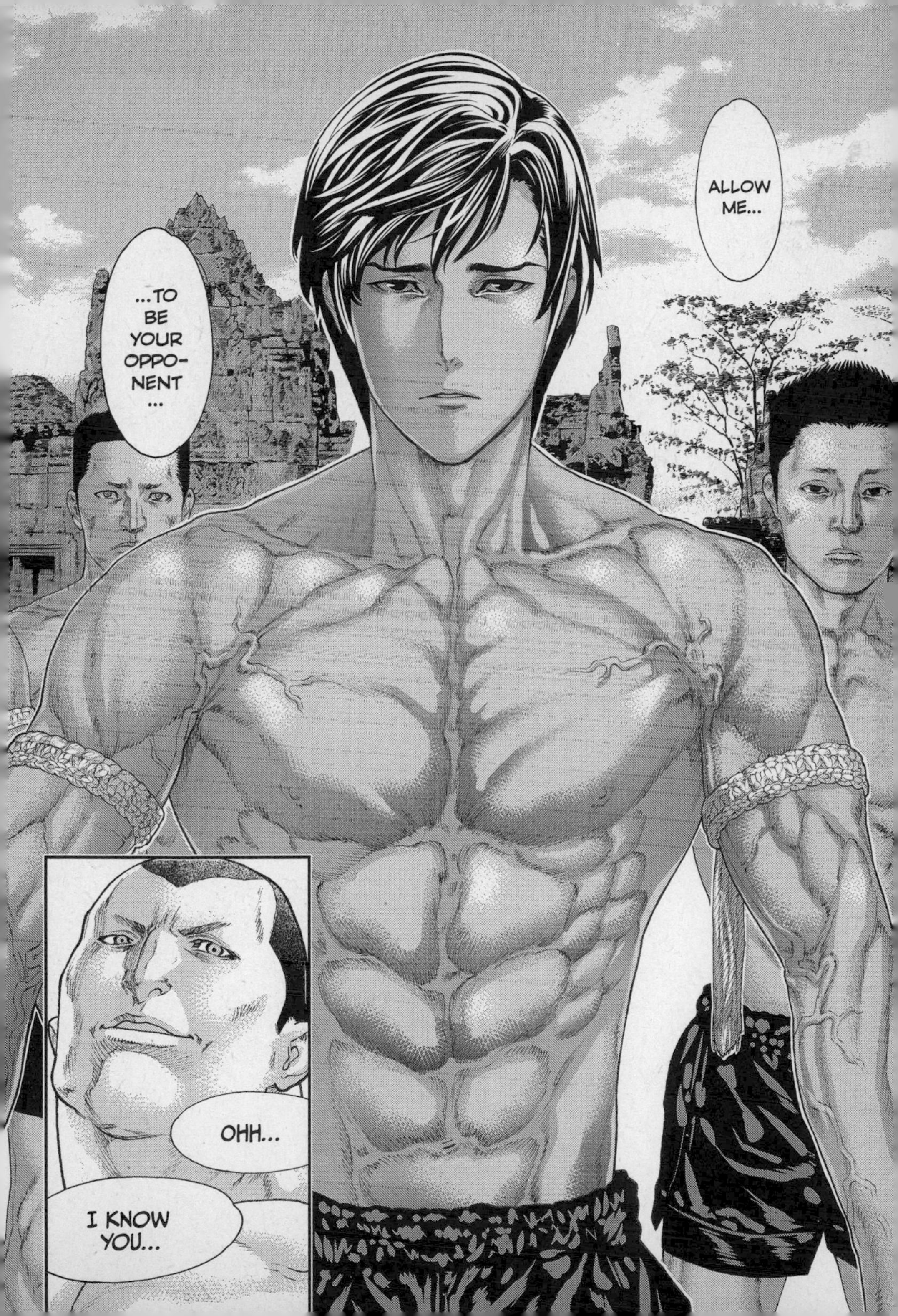
ALLOW ME...
...TO BE YOUR OPPO-NENT...
OHH...
I KNOW YOU...

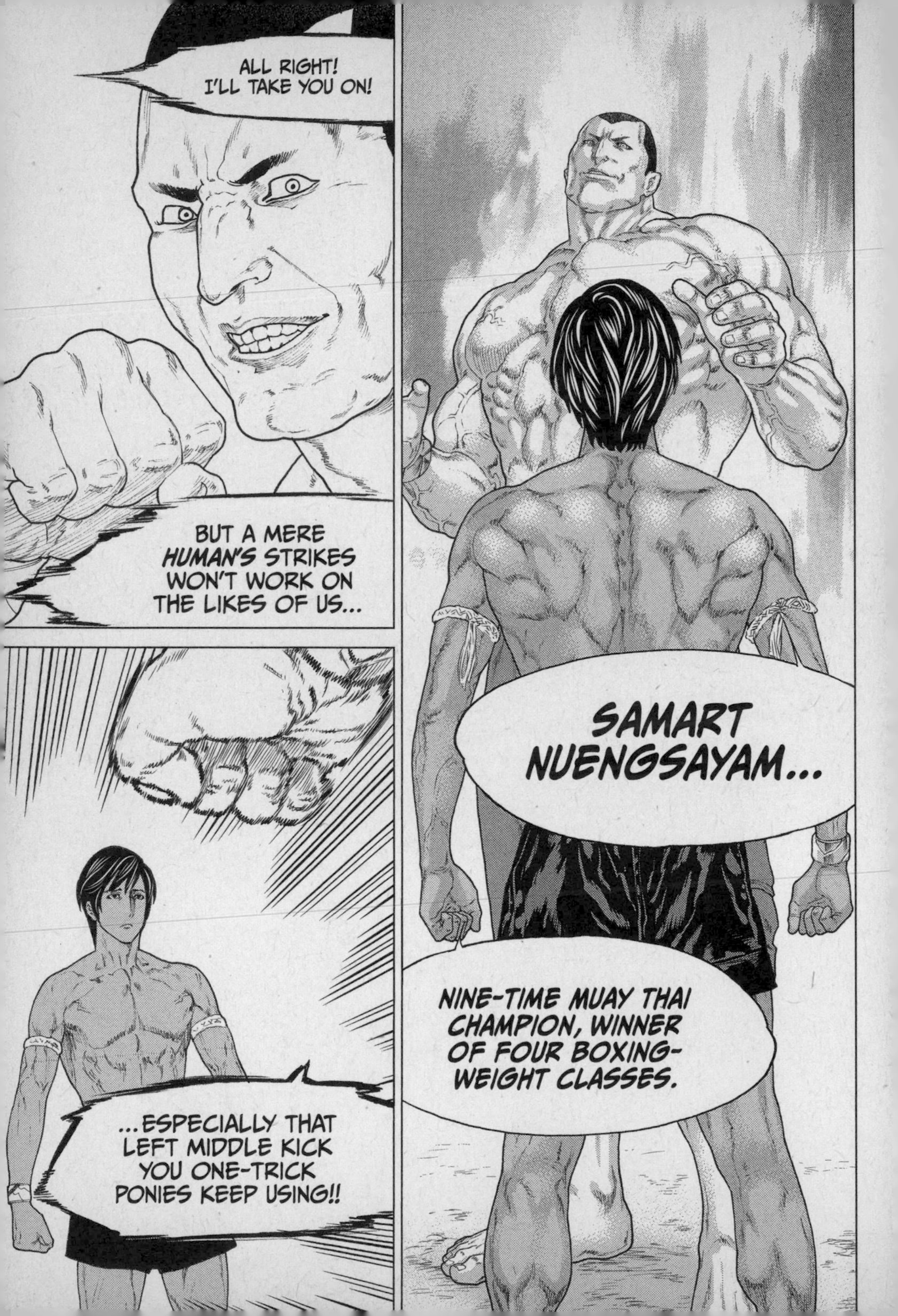
SAMART NUENGSAYAM...
NINE-TIME MUAY THAI CHAMPION, WINNER OF FOUR BOXING-WEIGHT CLASSES.
ALL RIGHT! I'LL TAKE YOU ON!
BUT A MERE *HUMAN'S* STRIKES WON'T WORK ON THE LIKES OF US...
...ESPECIALLY THAT LEFT MIDDLE KICK YOU ONE-TRICK PONIES KEEP USING!!

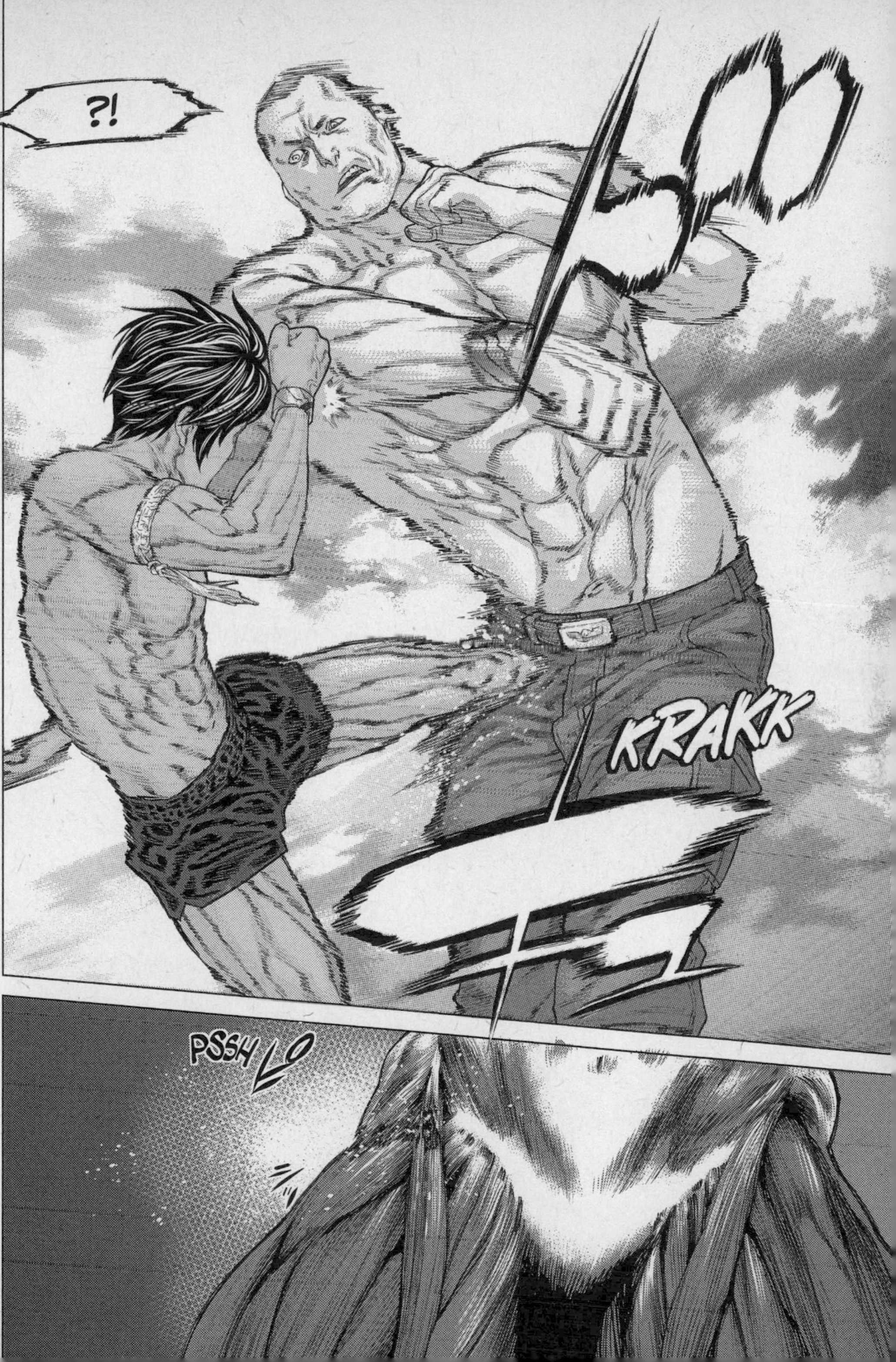
?!
KRAKK
PSSH

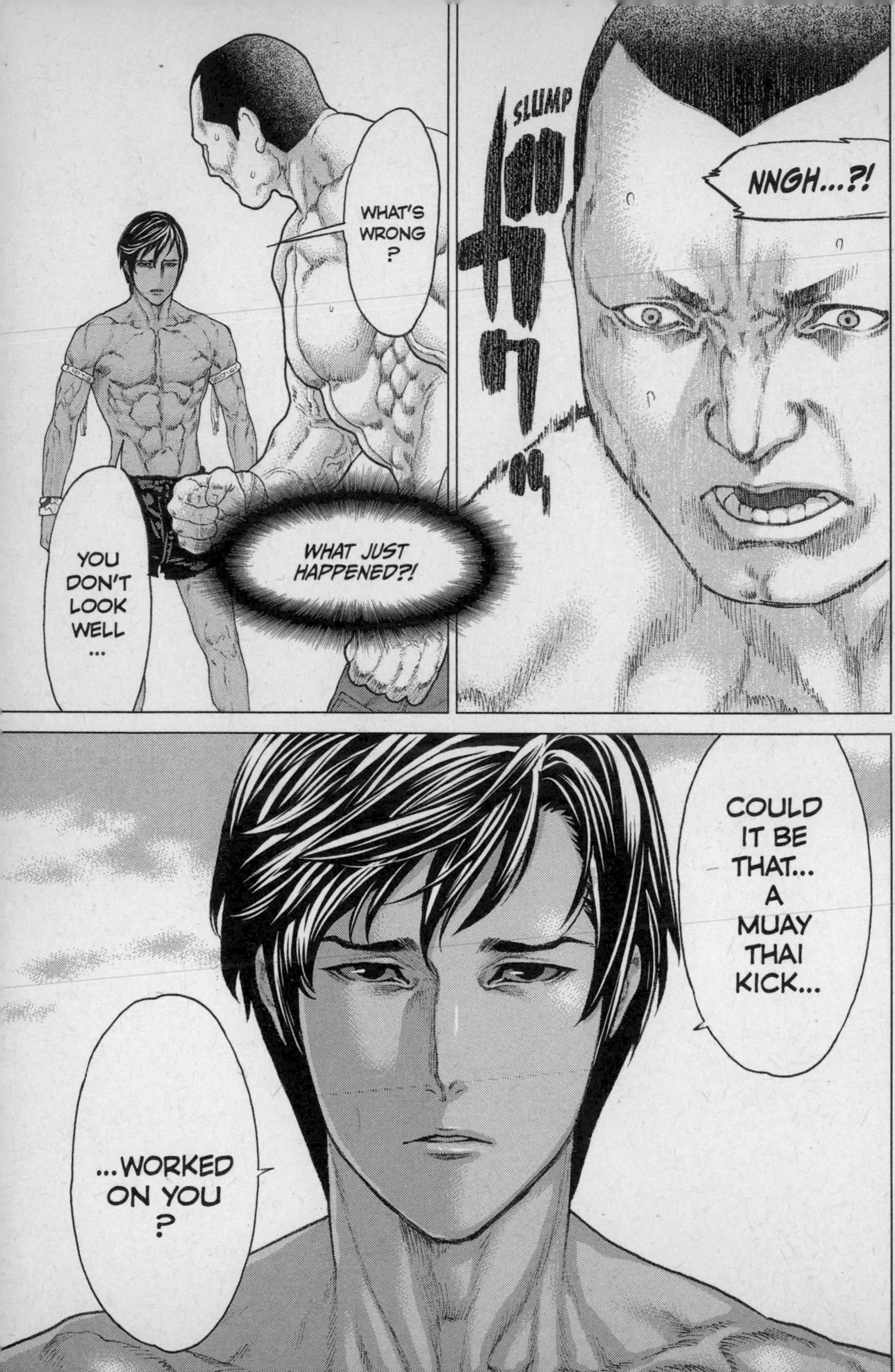
SLUMP
NNGH...?!
WHAT'S WRONG ?
WHAT JUST HAPPENED?!
YOU DON'T LOOK WELL ...
COULD IT BE THAT... A MUAY THAI KICK...
...WORKED ON YOU ?

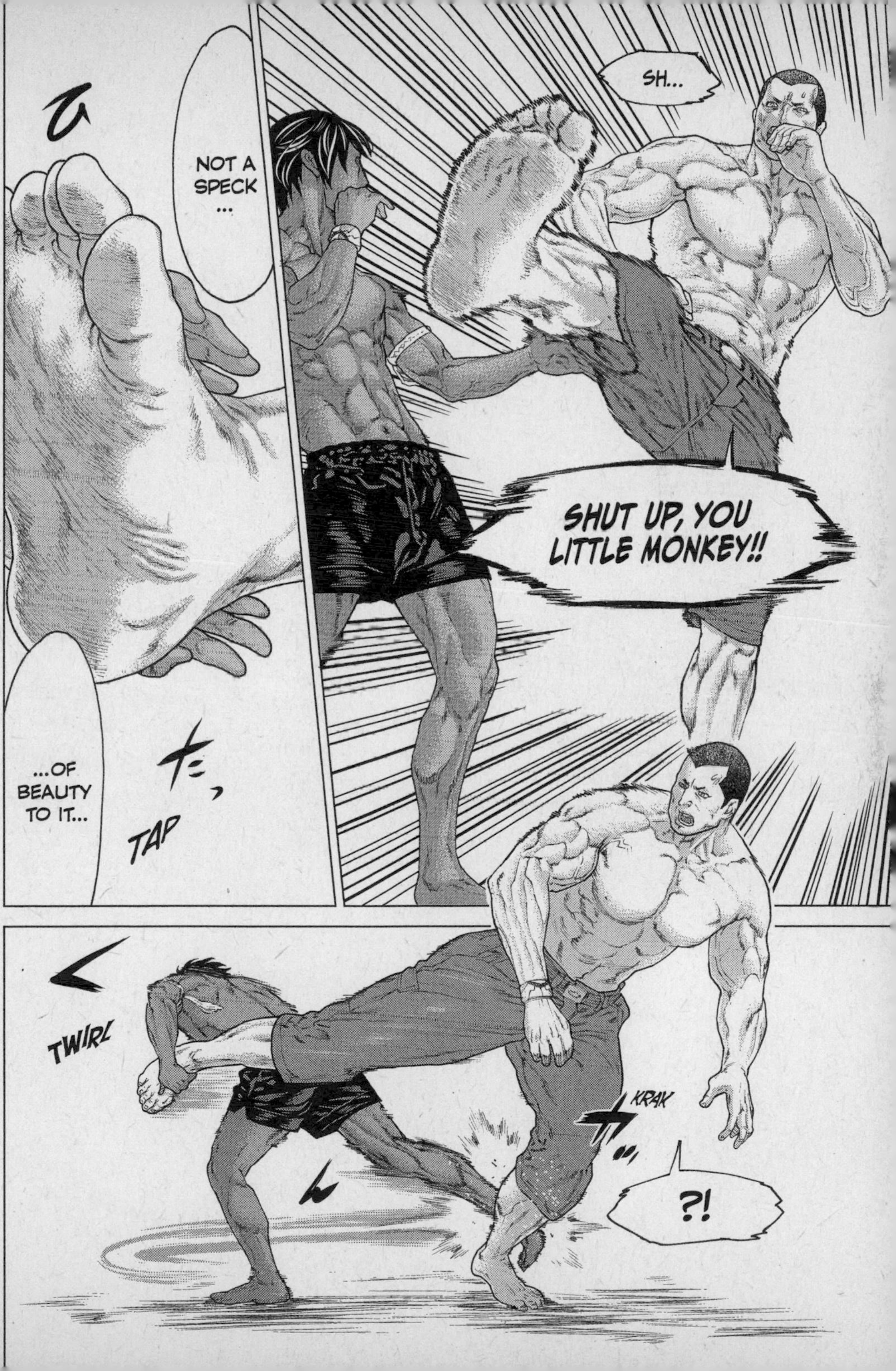

SH...
SHUT UP, YOU LITTLE MONKEY!!
NOT A SPECK ...
...OF BEAUTY TO IT...
TAP
TWIRL
KRAK
?!

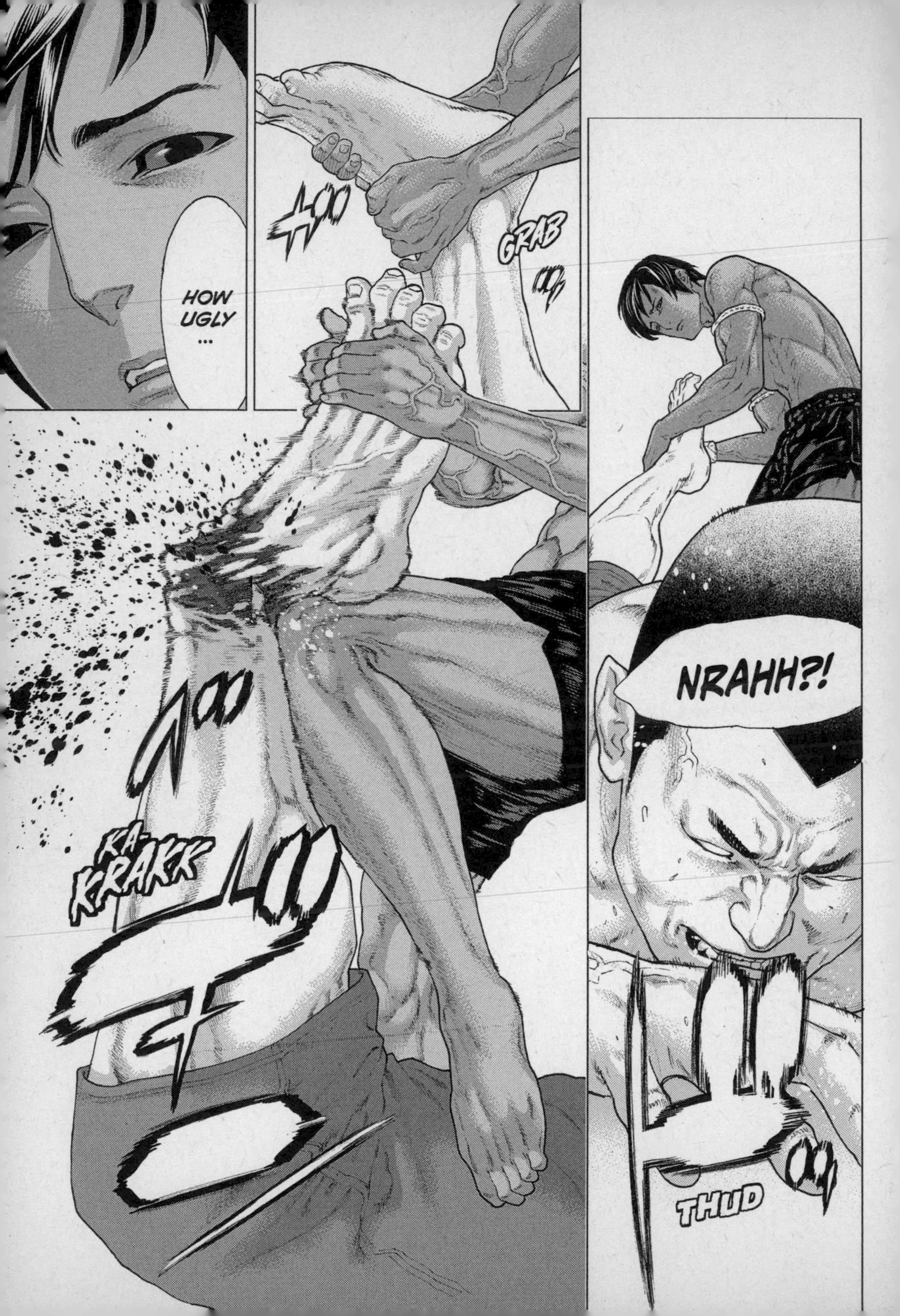
NRAHH?!
THUD
GRAB
HOW UGLY ...
KA-KRAKK

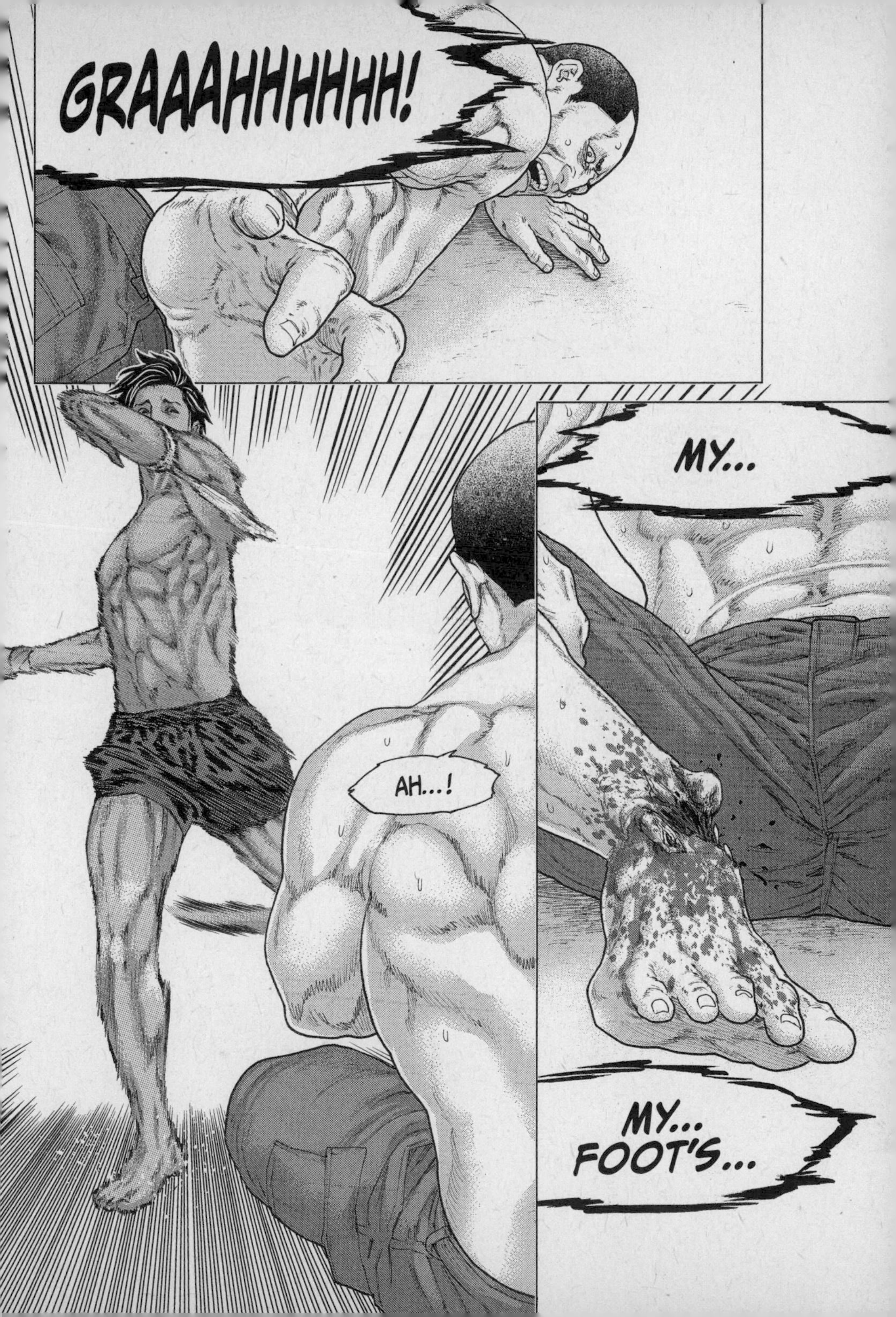
GRAAAHHHHHH!
MY...
MY... FOOT'S...
AH...!

GRAKK

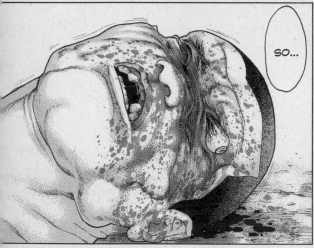

SO...

CLEAN THIS UP.

ONCE HIS HEART STOPS, RETRIEVE HIS PEACE-MAKER.

YES, SIR!

DOES THIS MEAN...

YOU'RE WITH THE RUSSIANS NOW?

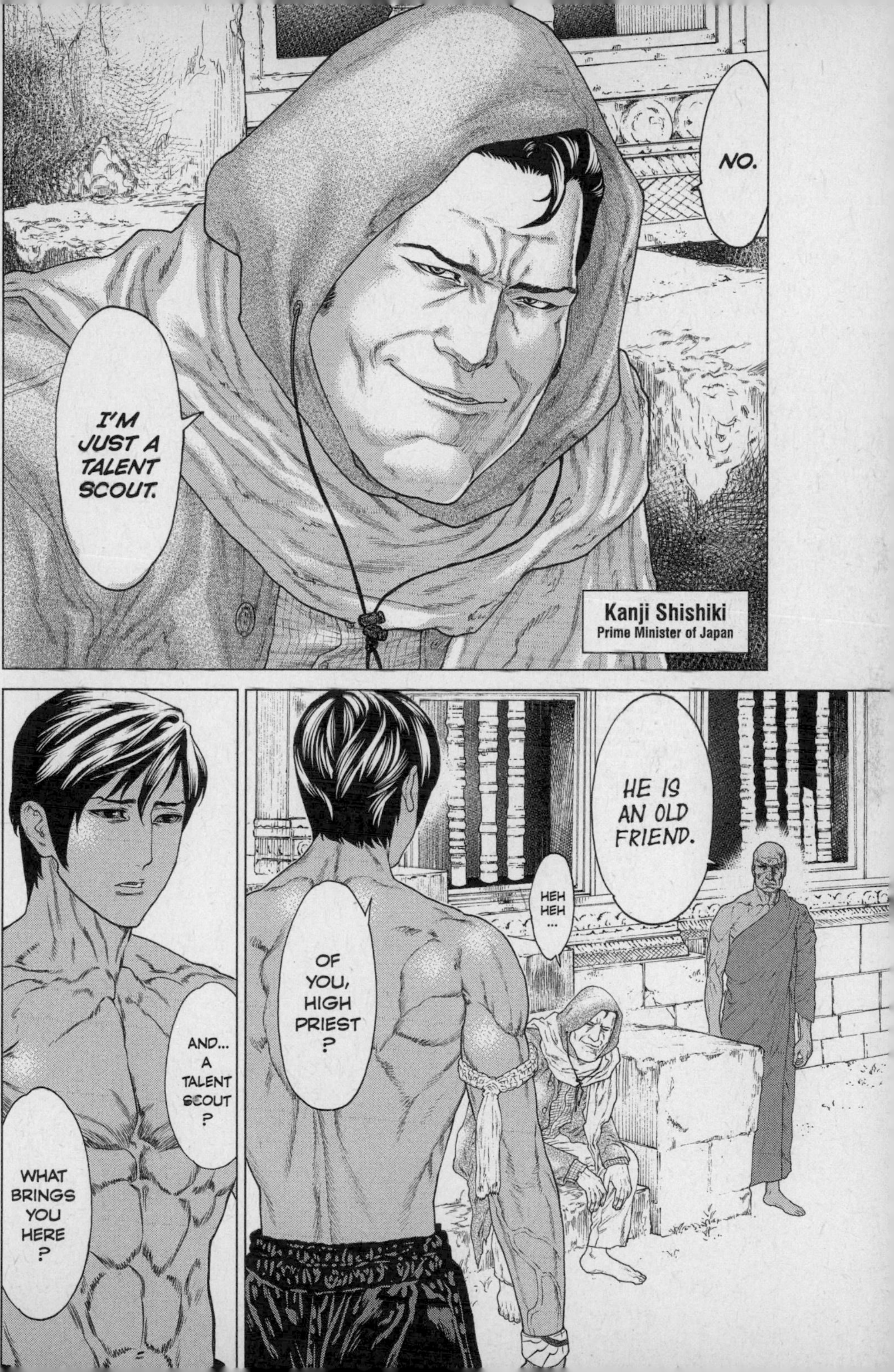
NO.
I'M JUST A TALENT SCOUT.
Kanji Shishiki
Prime Minister of Japan
HE IS AN OLD FRIEND.
HEH HEH...
OF YOU, HIGH PRIEST?
AND... A TALENT SCOUT?
WHAT BRINGS YOU HERE?

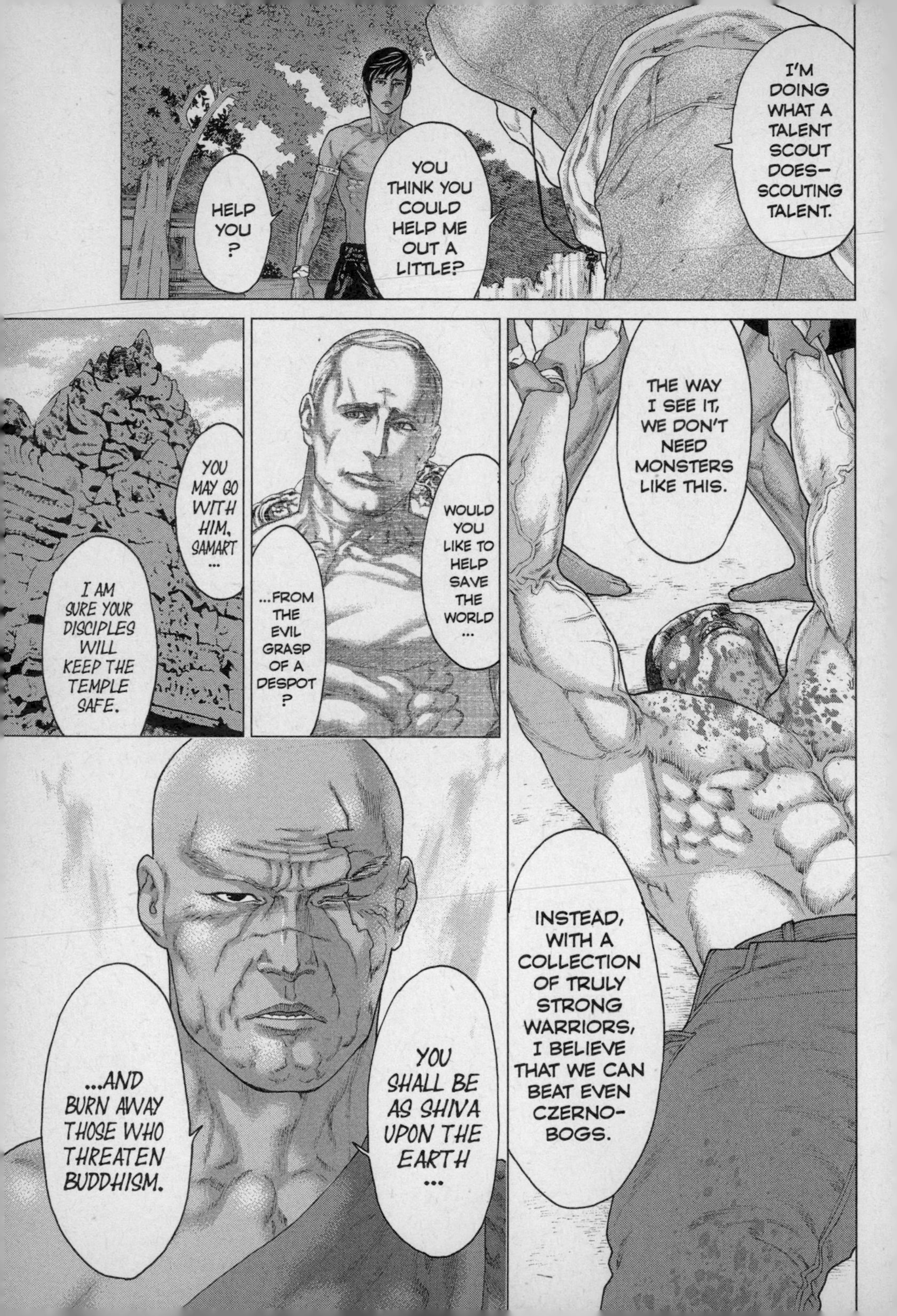
I'M DOING WHAT A TALENT SCOUT DOES—SCOUTING TALENT.
YOU THINK YOU COULD HELP ME OUT A LITTLE?
HELP YOU?
THE WAY I SEE IT, WE DON'T NEED MONSTERS LIKE THIS.
INSTEAD, WITH A COLLECTION OF TRULY STRONG WARRIORS, I BELIEVE THAT WE CAN BEAT EVEN CZERNO-BOGS.
WOULD YOU LIKE TO HELP SAVE THE WORLD...
...FROM THE EVIL GRASP OF A DESPOT?
YOU MAY GO WITH HIM, SAMART...
I AM SURE YOUR DISCIPLES WILL KEEP THE TEMPLE SAFE.
YOU SHALL BE AS SHIVA UPON THE EARTH...
...AND BURN AWAY THOSE WHO THREATEN BUDDHISM.

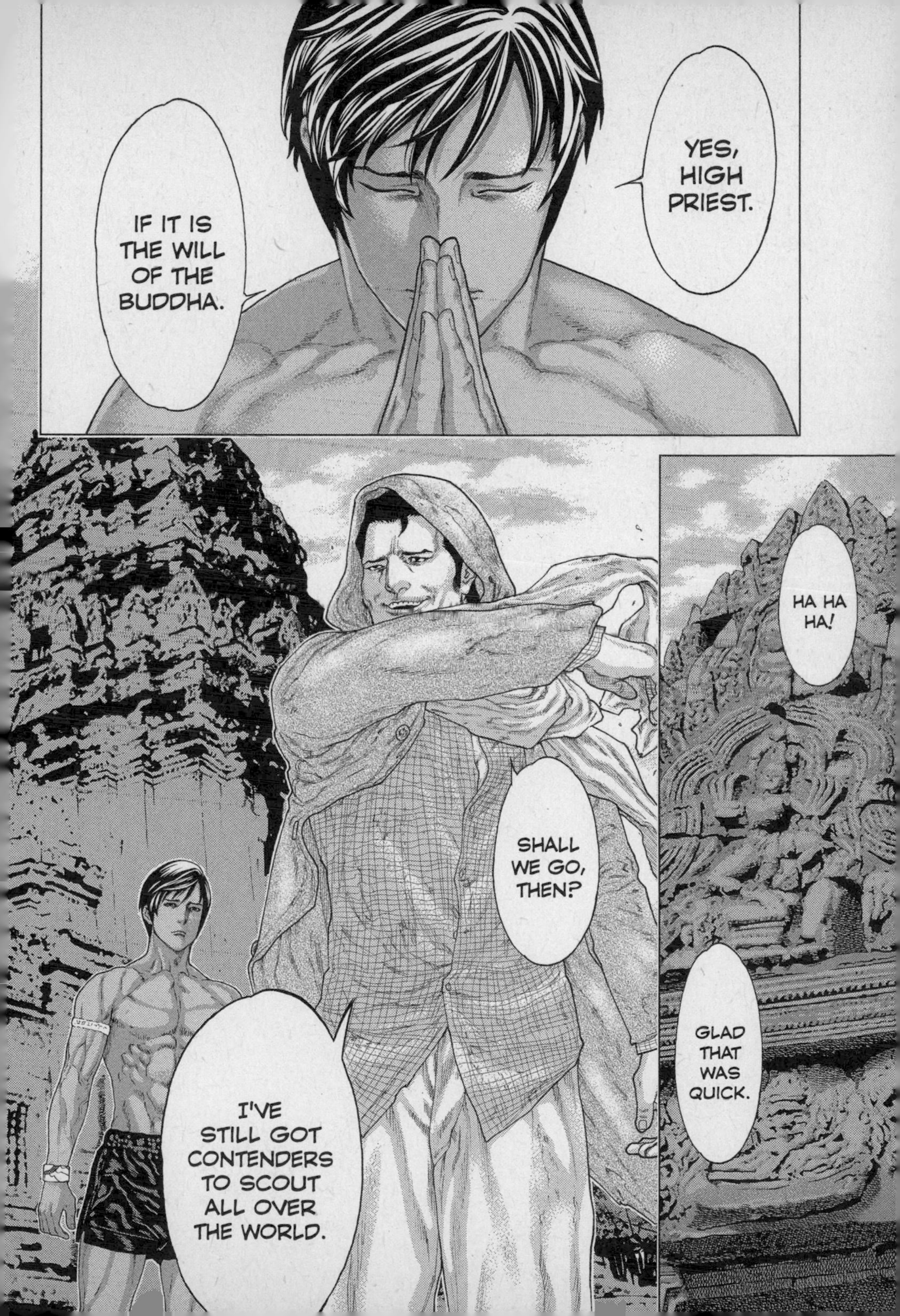
YES, HIGH PRIEST.
IF IT IS THE WILL OF THE BUDDHA.
HA HA HA!
GLAD THAT WAS QUICK.
SHALL WE GO, THEN?
I'VE STILL GOT CONTENDERS TO SCOUT ALL OVER THE WORLD.

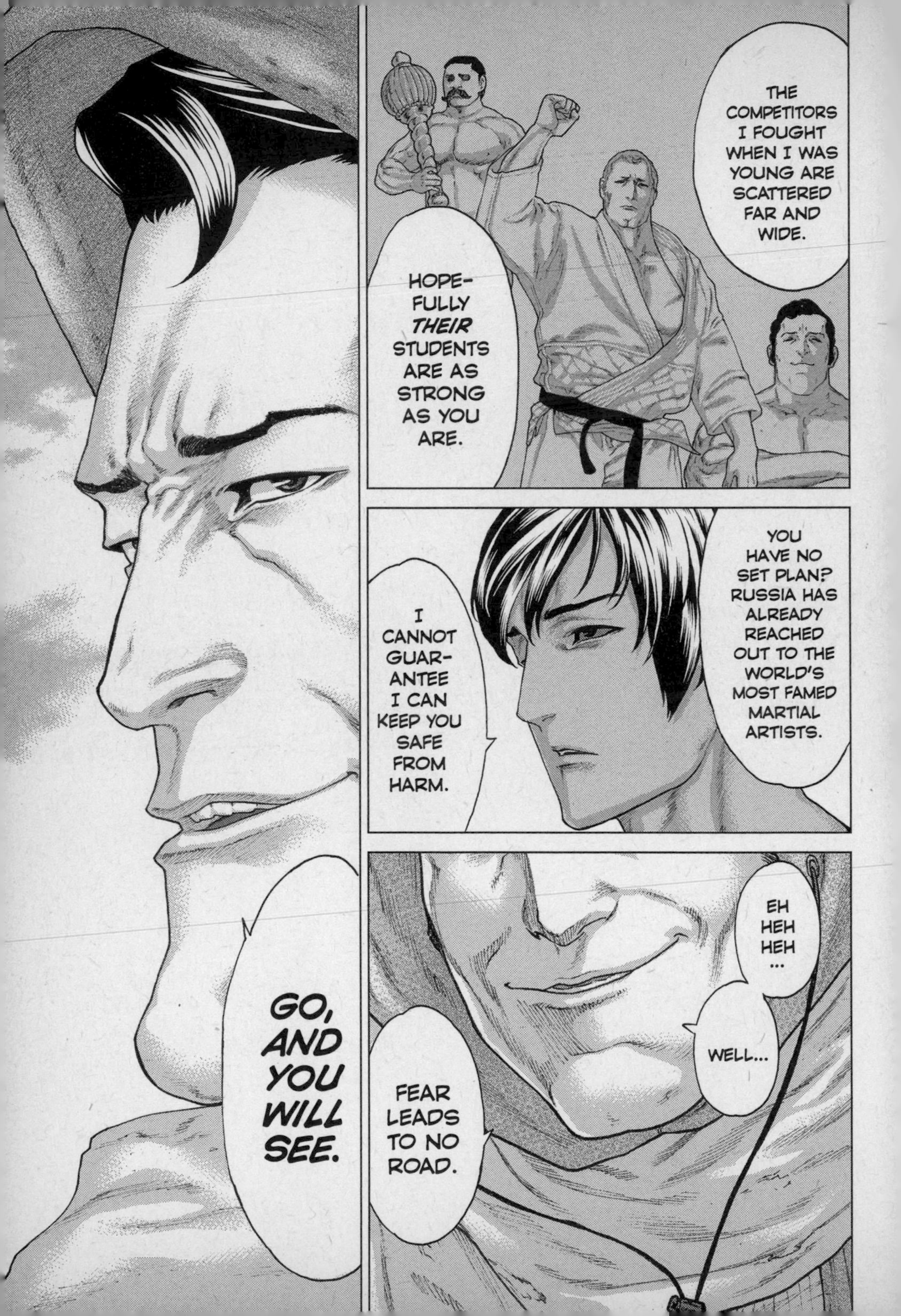
THE COMPETITORS I FOUGHT WHEN I WAS YOUNG ARE SCATTERED FAR AND WIDE.
HOPE-FULLY *THEIR* STUDENTS ARE AS STRONG AS YOU ARE.
YOU HAVE NO SET PLAN? RUSSIA HAS ALREADY REACHED OUT TO THE WORLD'S MOST FAMED MARTIAL ARTISTS.
I CANNOT GUAR-ANTEE I CAN KEEP YOU SAFE FROM HARM.
EH HEH HEH ...
WELL...
FEAR LEADS TO NO ROAD.
GO, AND YOU WILL SEE.

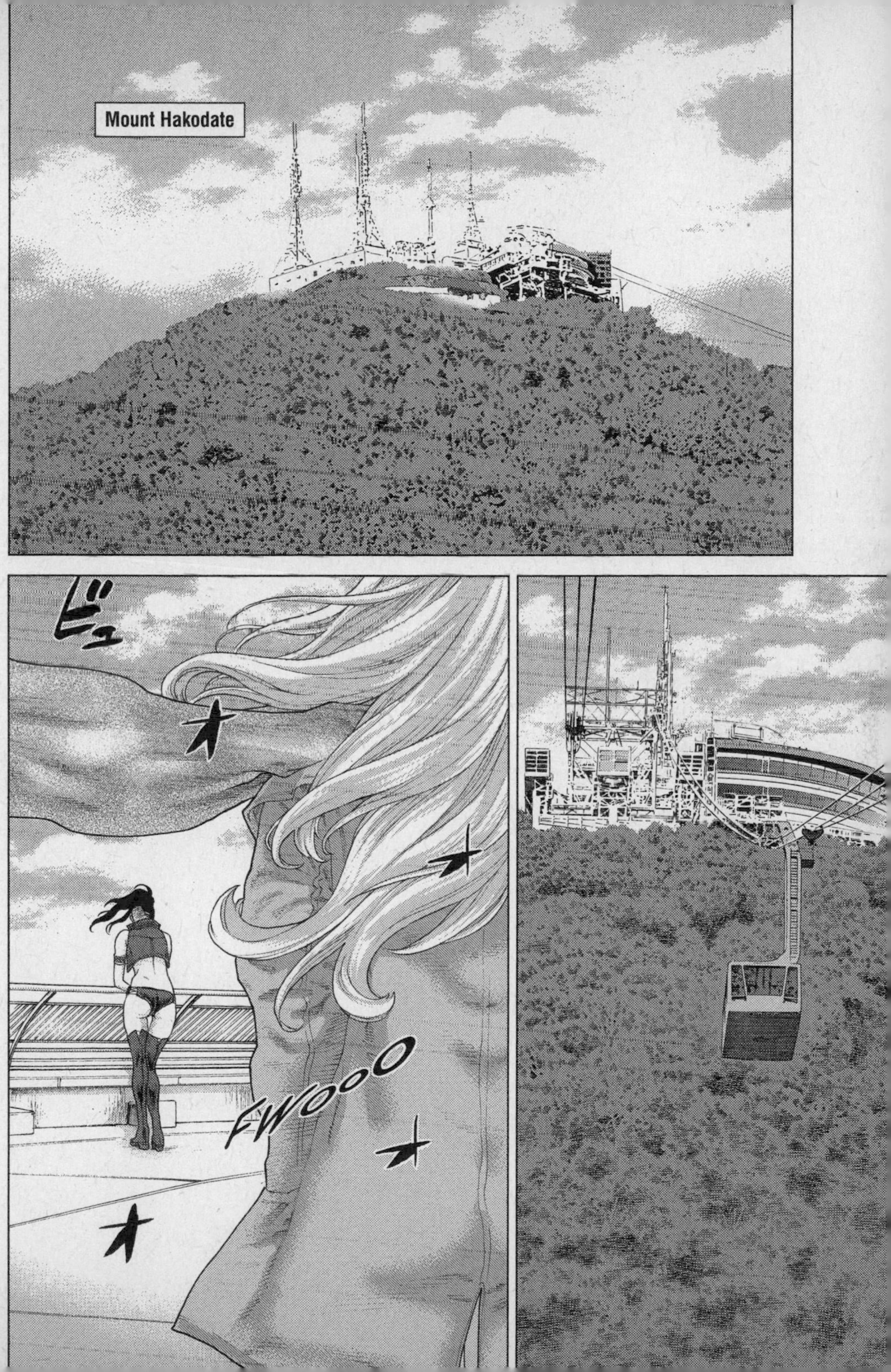
Mount Hakodate
ビュ
FWOOOO

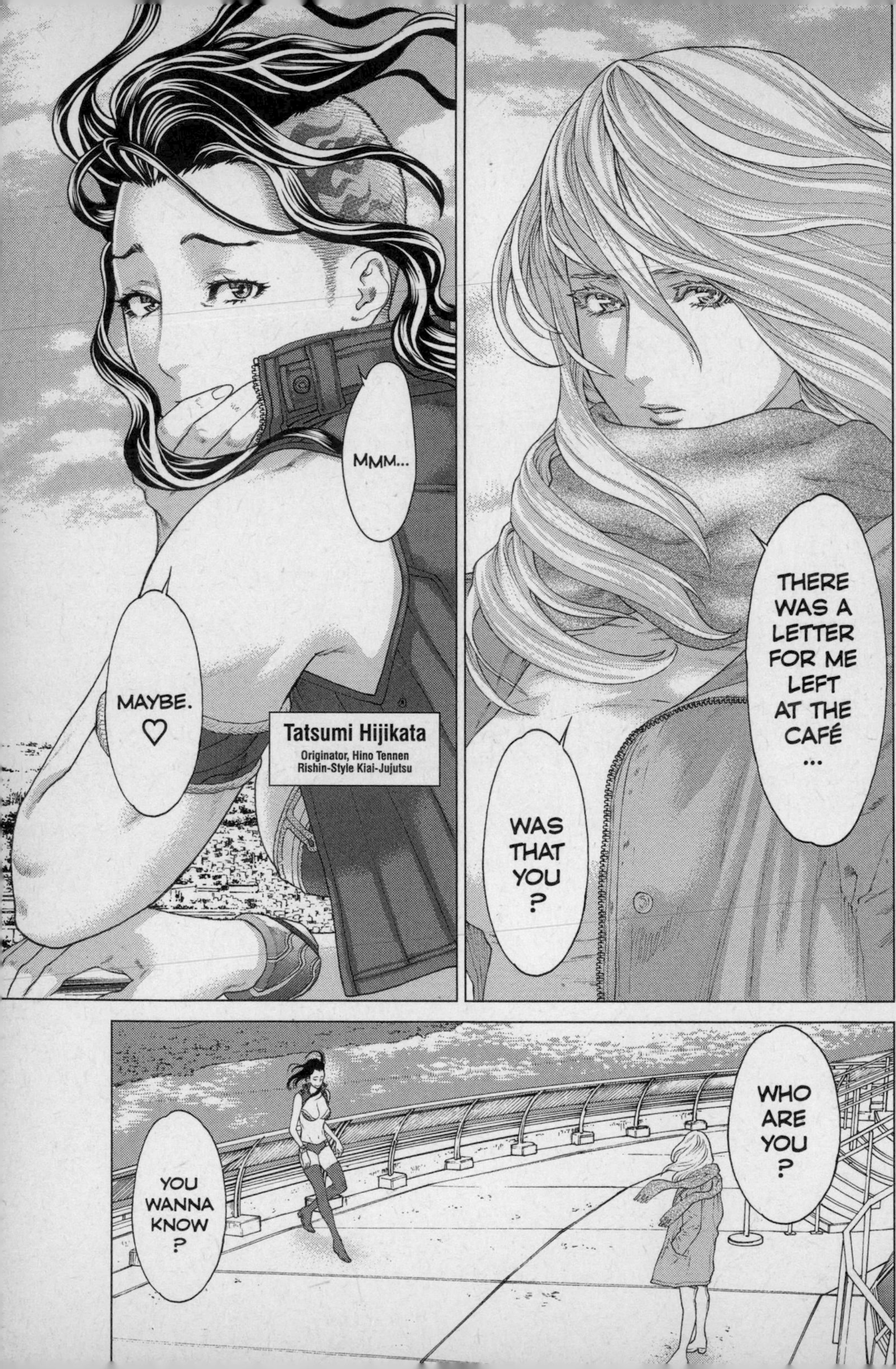
THERE WAS A LETTER FOR ME LEFT AT THE CAFÉ ...
WAS THAT YOU ?
MMM...
MAYBE. ♡
Tatsumi Hijikata
Originator, Hino Tennen Rishin-Style Kiai-Jujutsu
WHO ARE YOU ?
YOU WANNA KNOW ?

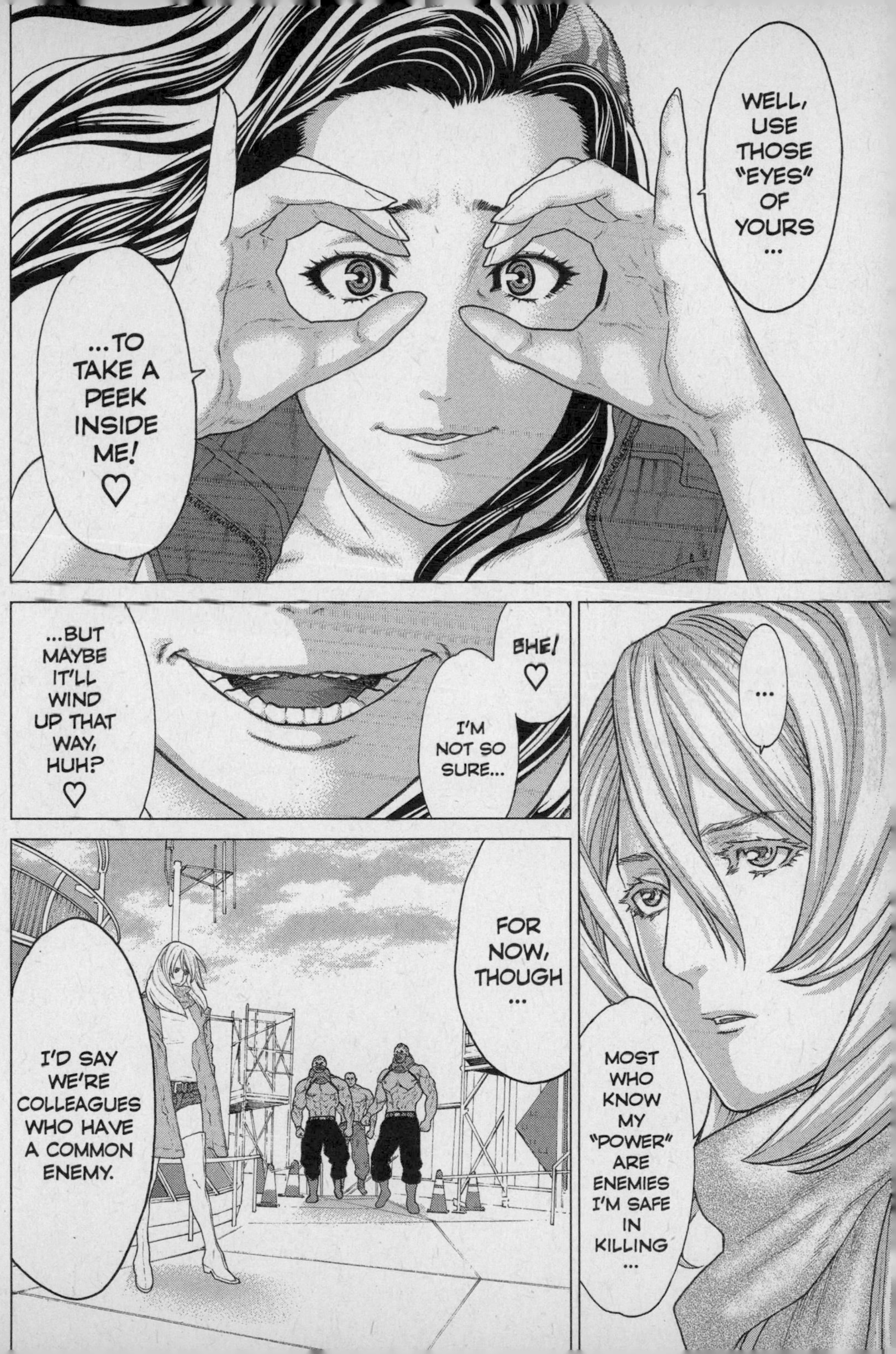
WELL, USE THOSE "EYES" OF YOURS ...
...TO TAKE A PEEK INSIDE ME! ♡
...
MOST WHO KNOW MY "POWER" ARE ENEMIES I'M SAFE IN KILLING ...
EHE! ♡
I'M NOT SO SURE...
...BUT MAYBE IT'LL WIND UP THAT WAY, HUH? ♡
FOR NOW, THOUGH ...
I'D SAY WE'RE COLLEAGUES WHO HAVE A COMMON ENEMY.

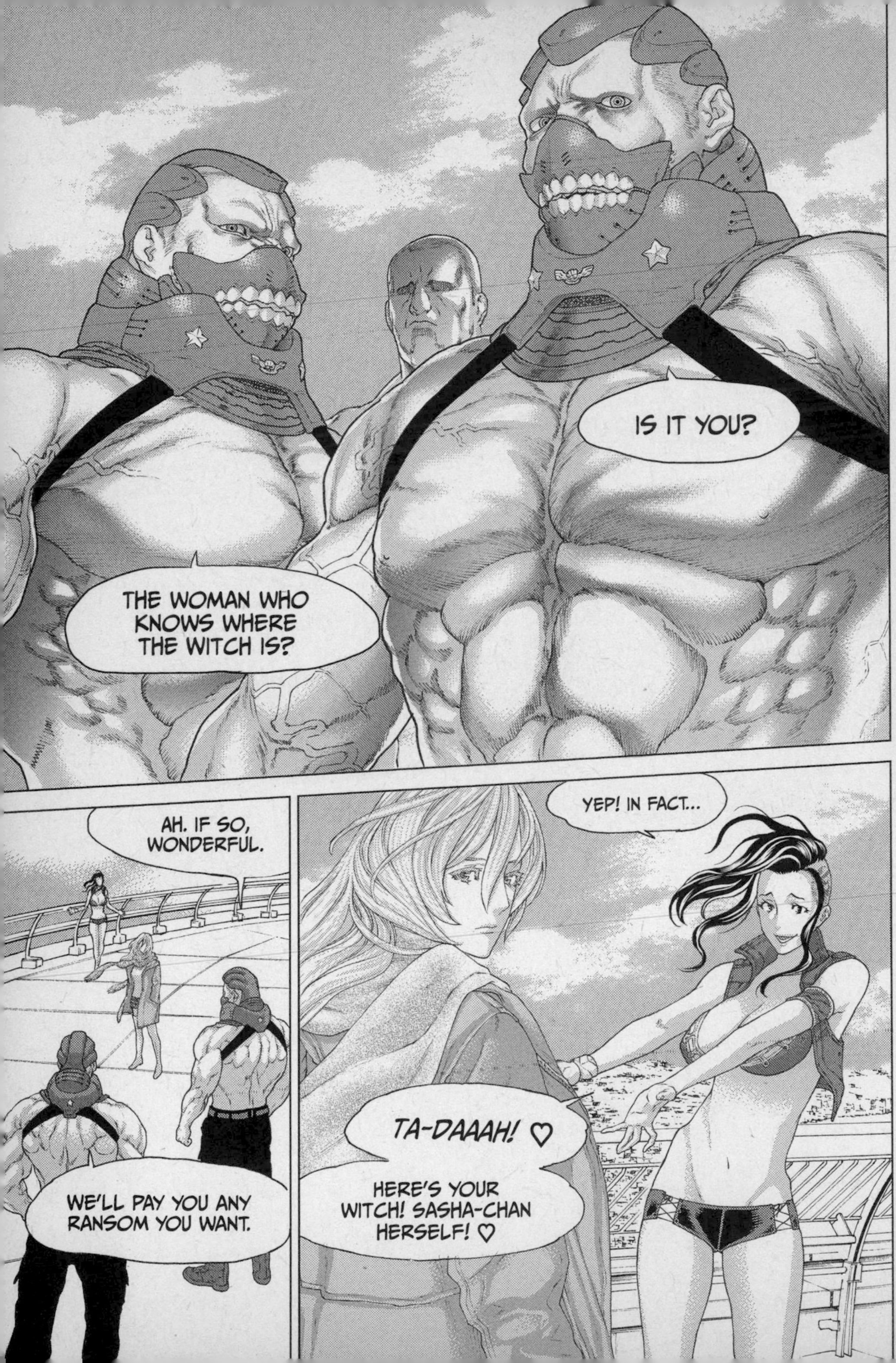
IS IT YOU?
THE WOMAN WHO KNOWS WHERE THE WITCH IS?
YEP! IN FACT...
TA-DAAAH! ♡
HERE'S YOUR WITCH! SASHA-CHAN HERSELF! ♡
AH. IF SO, WONDERFUL.
WE'LL PAY YOU ANY RANSOM YOU WANT.

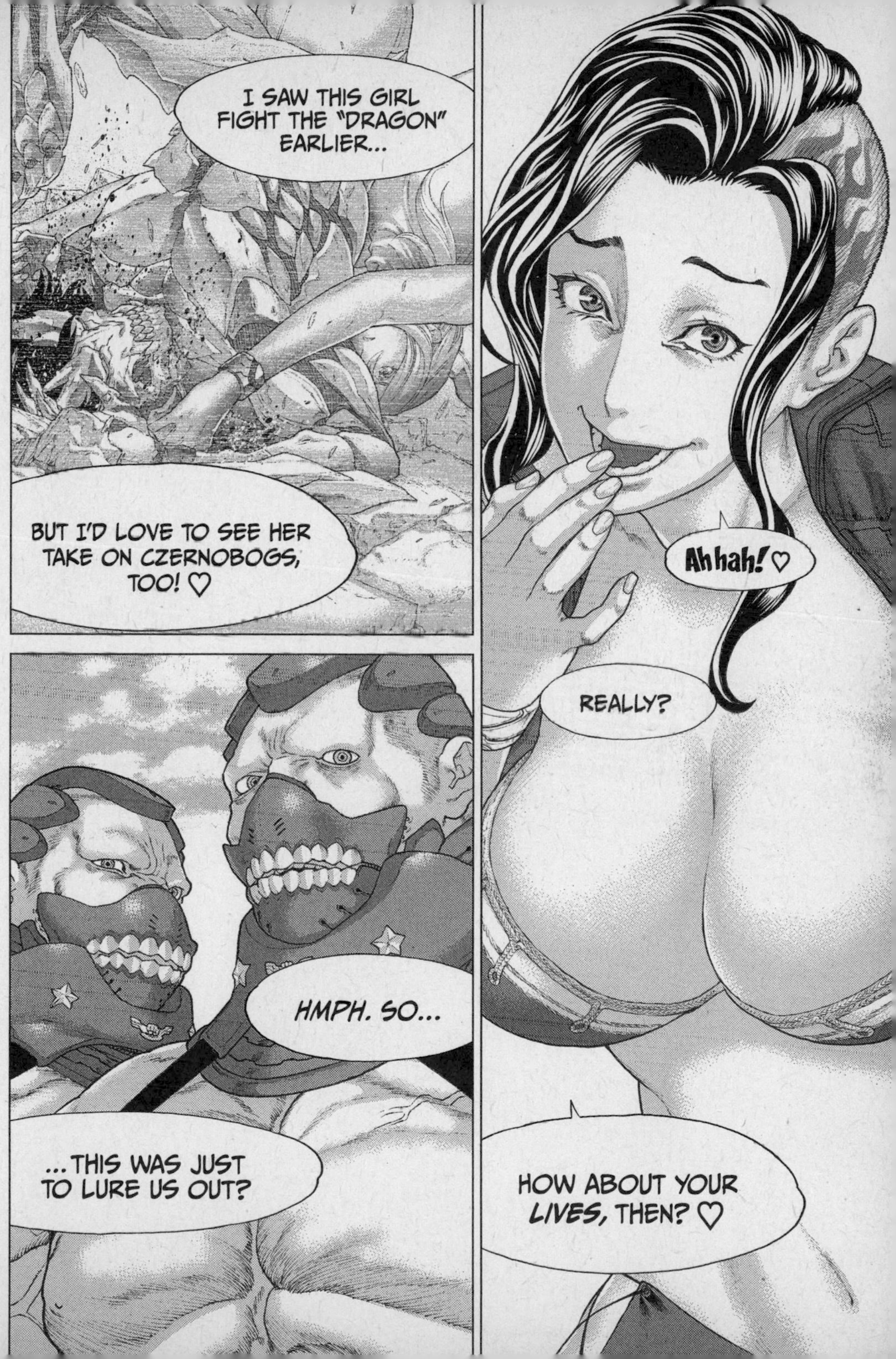
I SAW THIS GIRL FIGHT THE "DRAGON" EARLIER...
BUT I'D LOVE TO SEE HER TAKE ON CZERNOBOGS, TOO! ♡
HMPH. SO...
...THIS WAS JUST TO LURE US OUT?
Ahhah! ♡
REALLY?
HOW ABOUT YOUR *LIVES*, THEN? ♡

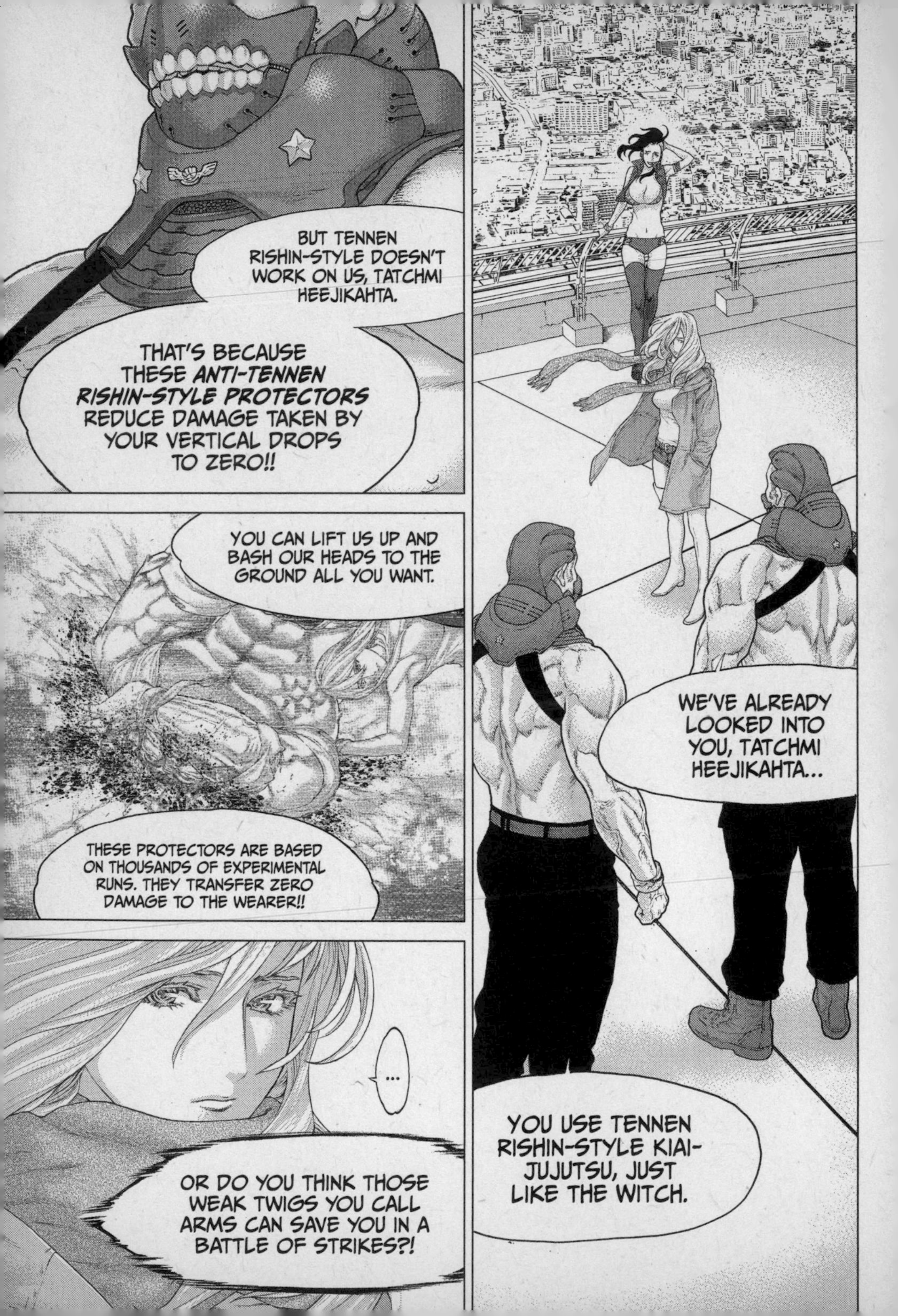
WE'VE ALREADY LOOKED INTO YOU, TATCHMI HEEJIKAHTA...
YOU USE TENNEN RISHIN-STYLE KIAI-JUJUTSU, JUST LIKE THE WITCH.
BUT TENNEN RISHIN-STYLE DOESN'T WORK ON US, TATCHMI HEEJIKAHTA.
THAT'S BECAUSE THESE *ANTI-TENNEN RISHIN-STYLE PROTECTORS* REDUCE DAMAGE TAKEN BY YOUR VERTICAL DROPS TO ZERO!!
YOU CAN LIFT US UP AND BASH OUR HEADS TO THE GROUND ALL YOU WANT.
THESE PROTECTORS ARE BASED ON THOUSANDS OF EXPERIMENTAL RUNS. THEY TRANSFER ZERO DAMAGE TO THE WEARER!!
...
OR DO YOU THINK THOSE WEAK TWIGS YOU CALL ARMS CAN SAVE YOU IN A BATTLE OF STRIKES?!

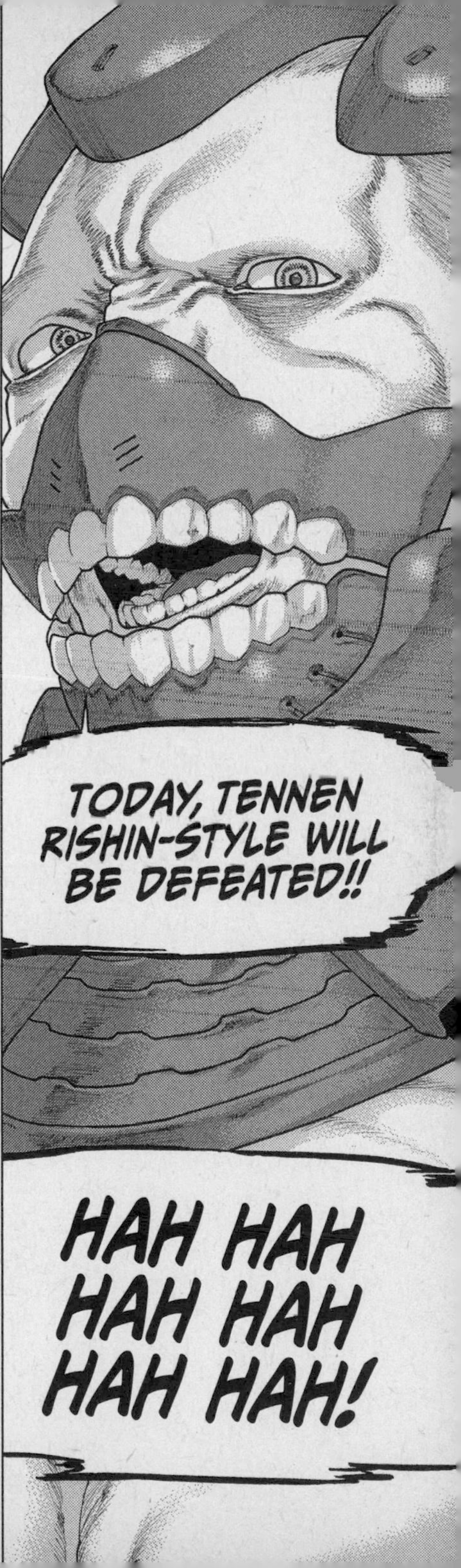
TODAY, TENNEN RISHIN-STYLE WILL BE DEFEATED!!
HAH HAH HAH HAH HAH HAH!

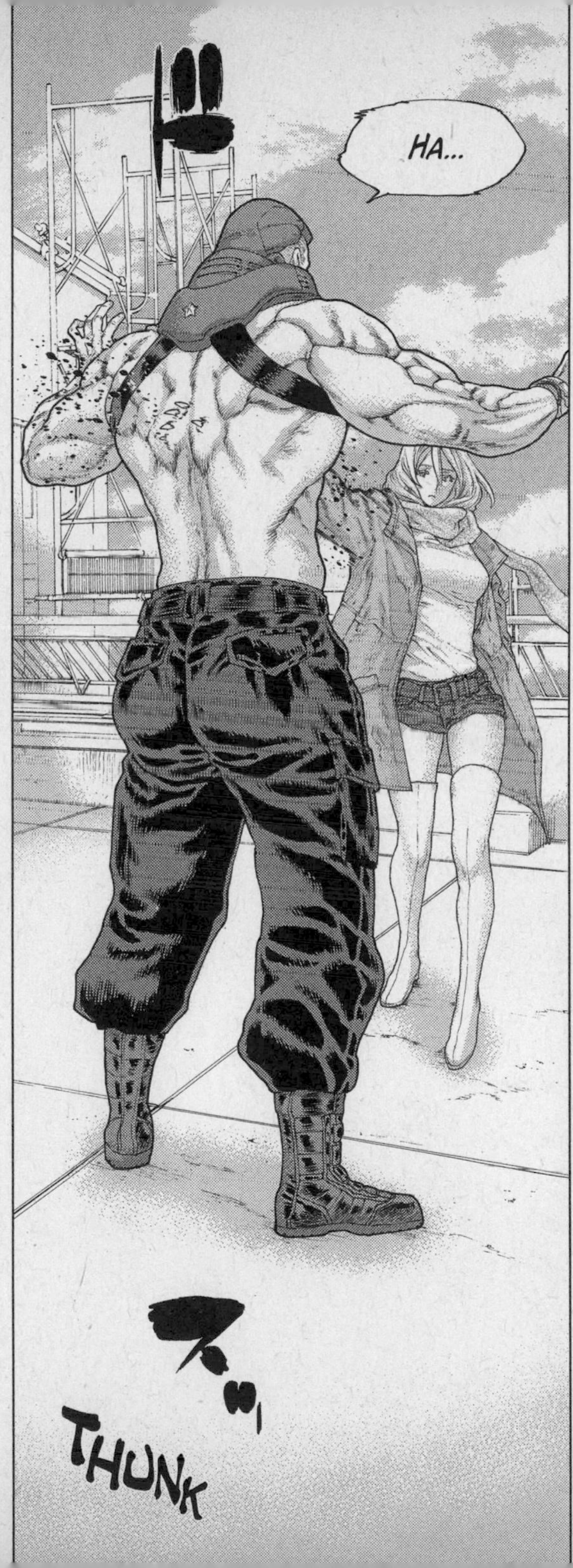
HA...
THUNK

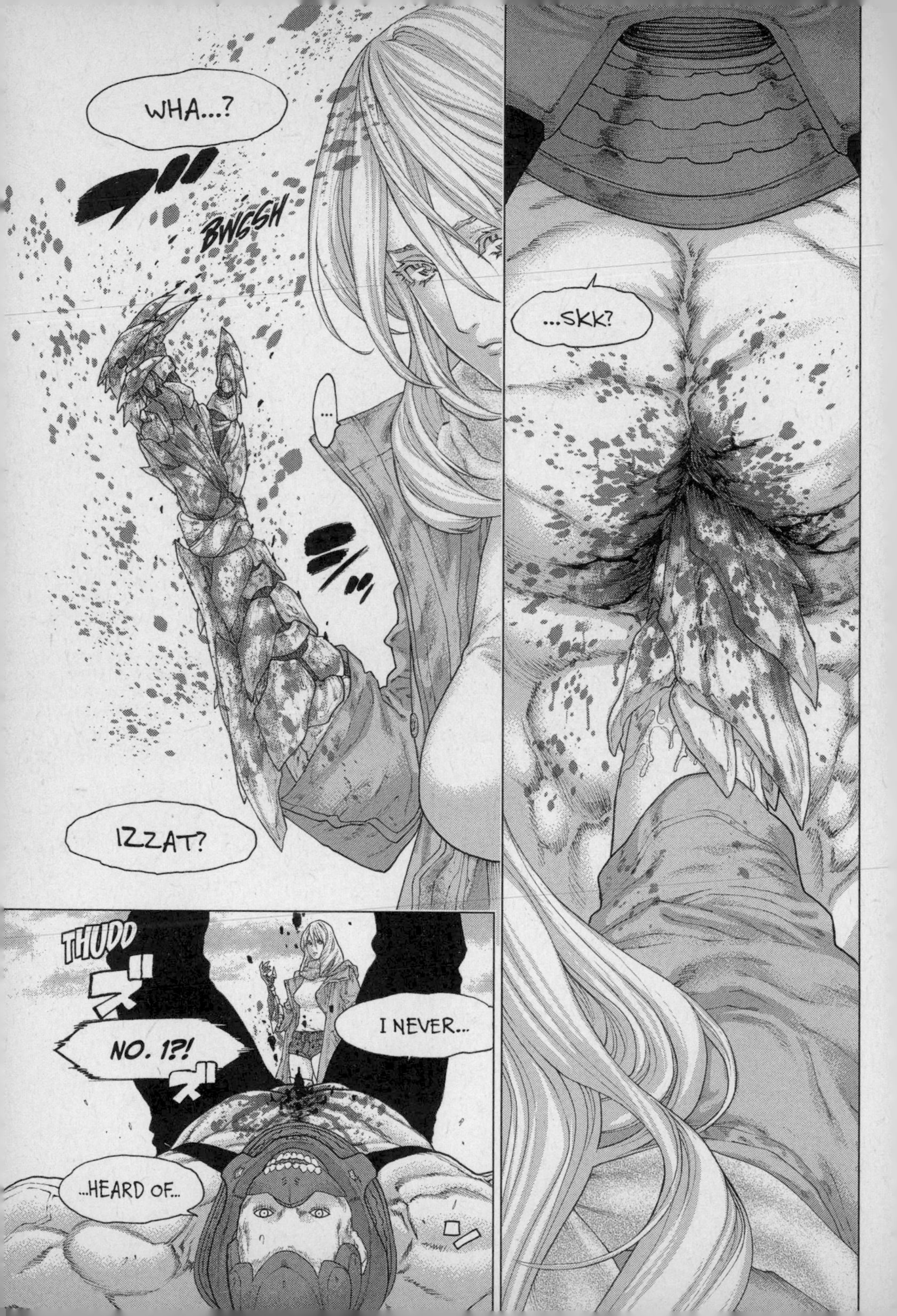
...SKK?
WHA...?
BWGSH
...
IZZAT?
THUDD
I NEVER...
NO. 1?!
...HEARD OF...

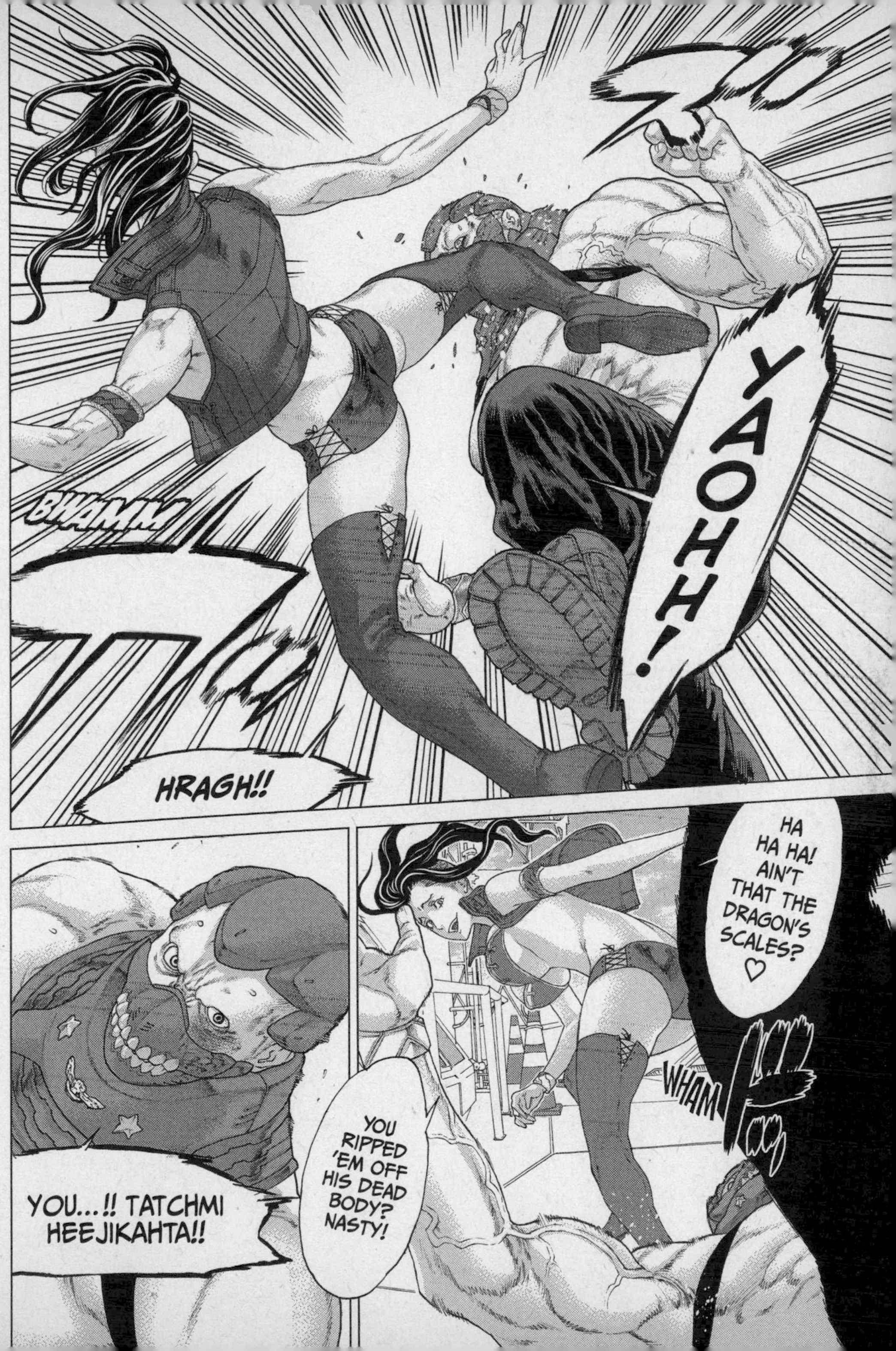
YAOHH!
BWAMM
HRAGH!!
HA HA HA! AIN'T THAT THE DRAGON'S SCALES? ♡
WHAM
YOU RIPPED 'EM OFF HIS DEAD BODY? NASTY!
YOU...!! TATCHMI HEEJIKAHTA!!

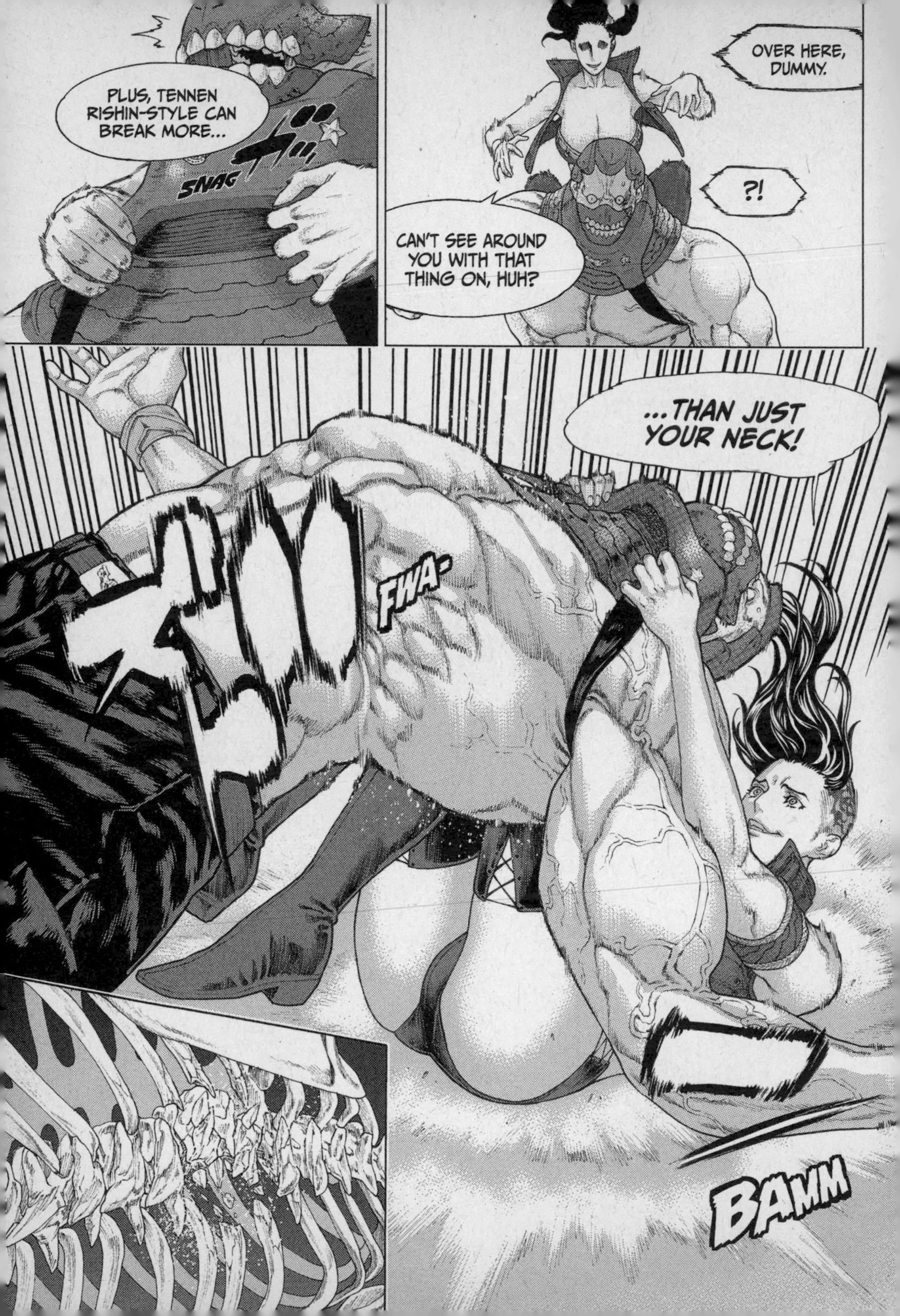
OVER HERE, DUMMY.
?!
CAN'T SEE AROUND YOU WITH THAT THING ON, HUH?
PLUS, TENNEN RISHIN-STYLE CAN BREAK MORE...
SNAG
...THAN JUST YOUR NECK!
FWA-
BAMM

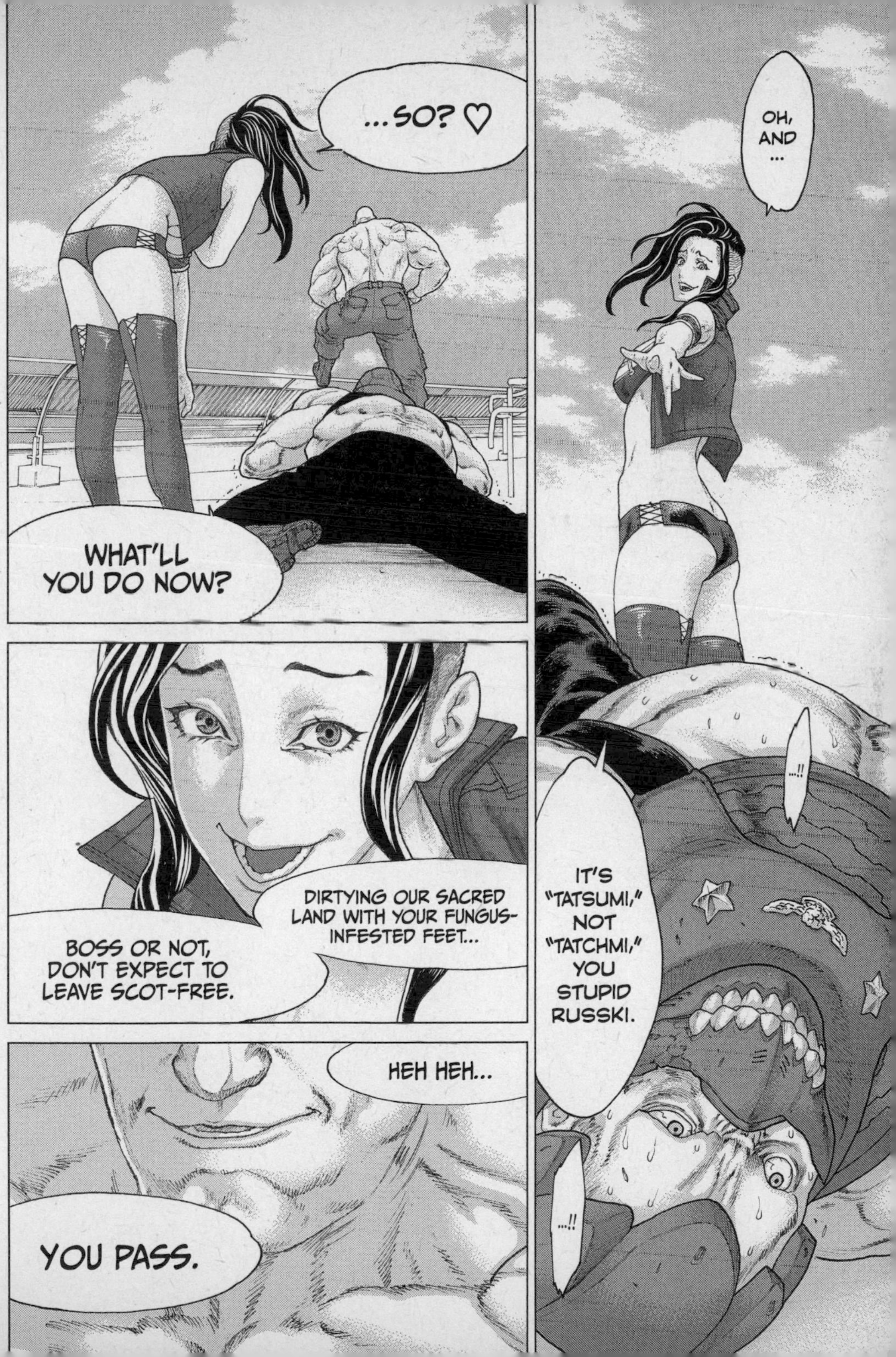
OH, AND ...
...!!
IT'S "TATSUMI," NOT "TATCHMI," YOU STUPID RUSSKI.
...!!
...SO? ♡
WHAT'LL YOU DO NOW?
DIRTYING OUR SACRED LAND WITH YOUR FUNGUS-INFESTED FEET...
BOSS OR NOT, DON'T EXPECT TO LEAVE SCOT-FREE.
HEH HEH...
YOU PASS.

I DON'T KNOW IF YOU'RE A WITCH OR NOT...

G-GENERAL...

BUT I FIGURED THESE IDIOTS WOULD BE ENOUGH TO HANDLE TWO GIRLS.

HELP ME...

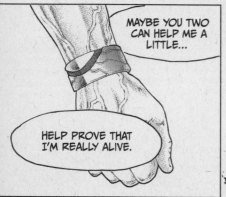

MAYBE YOU TWO CAN HELP ME A LITTLE...

HELP PROVE THAT I'M REALLY ALIVE.

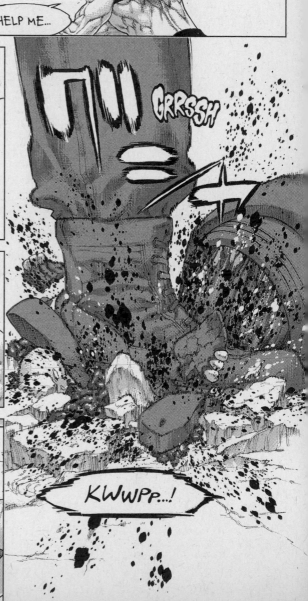

CRRSSH

HELP ME FEEL DEATH...

...BY WAGERING YOUR LIFE.

SUCH A PITIFUL MAN. ♡

BUT FINE. I'LL MAKE YOU FEEL IT, ALL RIGHT.

KWWPP...!

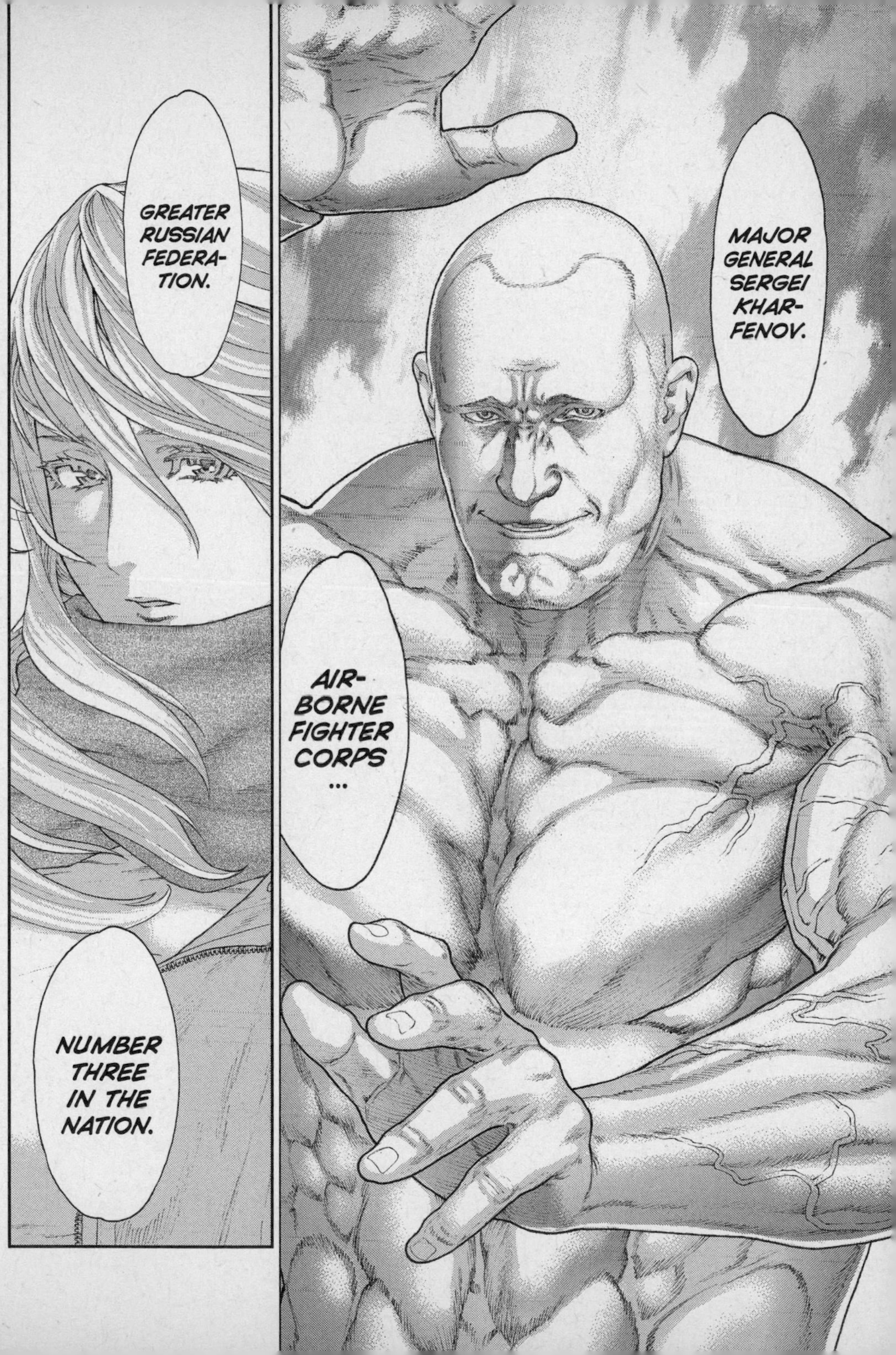
MAJOR GENERAL SERGEI KHAR-FENOV.
AIR-BORNE FIGHTER CORPS ...
GREATER RUSSIAN FEDERA-TION.
NUMBER THREE IN THE NATION.

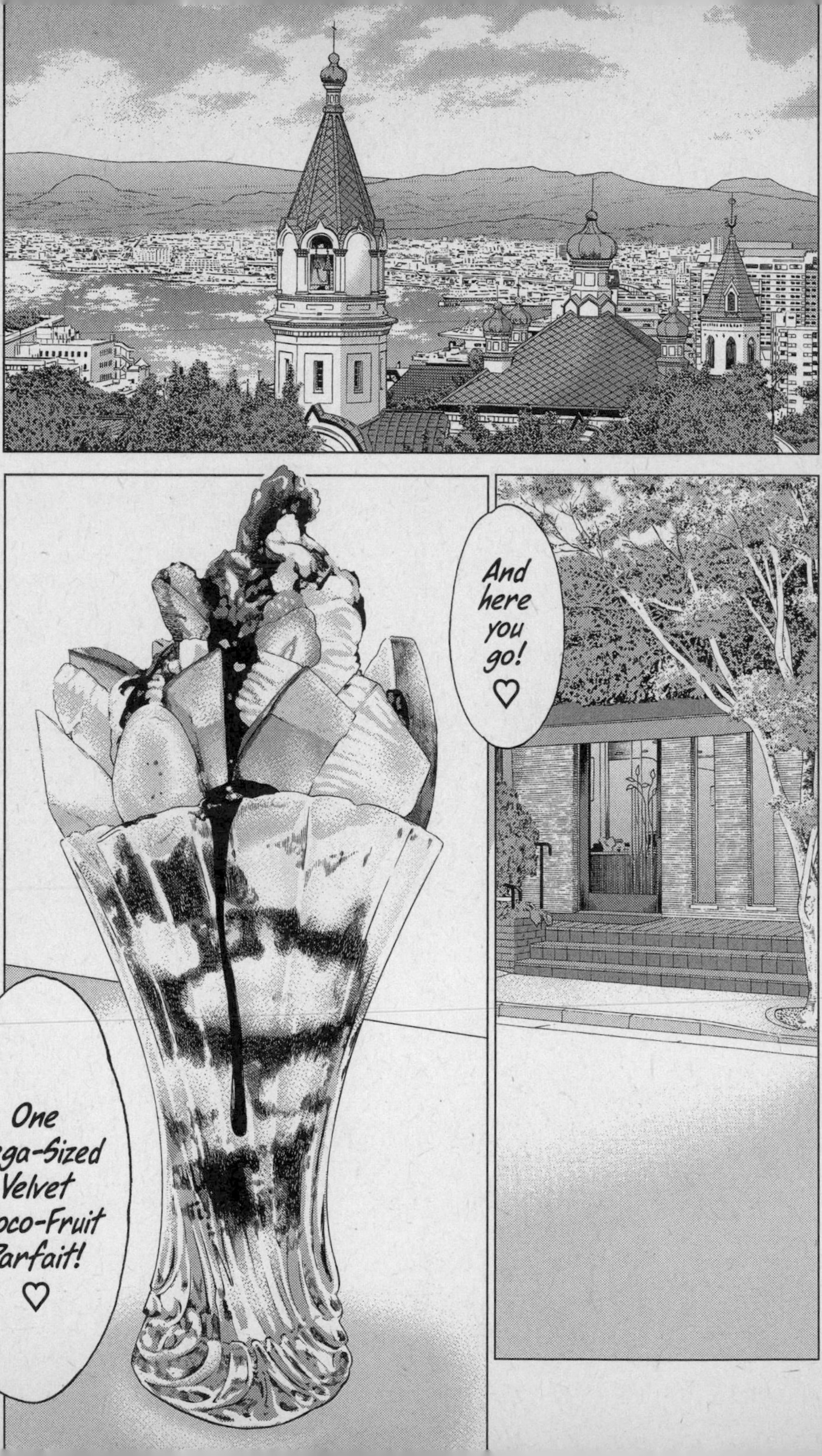
And here you go! ♡
One Mega-Sized Velvet Choco-Fruit Parfait! ♡

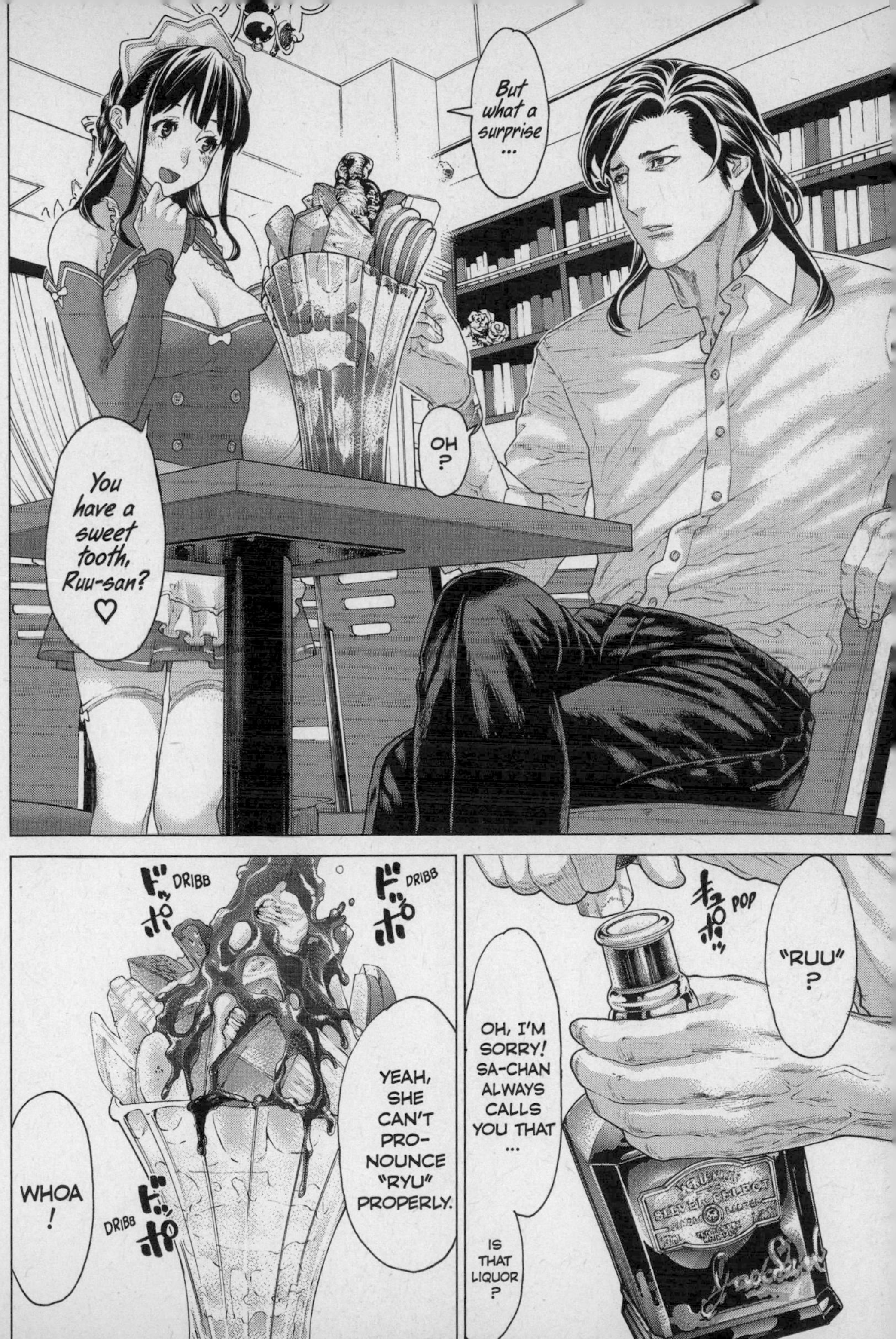
But what a surprise ...
OH?
You have a sweet tooth, Ruu-san? ♡
POP
"RUU"?
OH, I'M SORRY! SA-CHAN ALWAYS CALLS YOU THAT ...
IS THAT LIQUOR?
DRIBB
DRIBB
YEAH, SHE CAN'T PRO-NOUNCE "RYU" PROPERLY.
WHOA!
DRIBB

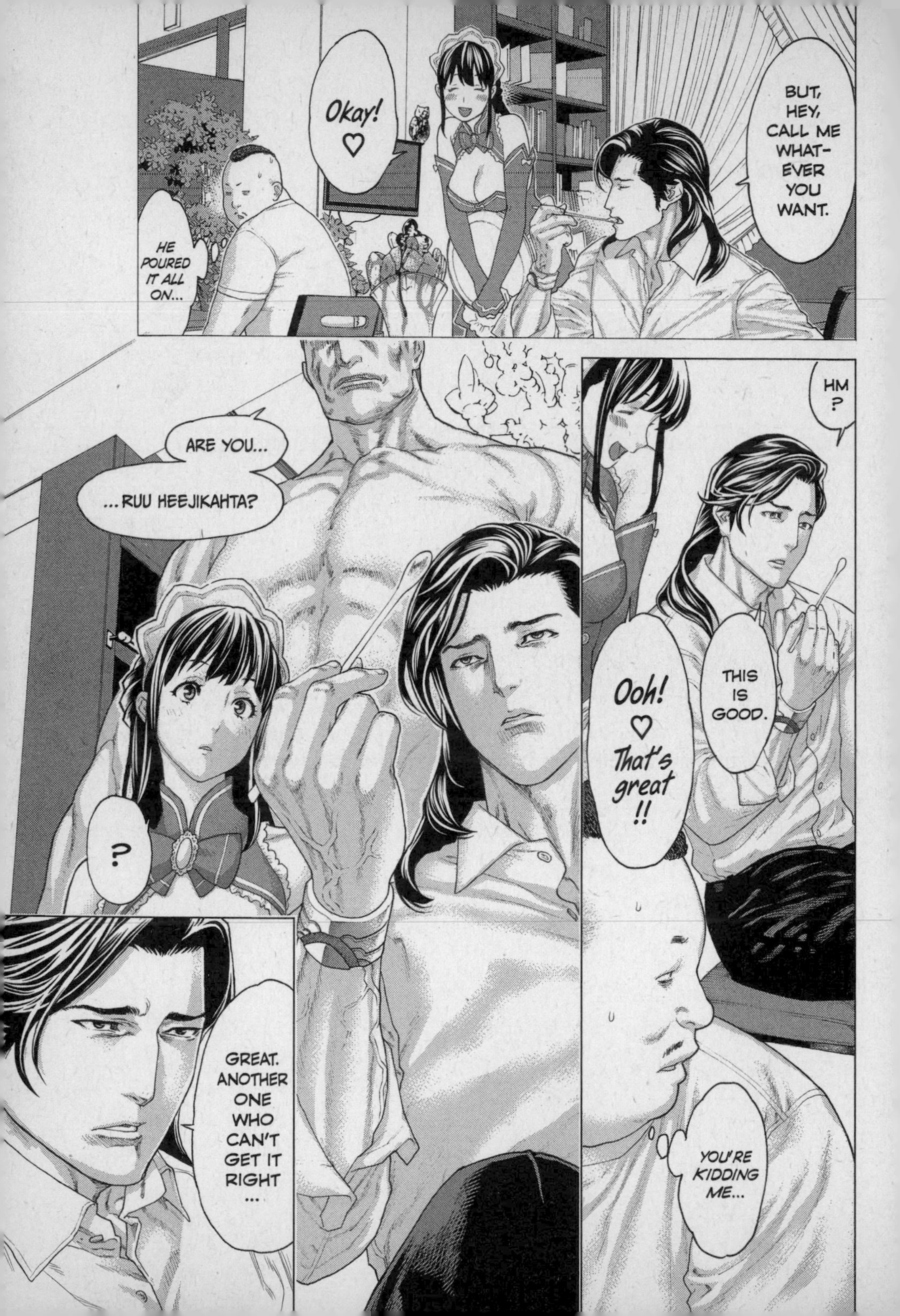
BUT, HEY, CALL ME WHATEVER YOU WANT.
Okay! ♡
HE POURED IT ALL ON...
HM ?
THIS IS GOOD.
Ooh! ♡ That's great !!
YOU'RE KIDDING ME...
ARE YOU...
...RUU HEEJIKAHTA?
?
GREAT. ANOTHER ONE WHO CAN'T GET IT RIGHT ...

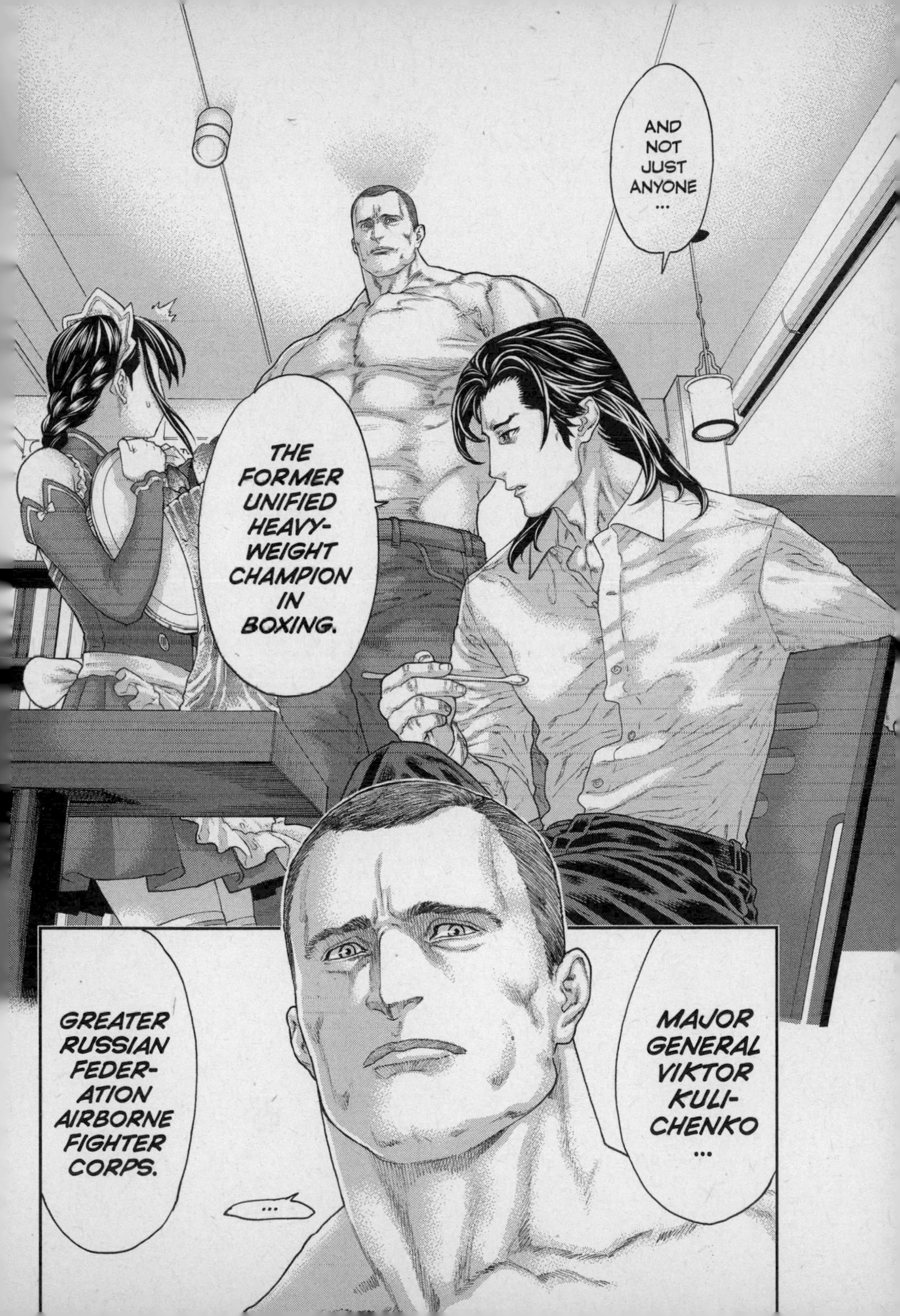
AND NOT JUST ANYONE ...
THE FORMER UNIFIED HEAVY-WEIGHT CHAMPION IN BOXING.
MAJOR GENERAL VIKTOR KULI-CHENKO ...
GREATER RUSSIAN FEDER-ATION AIRBORNE FIGHTER CORPS.
...

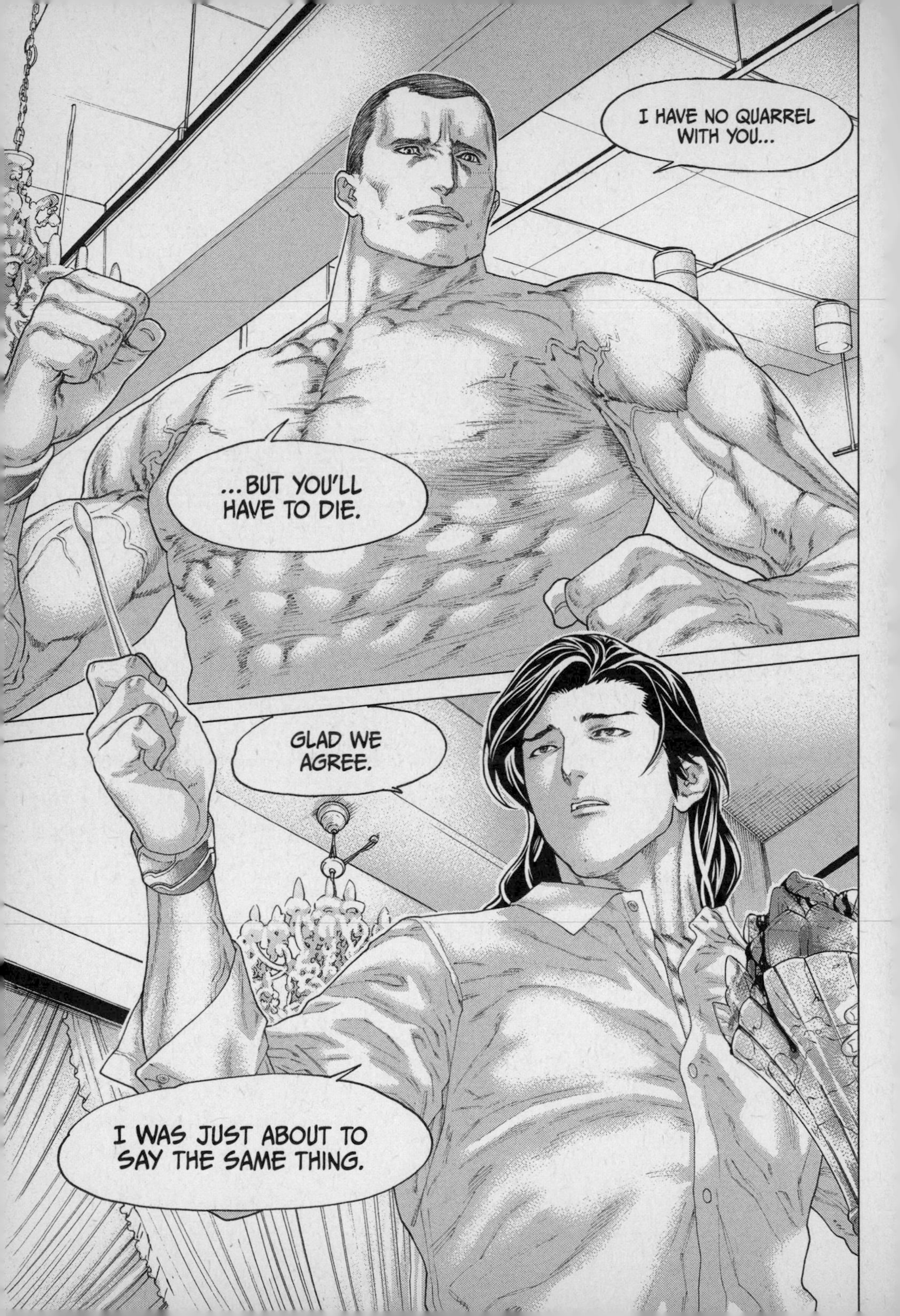
I HAVE NO QUARREL WITH YOU...
...BUT YOU'LL HAVE TO DIE.
GLAD WE AGREE.
I WAS JUST ABOUT TO SAY THE SAME THING.

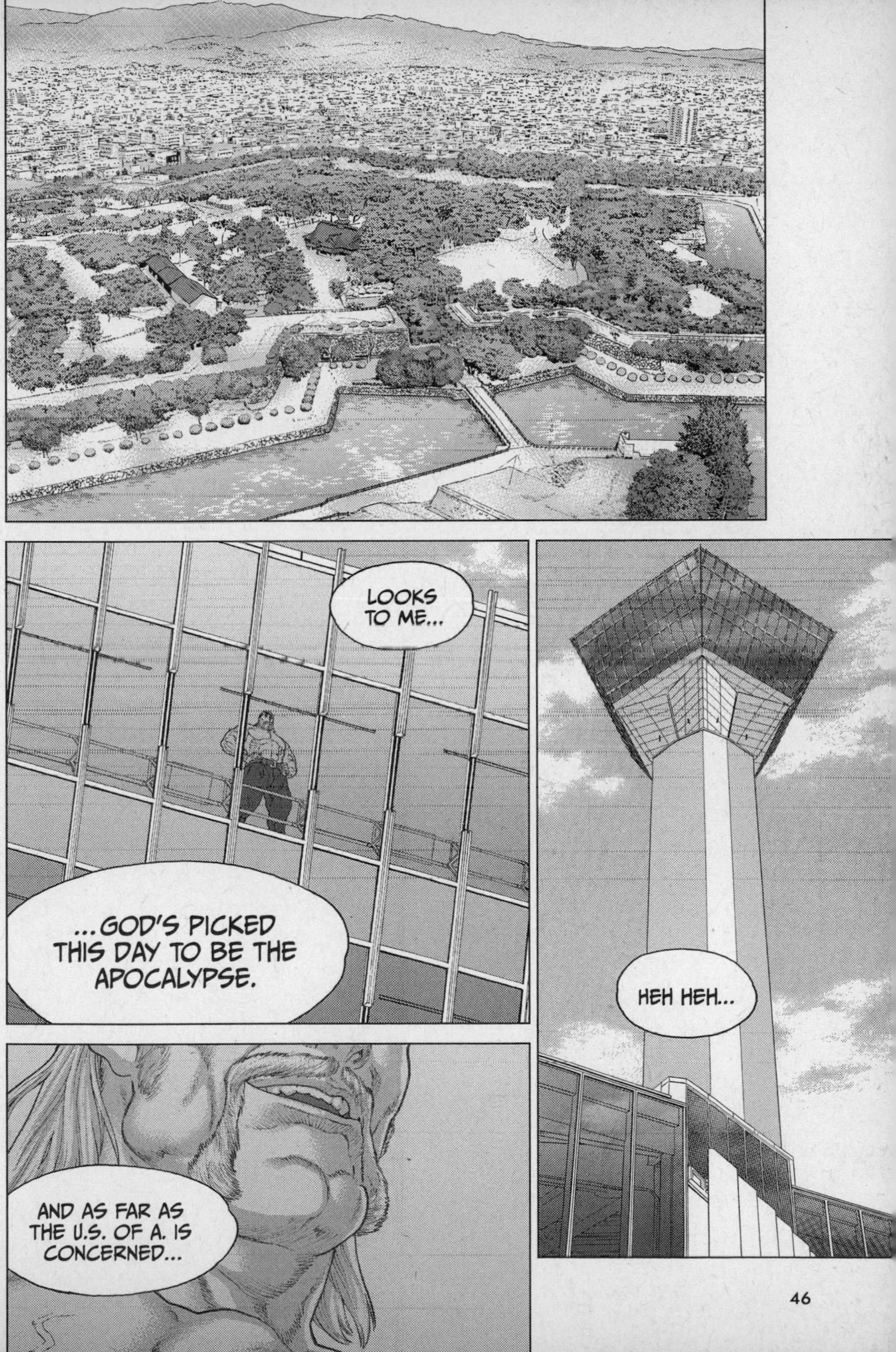
HEH HEH...
LOOKS TO ME...
...GOD'S PICKED THIS DAY TO BE THE APOCALYPSE.
AND AS FAR AS THE U.S. OF A. IS CONCERNED...

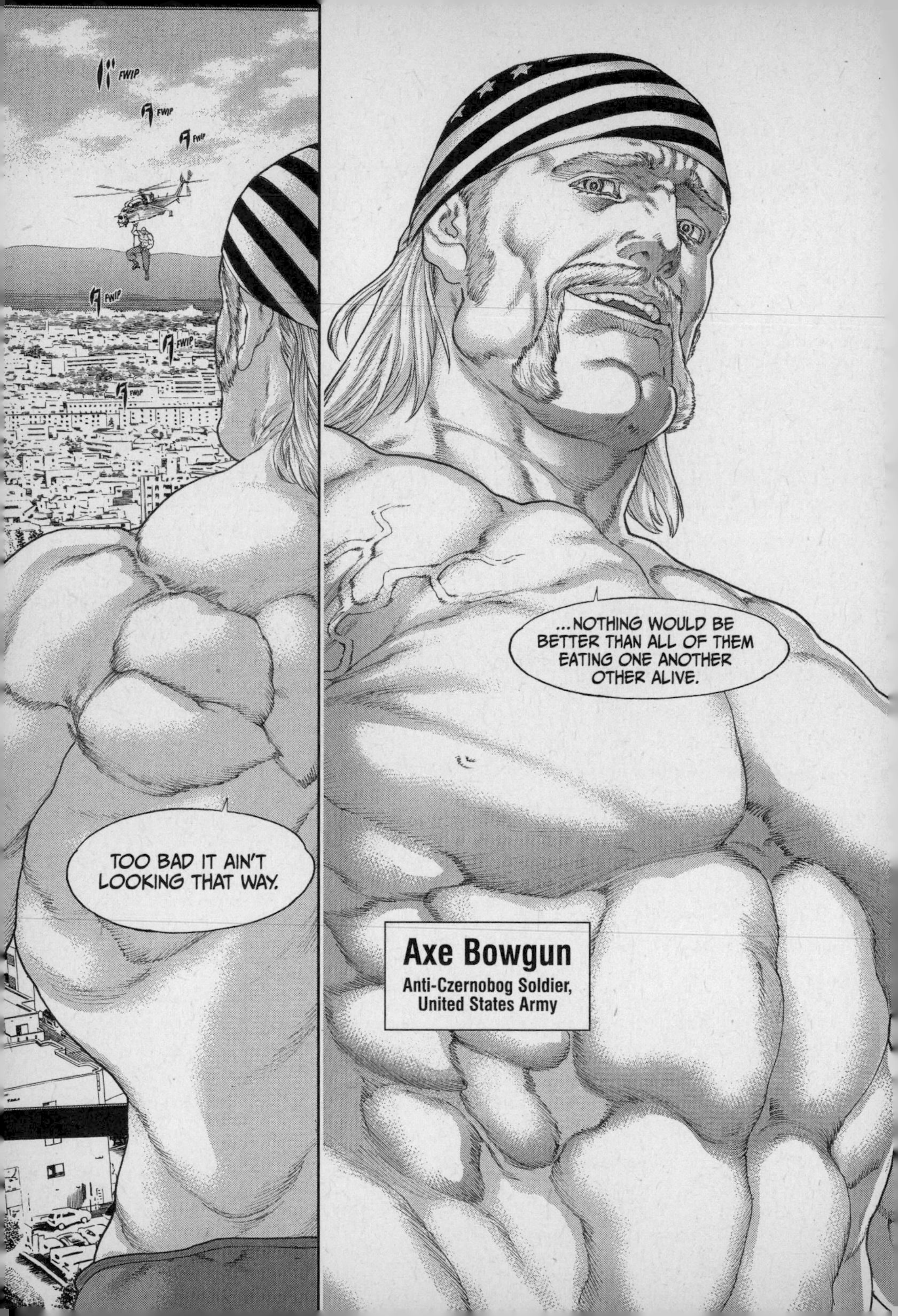
...NOTHING WOULD BE BETTER THAN ALL OF THEM EATING ONE ANOTHER OTHER ALIVE.
Axe Bowgun
Anti-Czernobog Soldier, United States Army
FWIP
FWIP
FWIP
FWIP
FWIP
FWIP
TOO BAD IT AIN'T LOOKING THAT WAY.

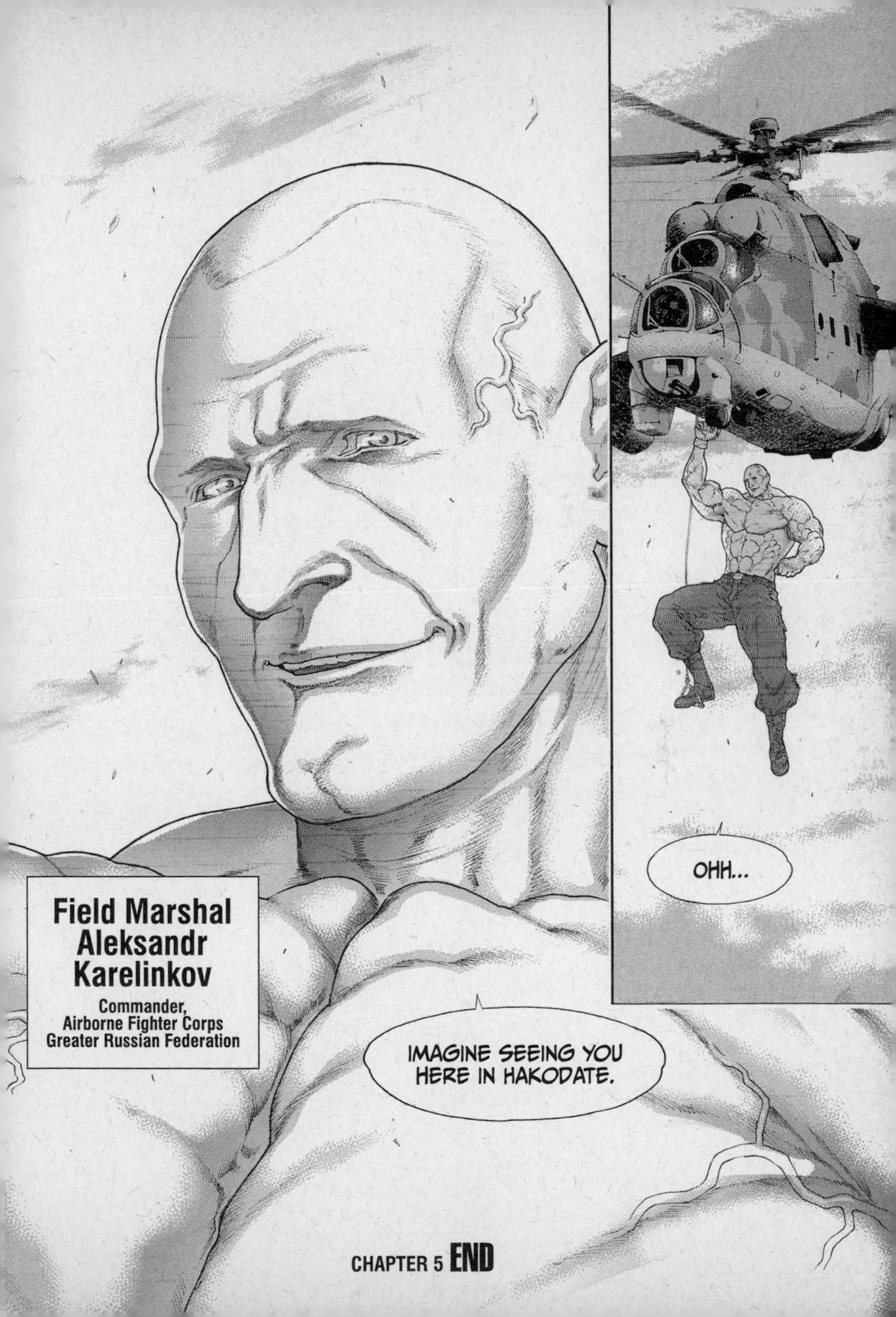
OHH...
Field Marshal Aleksandr Karelinkov
Commander, Airborne Fighter Corps Greater Russian Federation
IMAGINE SEEING YOU HERE IN HAKODATE.
CHAPTER 5 END

GOLOSSEUM

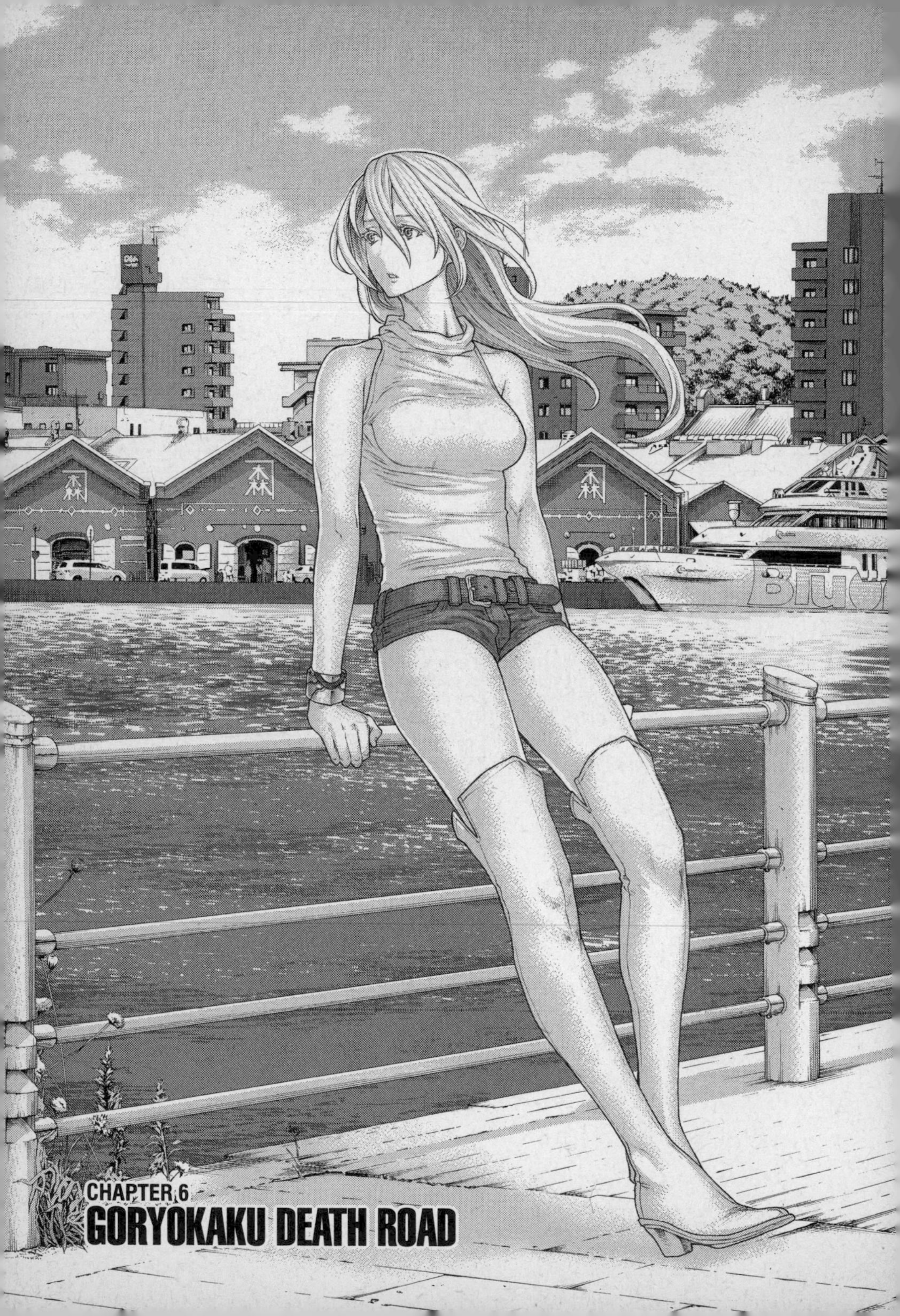

CHAPTER 6
GORYOKAKU DEATH ROAD

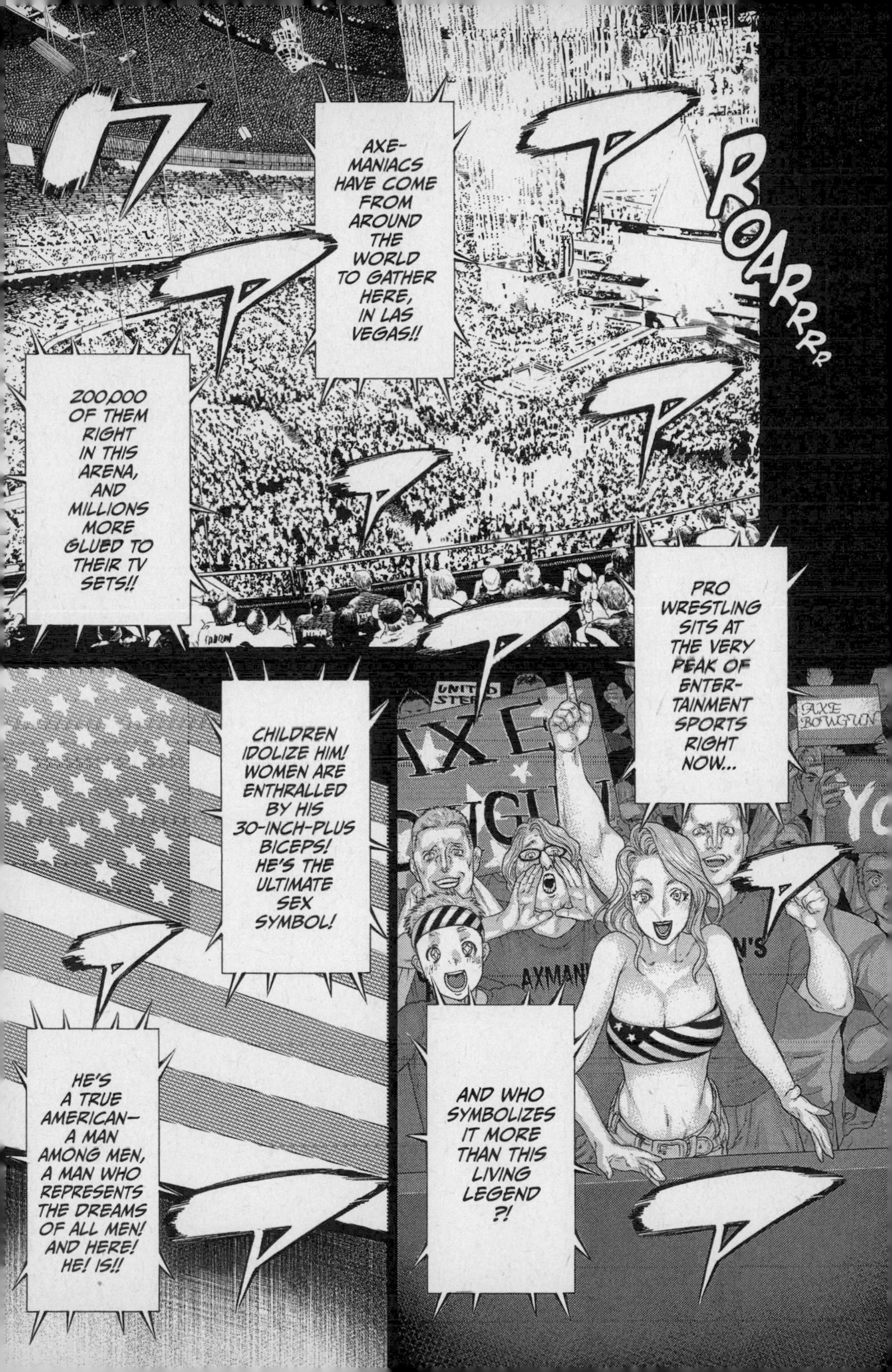
ROARRRR
AXE-MANIACS HAVE COME FROM AROUND THE WORLD TO GATHER HERE, IN LAS VEGAS!!
200,000 OF THEM RIGHT IN THIS ARENA, AND MILLIONS MORE GLUED TO THEIR TV SETS!!
PRO WRESTLING SITS AT THE VERY PEAK OF ENTER-TAINMENT SPORTS RIGHT NOW...
AND WHO SYMBOLIZES IT MORE THAN THIS LIVING LEGEND ?!
CHILDREN IDOLIZE HIM! WOMEN ARE ENTHRALLED BY HIS 30-INCH-PLUS BICEPS! HE'S THE ULTIMATE SEX SYMBOL!
HE'S A TRUE AMERICAN— A MAN AMONG MEN, A MAN WHO REPRESENTS THE DREAMS OF ALL MEN! AND HERE! HE! IS!!

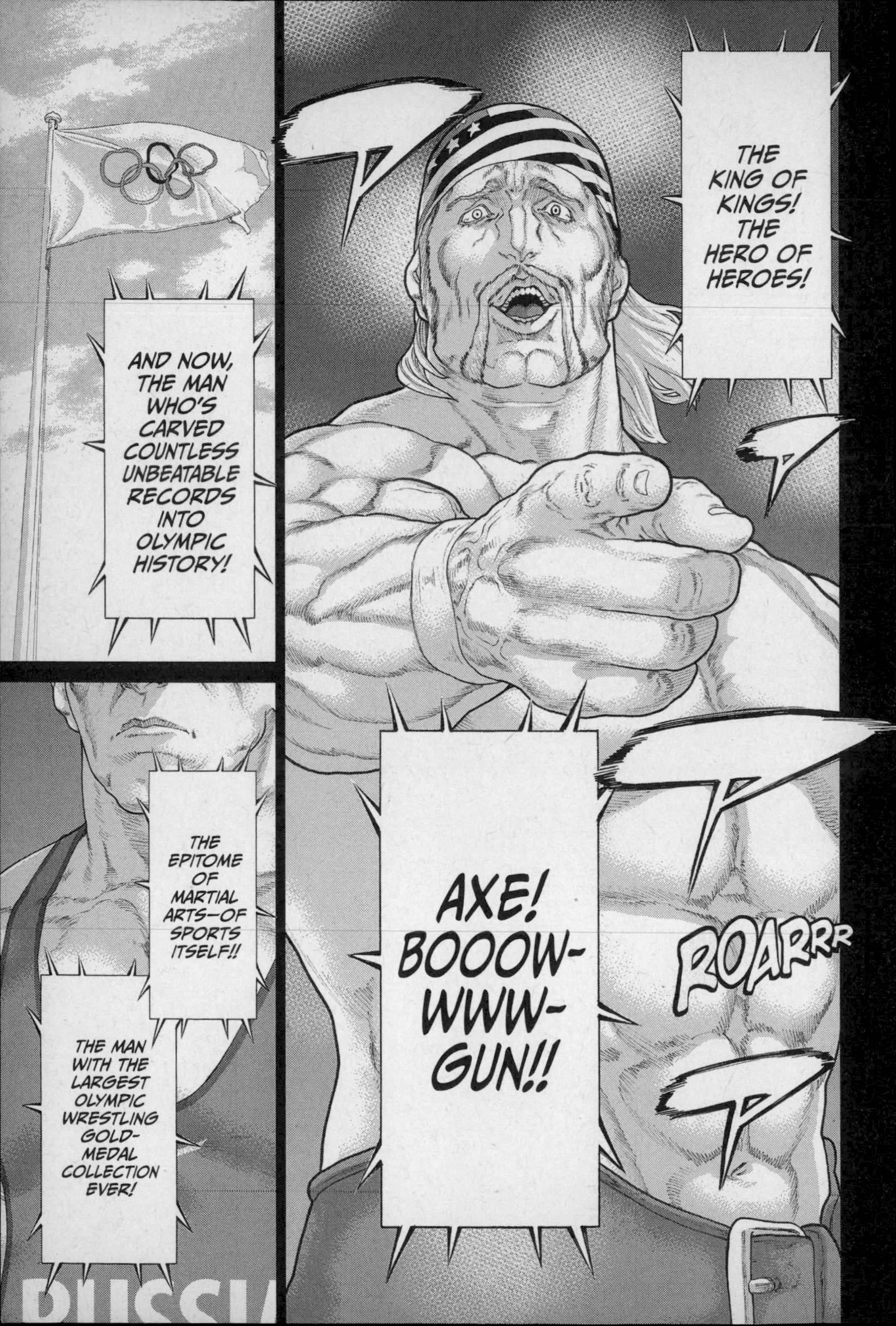
THE KING OF KINGS! THE HERO OF HEROES!
AXE! BOOOW-WWW-GUN!!
ROARRR
AND NOW, THE MAN WHO'S CARVED COUNTLESS UNBEATABLE RECORDS INTO OLYMPIC HISTORY!
THE EPITOME OF MARTIAL ARTS—OF SPORTS ITSELF!!
THE MAN WITH THE LARGEST OLYMPIC WRESTLING GOLD-MEDAL COLLECTION EVER!

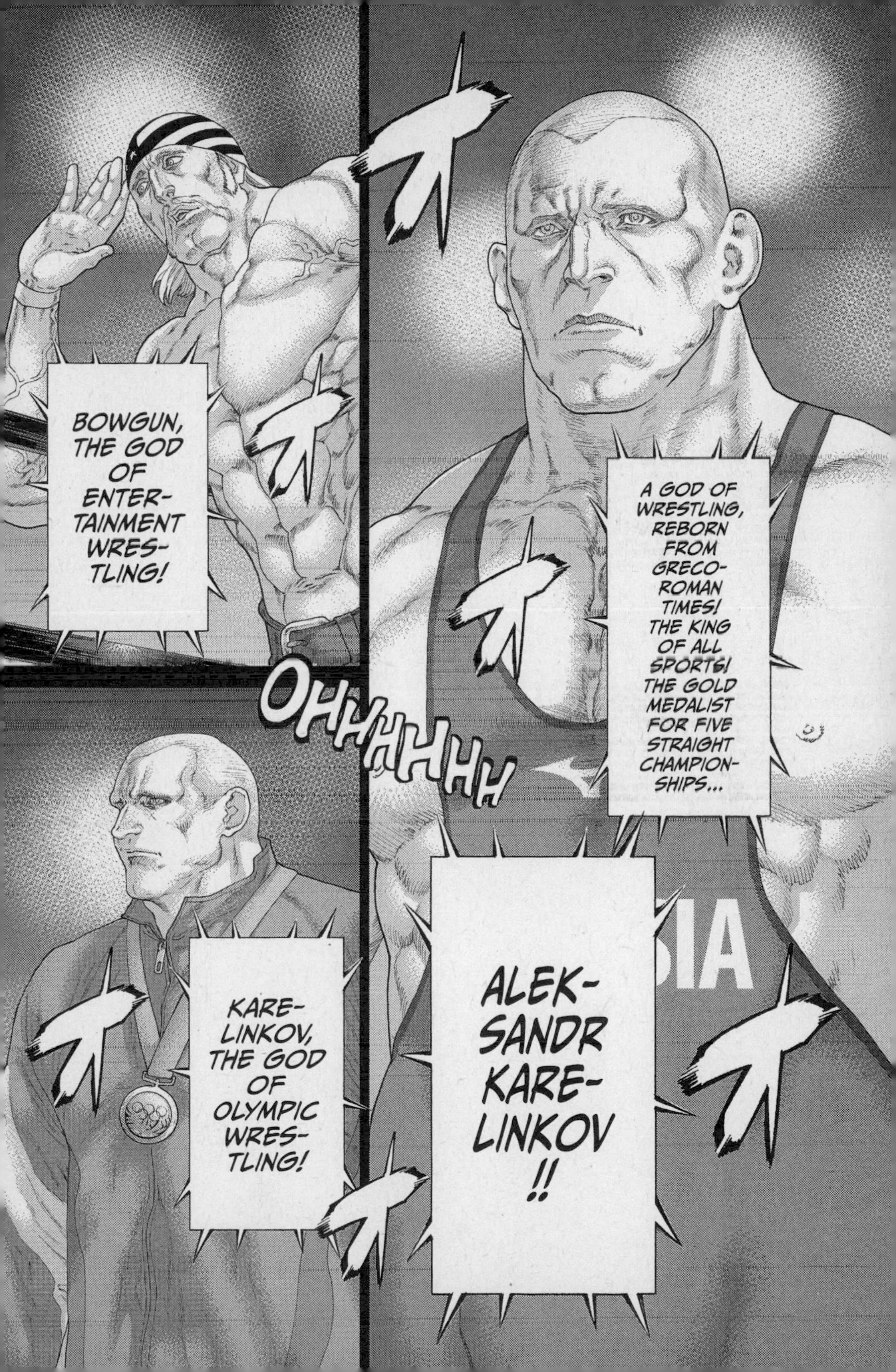
A GOD OF WRESTLING, REBORN FROM GRECO-ROMAN TIMES! THE KING OF ALL SPORTS! THE GOLD MEDALIST FOR FIVE STRAIGHT CHAMPION-SHIPS...
ALEK-SANDR KARE-LINKOV!!
OHHHHHHH
BOWGUN, THE GOD OF ENTER-TAINMENT WRES-TLING!
KARE-LINKOV, THE GOD OF OLYMPIC WRES-TLING!

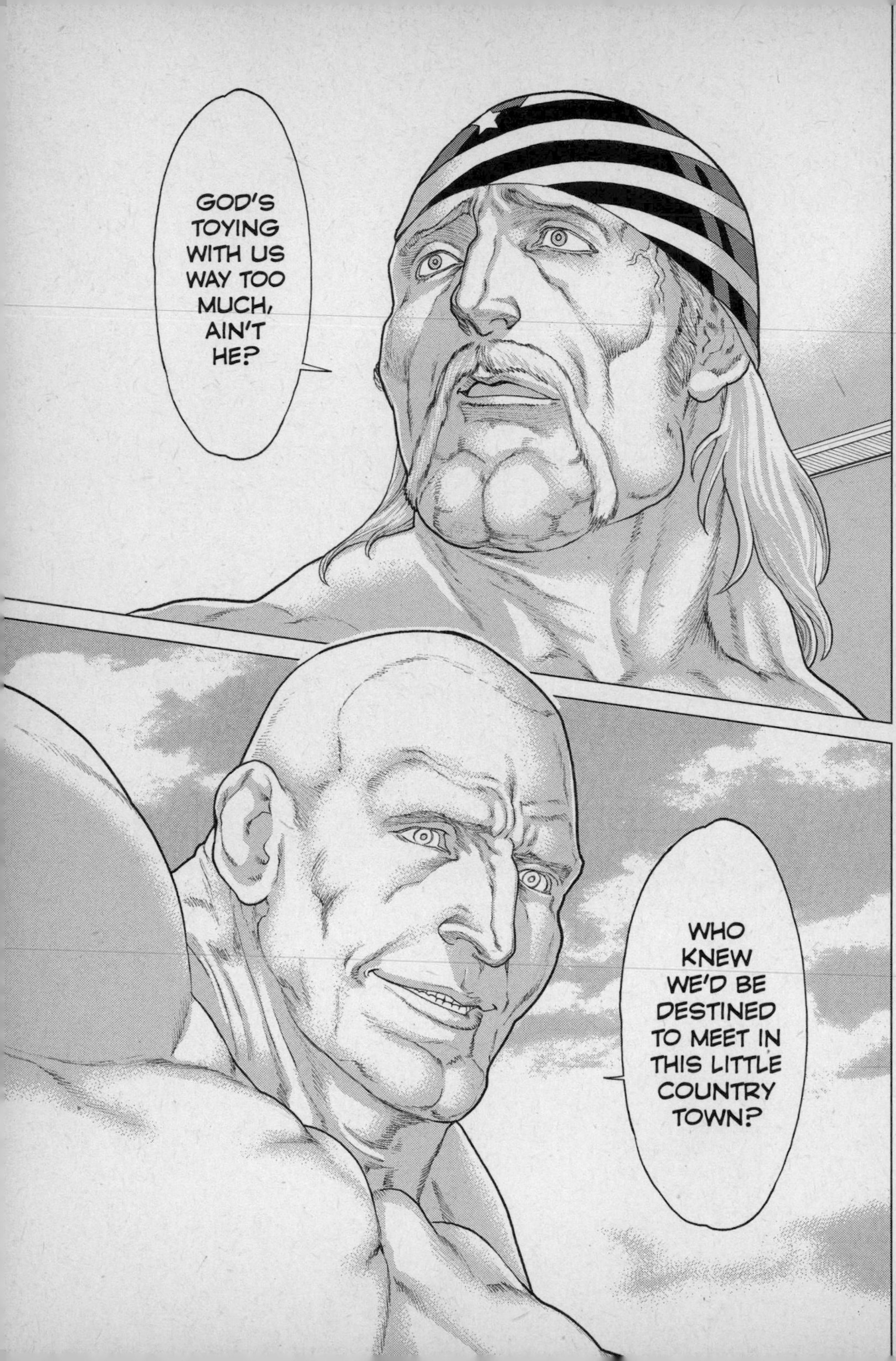
GOD'S TOYING WITH US WAY TOO MUCH, AIN'T HE?
WHO KNEW WE'D BE DESTINED TO MEET IN THIS LITTLE COUNTRY TOWN?

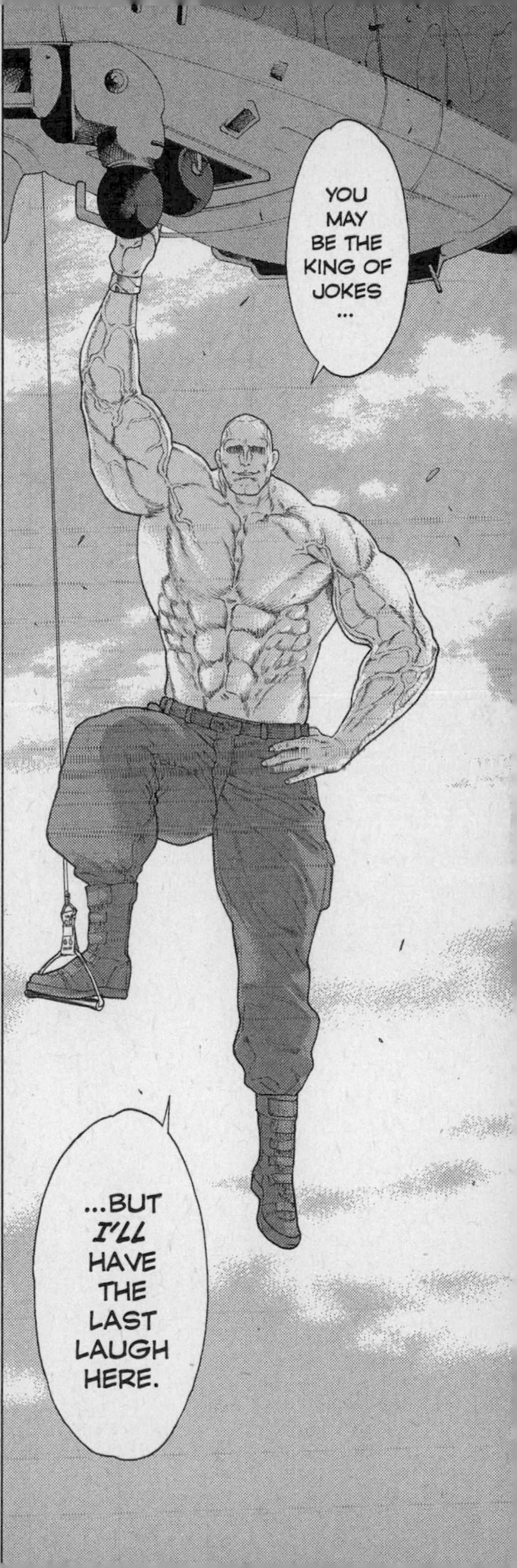
YOU MAY BE THE KING OF JOKES ...
...BUT *I'LL* HAVE THE LAST LAUGH HERE.
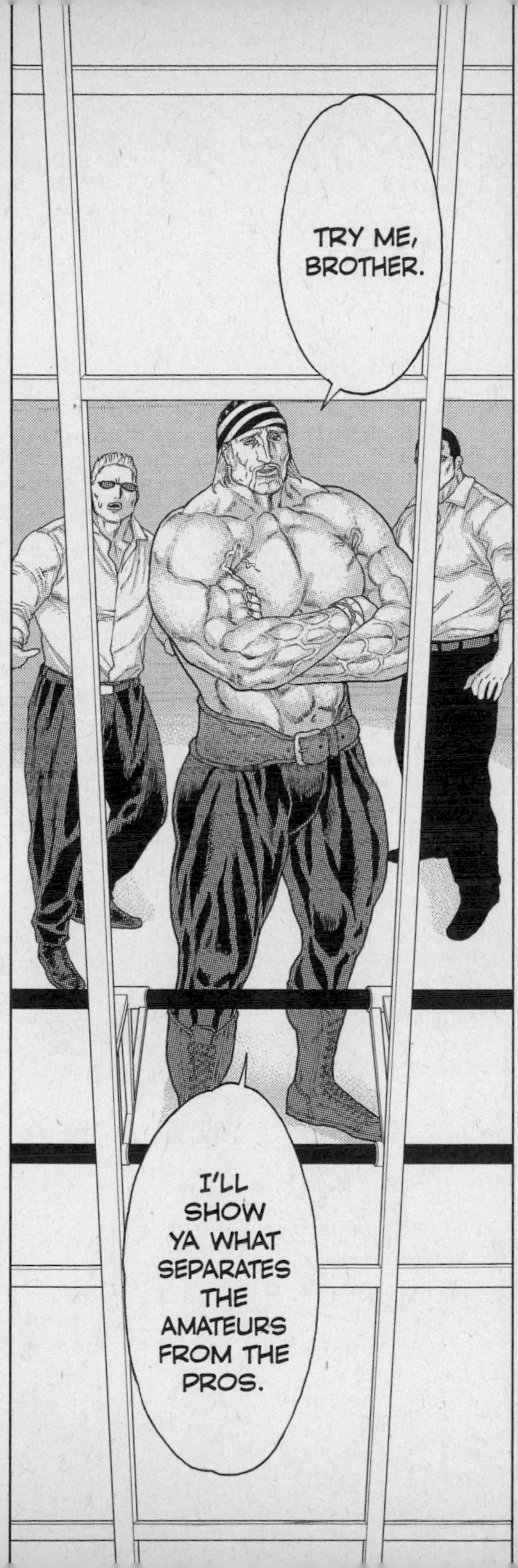
TRY ME, BROTHER.
I'LL SHOW YA WHAT SEPARATES THE AMATEURS FROM THE PROS.

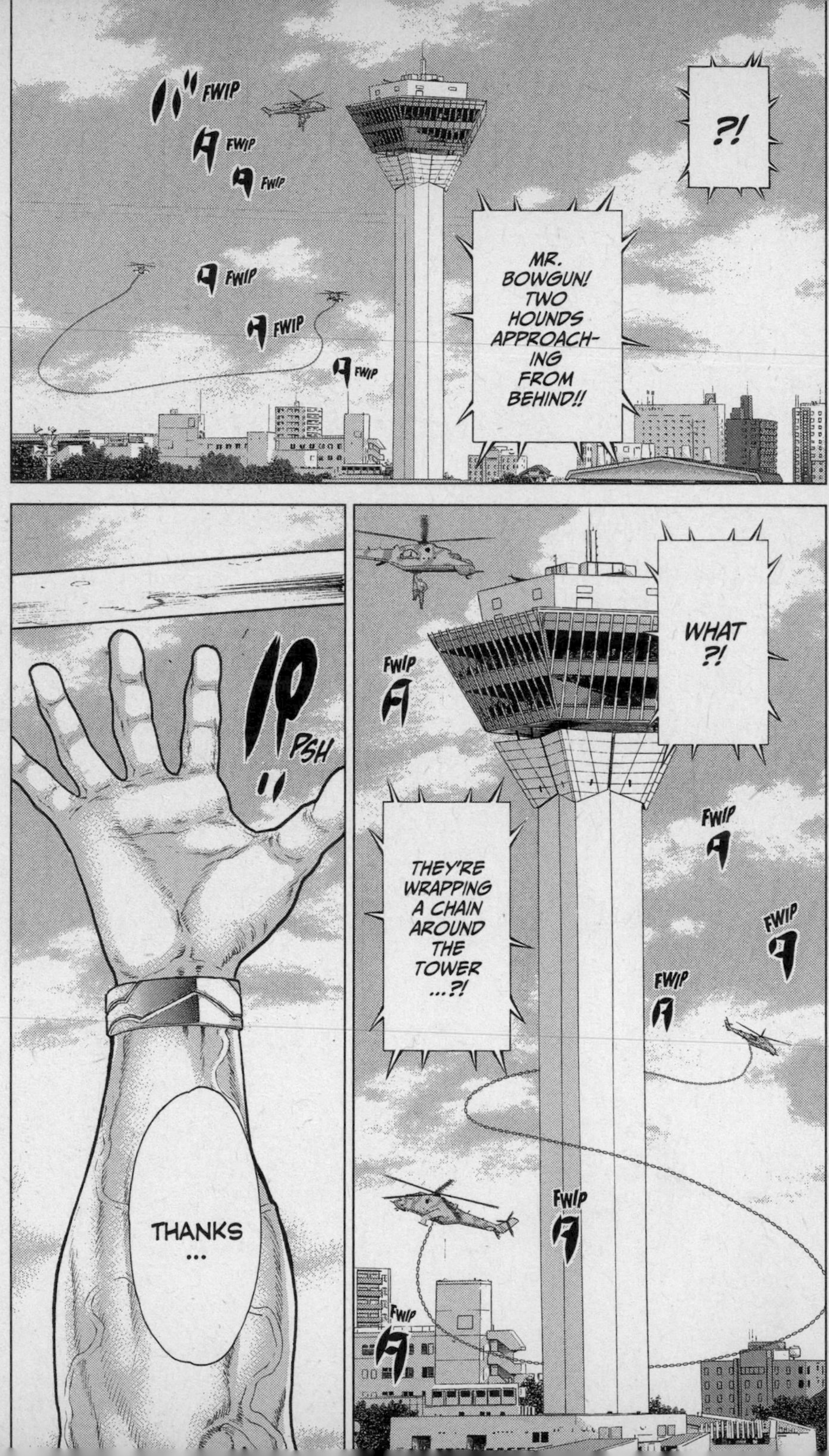
?!
MR. BOWGUN! TWO HOUNDS APPROACHING FROM BEHIND!!
FWIP
FWIP
FWIP
FWIP
FWIP
FWIP
WHAT ?!
FWIP
THEY'RE WRAPPING A CHAIN AROUND THE TOWER ...?!
FWIP
FWIP
FWIP
FWIP
FWIP
PSH
THANKS ...

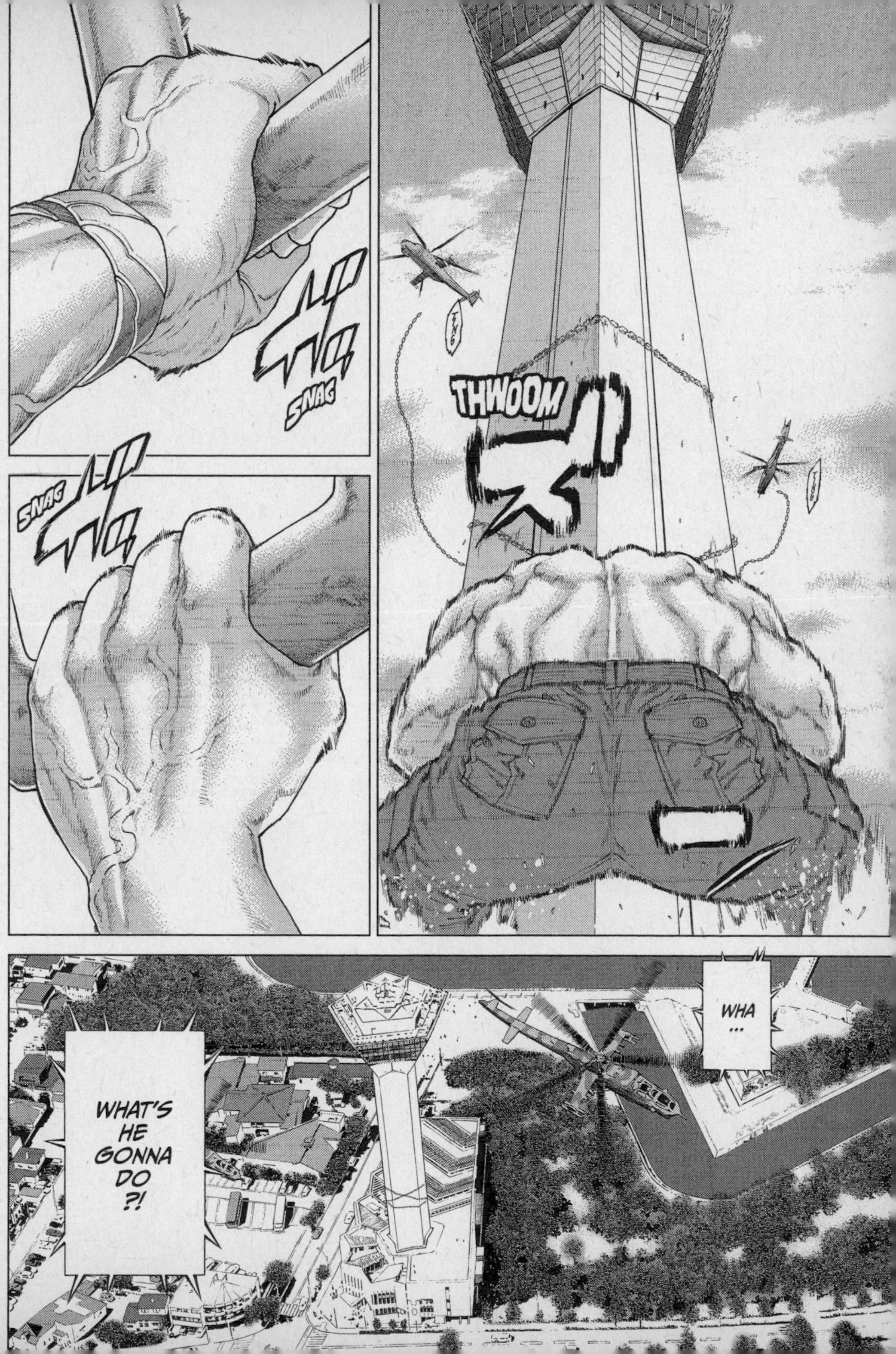
THWOOM
SNAG
SNAG
WHA...
WHAT'S HE GONNA DO?!

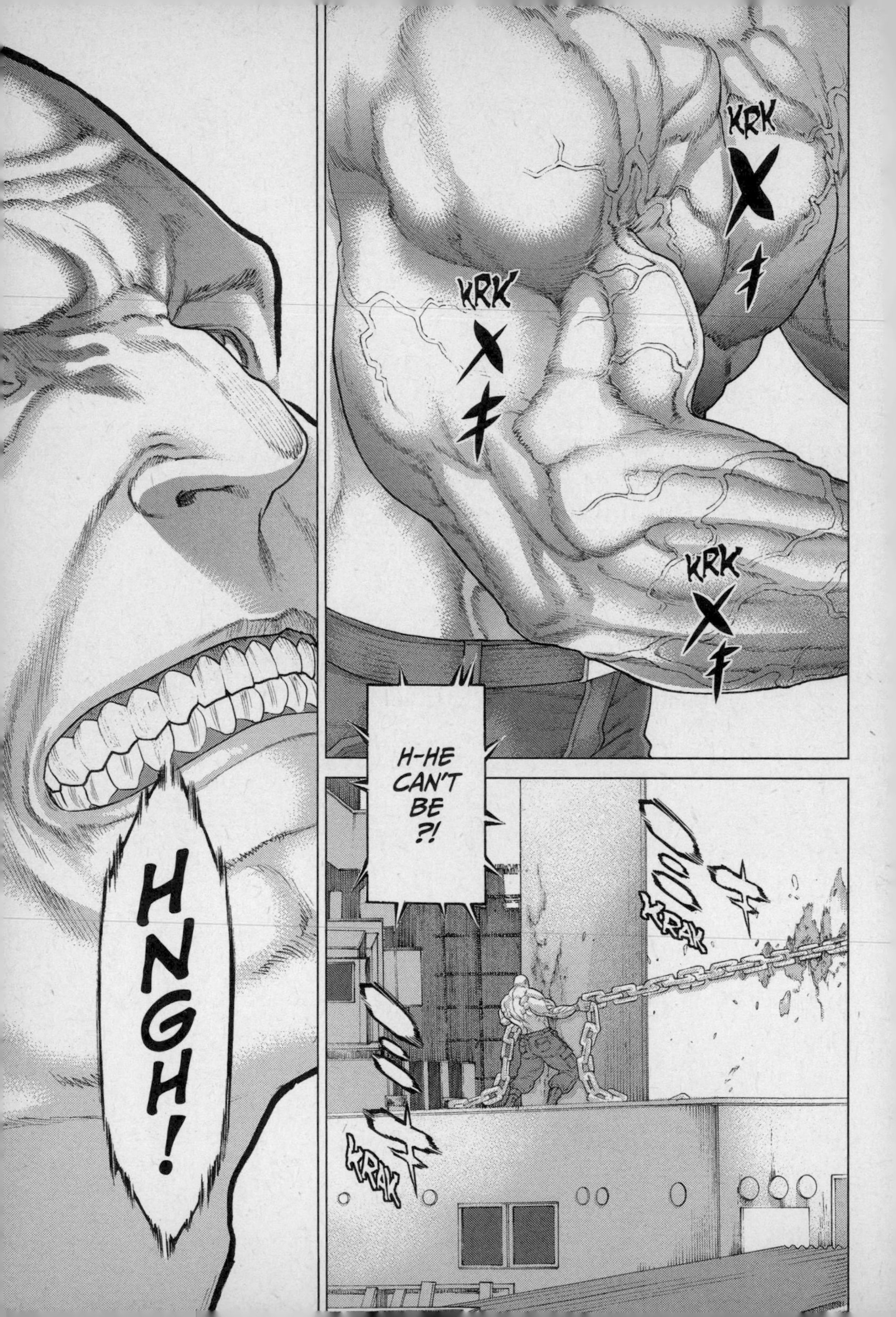
KRK
KRK
KRK
H-HE CAN'T BE ?!
KRAK
KRAK
HNGH!

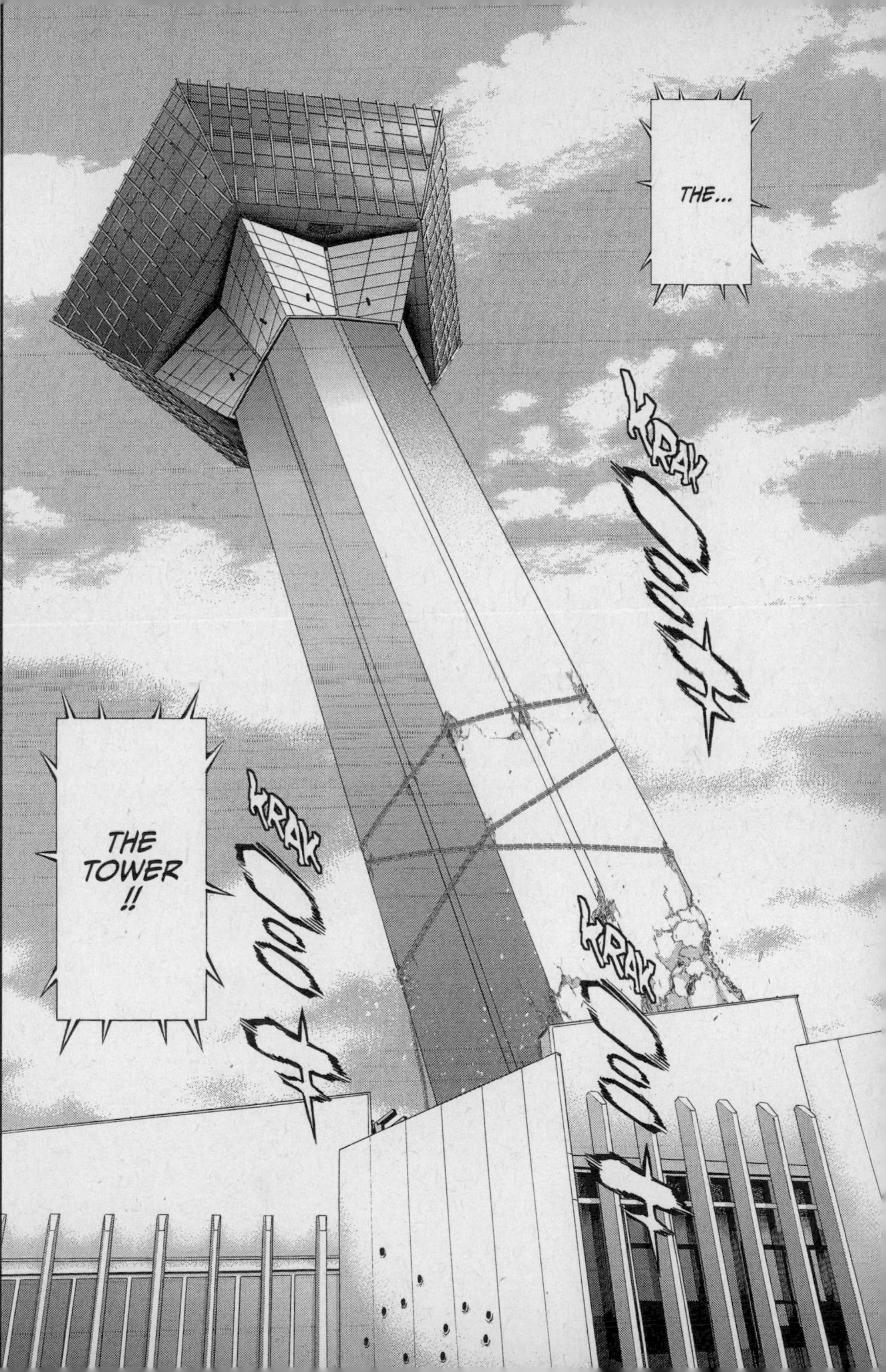
THE...
KRAK
KRAK
KRAK
THE TOWER !!

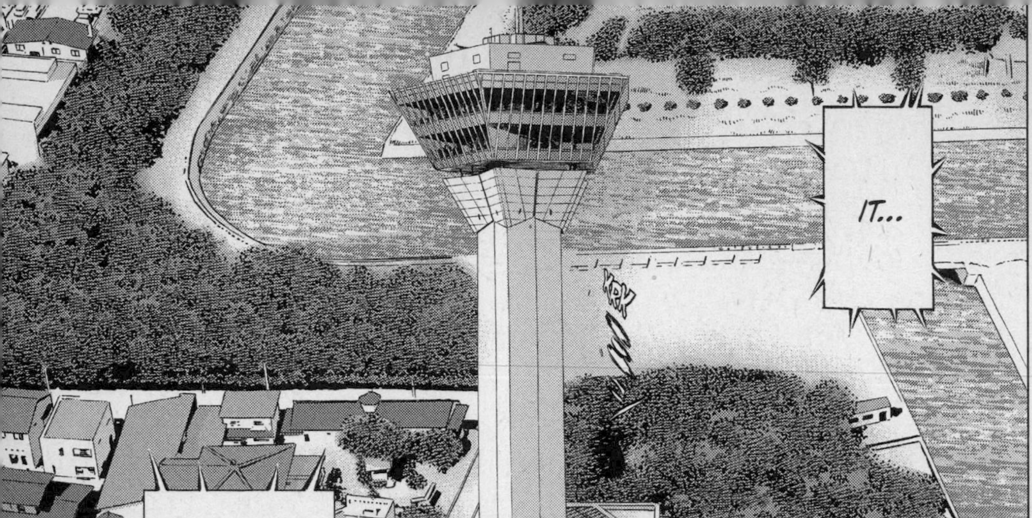
IT...
KRK
KRK
IT'S FALLING !!
KRK

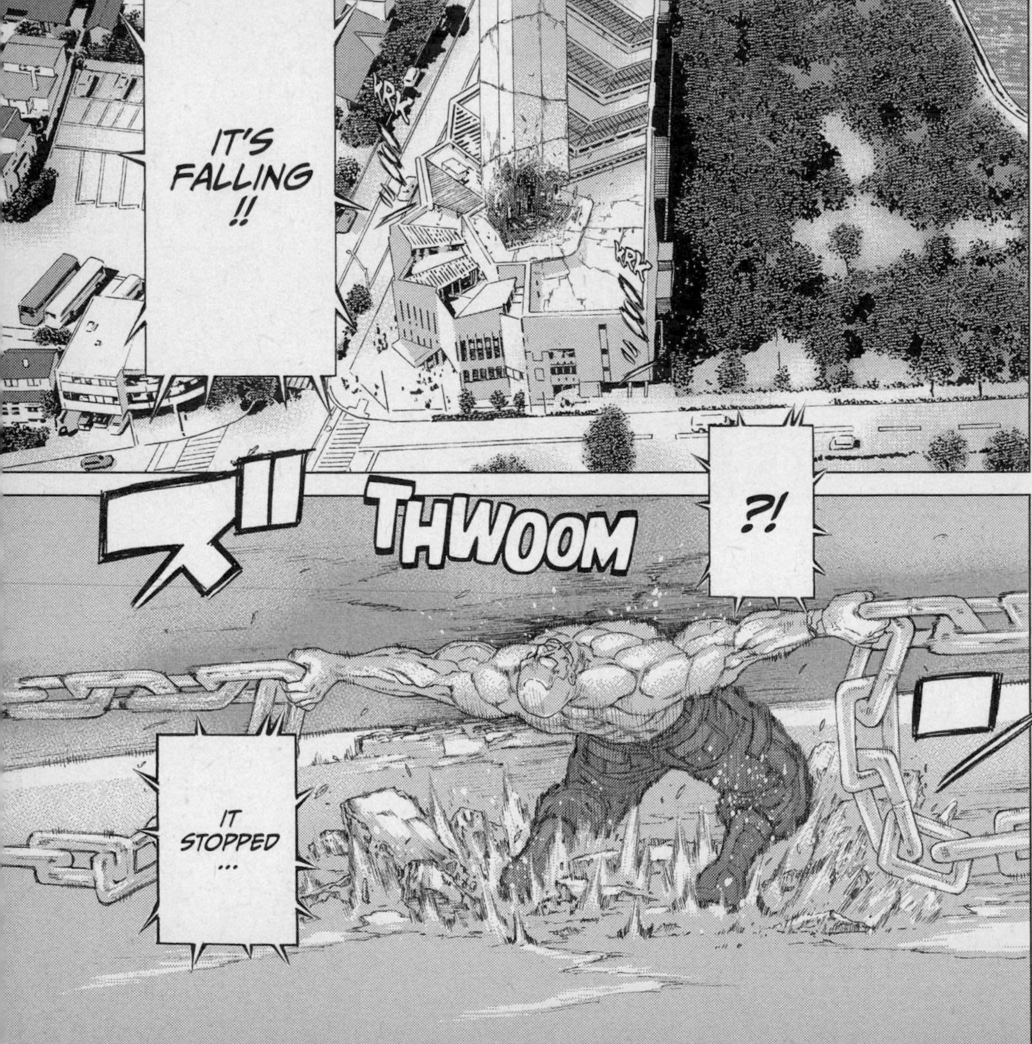
?!
THWOOM
IT STOPPED ...

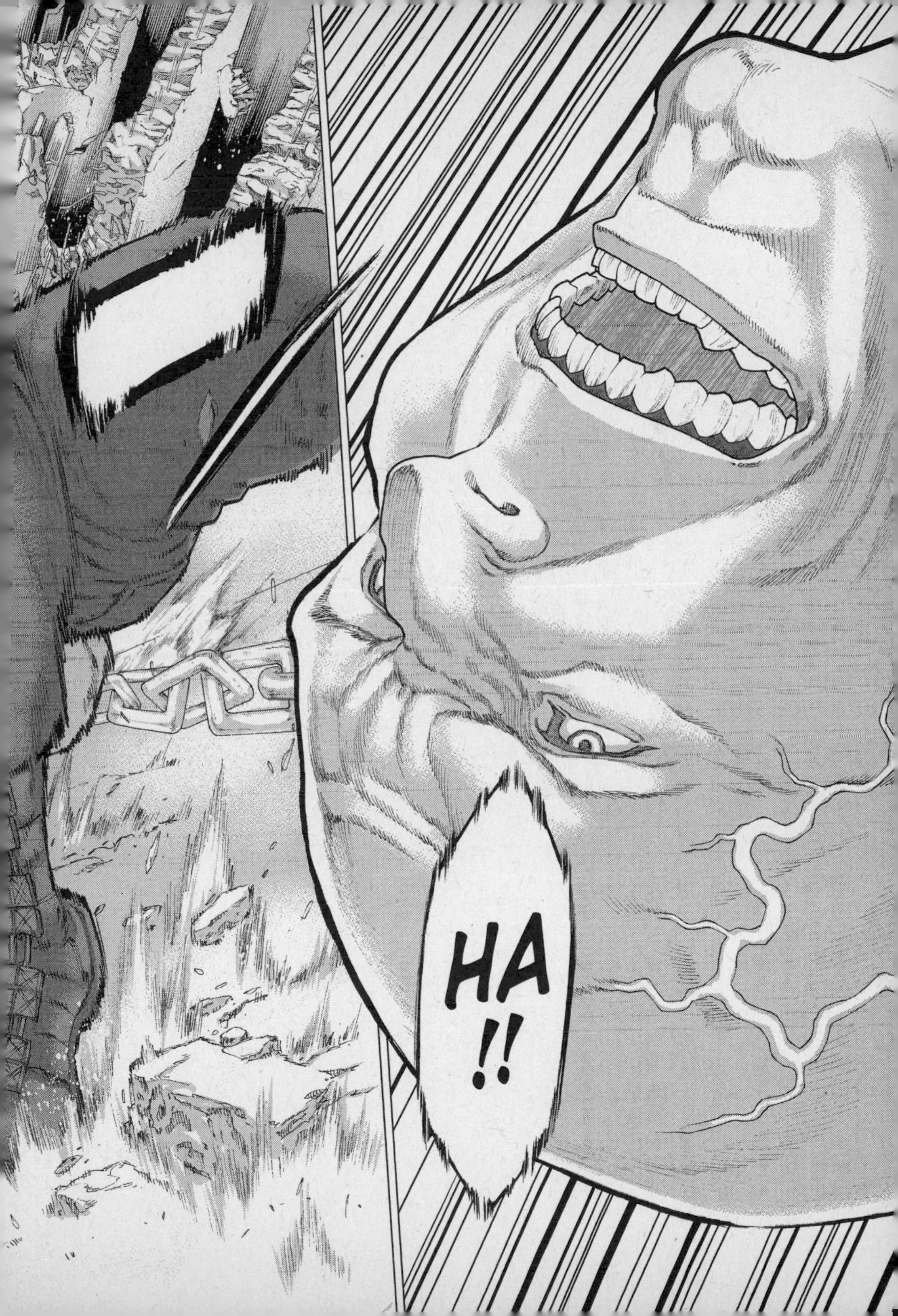
HA !!

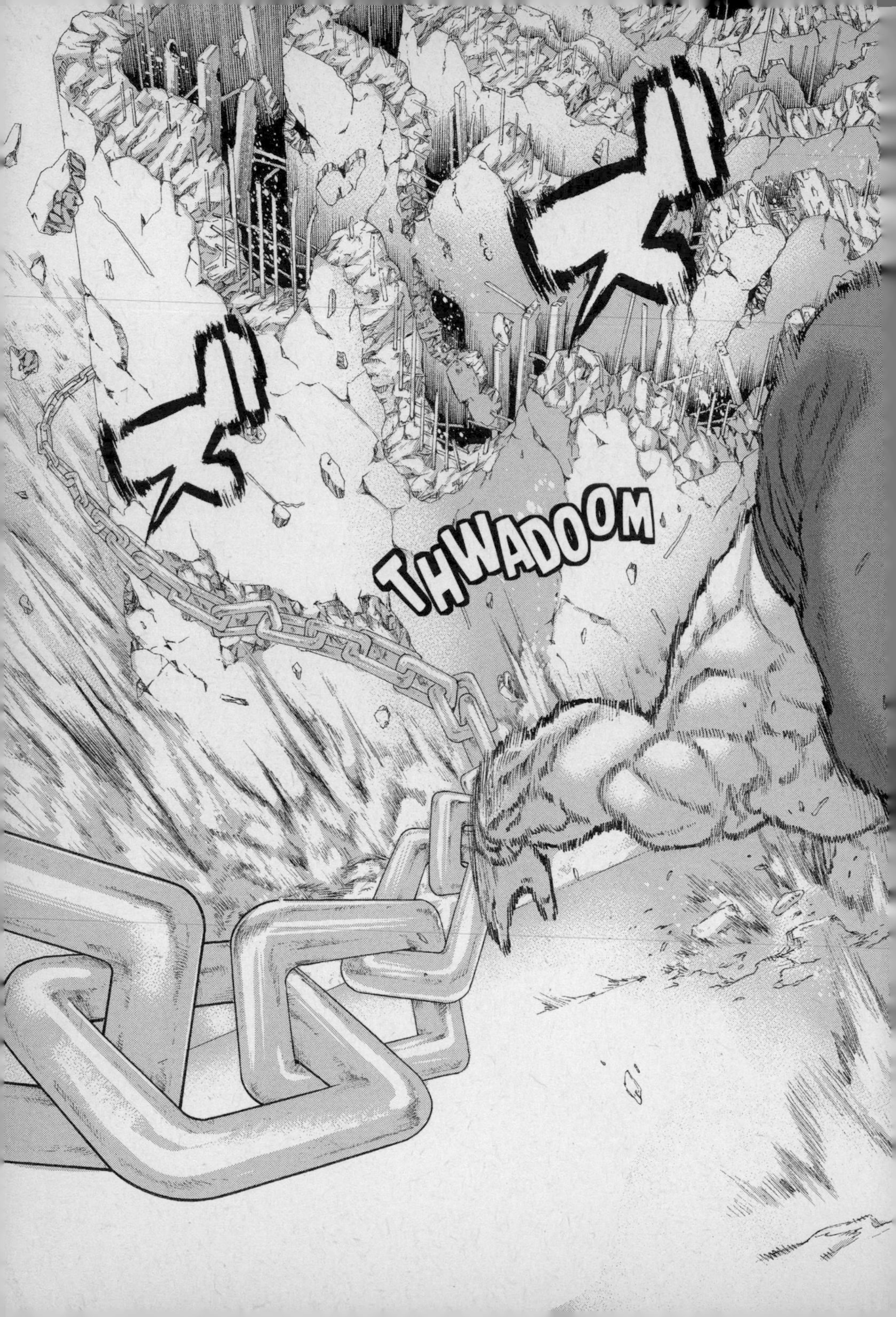
THWADOOM

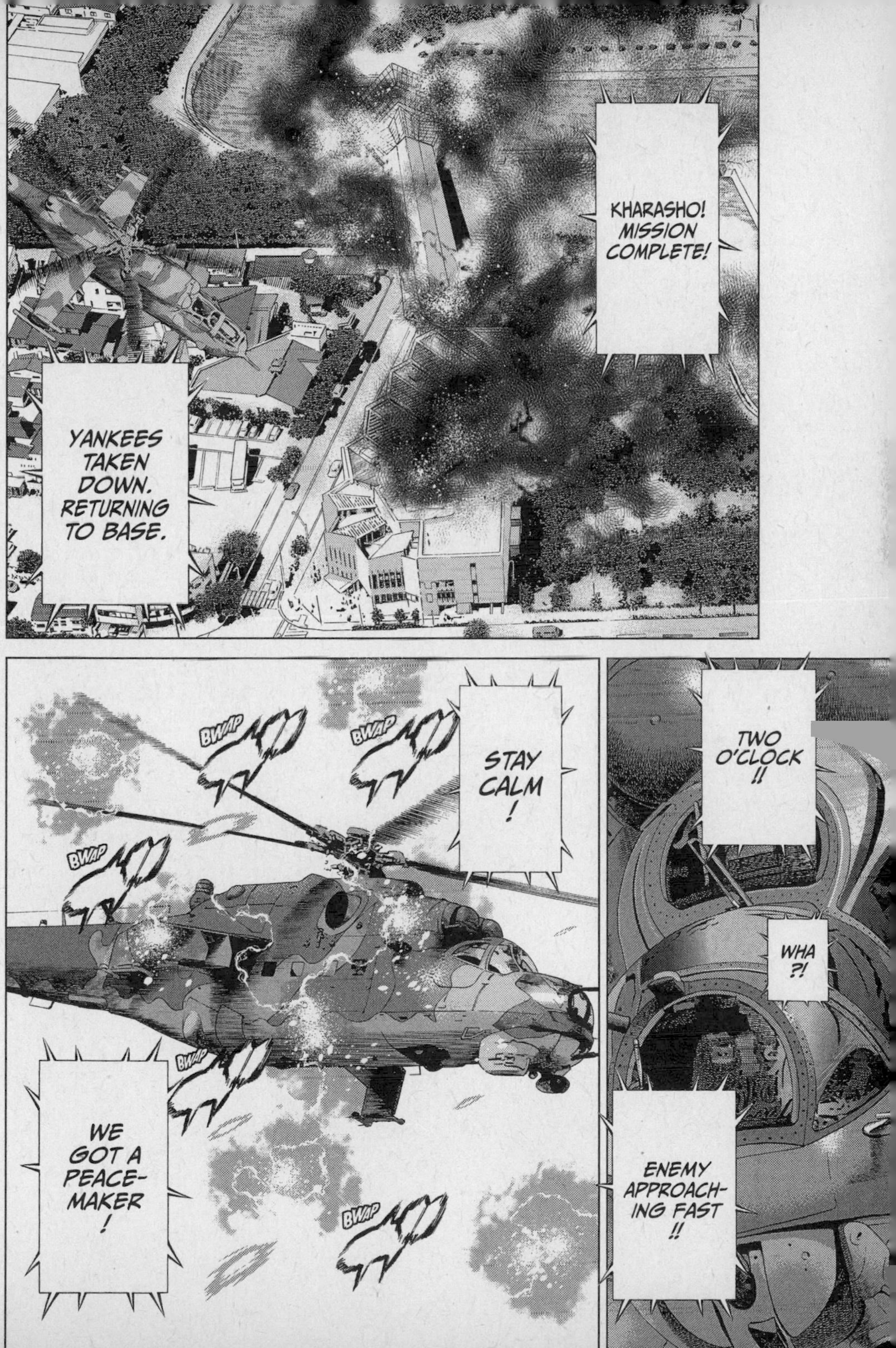
KHARASHO! MISSION COMPLETE!
YANKEES TAKEN DOWN. RETURNING TO BASE.
TWO O'CLOCK !!
WHA ?!
ENEMY APPROACHING FAST !!
STAY CALM !
BWAP
BWAP
BWAP
BWAP
WE GOT A PEACEMAKER !
BWAP

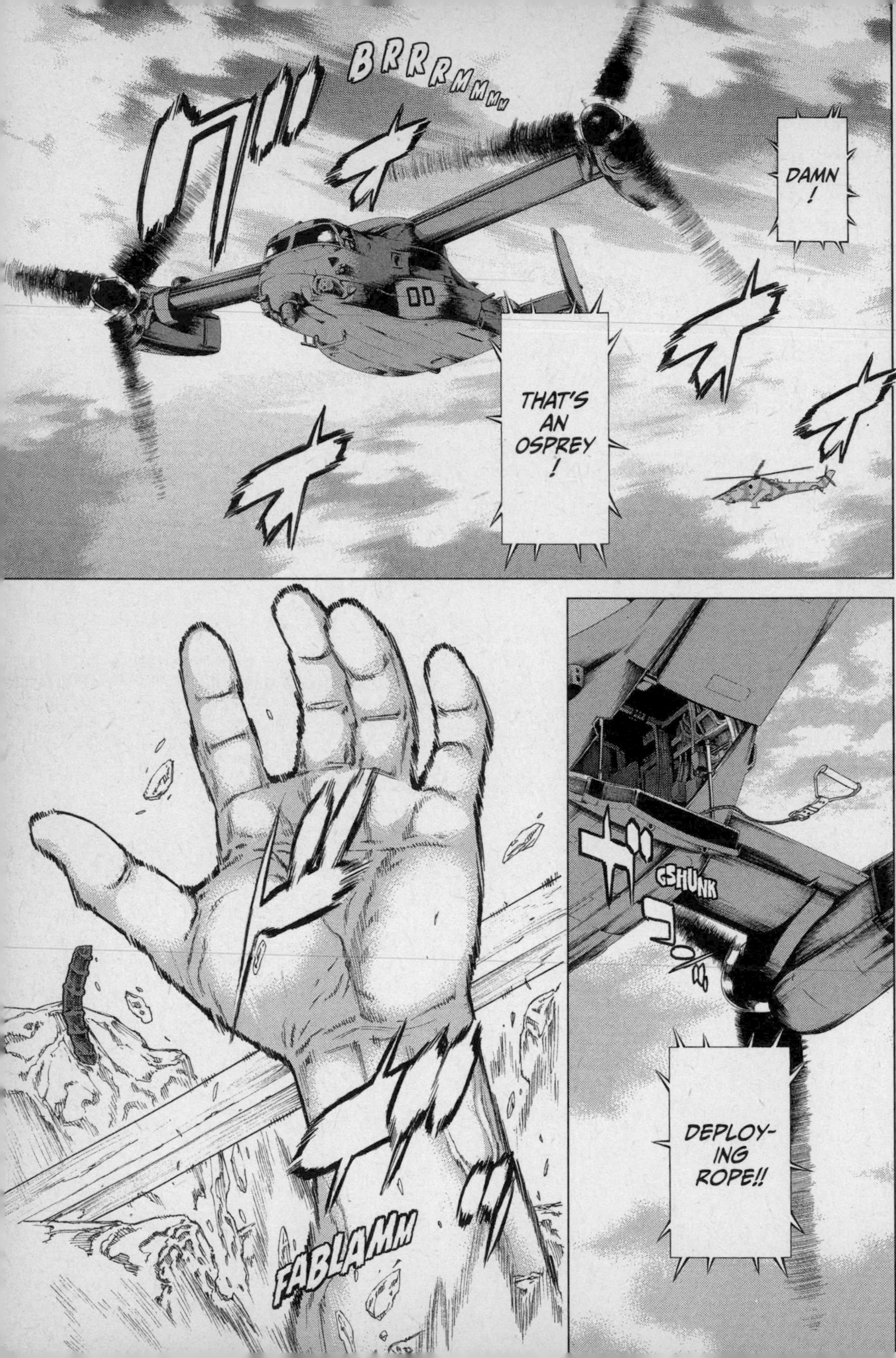
DAMN!
BRRRRMMMMM
THAT'S AN OSPREY!
GSHUNK
DEPLOY-ING ROPE!!
FABLAMM

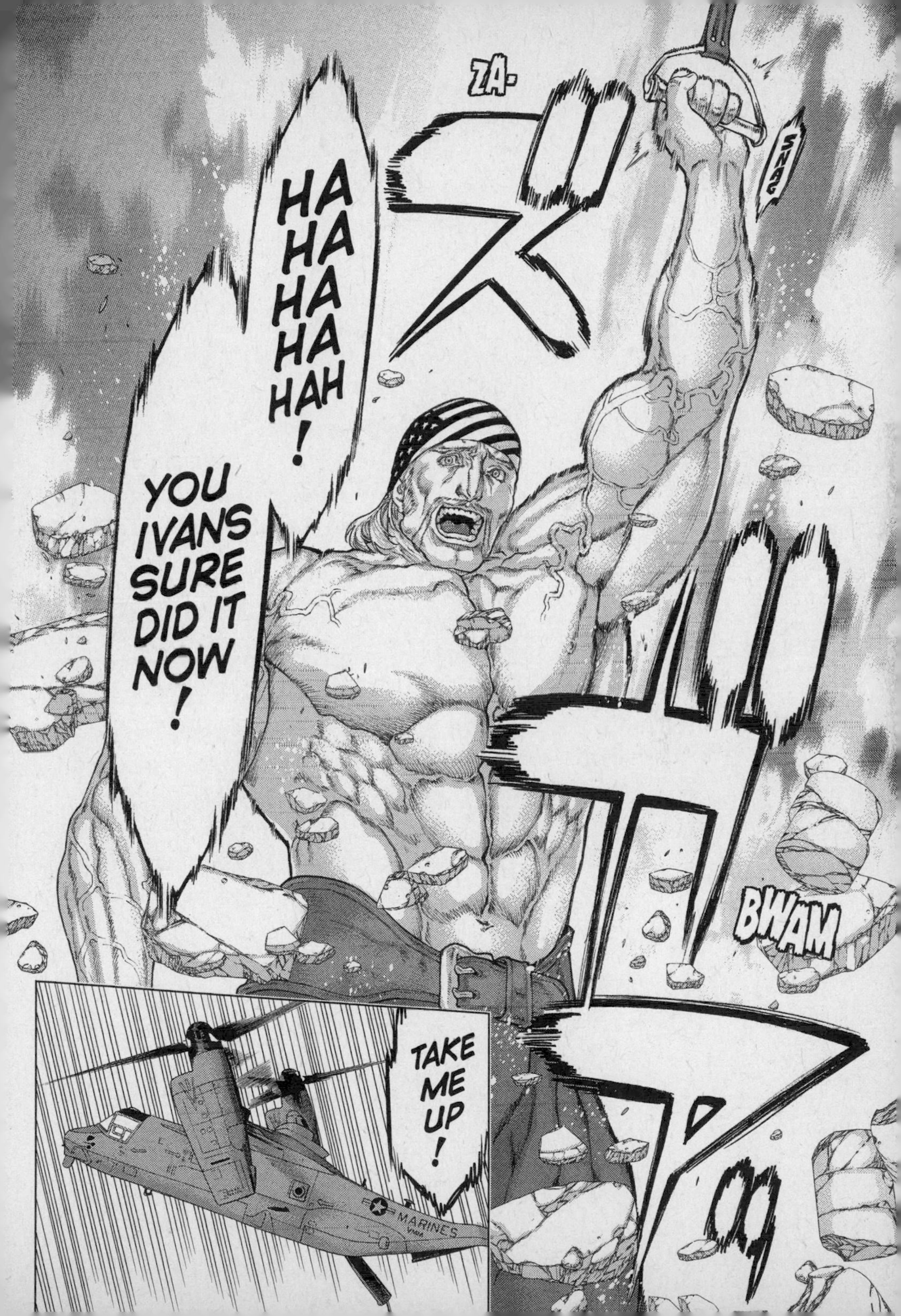
ZA-
SNAG
HAHAHAHAHAHAHAH!
YOU IVANS SURE DID IT NOW!
BWAM
TAKE ME UP!
MARINES

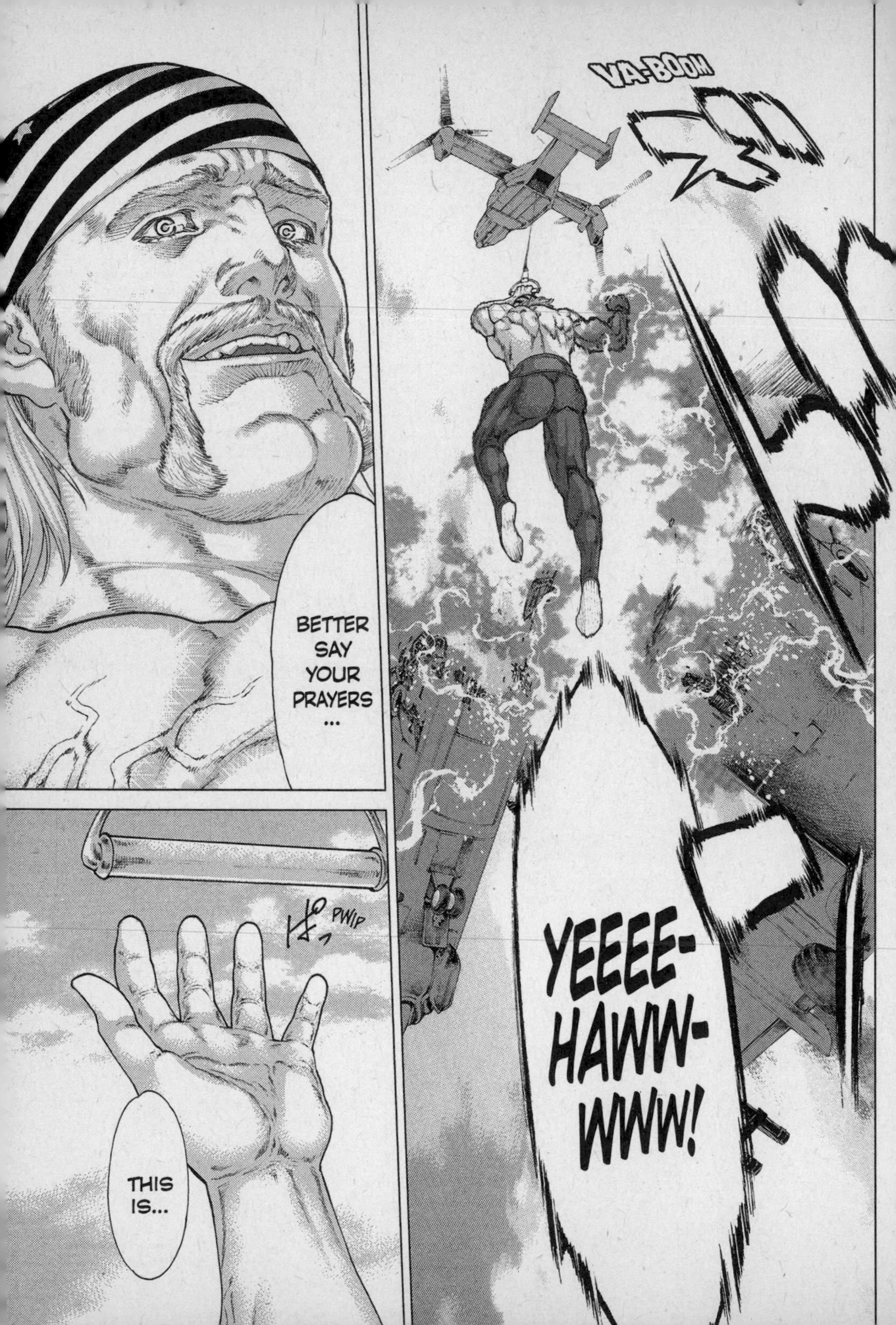
VA-BOOM
YEEEE-HAWW-WWW!
BETTER SAY YOUR PRAYERS...
PWIP
THIS IS...

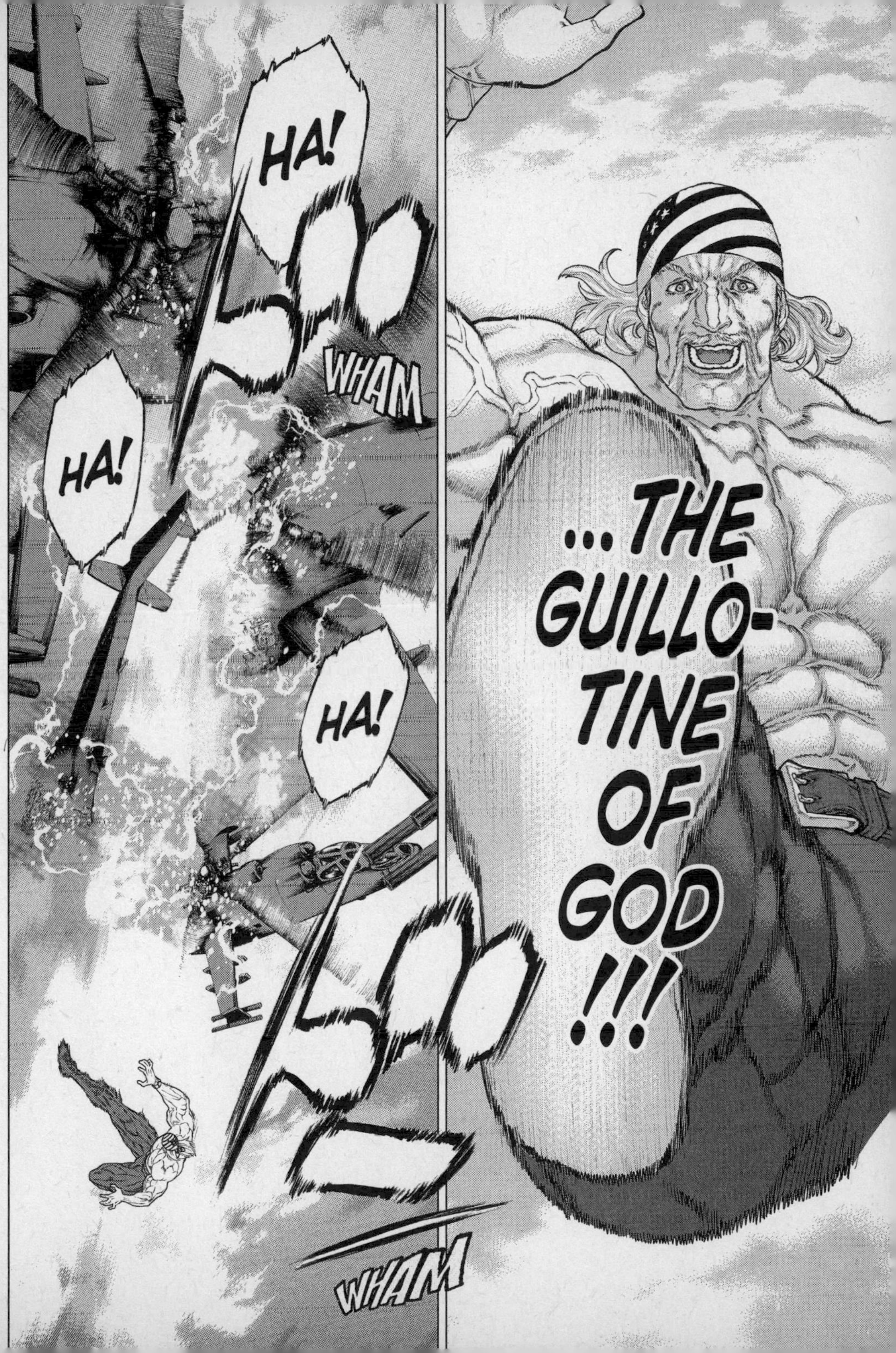
...THE GUILLO-TINE OF GOD!!!
HA!
WHAM
HA!
HA!
WHAM

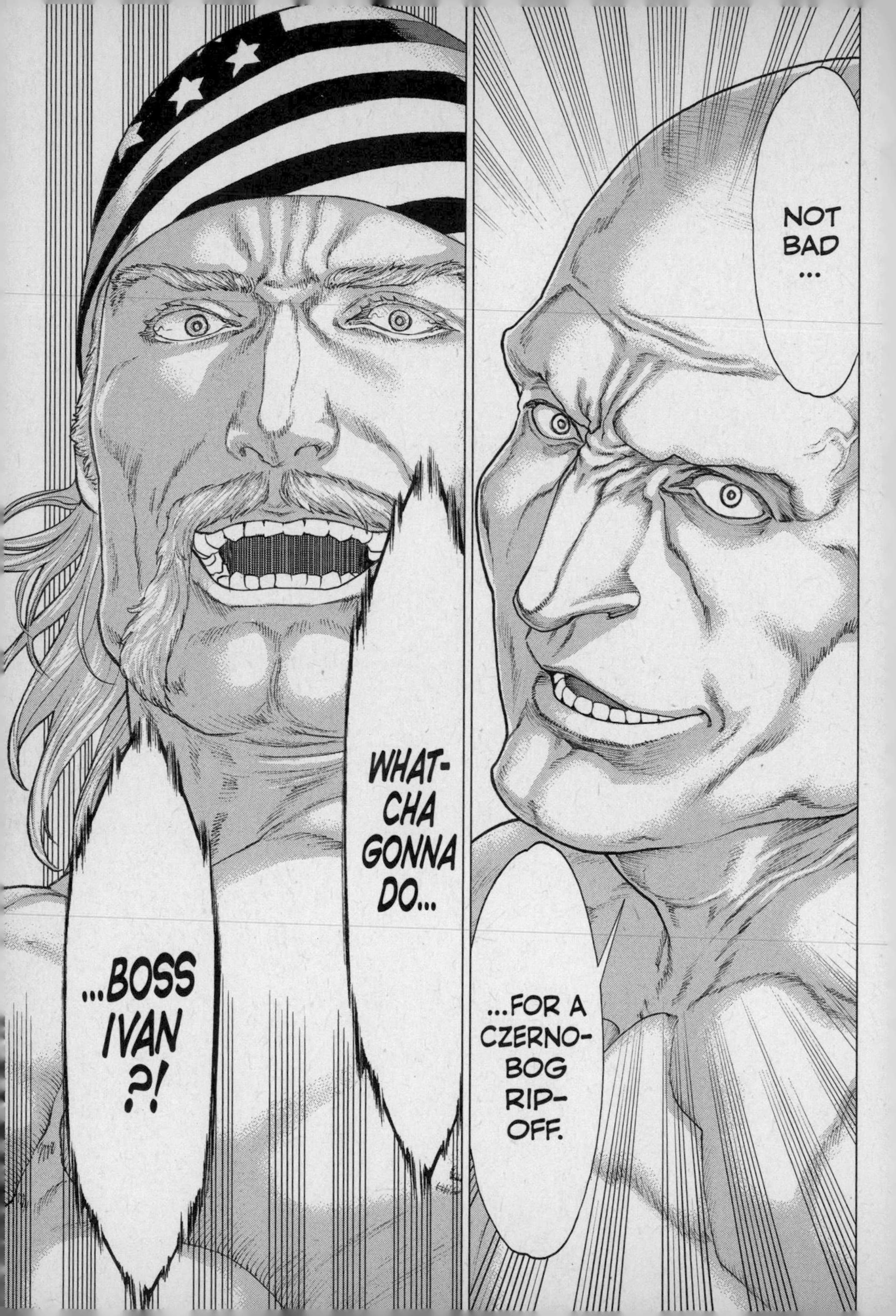
NOT BAD ...
...FOR A CZERNO-BOG RIP-OFF.
WHAT-CHA GONNA DO...
...BOSS IVAN ?!

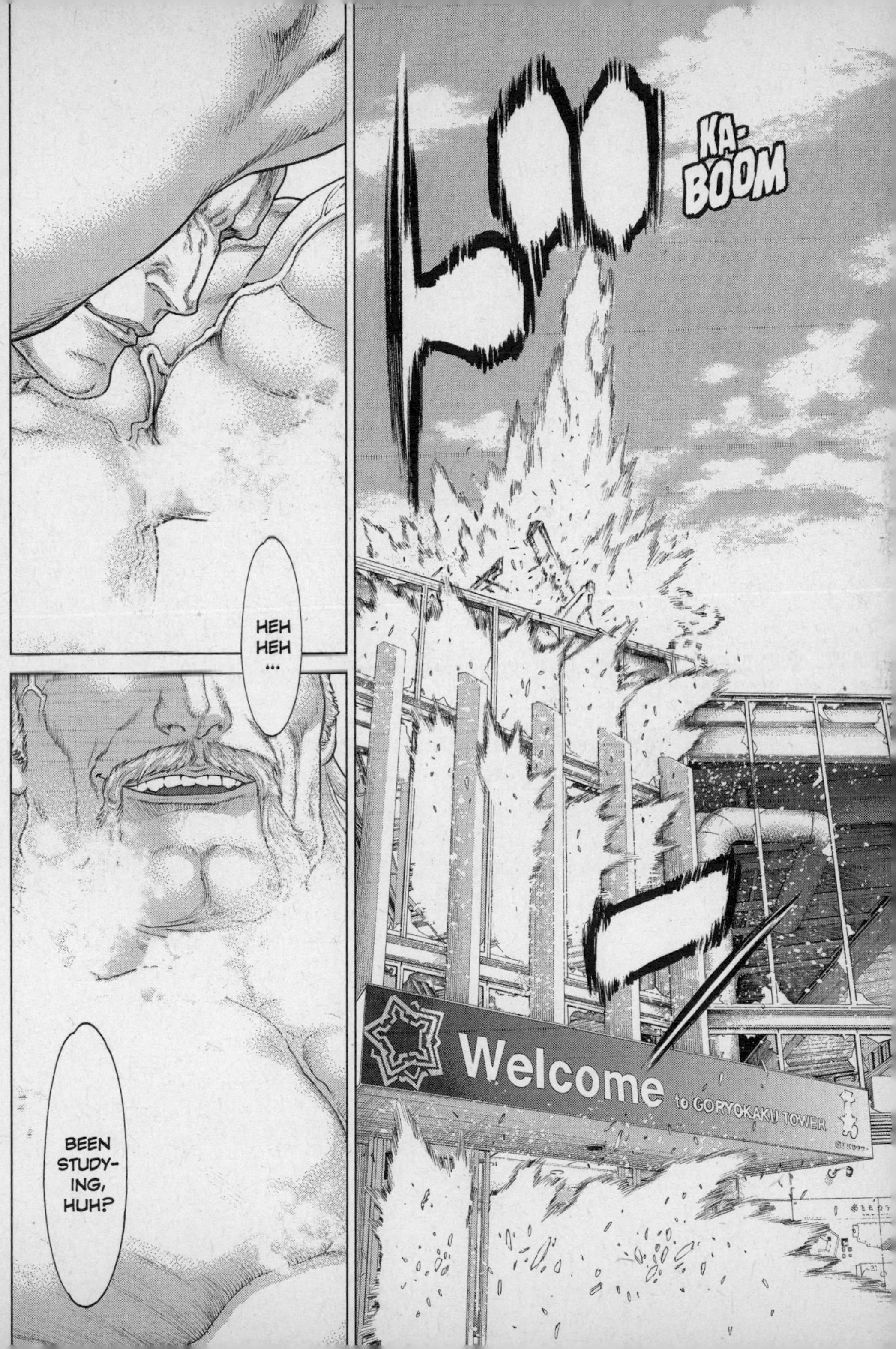
KA-
BOOM
Welcome
to GORYOKAKU TOWER
HEH
HEH
...
BEEN
STUDY-
ING,
HUH?

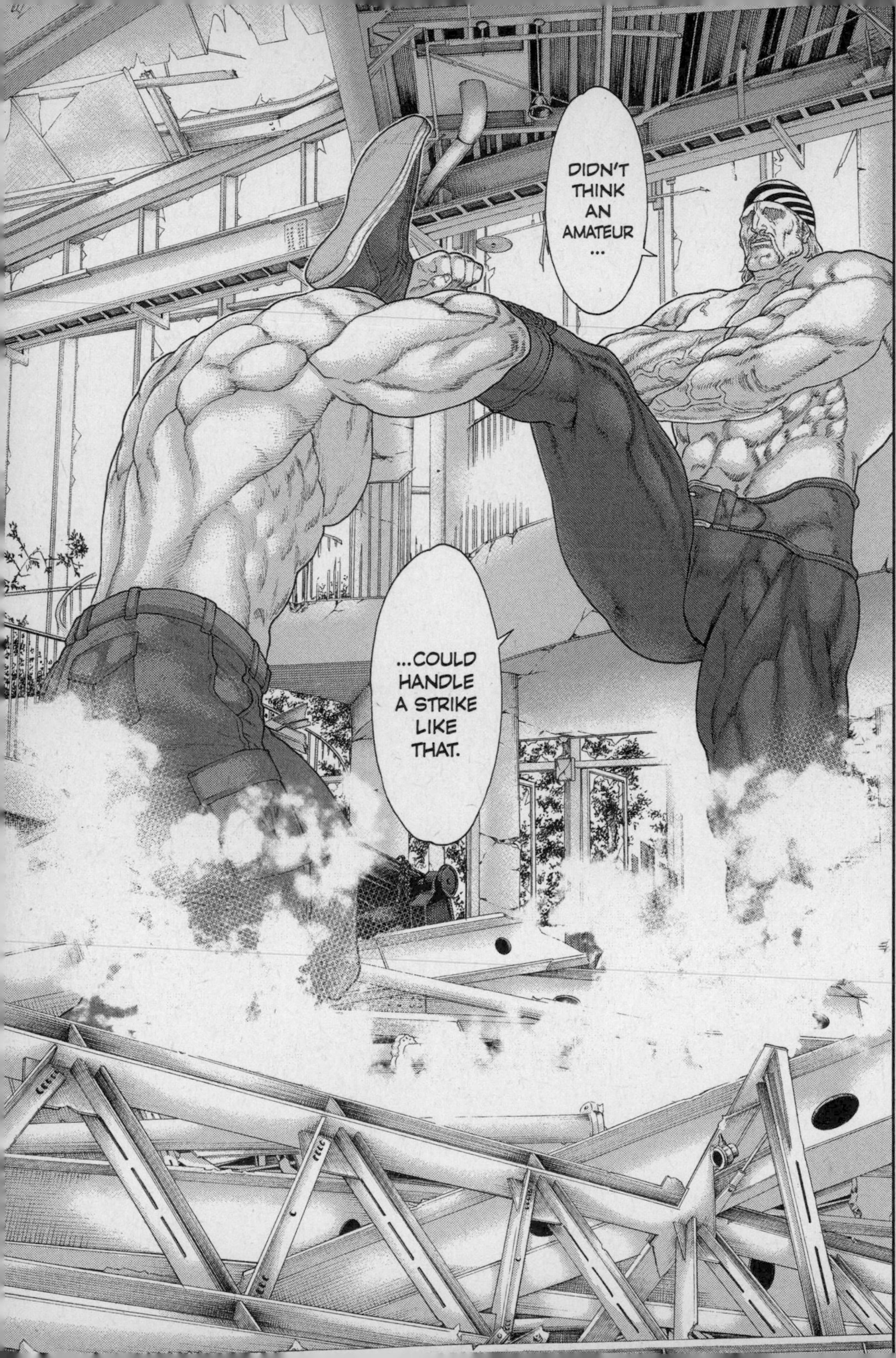
DIDN'T THINK AN AMATEUR ...
...COULD HANDLE A STRIKE LIKE THAT.

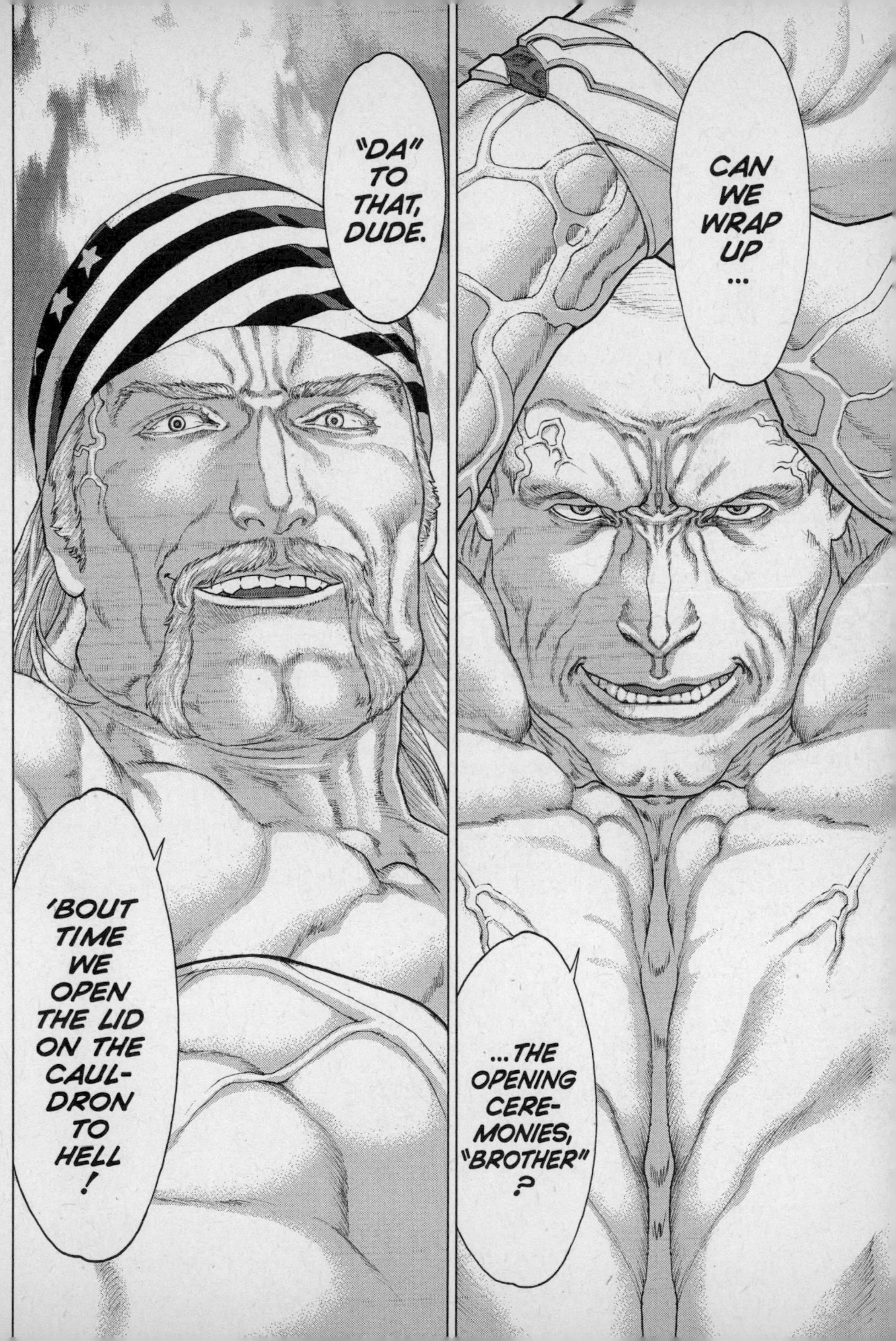
CAN WE WRAP UP ...
...THE OPENING CEREMONIES, "BROTHER"?
"DA" TO THAT, DUDE.
'BOUT TIME WE OPEN THE LID ON THE CAULDRON TO HELL!

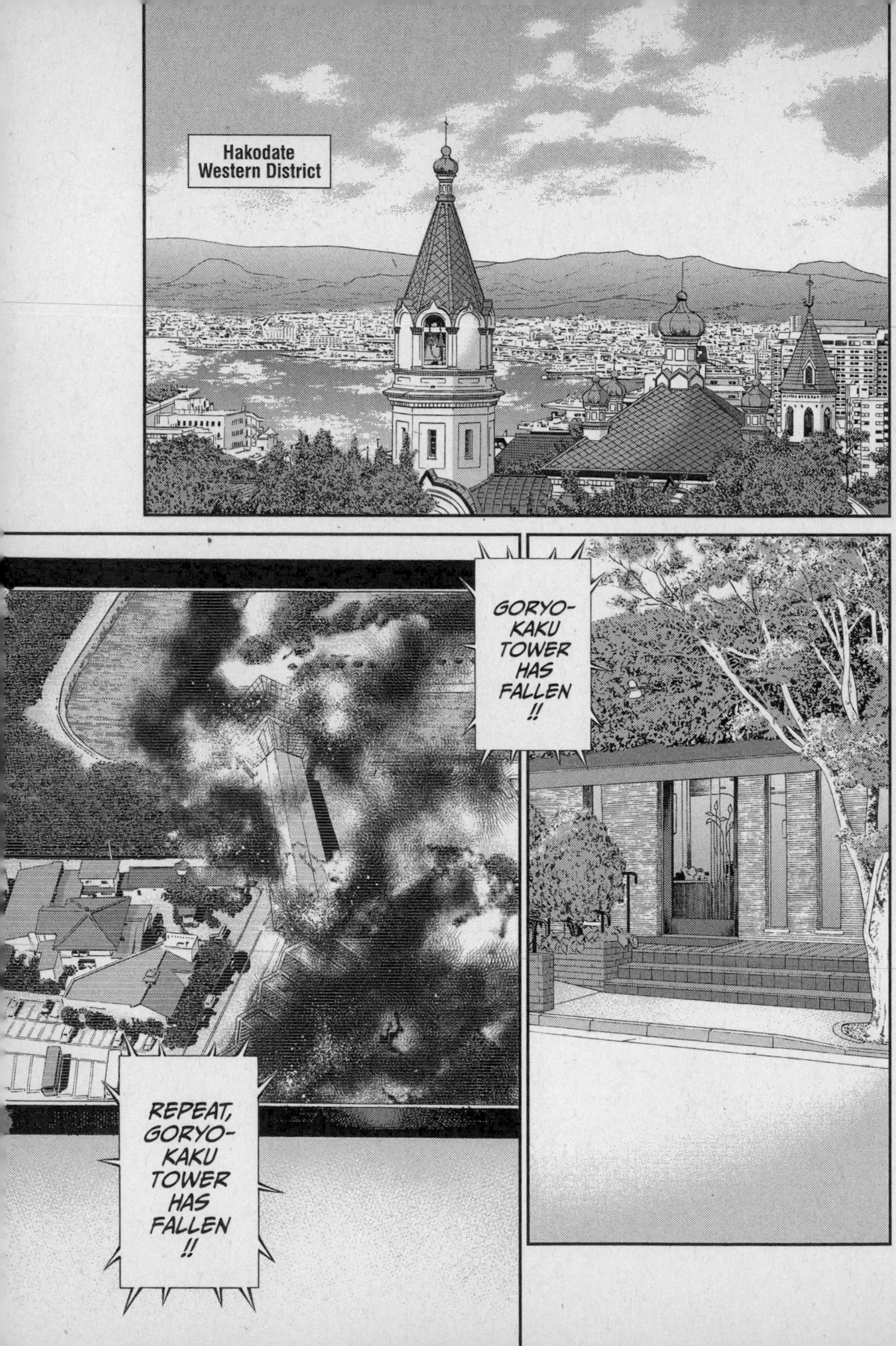
Hakodate Western District
GORYO-KAKU TOWER HAS FALLEN !!
REPEAT, GORYO-KAKU TOWER HAS FALLEN !!

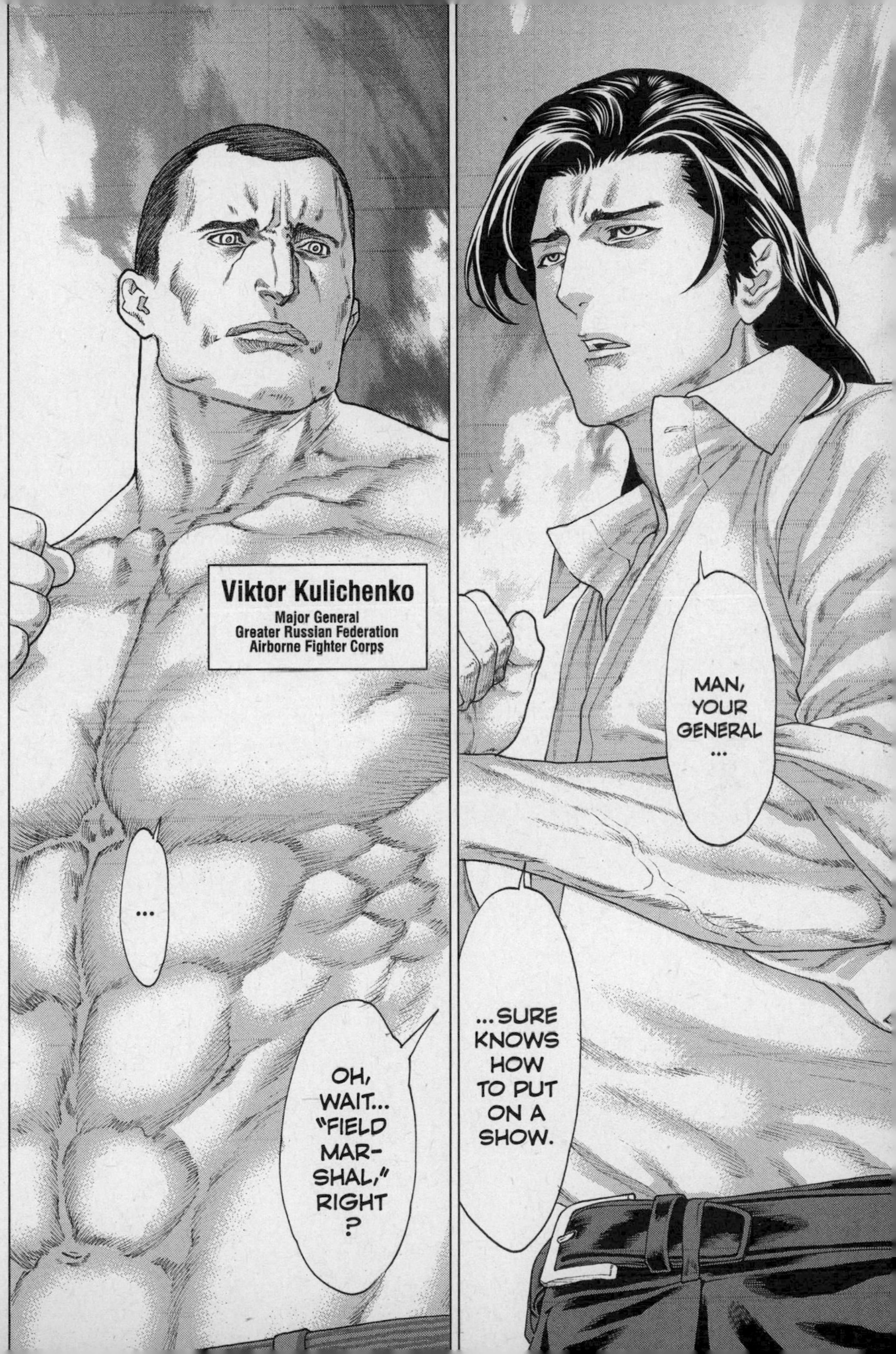
MAN, YOUR GENERAL ...
...SURE KNOWS HOW TO PUT ON A SHOW.
Viktor Kulichenko
Major General
Greater Russian Federation
Airborne Fighter Corps
...
OH, WAIT... "FIELD MAR-SHAL," RIGHT?

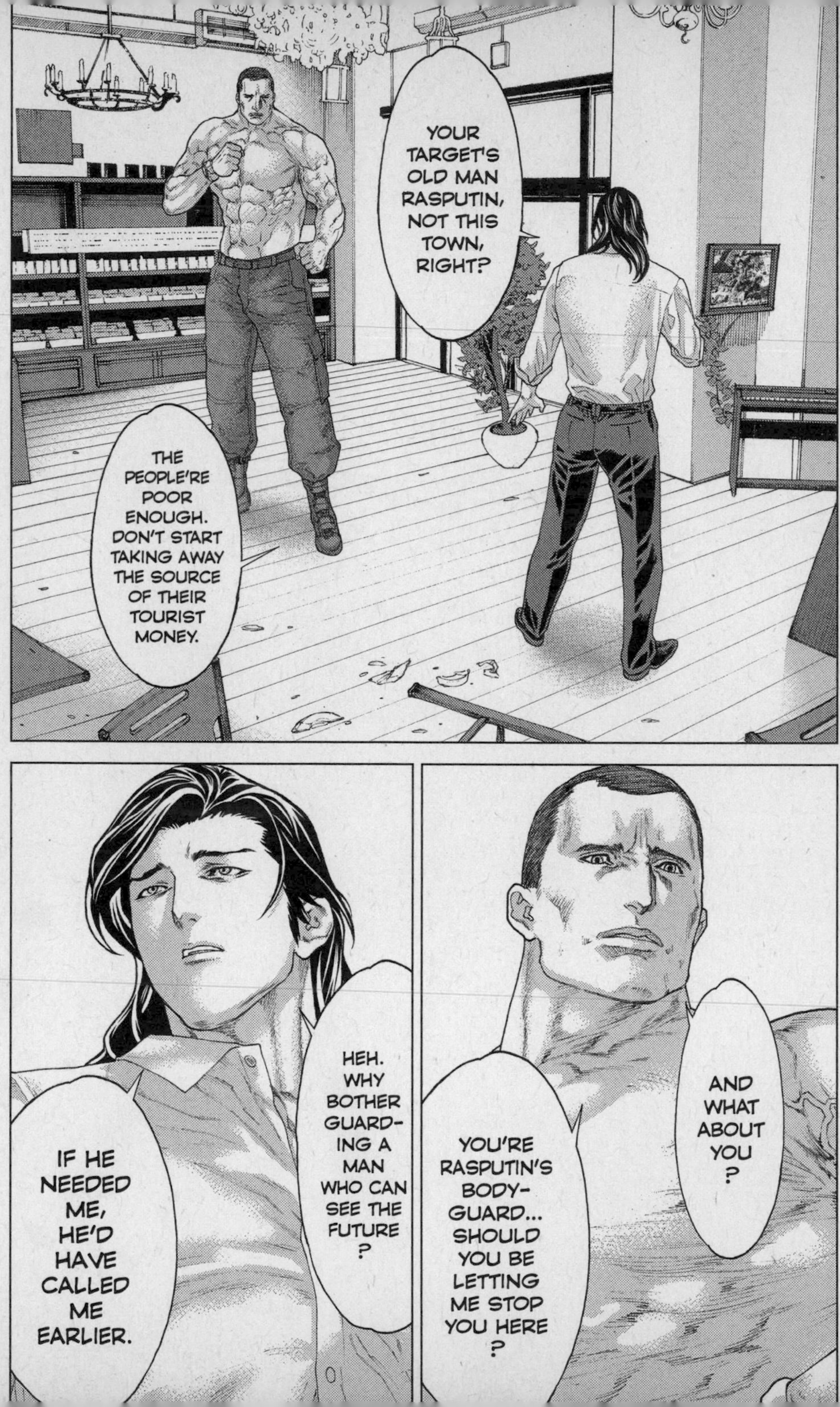
YOUR TARGET'S OLD MAN RASPUTIN, NOT THIS TOWN, RIGHT?
THE PEOPLE'RE POOR ENOUGH. DON'T START TAKING AWAY THE SOURCE OF THEIR TOURIST MONEY.
AND WHAT ABOUT YOU ?
YOU'RE RASPUTIN'S BODY-GUARD... SHOULD YOU BE LETTING ME STOP YOU HERE ?
HEH. WHY BOTHER GUARD-ING A MAN WHO CAN SEE THE FUTURE ?
IF HE NEEDED ME, HE'D HAVE CALLED ME EARLIER.

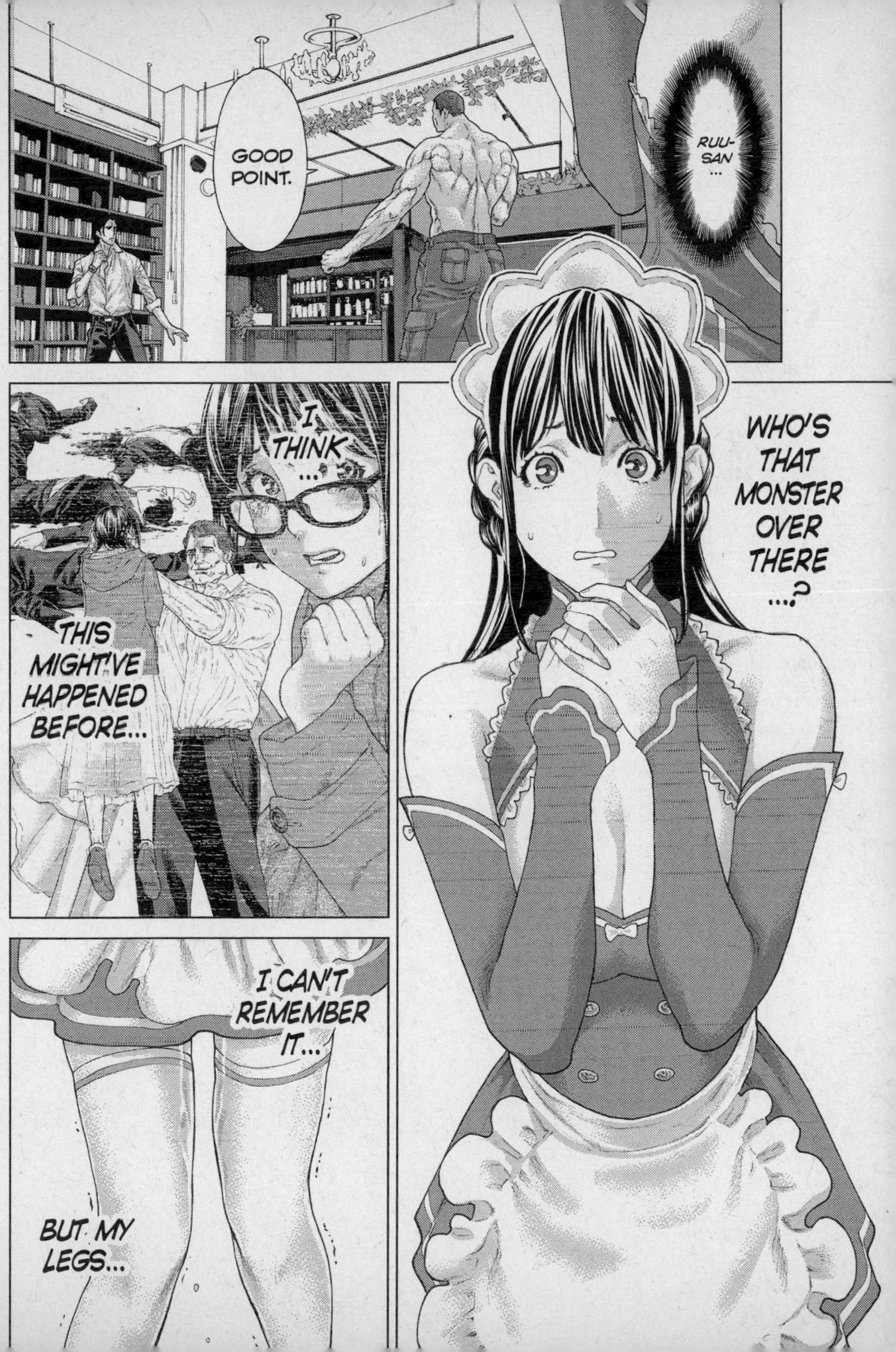
RUU-SAN ...
GOOD POINT.
WHO'S THAT MONSTER OVER THERE ...?
I THINK ...
THIS MIGHT'VE HAPPENED BEFORE...
I CAN'T REMEMBER IT...
BUT MY LEGS...

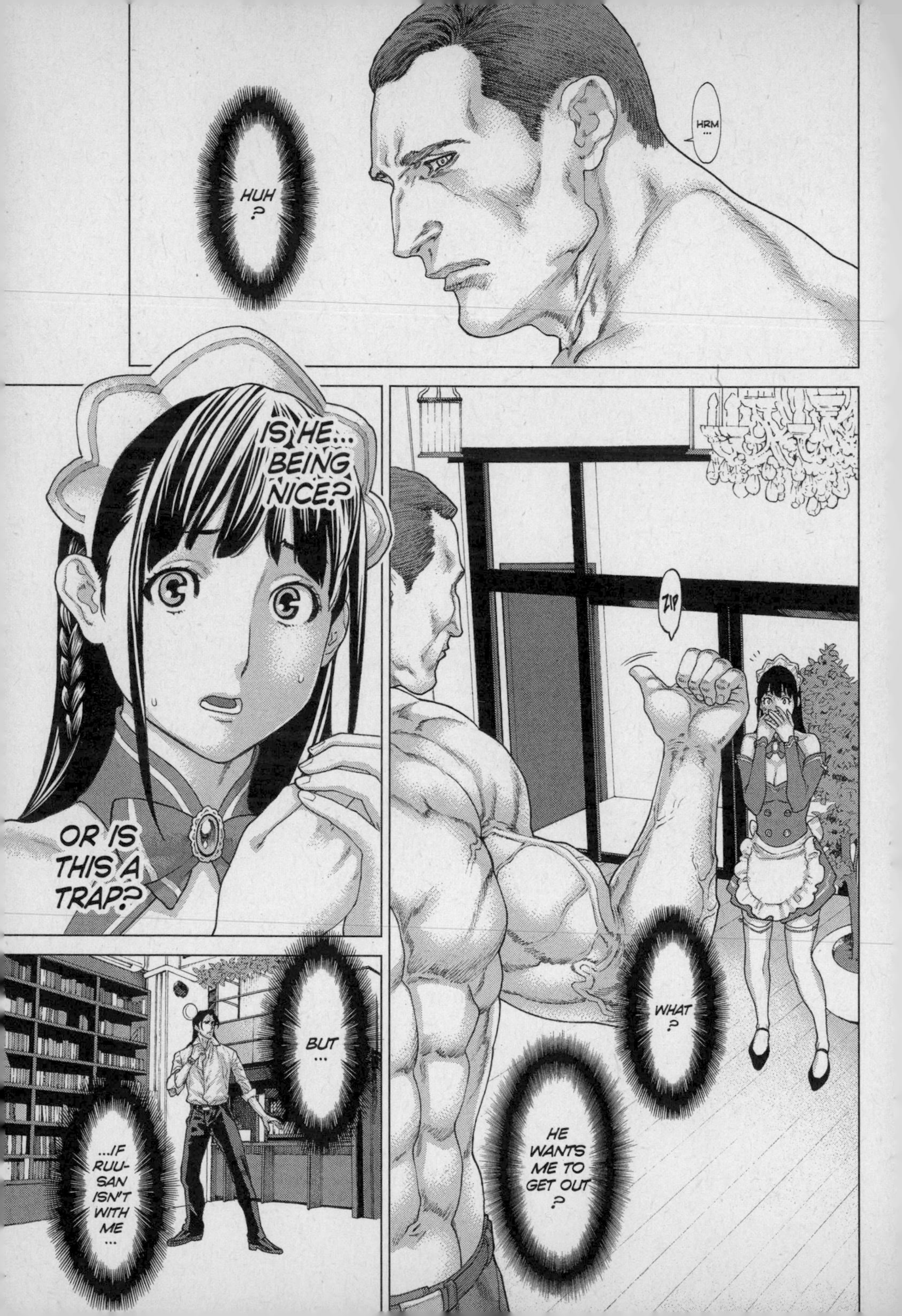
HRM...
HUH?
ZIP
WHAT?
HE WANTS ME TO GET OUT?
IS HE... BEING NICE?
OR IS THIS A TRAP?
BUT...
...IF RUU-SAN ISN'T WITH ME...

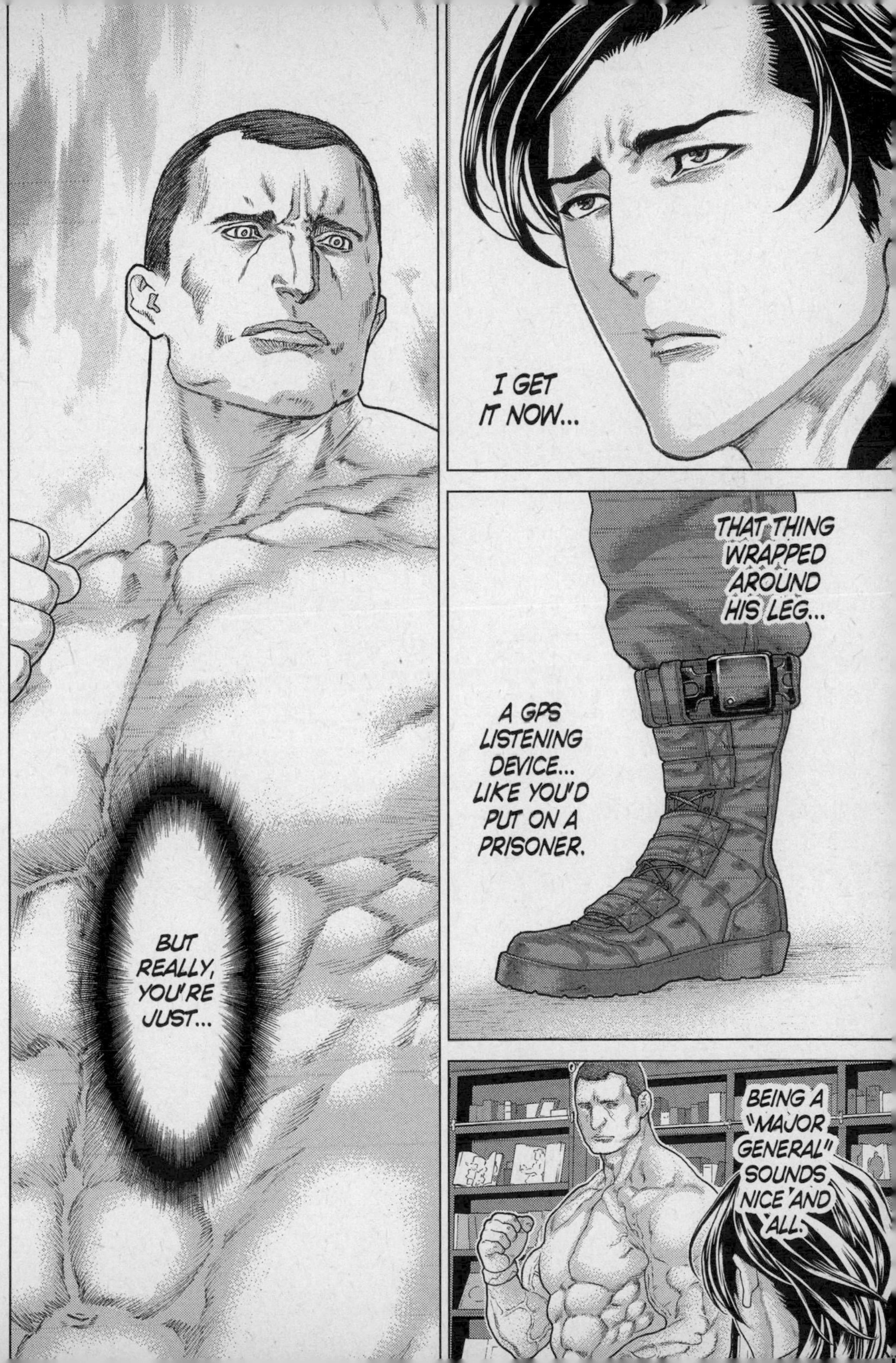
I GET IT NOW...
THAT THING WRAPPED AROUND HIS LEG...
A GPS LISTENING DEVICE... LIKE YOU'D PUT ON A PRISONER.
BEING A "MAJOR GENERAL" SOUNDS NICE AND ALL.
BUT REALLY, YOU'RE JUST...

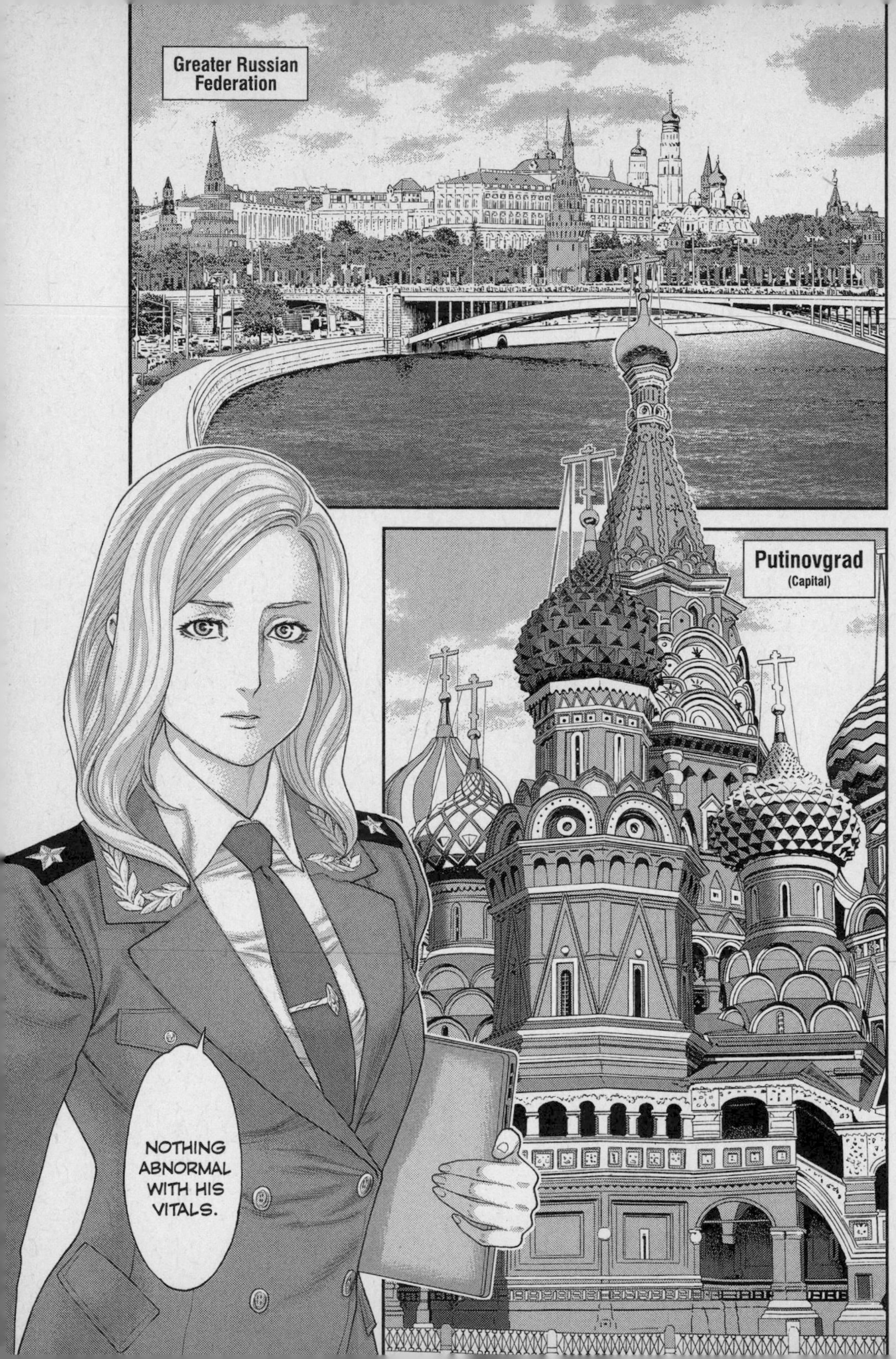
Greater Russian Federation
Putinovgrad (Capital)
NOTHING ABNORMAL WITH HIS VITALS.

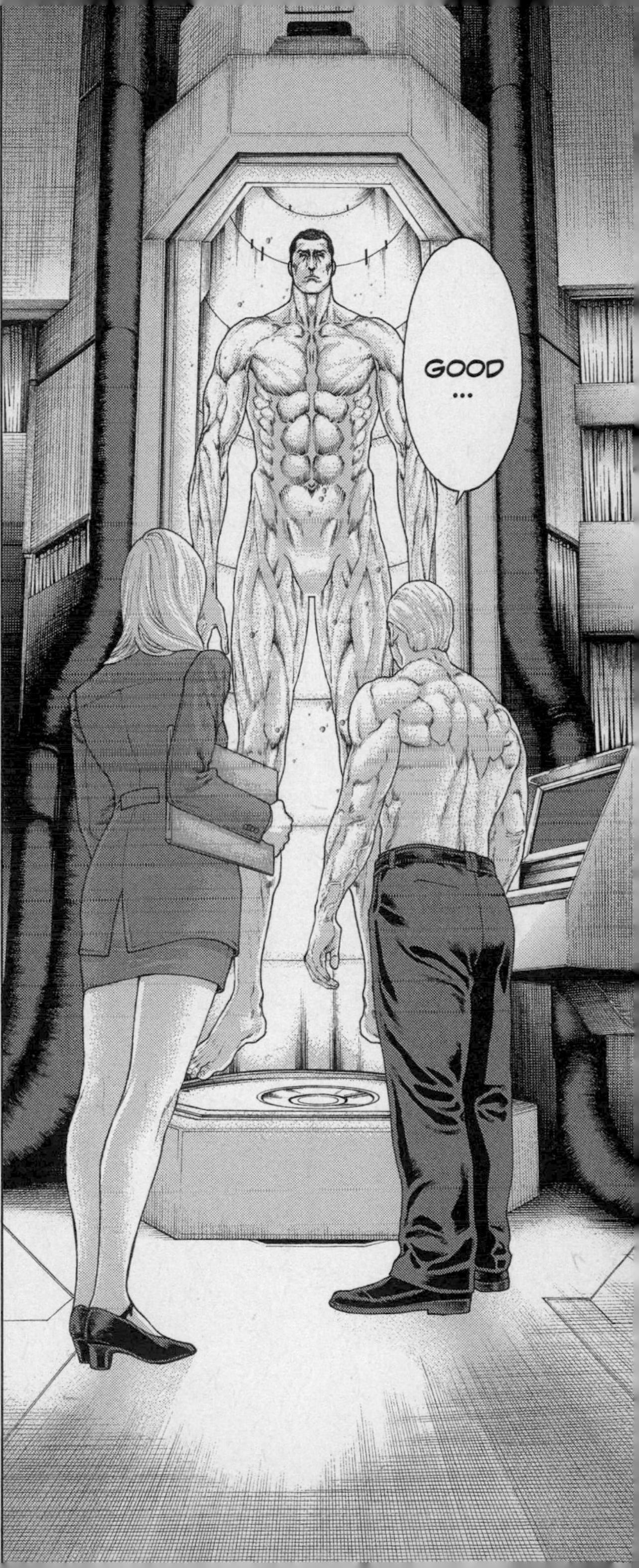
GOOD...

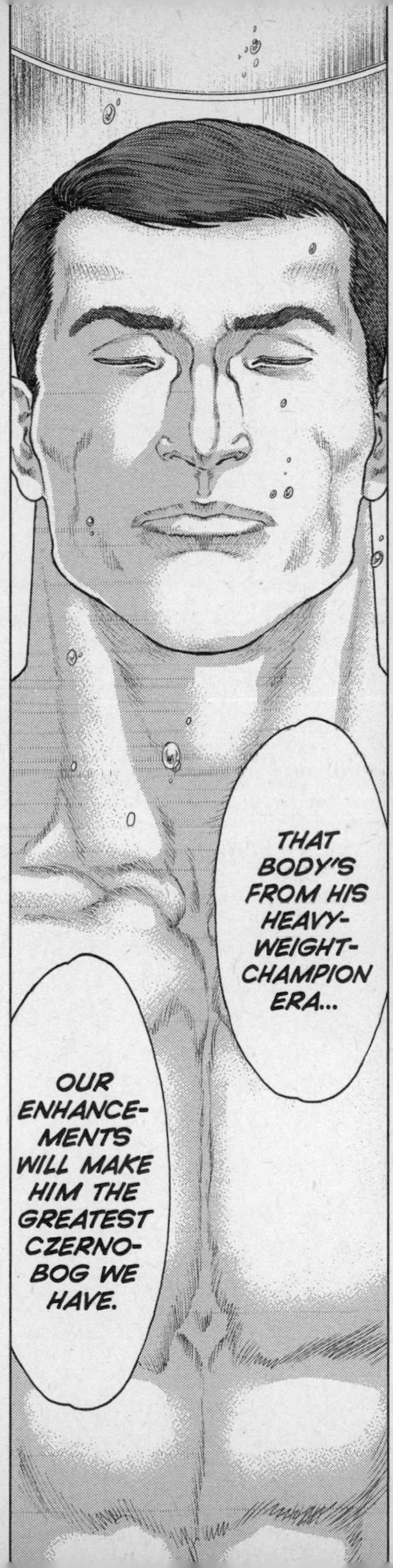
THAT BODY'S FROM HIS HEAVY-WEIGHT-CHAMPION ERA...
OUR ENHANCE-MENTS WILL MAKE HIM THE GREATEST CZERNO-BOG WE HAVE.

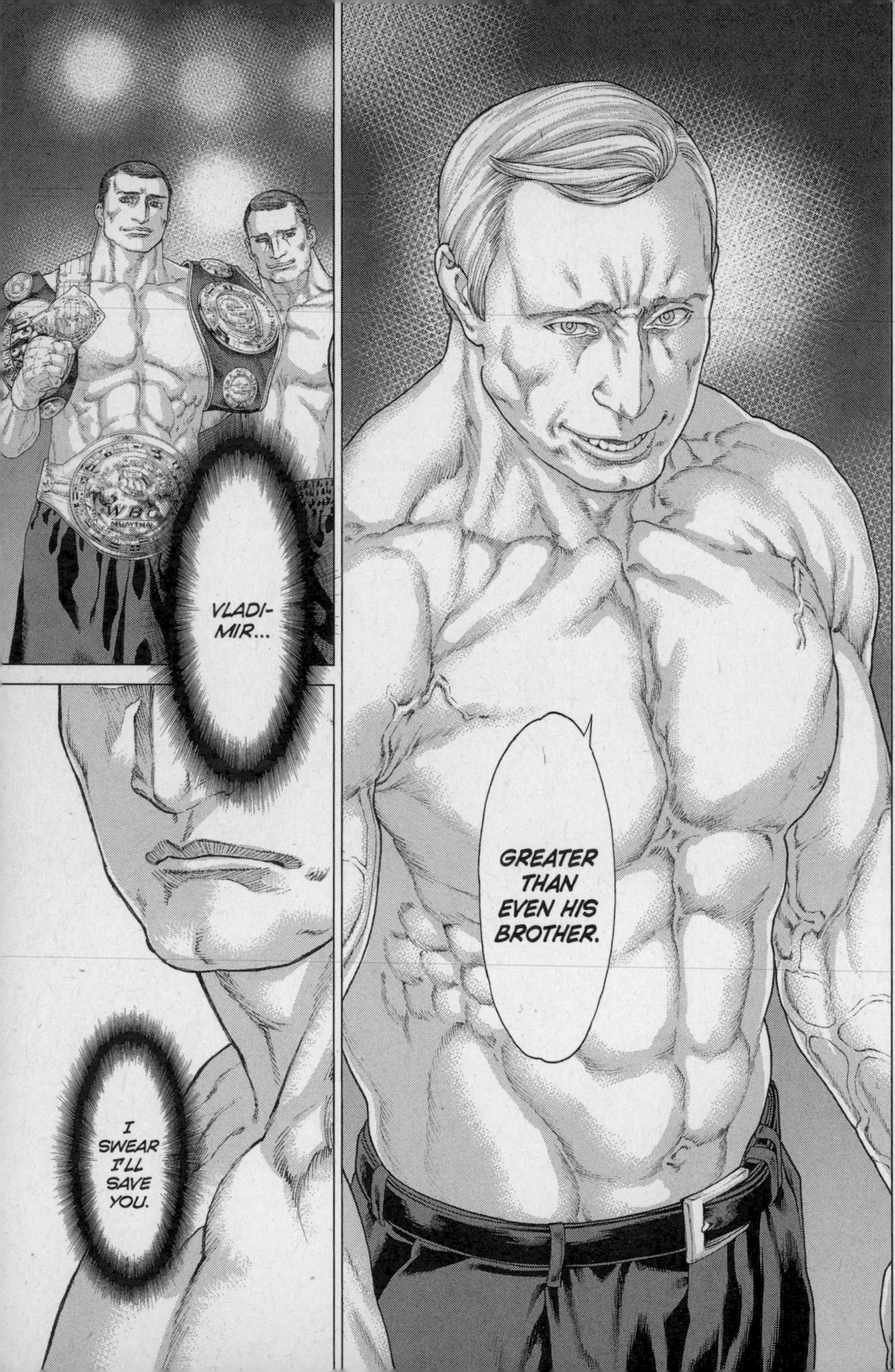
GREATER THAN EVEN HIS BROTHER.
VLADI-MIR...
I SWEAR I'LL SAVE YOU.

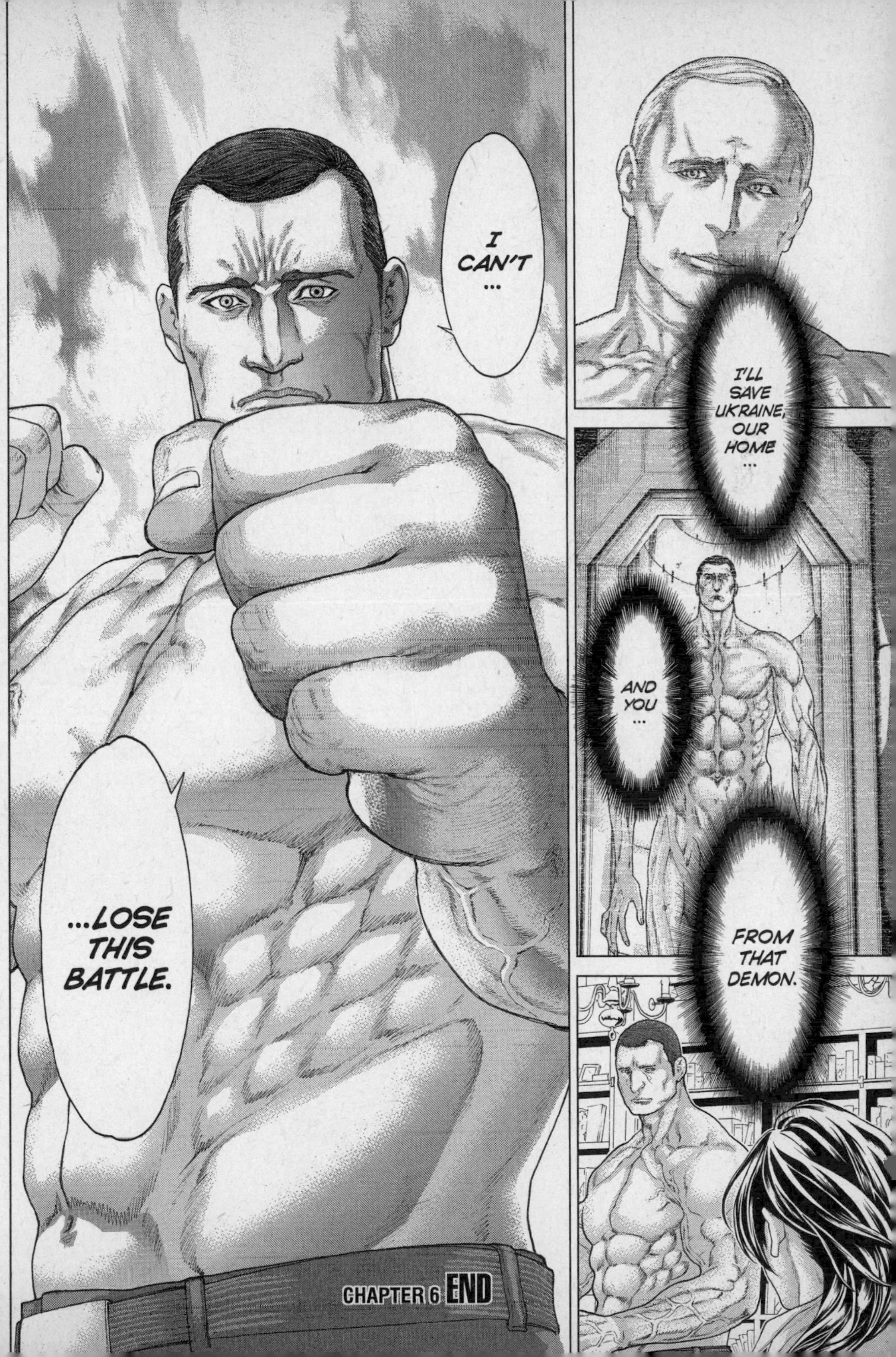
I'LL SAVE UKRAINE, OUR HOME ...
AND YOU ...
FROM THAT DEMON.
I CAN'T ...
...LOSE THIS BATTLE.
CHAPTER 6 END

ゴロセウム

GOLOSSEUM

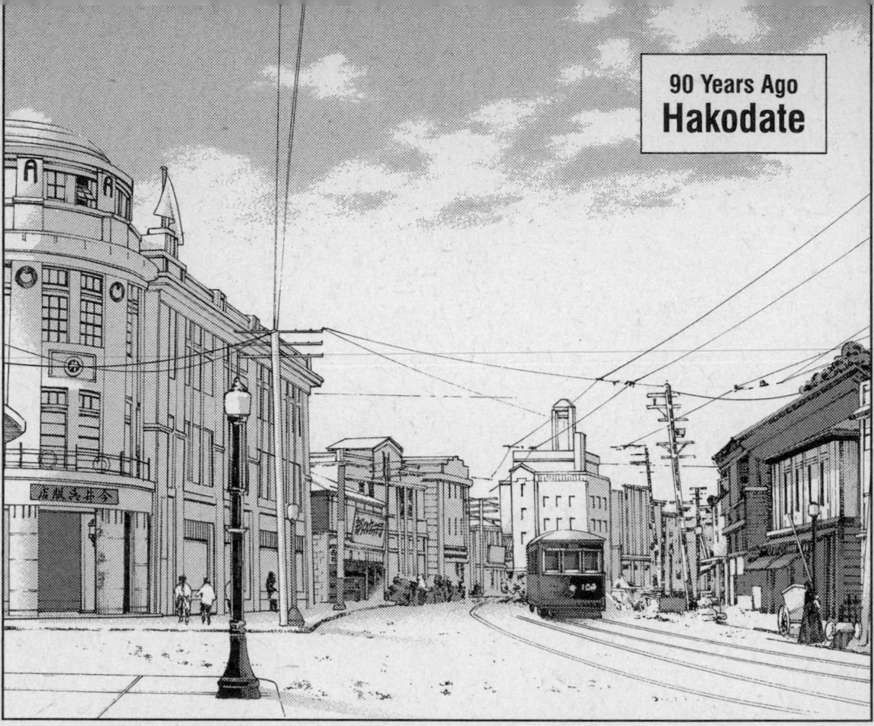
90 Years Ago
Hakodate
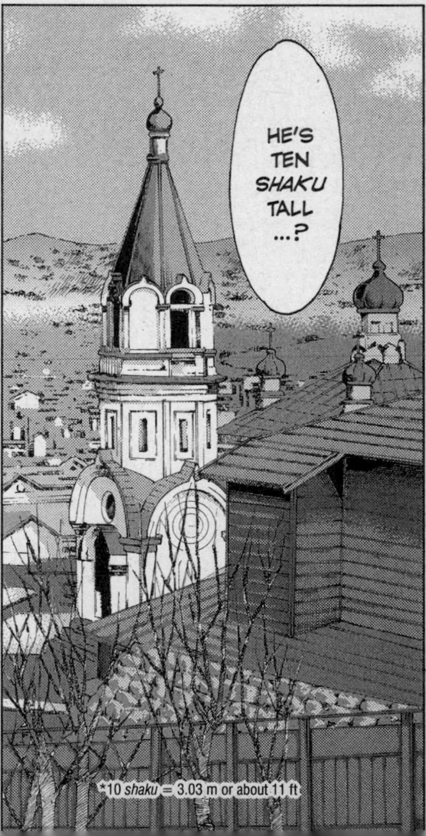
HE'S TEN SHAKU TALL ...?
*10 shaku = 3.03 m or about 11 ft
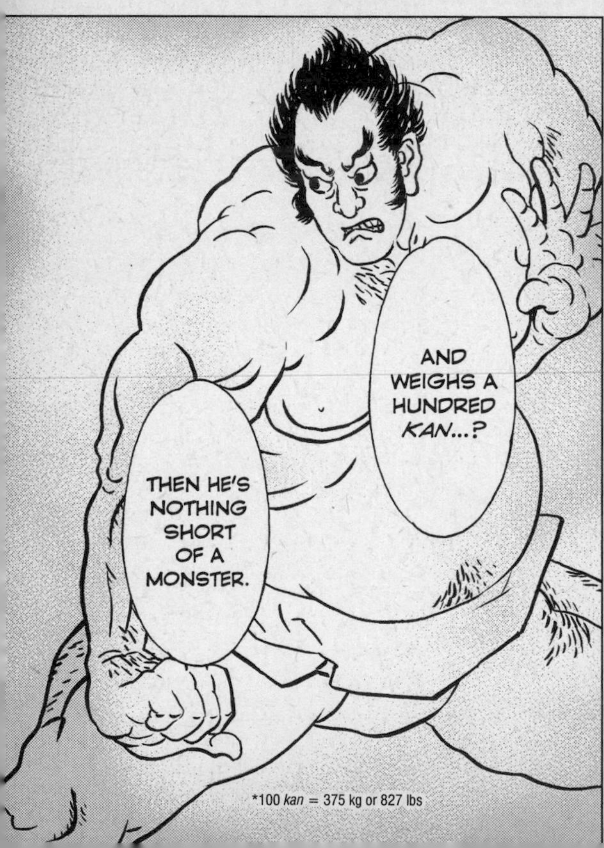
AND WEIGHS A HUNDRED KAN...?
THEN HE'S NOTHING SHORT OF A MONSTER.
*100 kan = 375 kg or 827 lbs

CHAPTER 7

THE PREDESTINED FAMILY

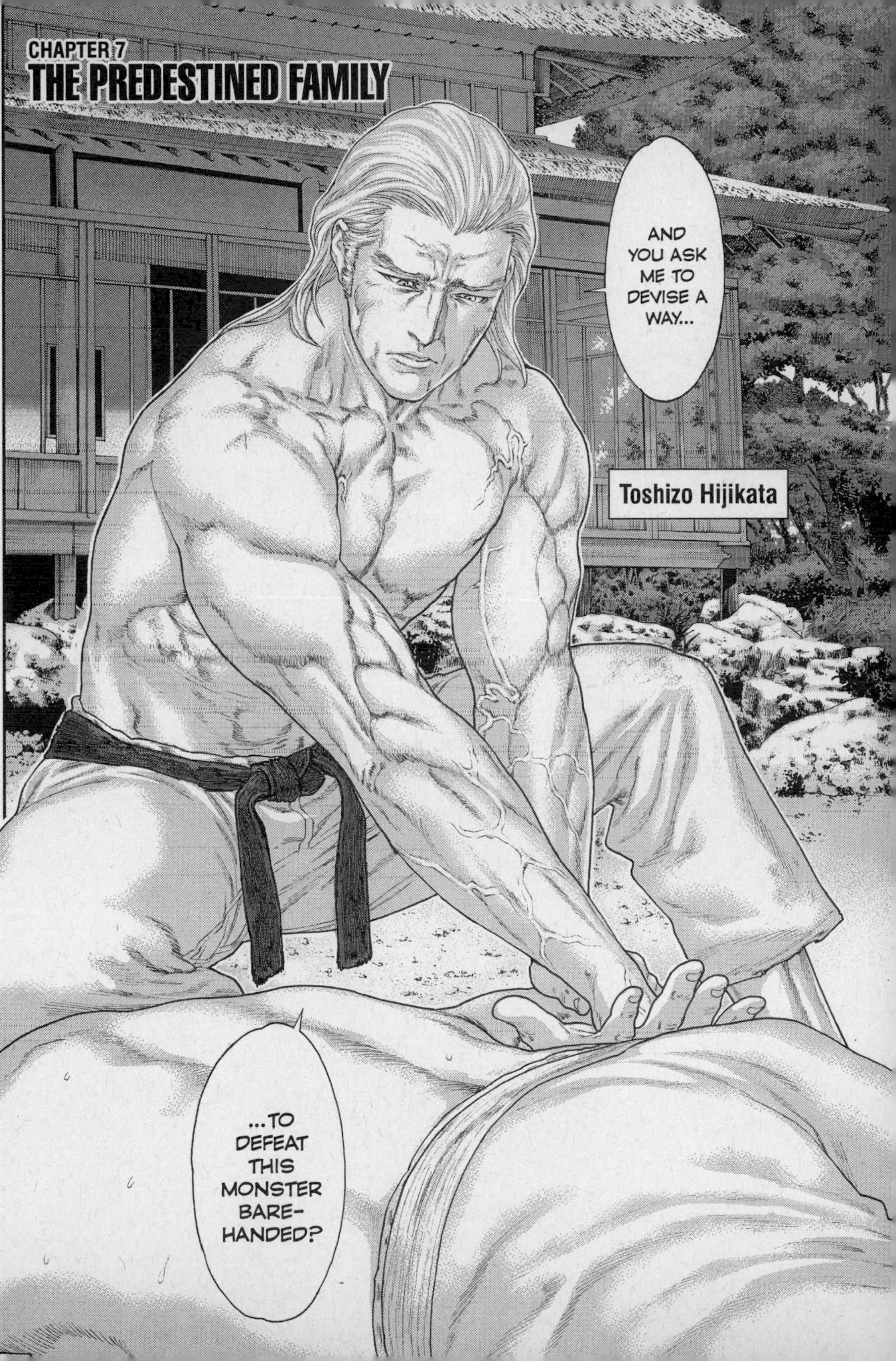
AND YOU ASK ME TO DEVISE A WAY...
Toshizo Hijikata
...TO DEFEAT THIS MONSTER BARE-HANDED?

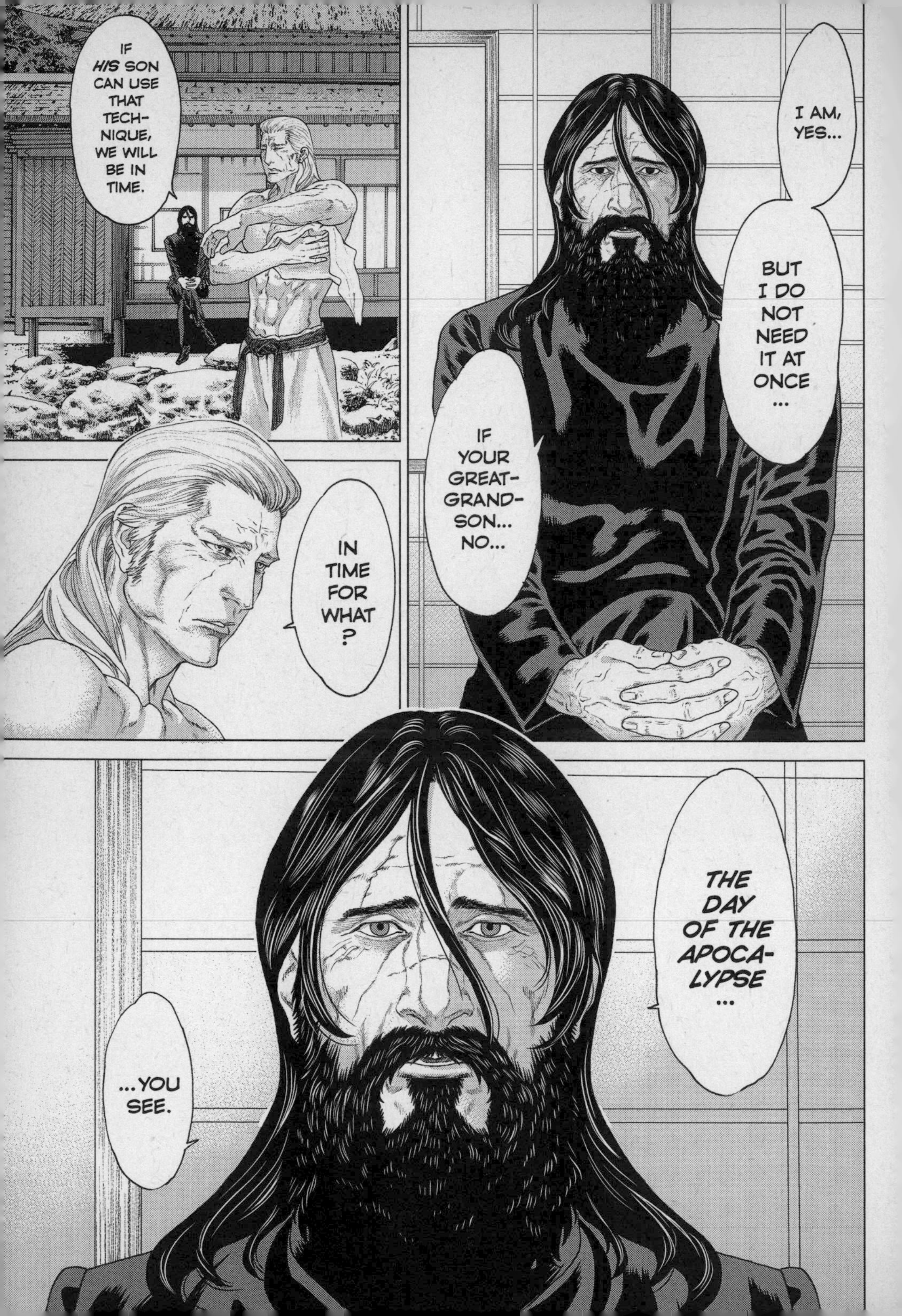
I AM, YES...
BUT I DO NOT NEED IT AT ONCE ...
IF YOUR GREAT-GRANDSON... NO...
IF *HIS* SON CAN USE THAT TECHNIQUE, WE WILL BE IN TIME.
IN TIME FOR WHAT?
THE DAY OF THE APOCALYPSE ...
...YOU SEE.

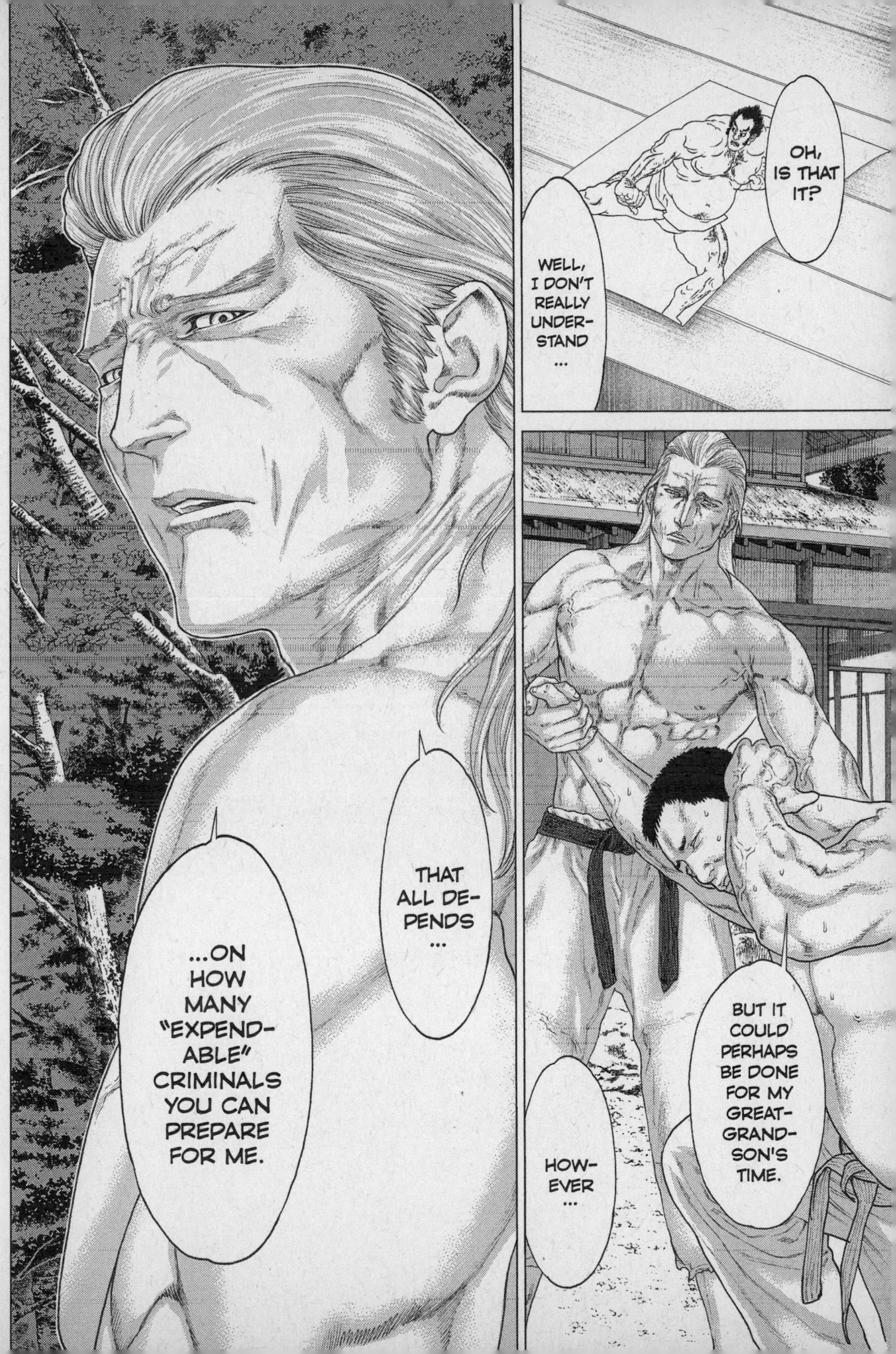
OH, IS THAT IT?
WELL, I DON'T REALLY UNDER-STAND ...
BUT IT COULD PERHAPS BE DONE FOR MY GREAT-GRAND-SON'S TIME.
HOW-EVER ...
THAT ALL DE-PENDS ...
...ON HOW MANY "EXPEND-ABLE" CRIMINALS YOU CAN PREPARE FOR ME.

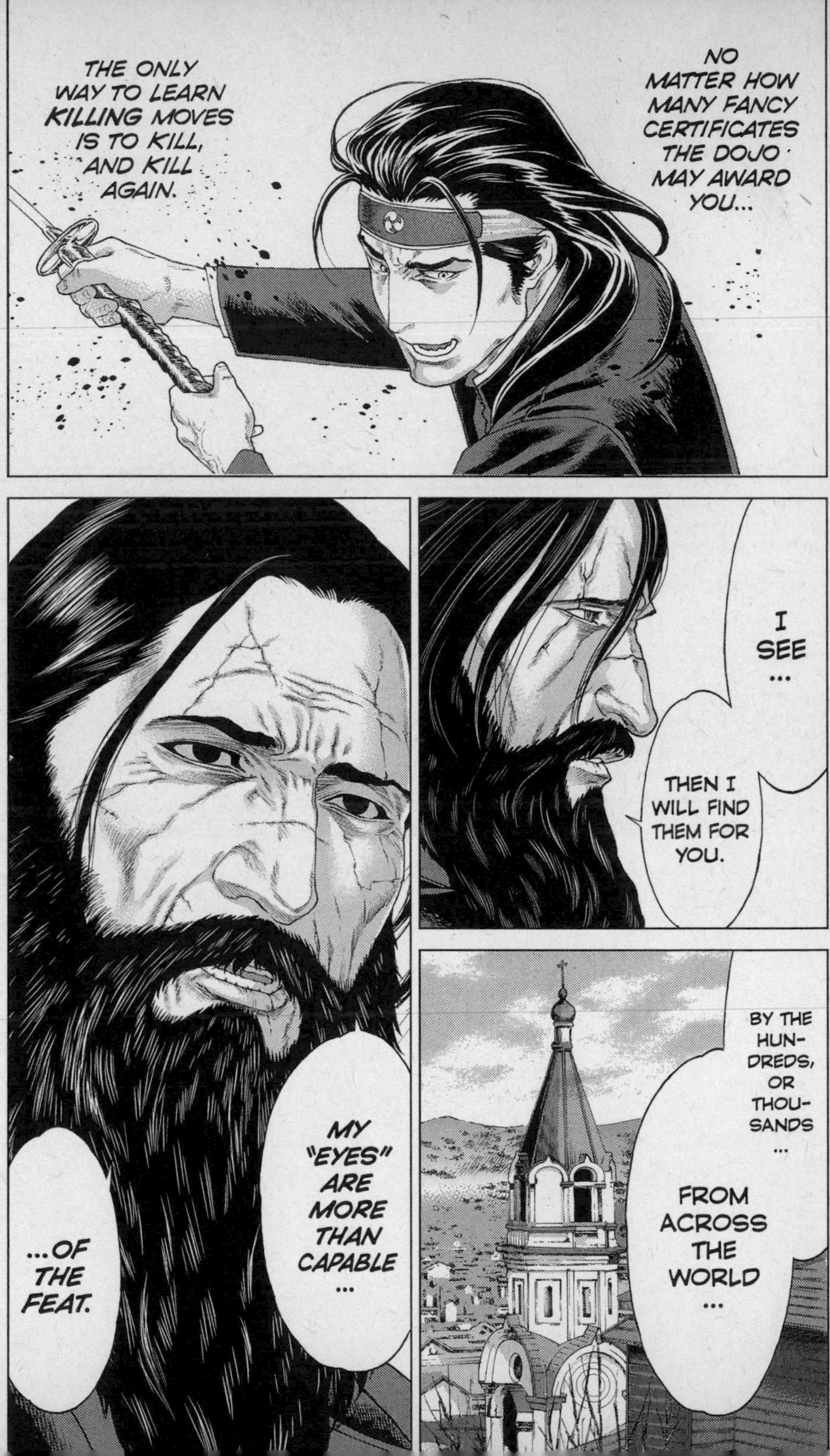
NO MATTER HOW MANY FANCY CERTIFICATES THE DOJO MAY AWARD YOU...
THE ONLY WAY TO LEARN KILLING MOVES IS TO KILL, AND KILL AGAIN.
I SEE ...
THEN I WILL FIND THEM FOR YOU.
BY THE HUN-DREDS, OR THOU-SANDS ...
FROM ACROSS THE WORLD ...
MY "EYES" ARE MORE THAN CAPABLE ...
...OF THE FEAT.

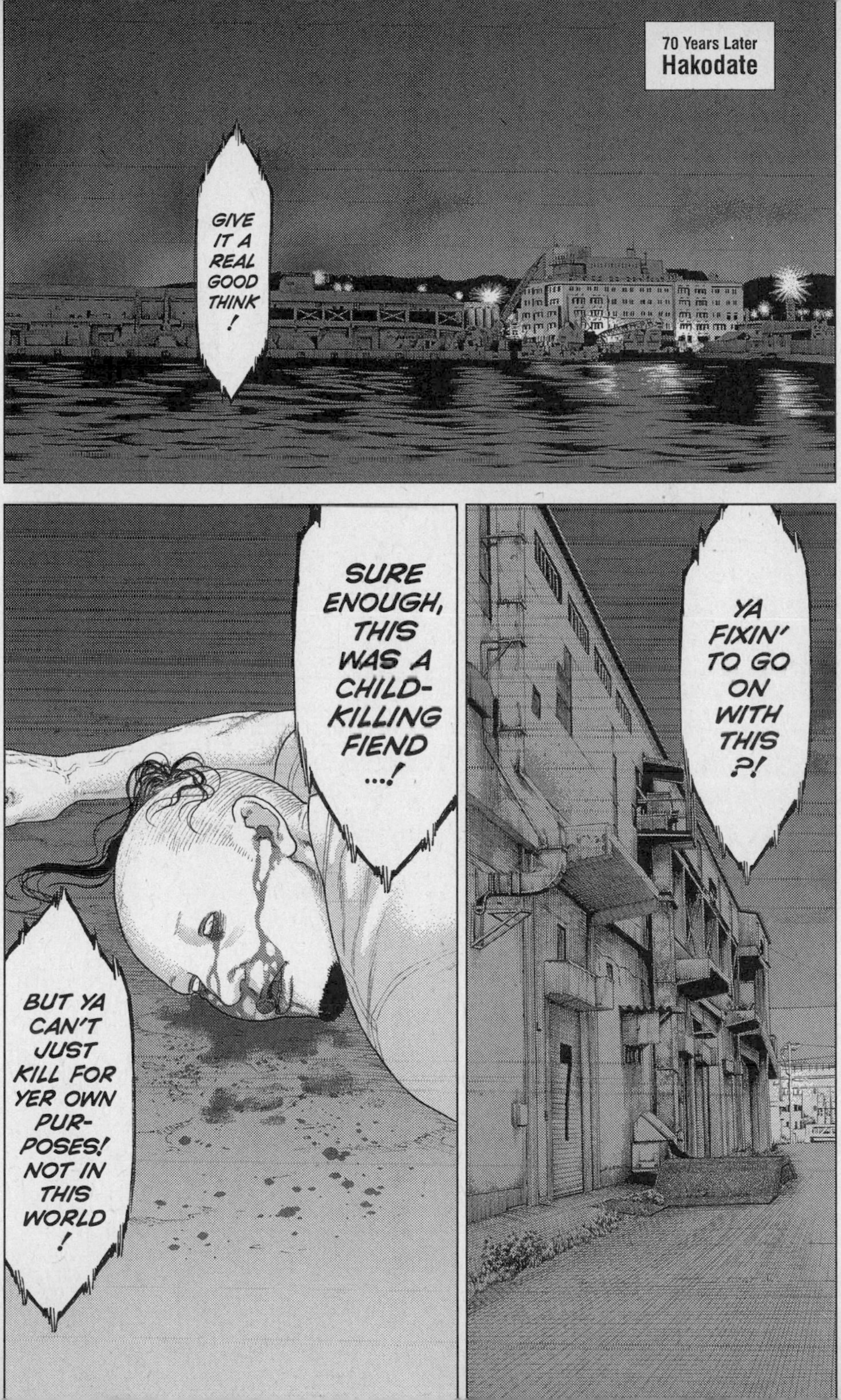
70 Years Later
Hakodate
GIVE IT A REAL GOOD THINK !
YA FIXIN' TO GO ON WITH THIS ?!
SURE ENOUGH, THIS WAS A CHILD-KILLING FIEND ...!
BUT YA CAN'T JUST KILL FOR YER OWN PUR-POSES! NOT IN THIS WORLD !

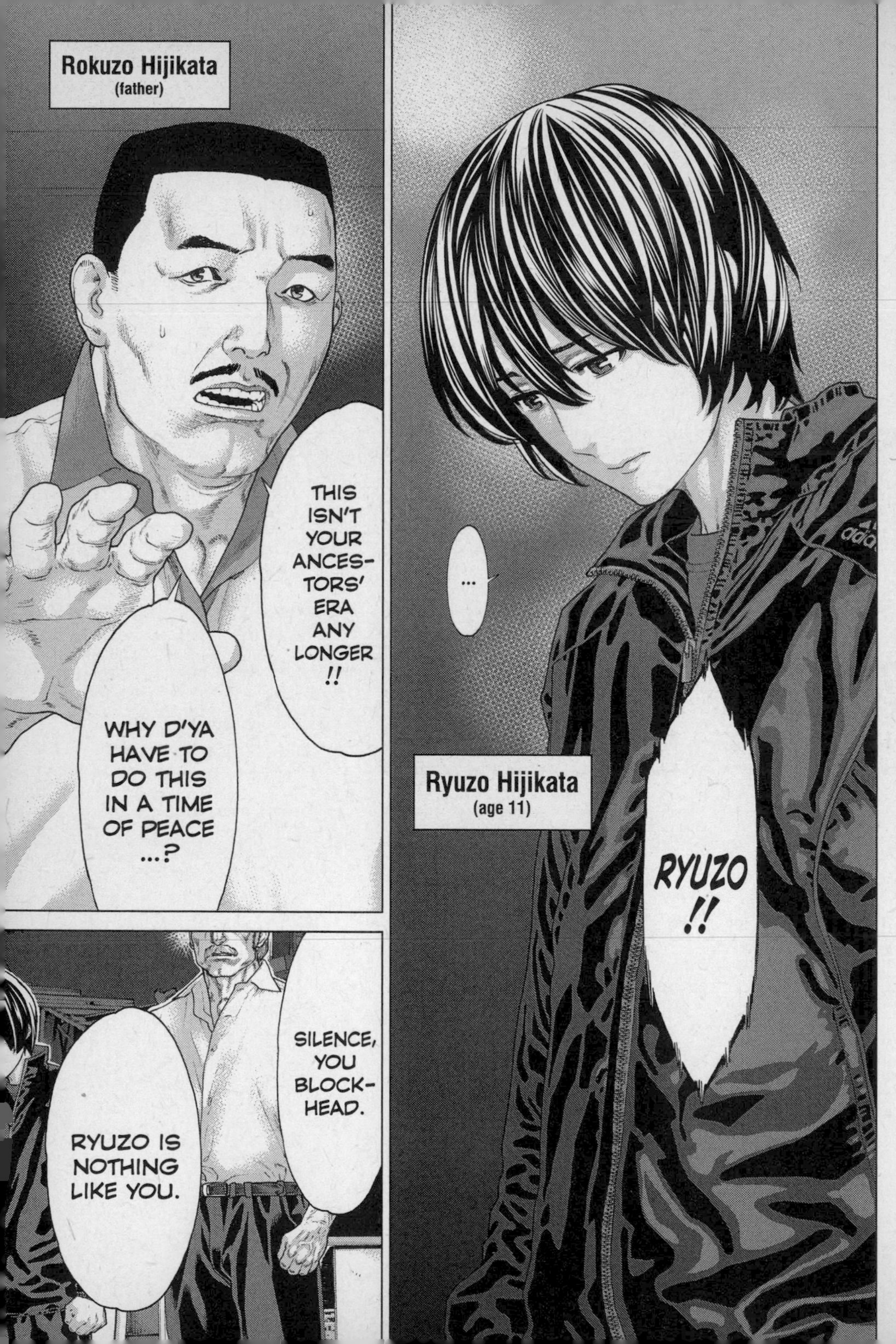
...
RYUZO!!
Ryuzo Hijikata
(age 11)
Rokuzo Hijikata
(father)
THIS ISN'T YOUR ANCESTORS' ERA ANY LONGER!!
WHY D'YA HAVE TO DO THIS IN A TIME OF PEACE ...?
SILENCE, YOU BLOCKHEAD.
RYUZO IS NOTHING LIKE YOU.

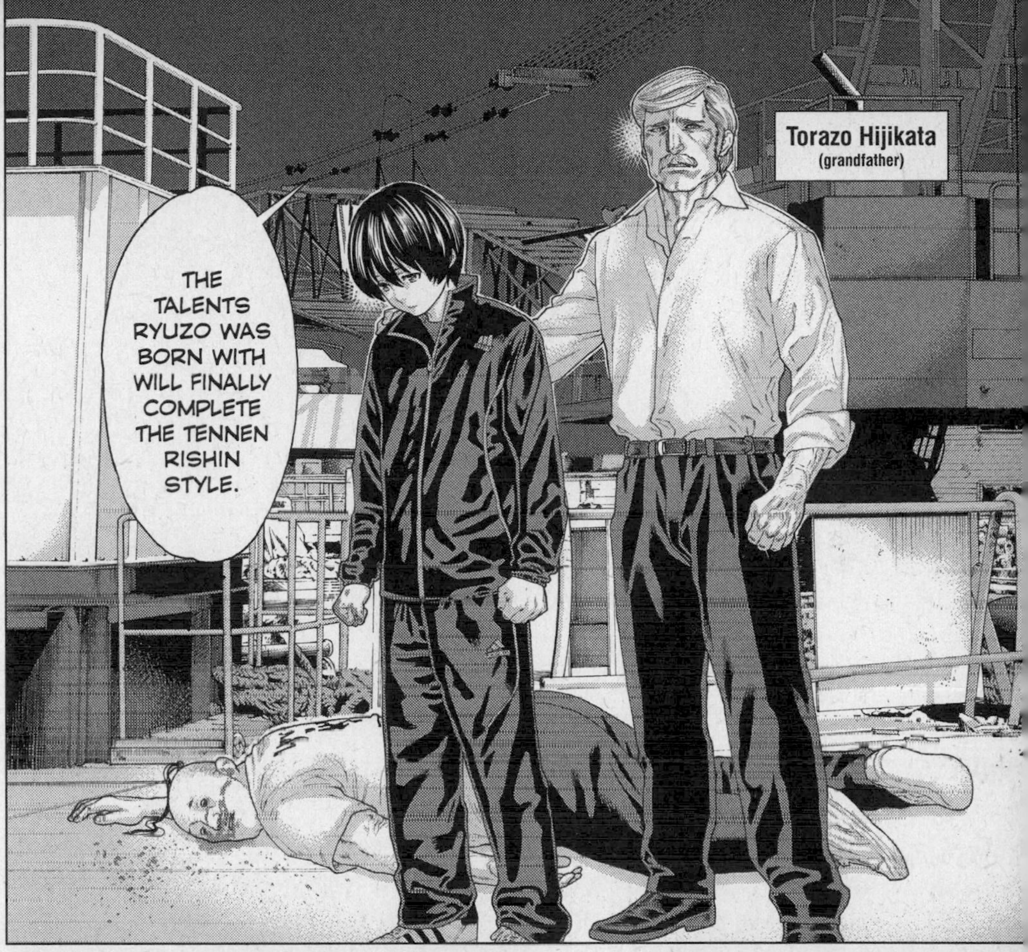
Torazo Hijikata
(grandfather)
THE TALENTS RYUZO WAS BORN WITH WILL FINALLY COMPLETE THE TENNEN RISHIN STYLE.
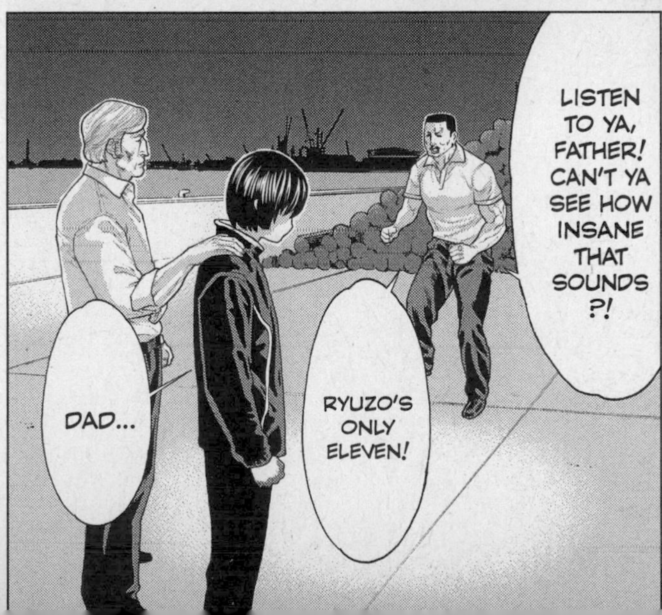
DAD...
RYUZO'S ONLY ELEVEN!
LISTEN TO YA, FATHER! CAN'T YA SEE HOW INSANE THAT SOUNDS ?!
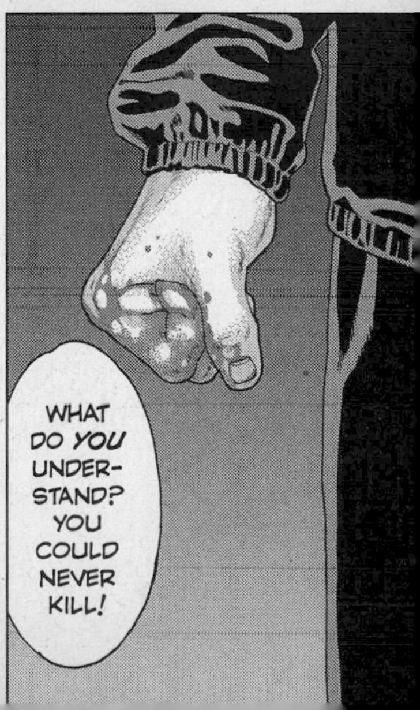
WHAT DO *YOU* UNDER-STAND? YOU COULD NEVER KILL!

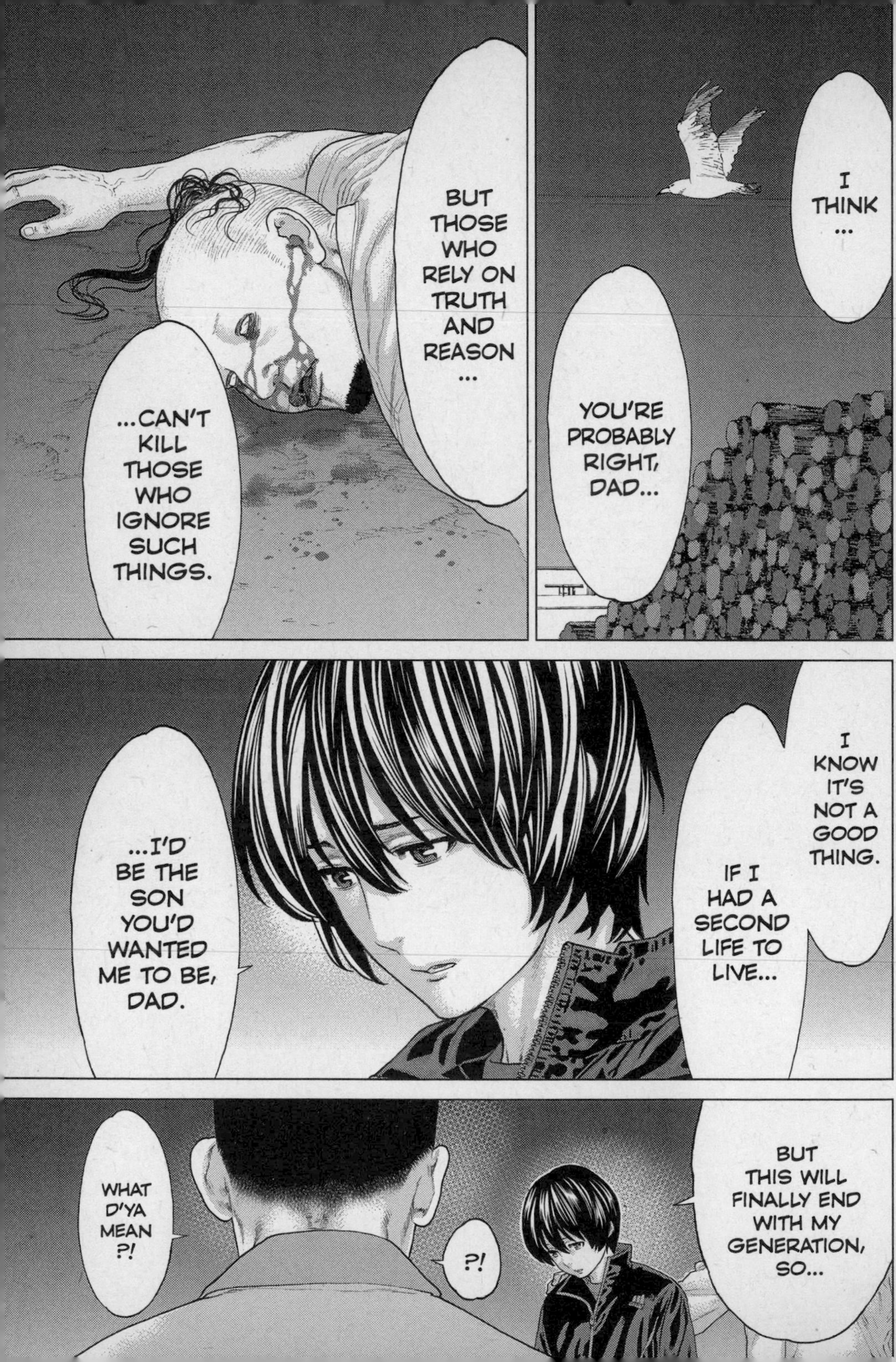
I THINK...
YOU'RE PROBABLY RIGHT, DAD...
BUT THOSE WHO RELY ON TRUTH AND REASON...
...CAN'T KILL THOSE WHO IGNORE SUCH THINGS.
I KNOW IT'S NOT A GOOD THING.
IF I HAD A SECOND LIFE TO LIVE...
...I'D BE THE SON YOU'D WANTED ME TO BE, DAD.
BUT THIS WILL FINALLY END WITH MY GENERATION, SO...
?!
WHAT D'YA MEAN?!

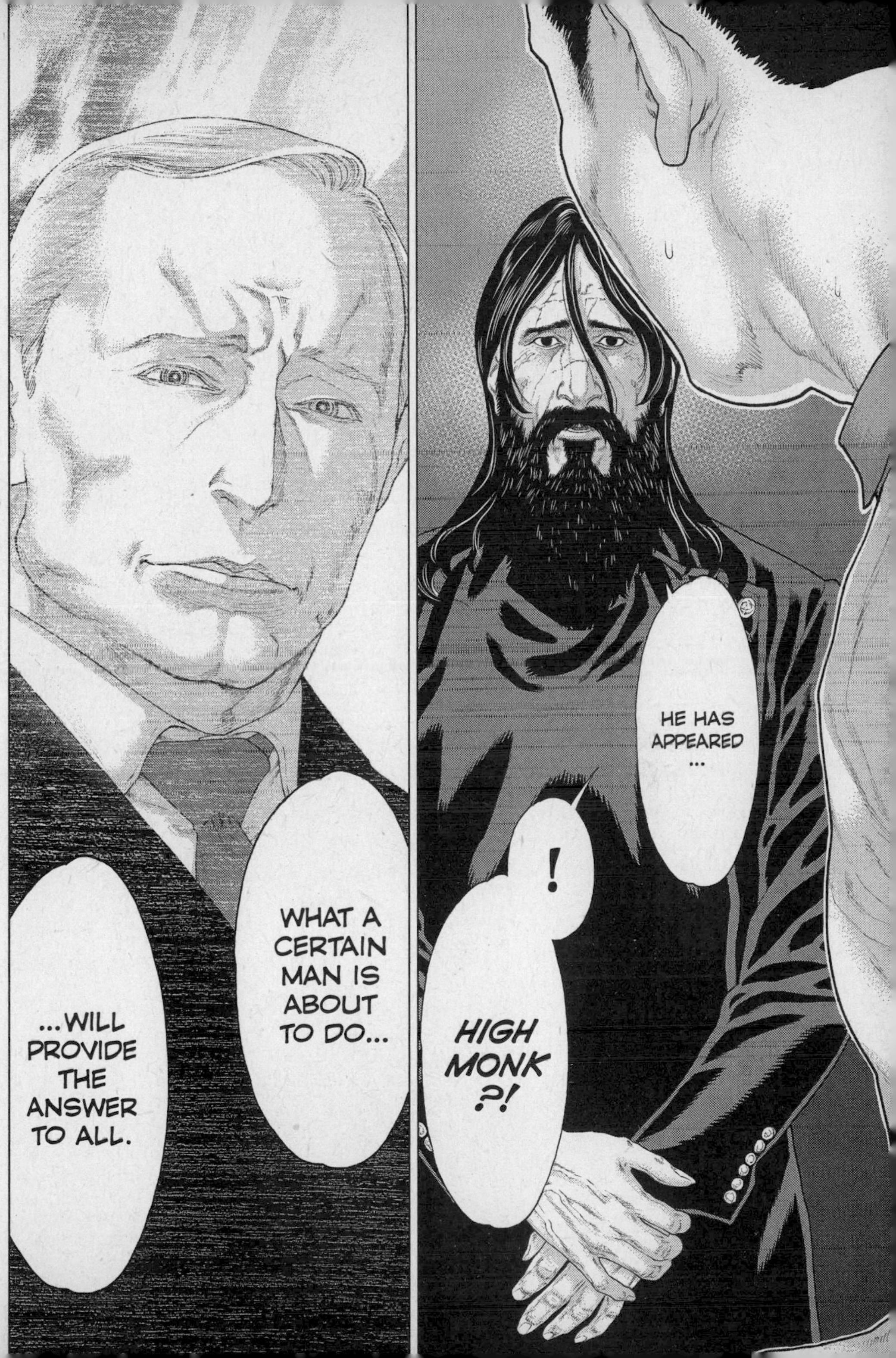
HE HAS APPEARED ...
!
HIGH MONK ?!
WHAT A CERTAIN MAN IS ABOUT TO DO...
...WILL PROVIDE THE ANSWER TO ALL.

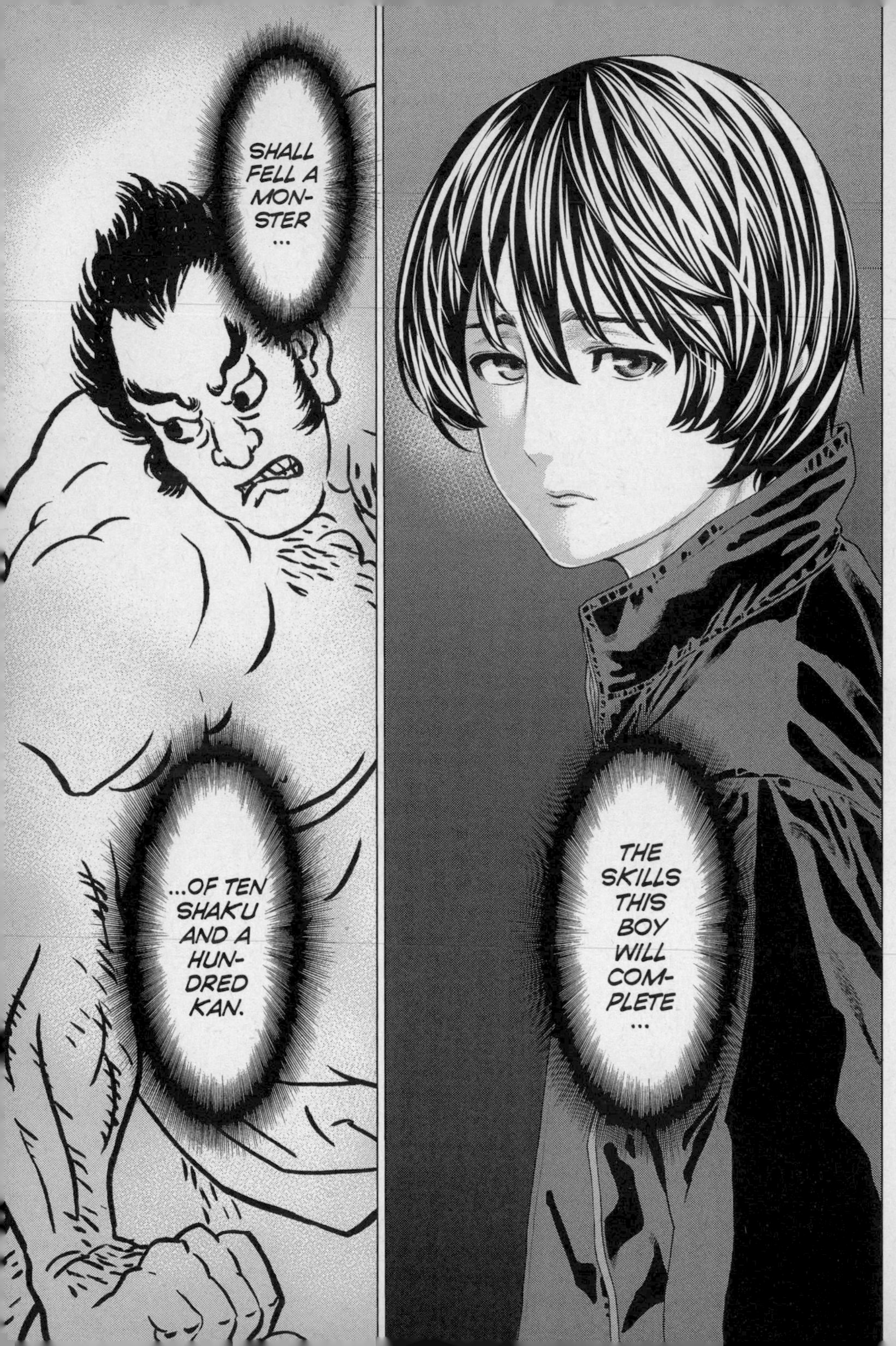
THE SKILLS THIS BOY WILL COMPLETE ...
SHALL FELL A MONSTER ...
...OF TEN SHAKU AND A HUNDRED KAN.

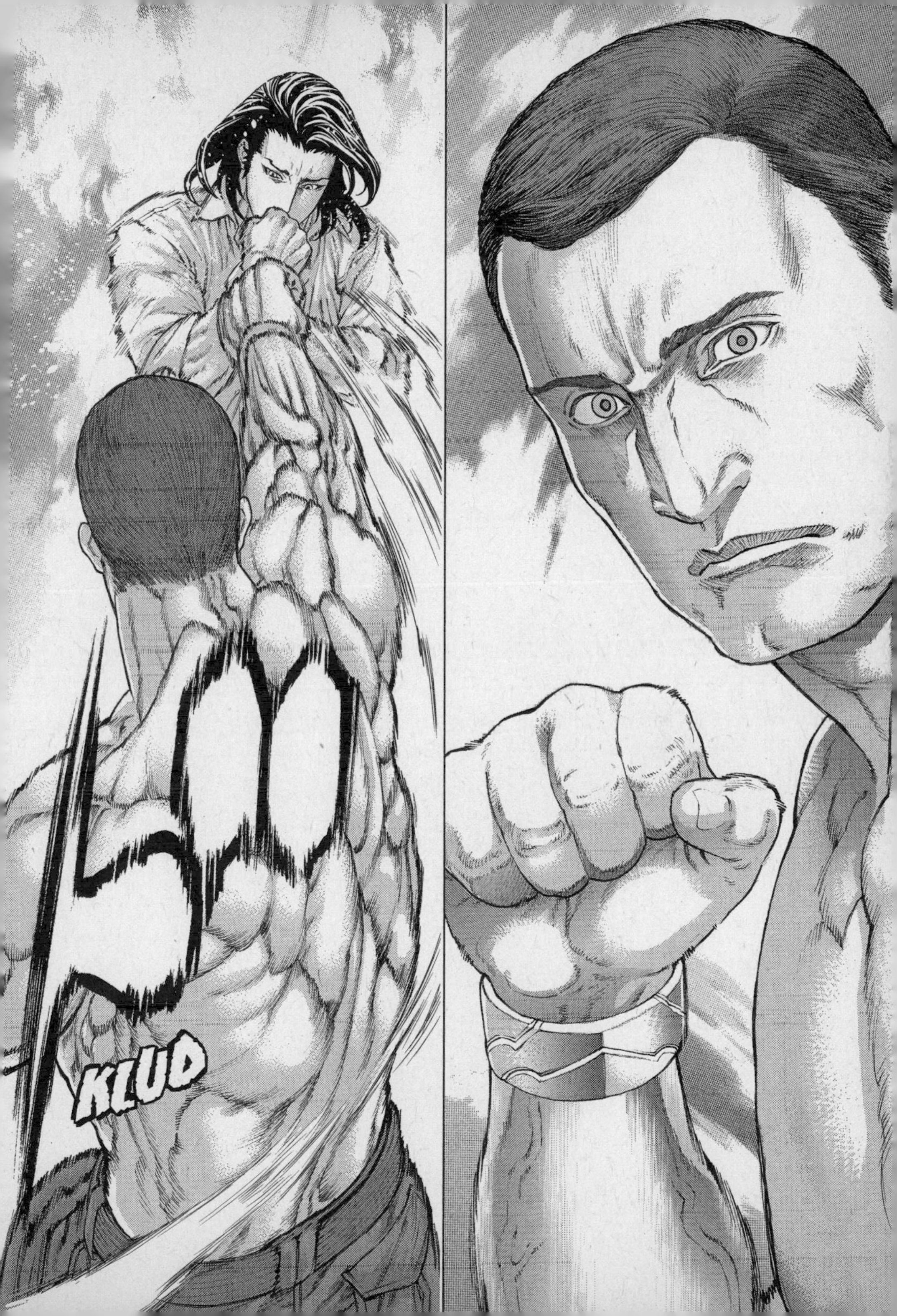
KLUD

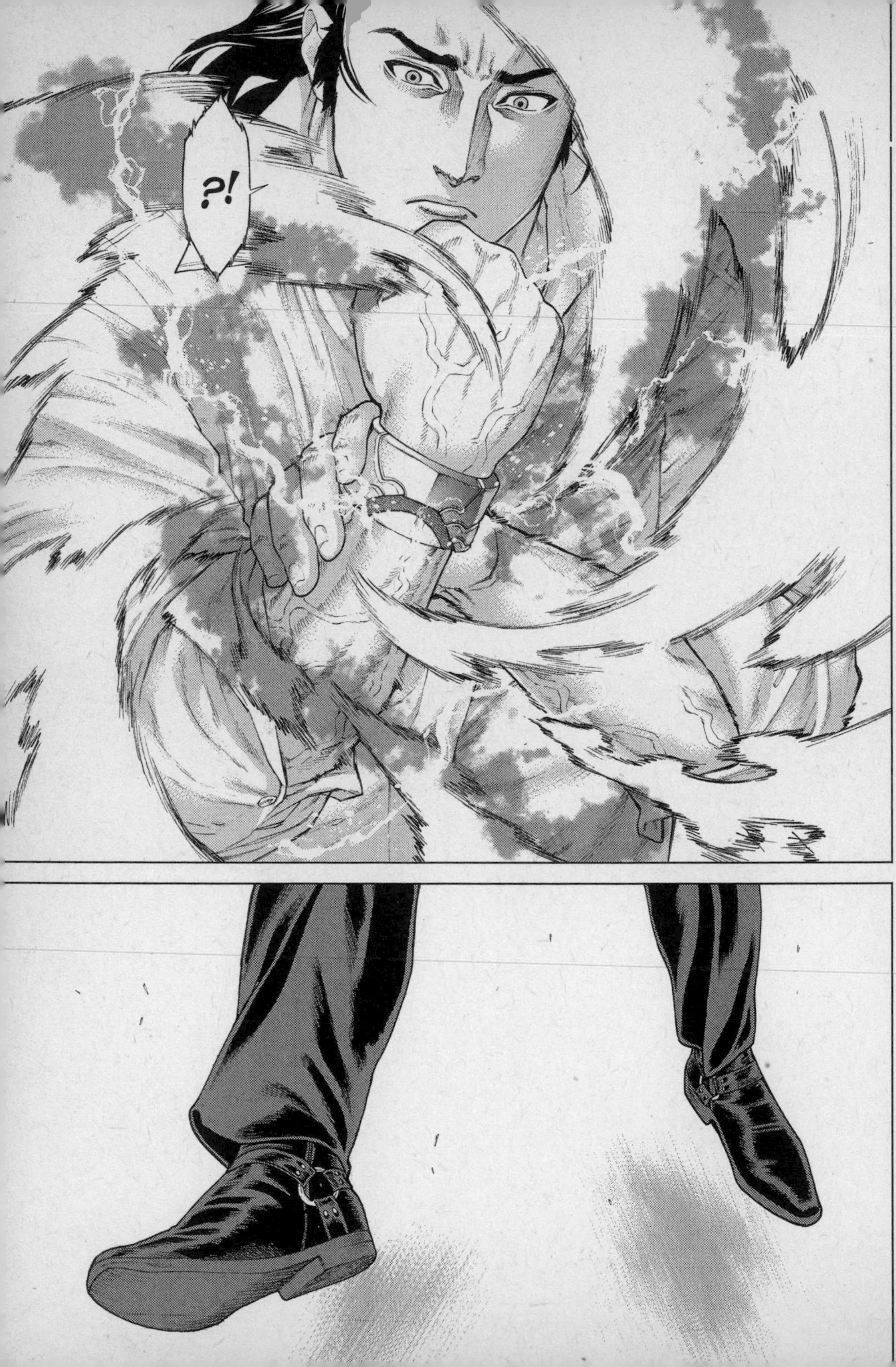
?!

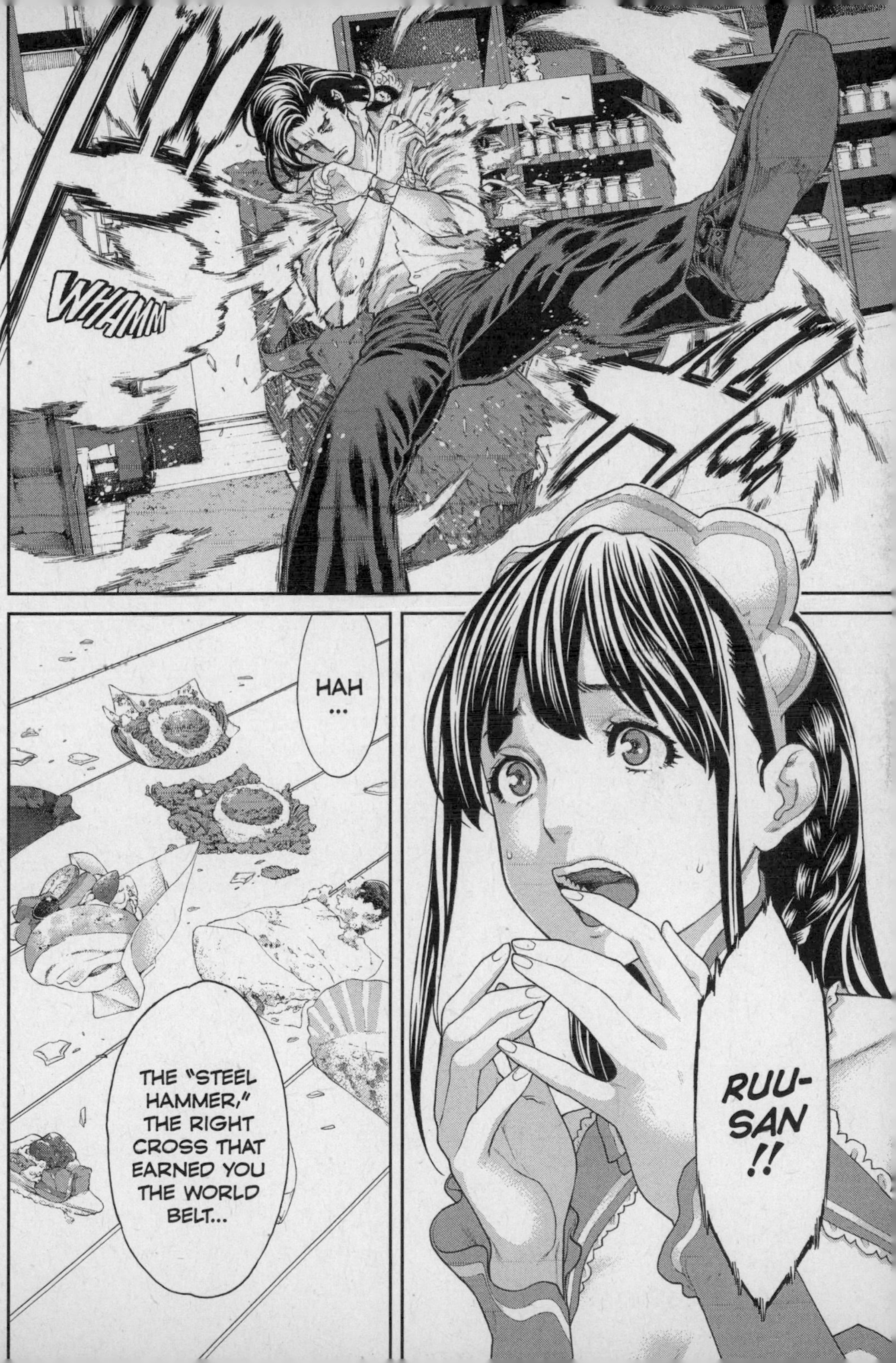
WHAMM
RUU-SAN!!
HAH ...
THE "STEEL HAMMER," THE RIGHT CROSS THAT EARNED YOU THE WORLD BELT...

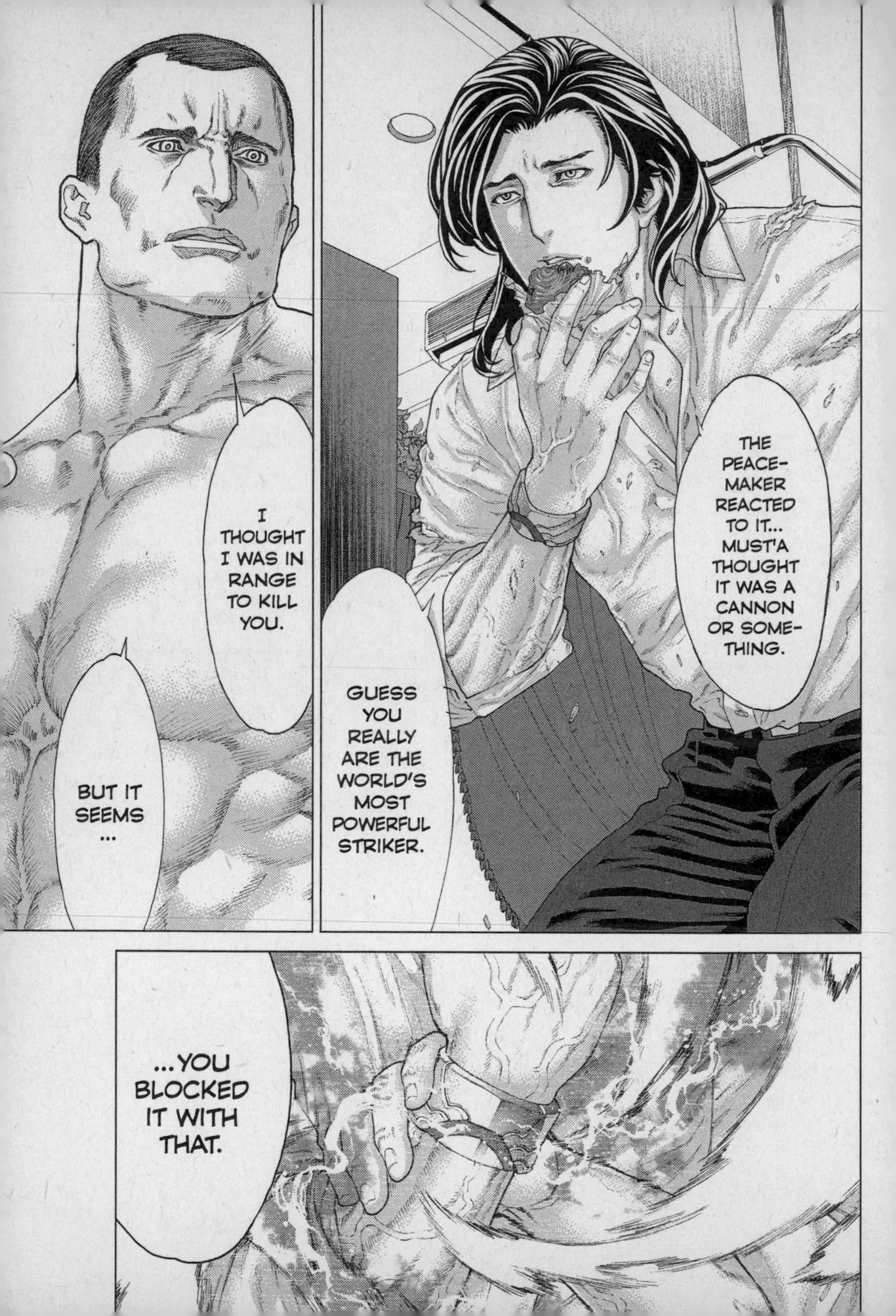
THE PEACE-MAKER REACTED TO IT... MUST'A THOUGHT IT WAS A CANNON OR SOME-THING.
GUESS YOU REALLY ARE THE WORLD'S MOST POWERFUL STRIKER.
I THOUGHT I WAS IN RANGE TO KILL YOU.
BUT IT SEEMS ...
...YOU BLOCKED IT WITH THAT.

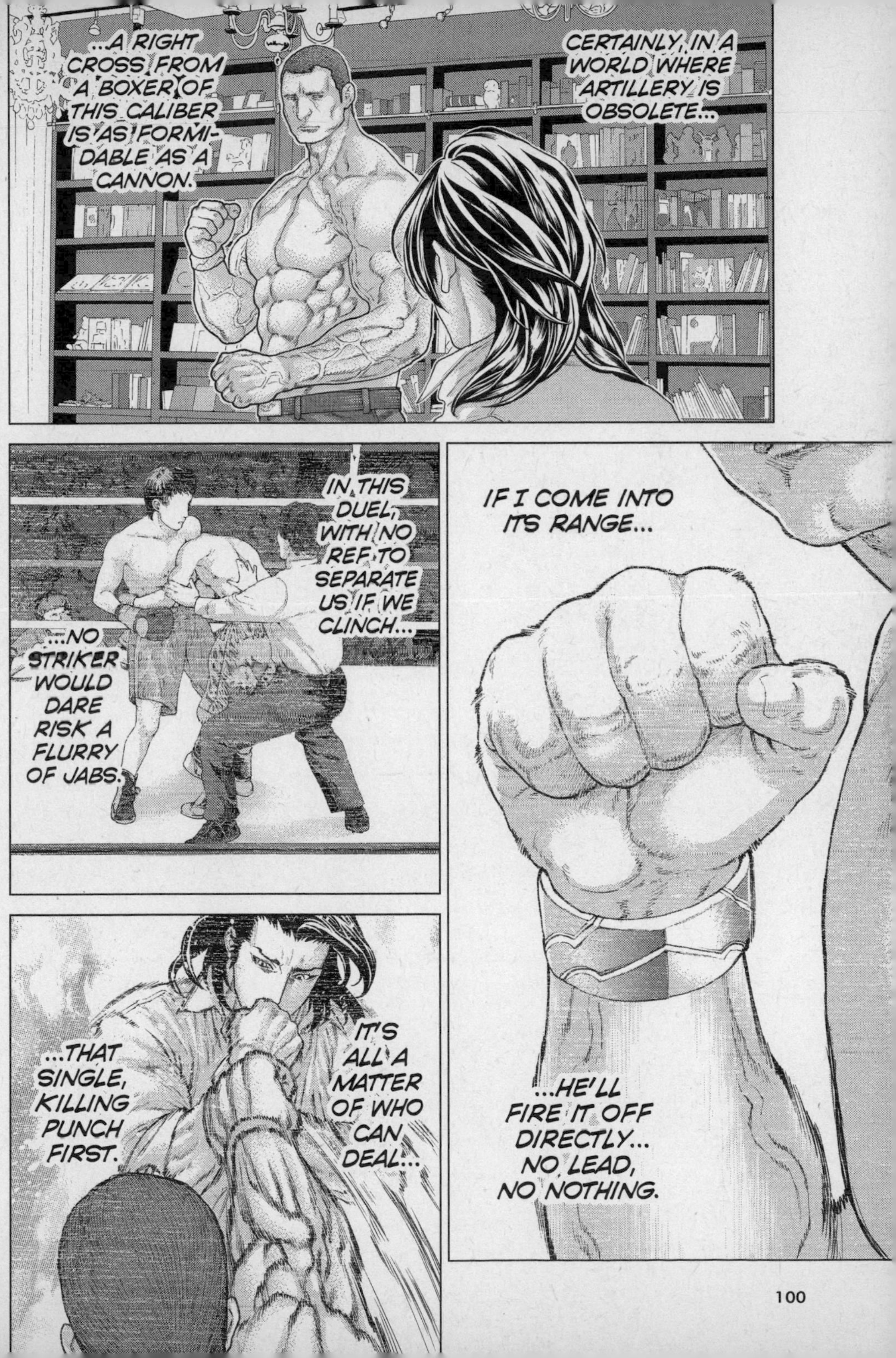
CERTAINLY, IN A WORLD WHERE ARTILLERY IS OBSOLETE...
...A RIGHT CROSS FROM A BOXER OF THIS CALIBER IS AS FORMIDABLE AS A CANNON.
IF I COME INTO ITS RANGE...
...HE'LL FIRE IT OFF DIRECTLY... NO LEAD, NO NOTHING.
IN THIS DUEL, WITH NO REF TO SEPARATE US IF WE CLINCH...
...NO STRIKER WOULD DARE RISK A FLURRY OF JABS.
IT'S ALL A MATTER OF WHO CAN DEAL...
...THAT SINGLE, KILLING PUNCH FIRST.

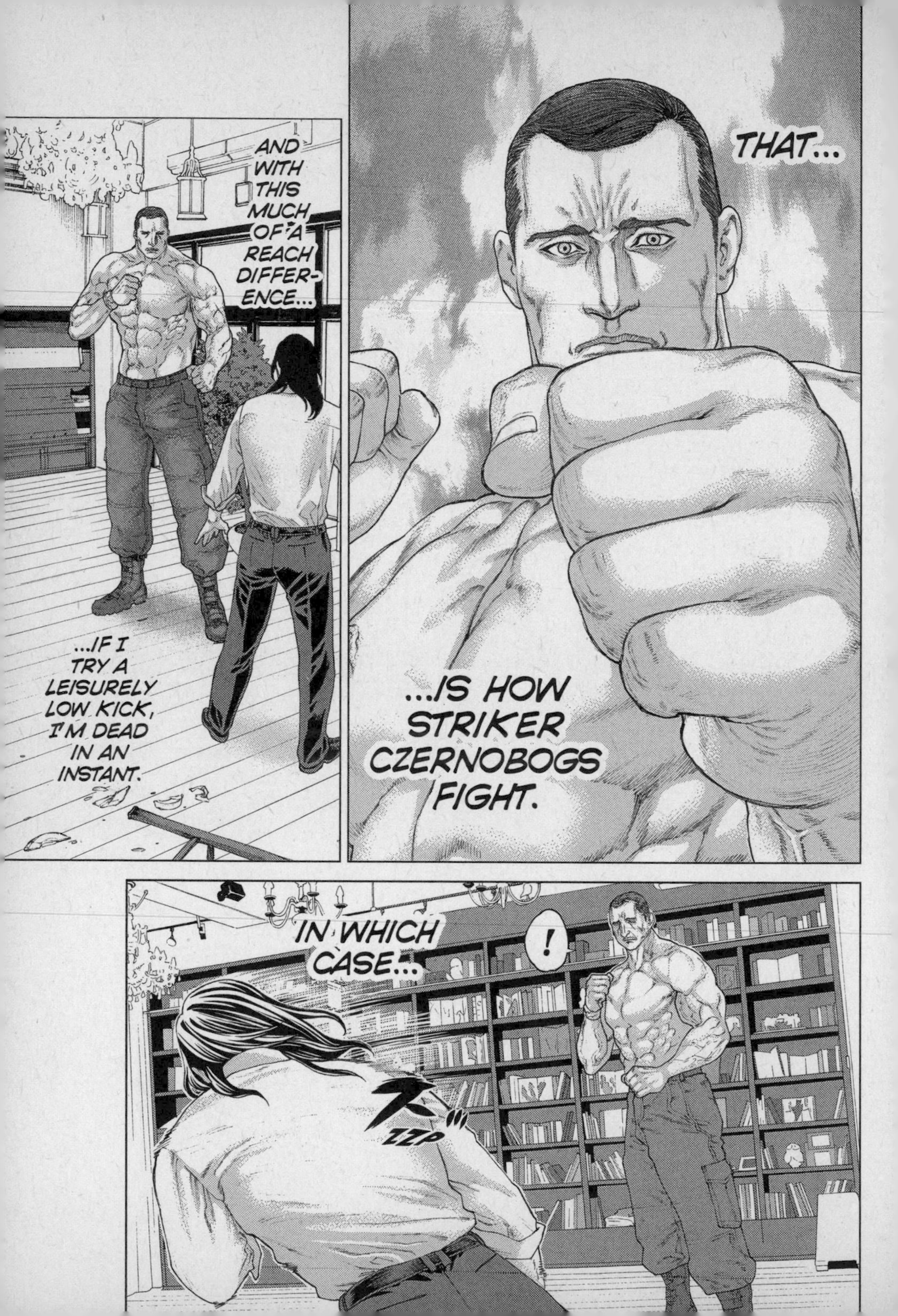
THAT...
...IS HOW STRIKER CZERNOBOGS FIGHT.
AND WITH THIS MUCH OF A REACH DIFFERENCE...
...IF I TRY A LEISURELY LOW KICK, I'M DEAD IN AN INSTANT.
IN WHICH CASE...
!
ZZP

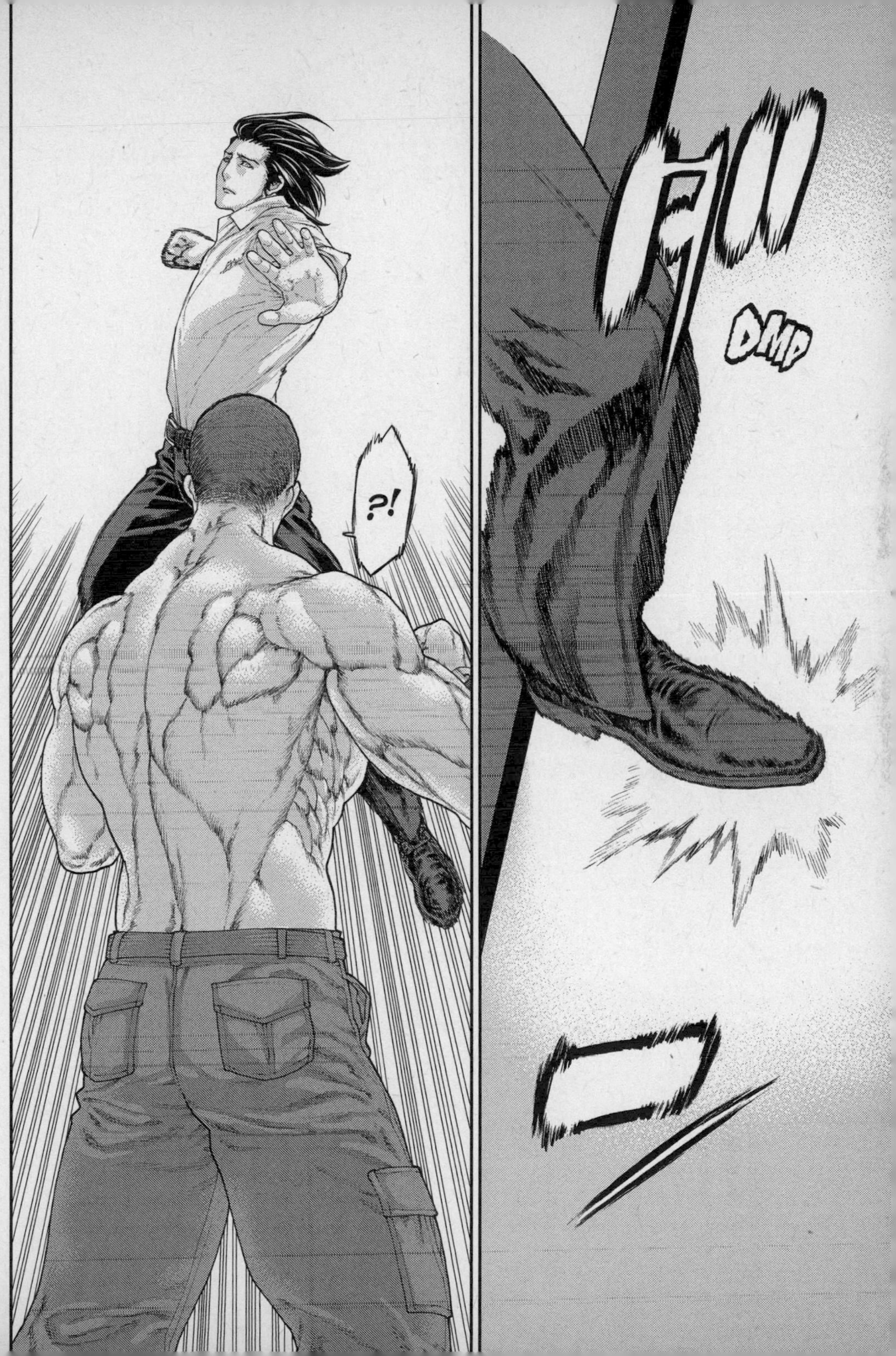
DMP
?!

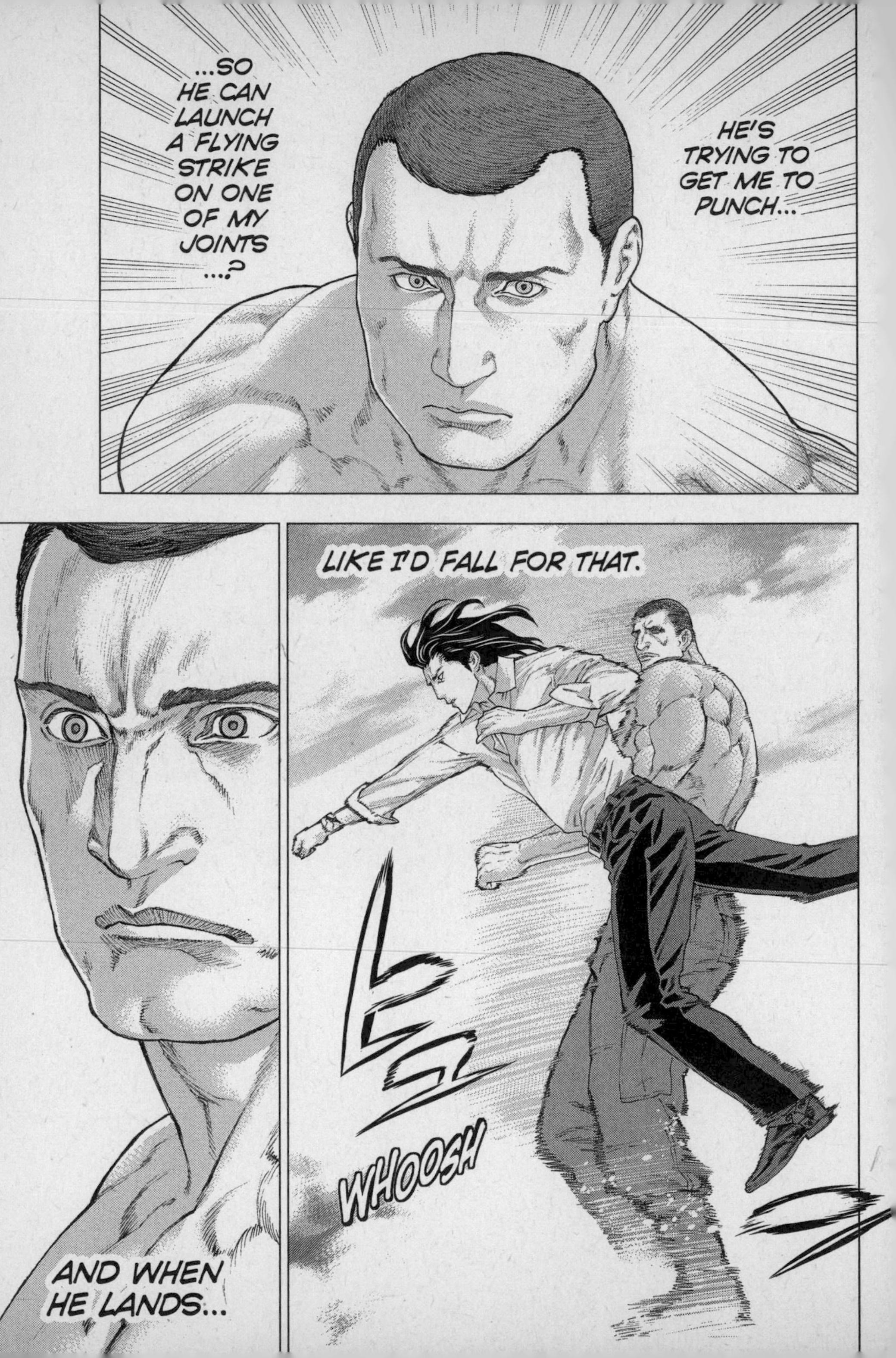
HE'S TRYING TO GET ME TO PUNCH...
...SO HE CAN LAUNCH A FLYING STRIKE ON ONE OF MY JOINTS ...?
LIKE I'D FALL FOR THAT.
WHOOSH
AND WHEN HE LANDS...

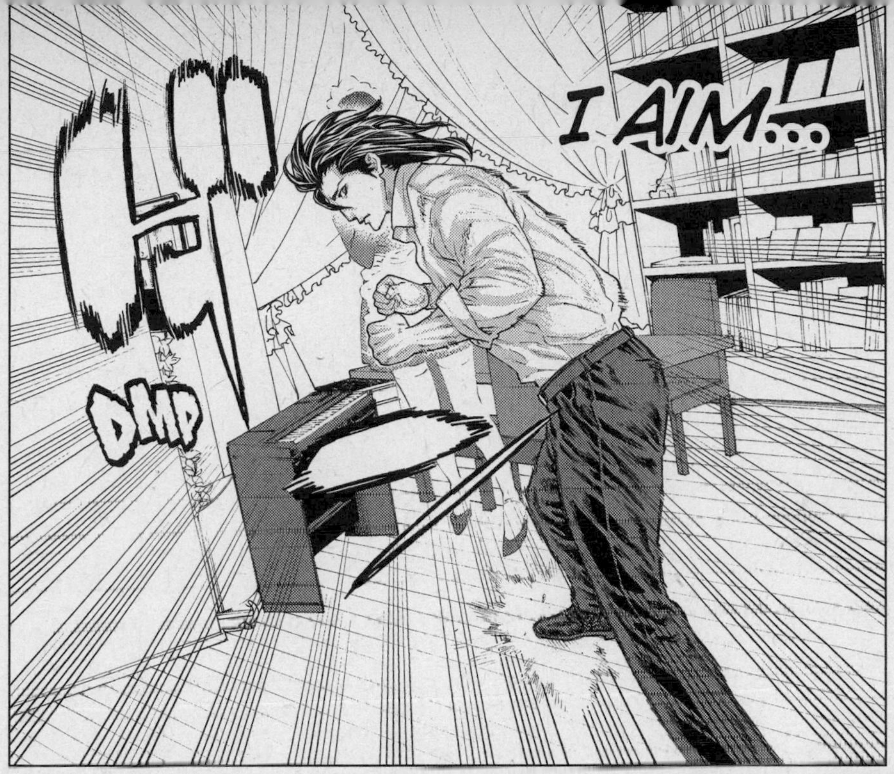
I AIM...
CLOP
DMP
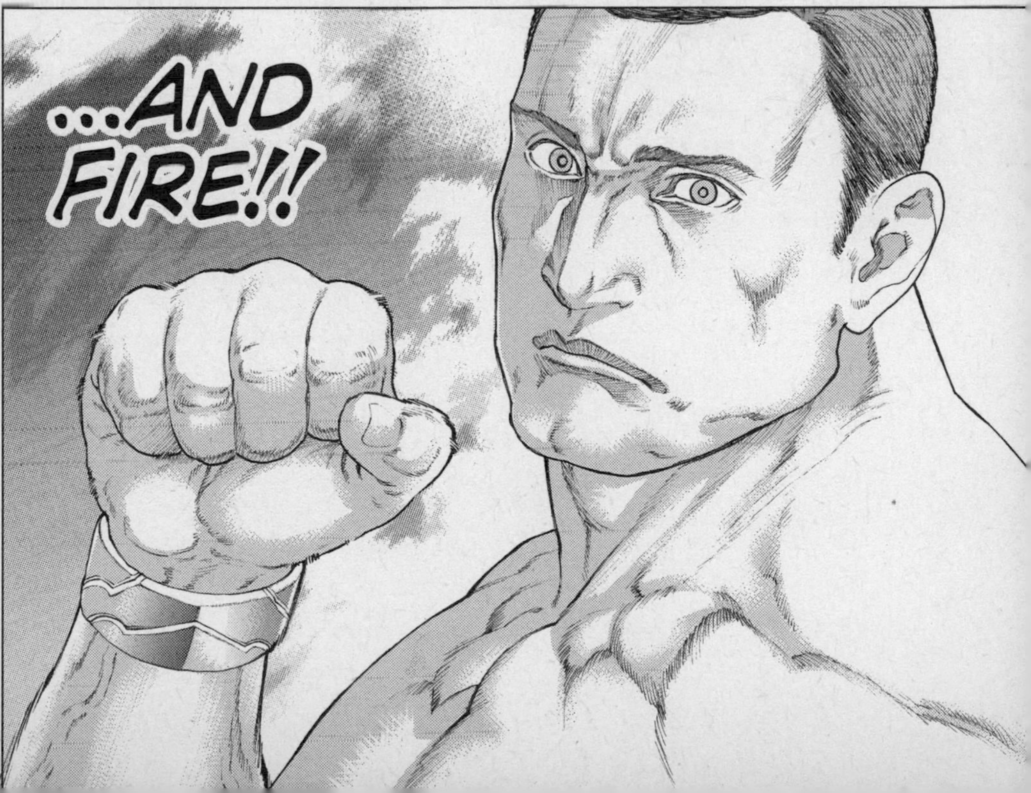
...AND FIRE!!

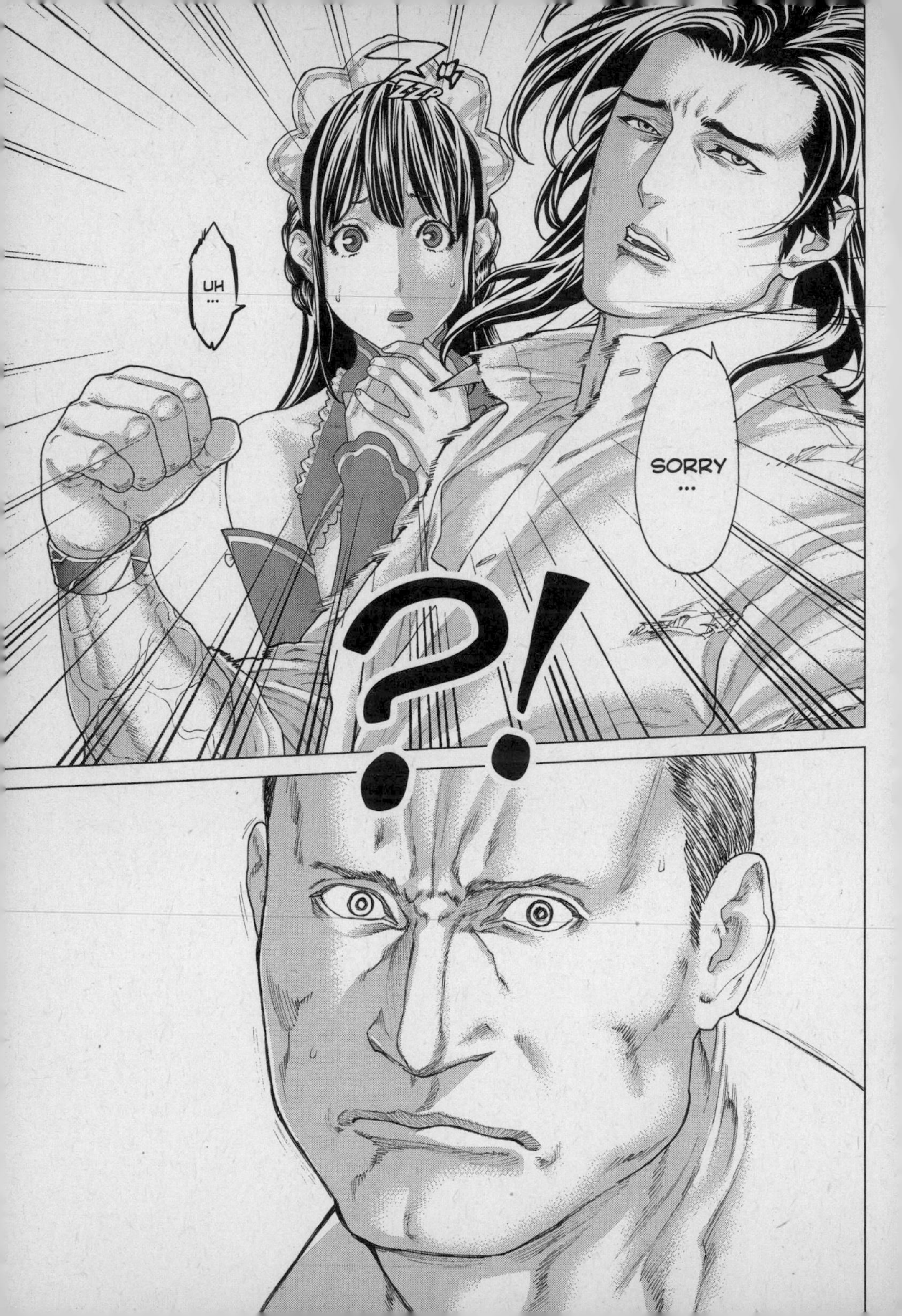
SORRY ...
UH ...
?!

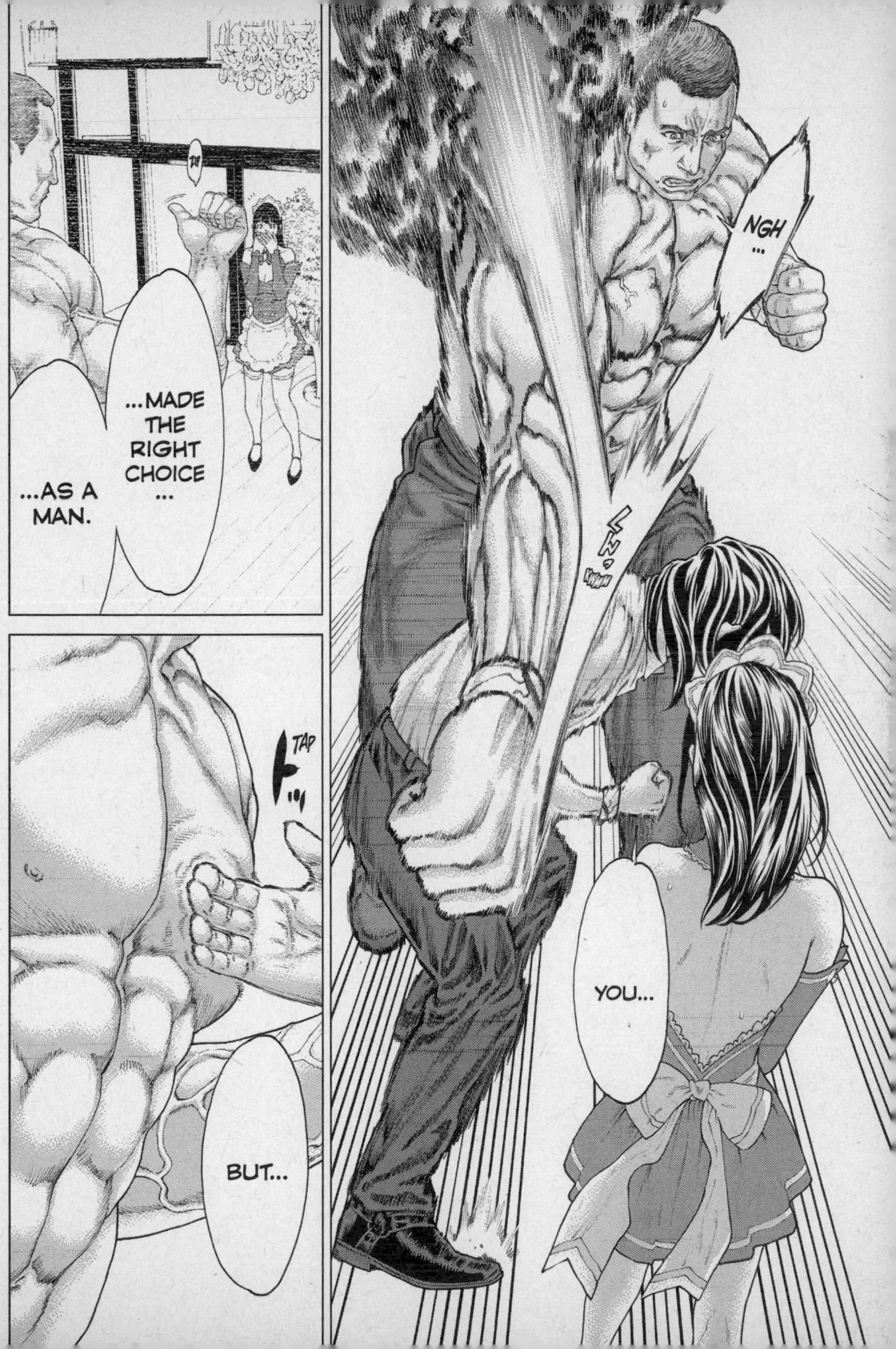
NGH ...
YOU...
TAP
...MADE THE RIGHT CHOICE ...
...AS A MAN.
TAP
BUT...

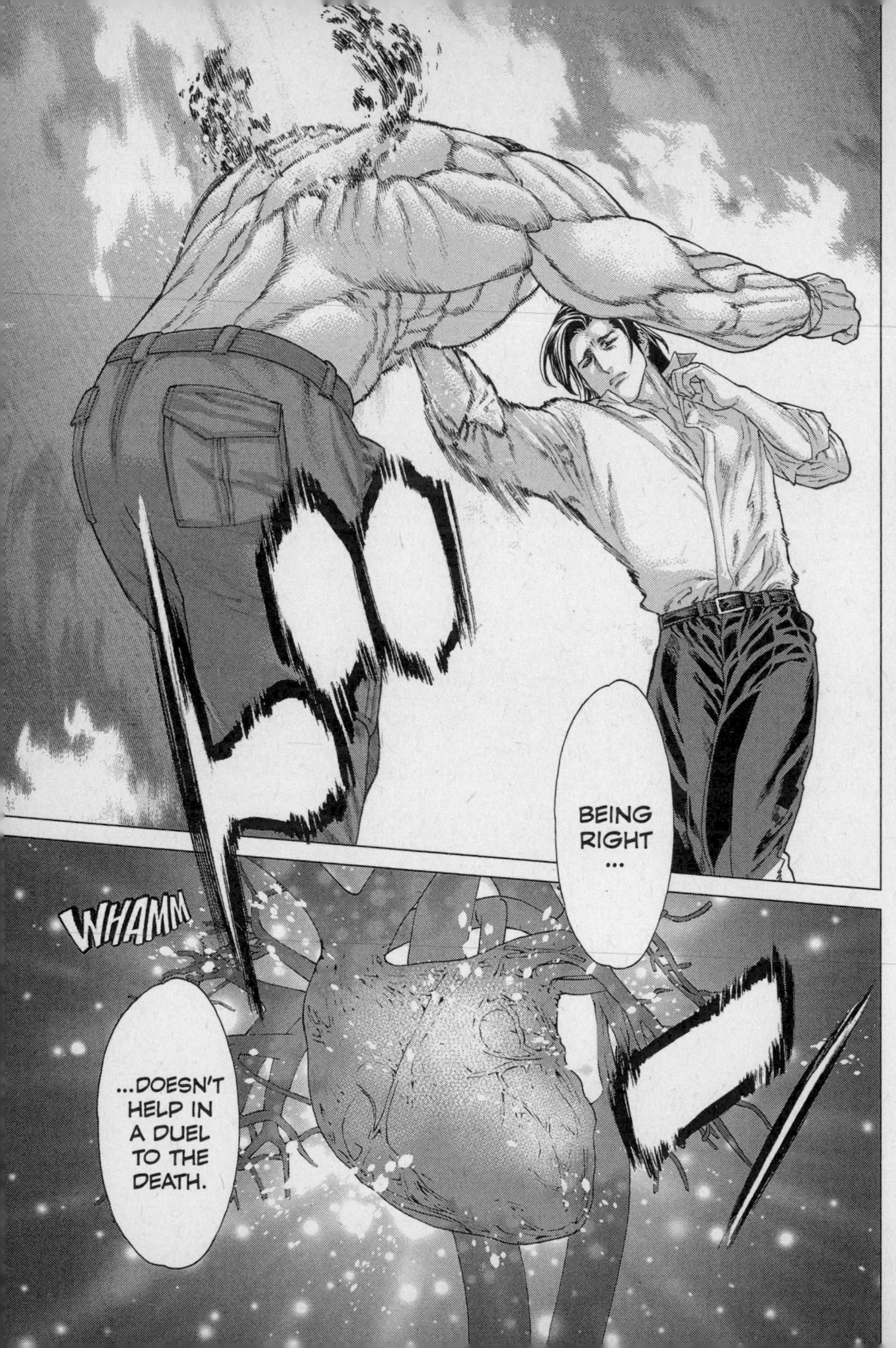
BEING RIGHT ...
WHAMM
...DOESN'T HELP IN A DUEL TO THE DEATH.

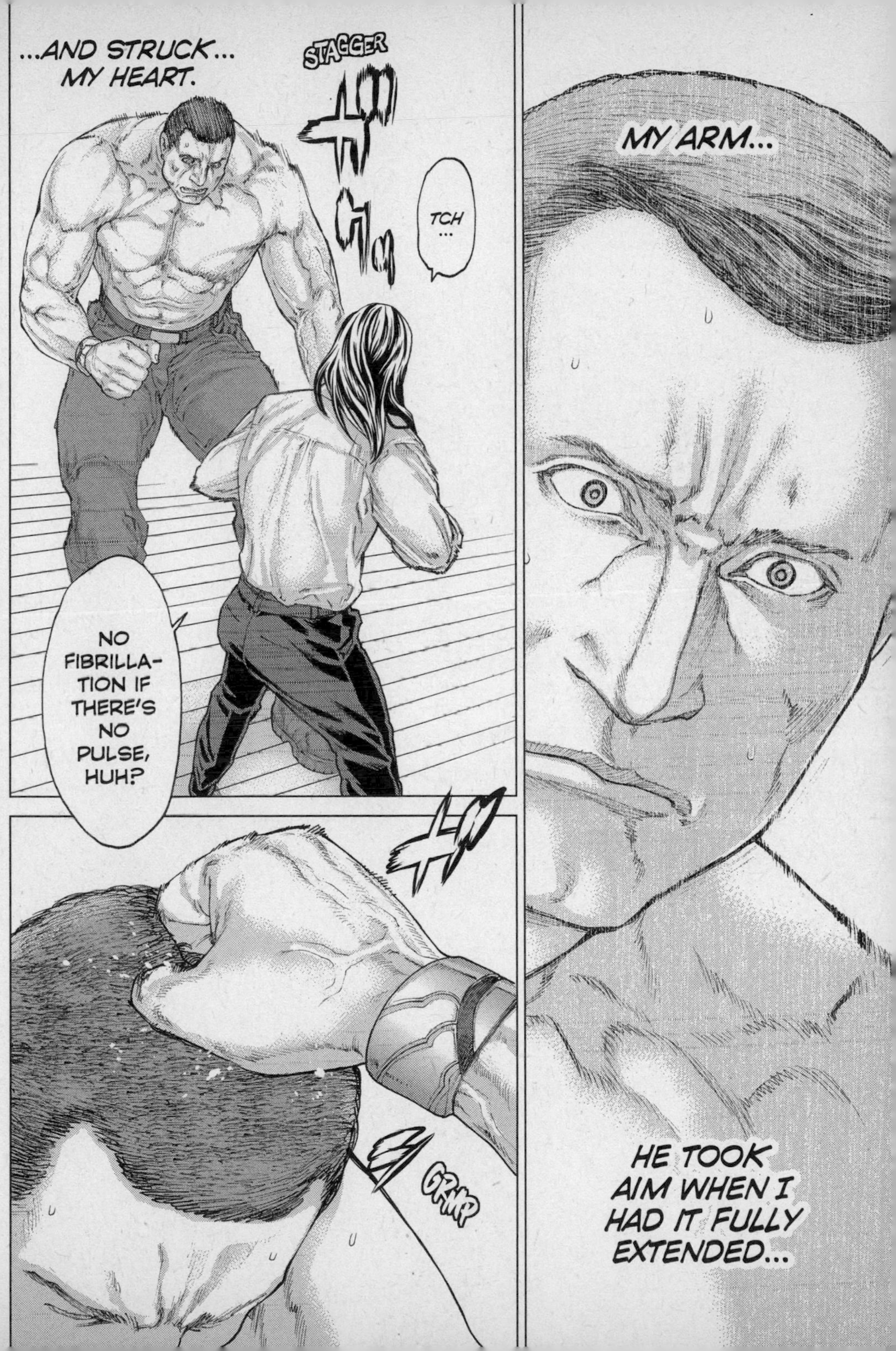
MY ARM...
HE TOOK AIM WHEN I HAD IT FULLY EXTENDED...
...AND STRUCK... MY HEART.
STAGGER
TCH...
NO FIBRILLATION IF THERE'S NO PULSE, HUH?
GRMP

THUDD

IN THAT CASE...

?!

I GUESS YOU'LL JUST HAVE TO DIE FOR ME.

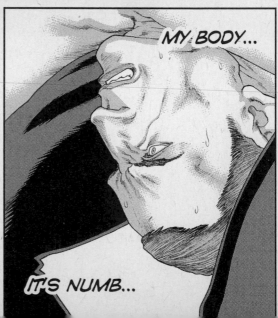

MY BODY...

IT'S NUMB...

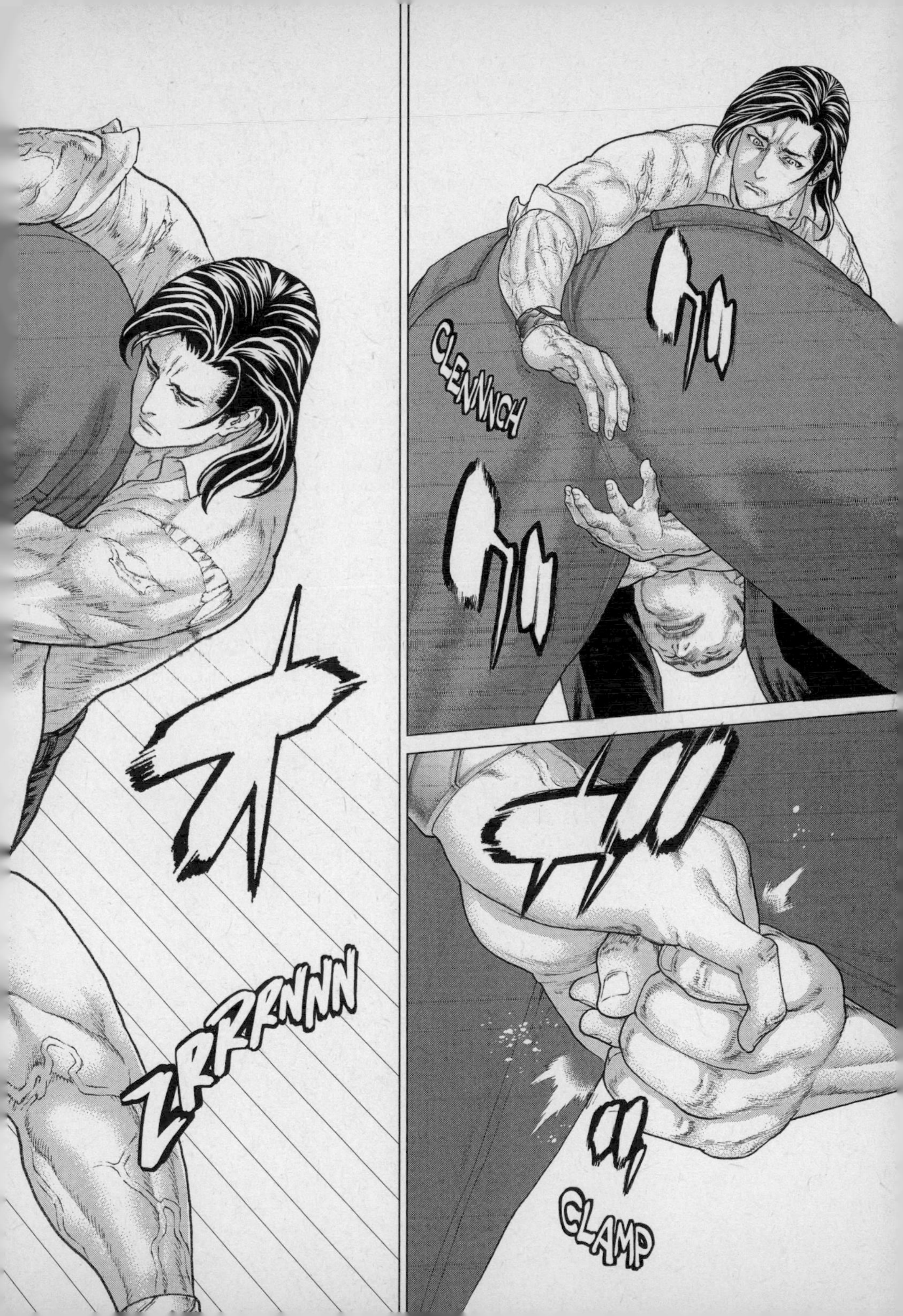
CLENNNCH
CLAMP
ZRRRNNNN

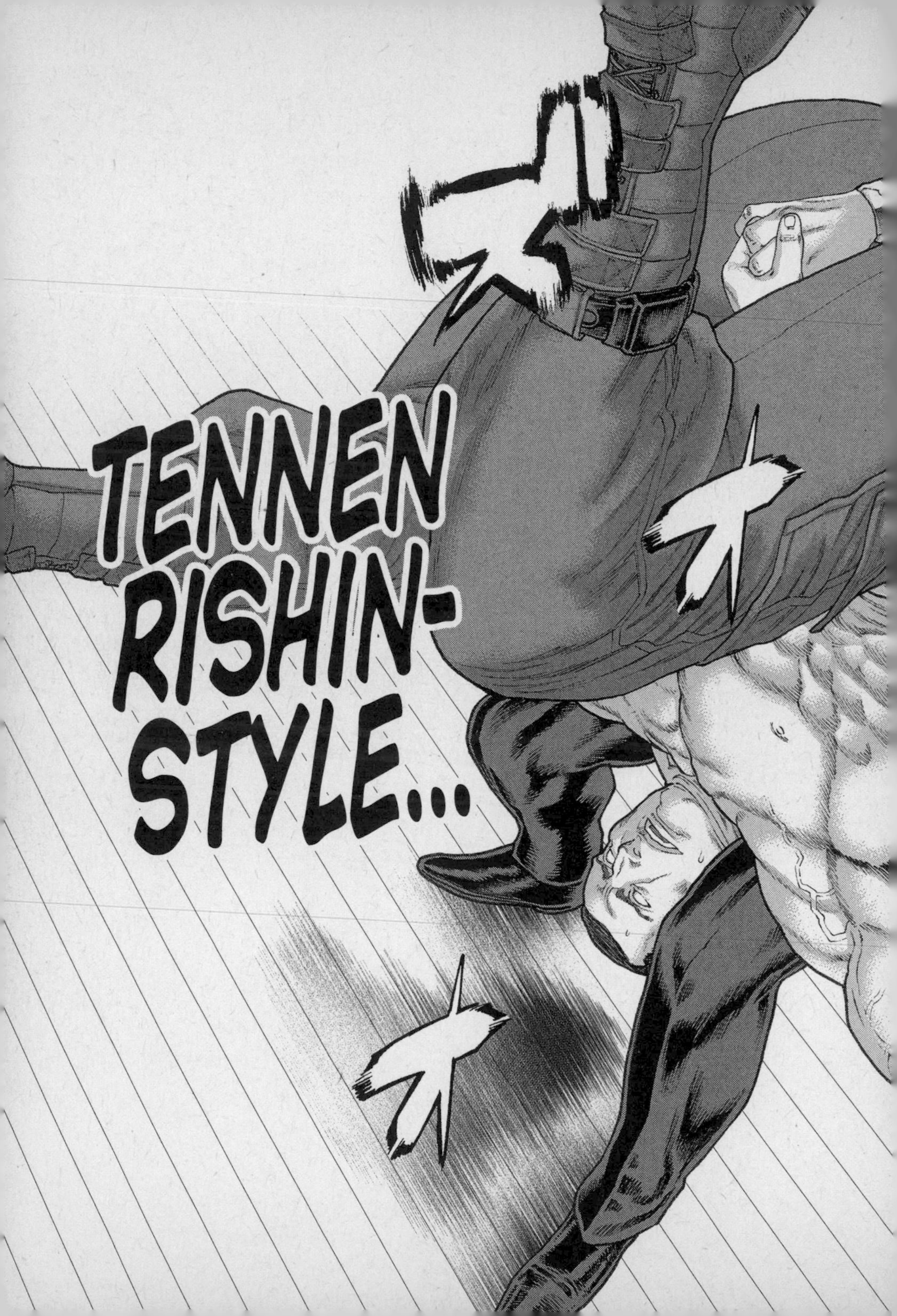
TENNEN RISHIN-STYLE...

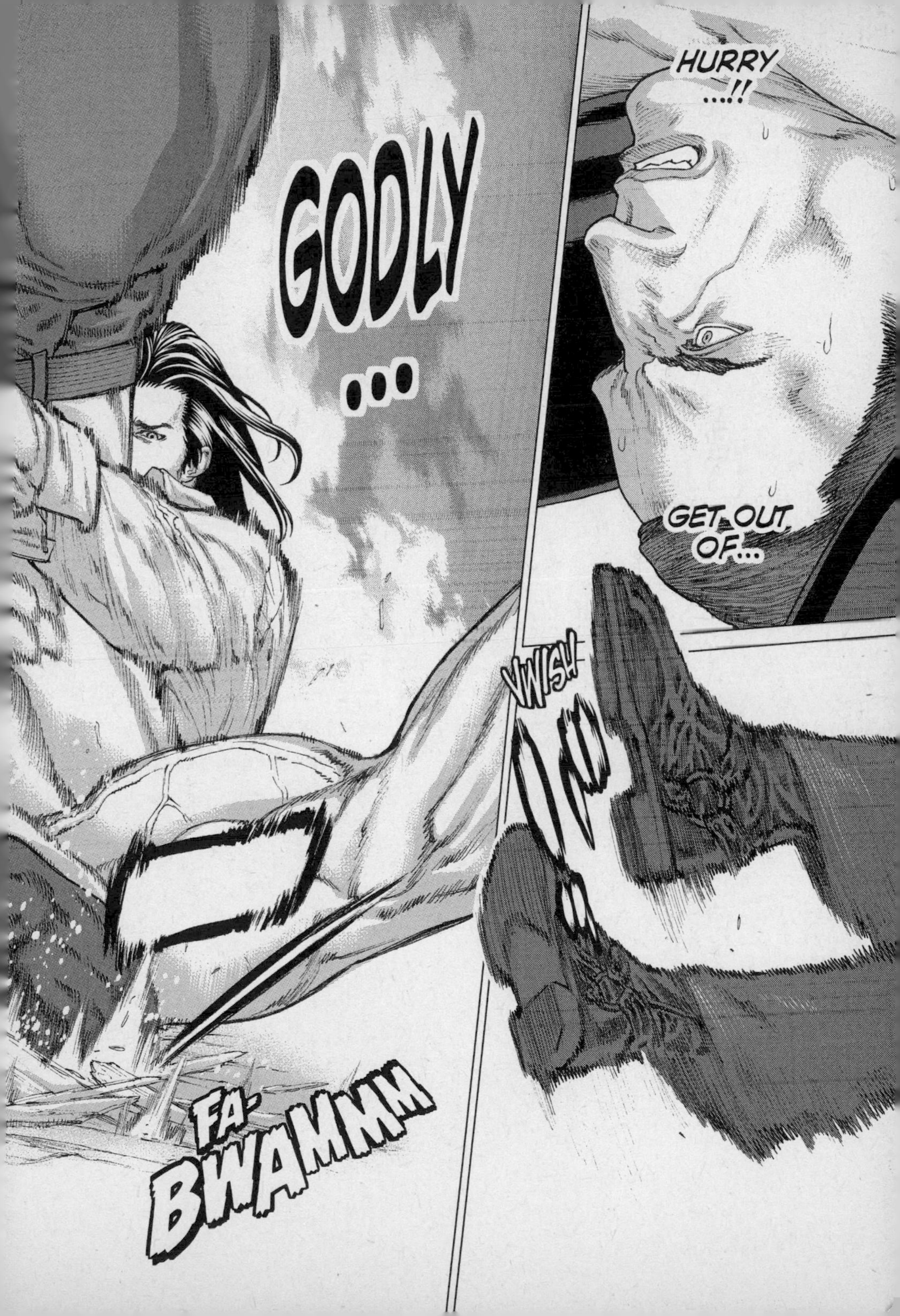
HURRY ...!!
GET OUT OF...
VWISH
GODLY ...
FA-BWAMMM

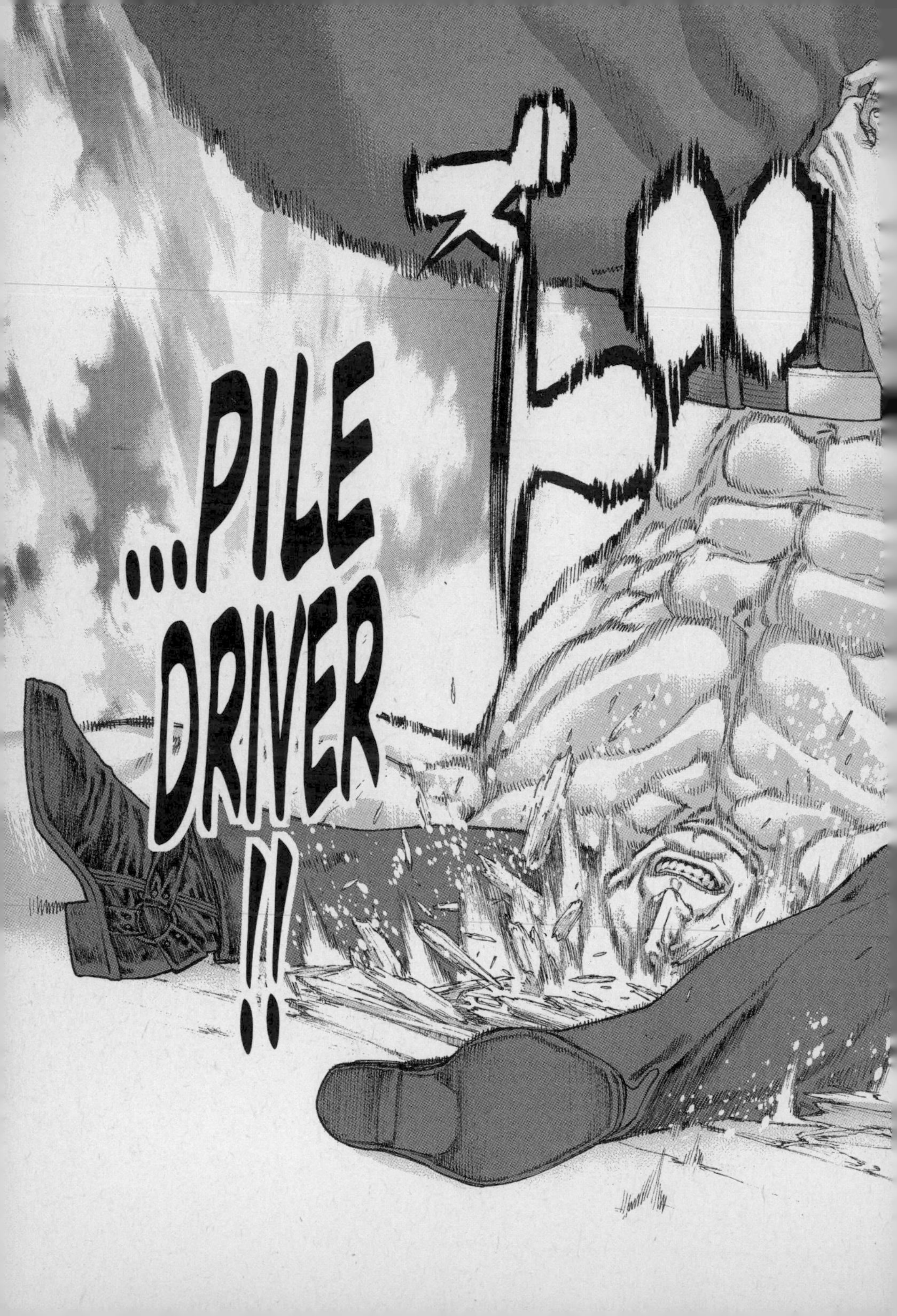
...PILE DRIVER!!

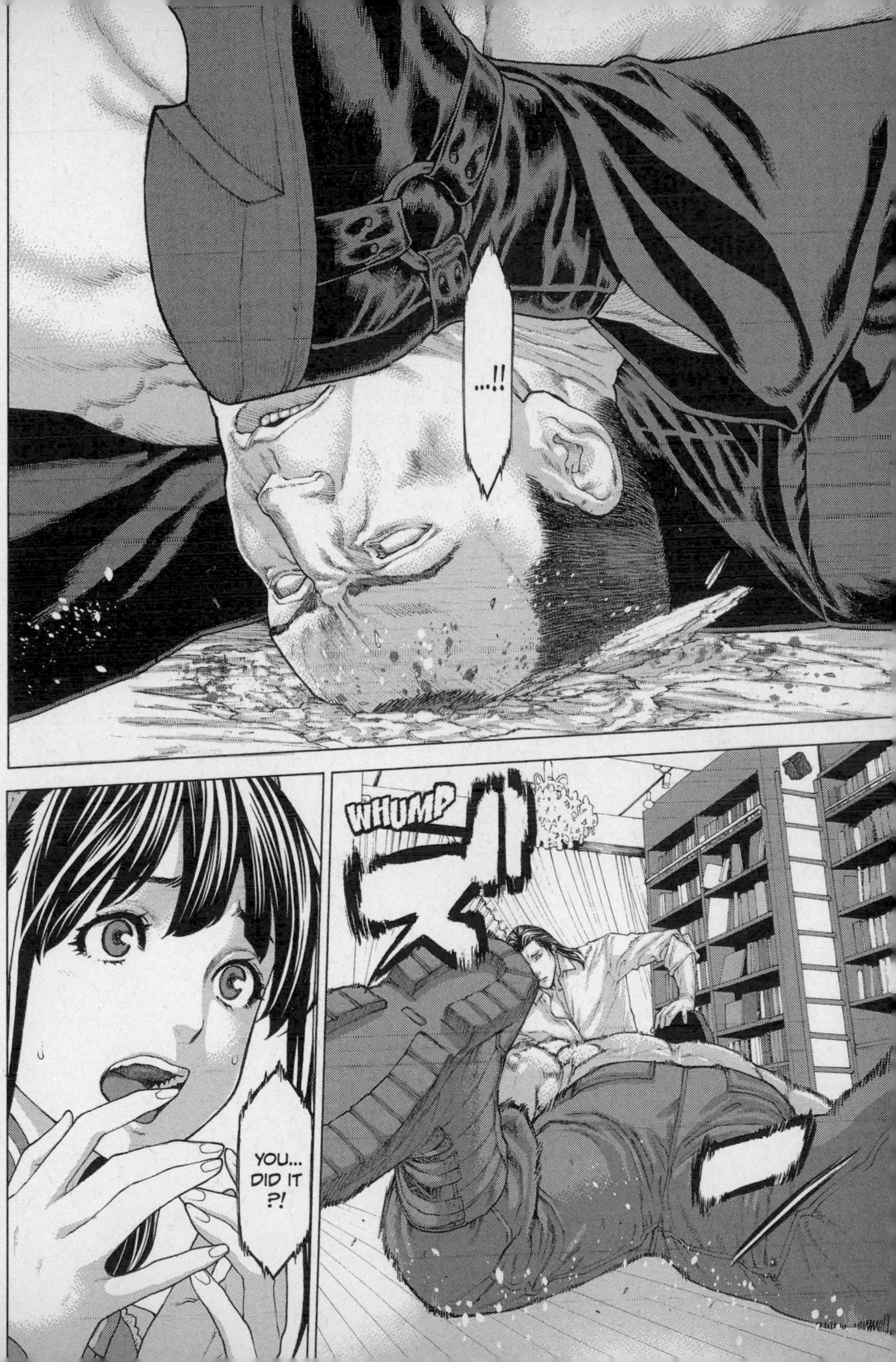
...!!
WHUMP
YOU... DID IT ?!

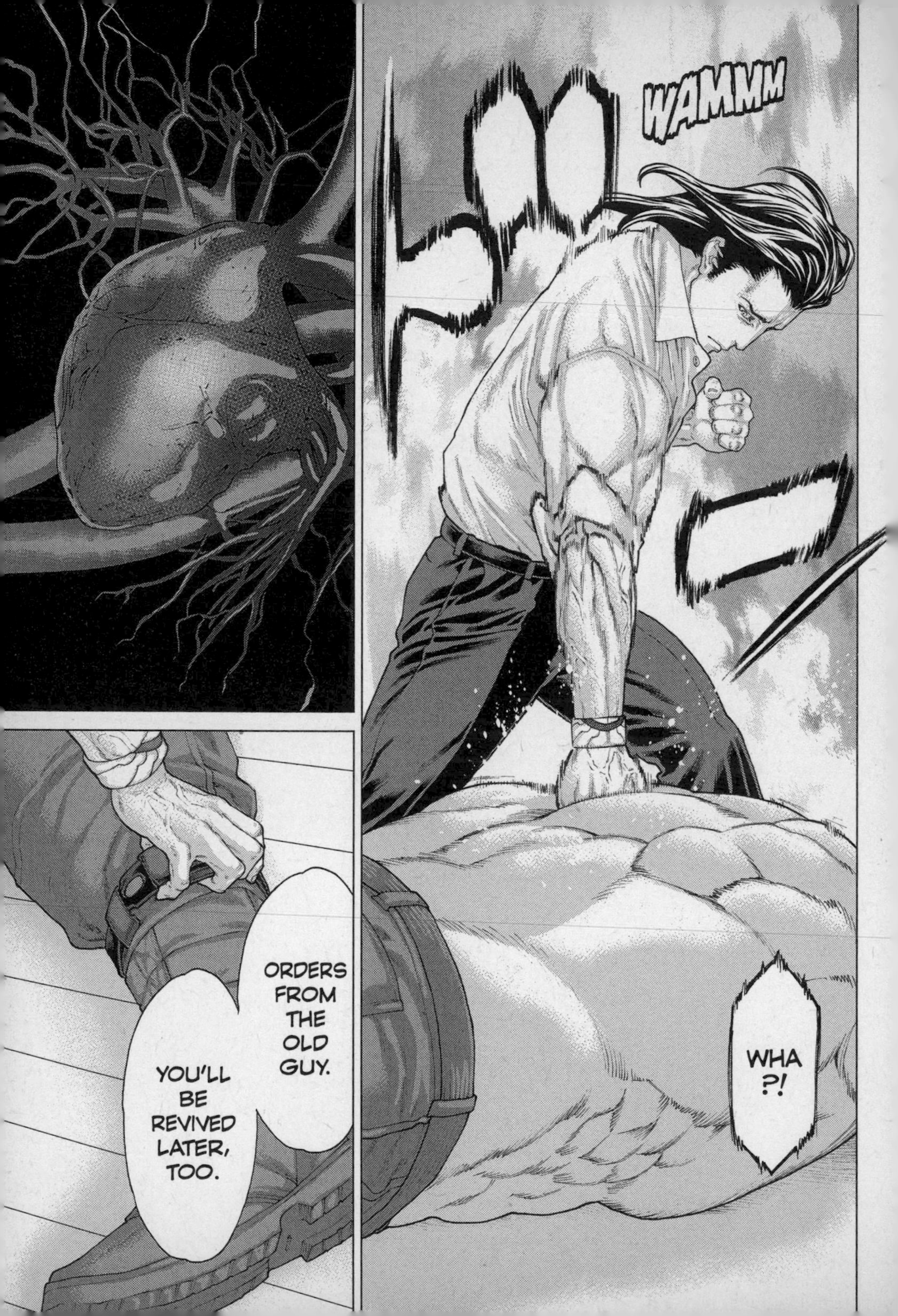
WAMMM
WHA ?!
ORDERS FROM THE OLD GUY.
YOU'LL BE REVIVED LATER, TOO.

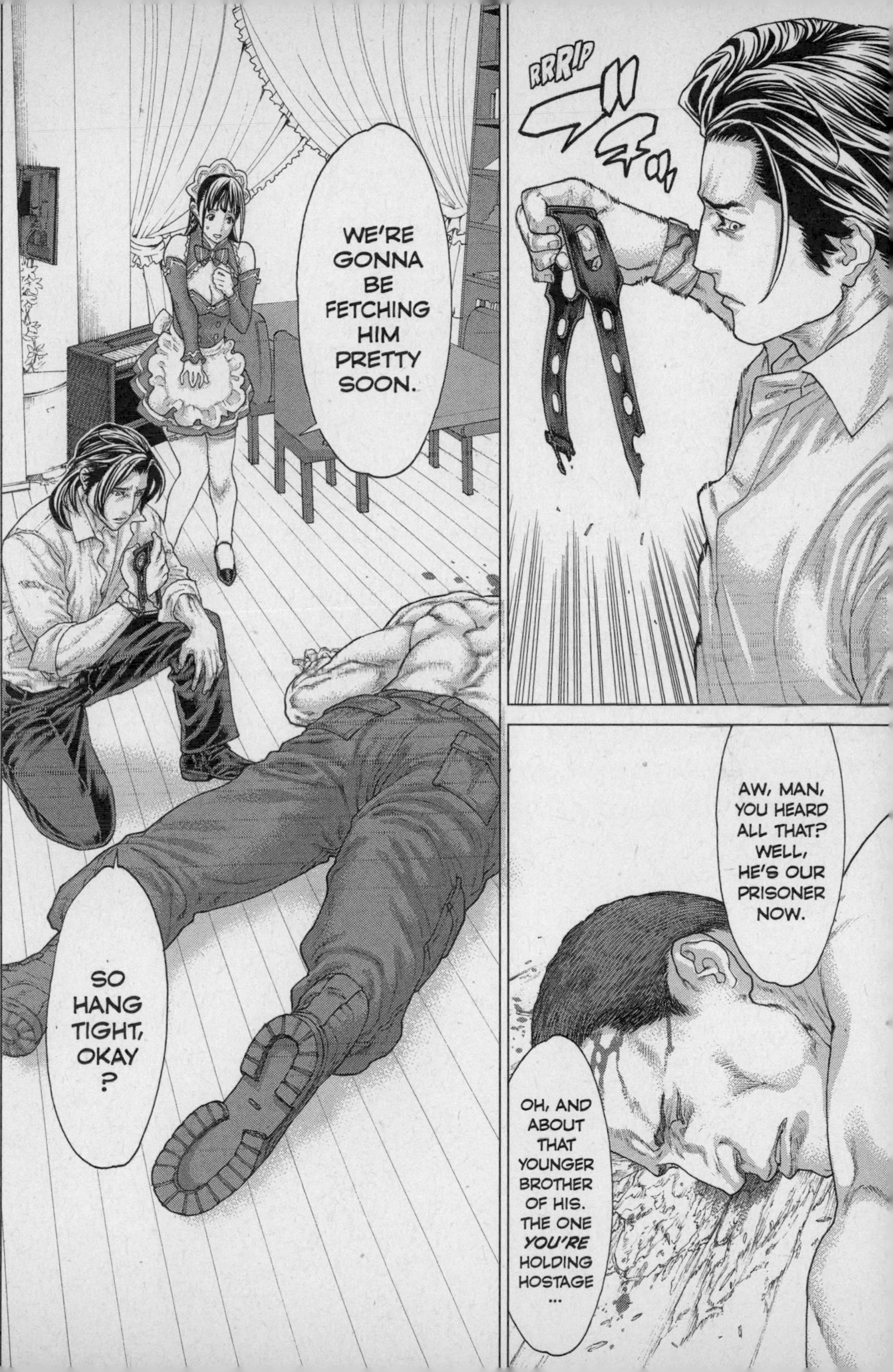
RRRIP
AW, MAN, YOU HEARD ALL THAT? WELL, HE'S OUR PRISONER NOW.
OH, AND ABOUT THAT YOUNGER BROTHER OF HIS. THE ONE *YOU'RE* HOLDING HOSTAGE ...
WE'RE GONNA BE FETCHING HIM PRETTY SOON.
SO HANG TIGHT, OKAY ?

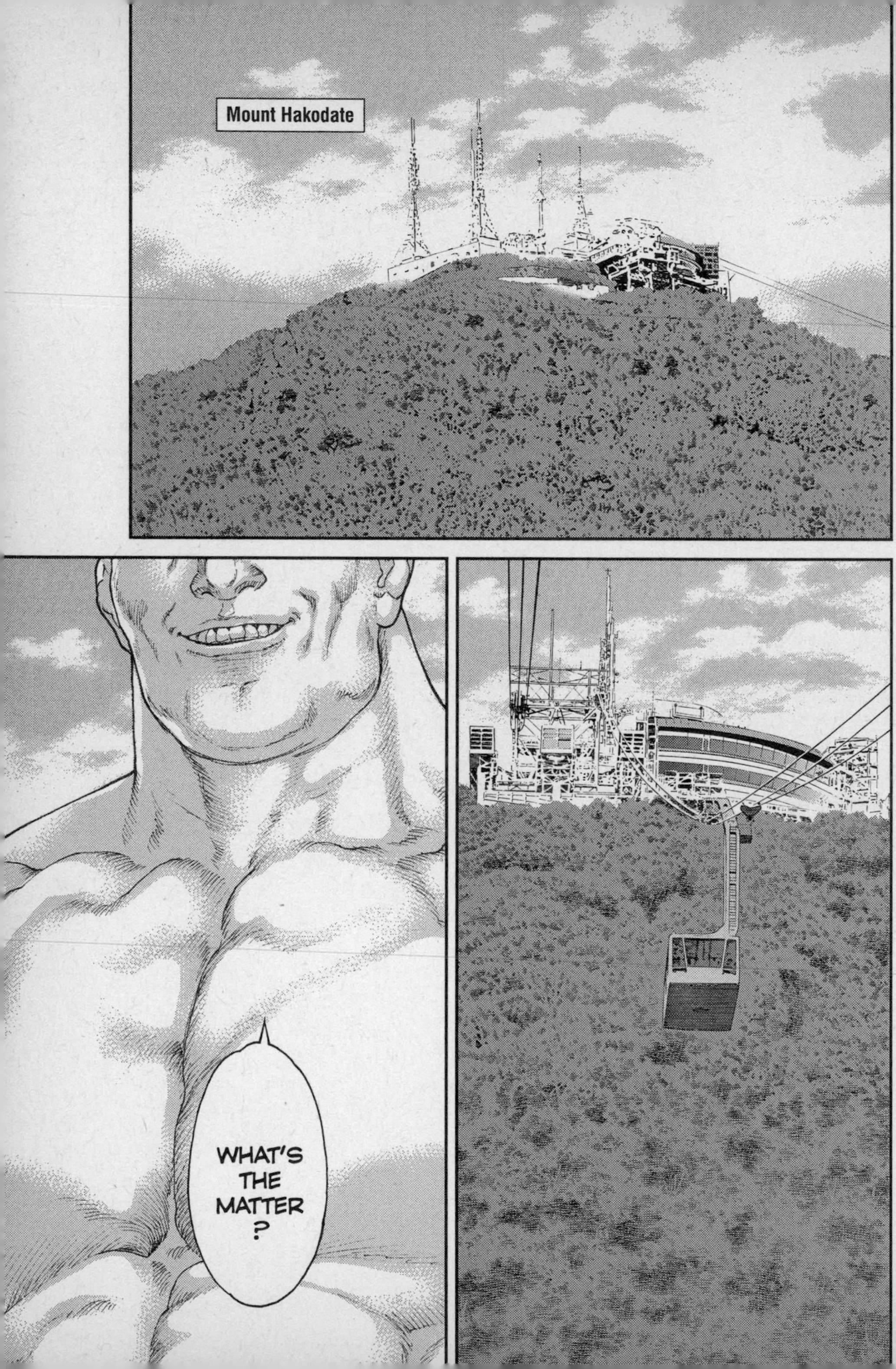
Mount Hakodate
WHAT'S THE MATTER ?

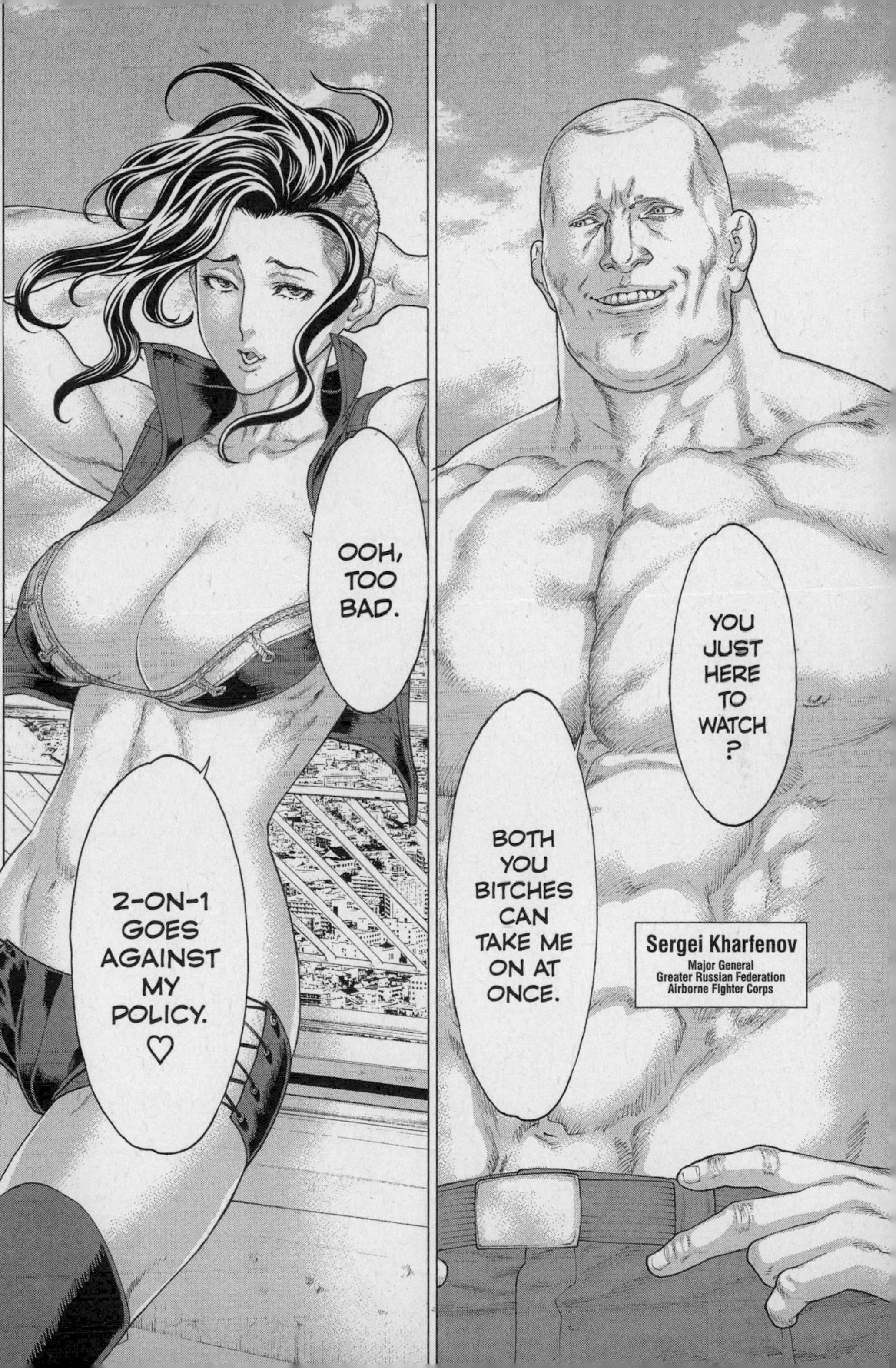
YOU JUST HERE TO WATCH?
BOTH YOU BITCHES CAN TAKE ME ON AT ONCE.
Sergei Kharfenov
Major General
Greater Russian Federation
Airborne Fighter Corps
OOH, TOO BAD.
2-ON-1 GOES AGAINST MY POLICY. ♡

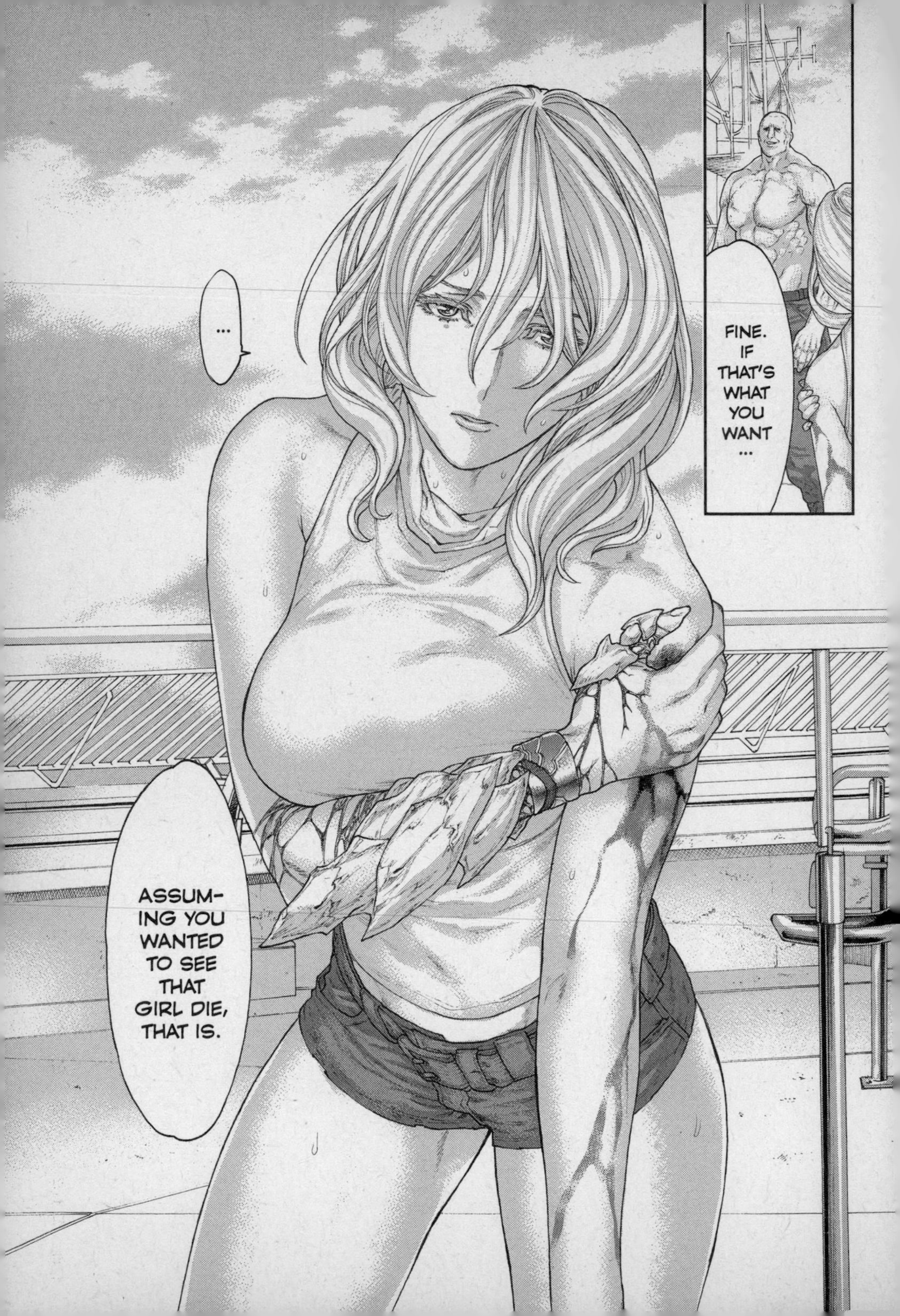
FINE. IF THAT'S WHAT YOU WANT ...
...
ASSUM-ING YOU WANTED TO SEE THAT GIRL DIE, THAT IS.

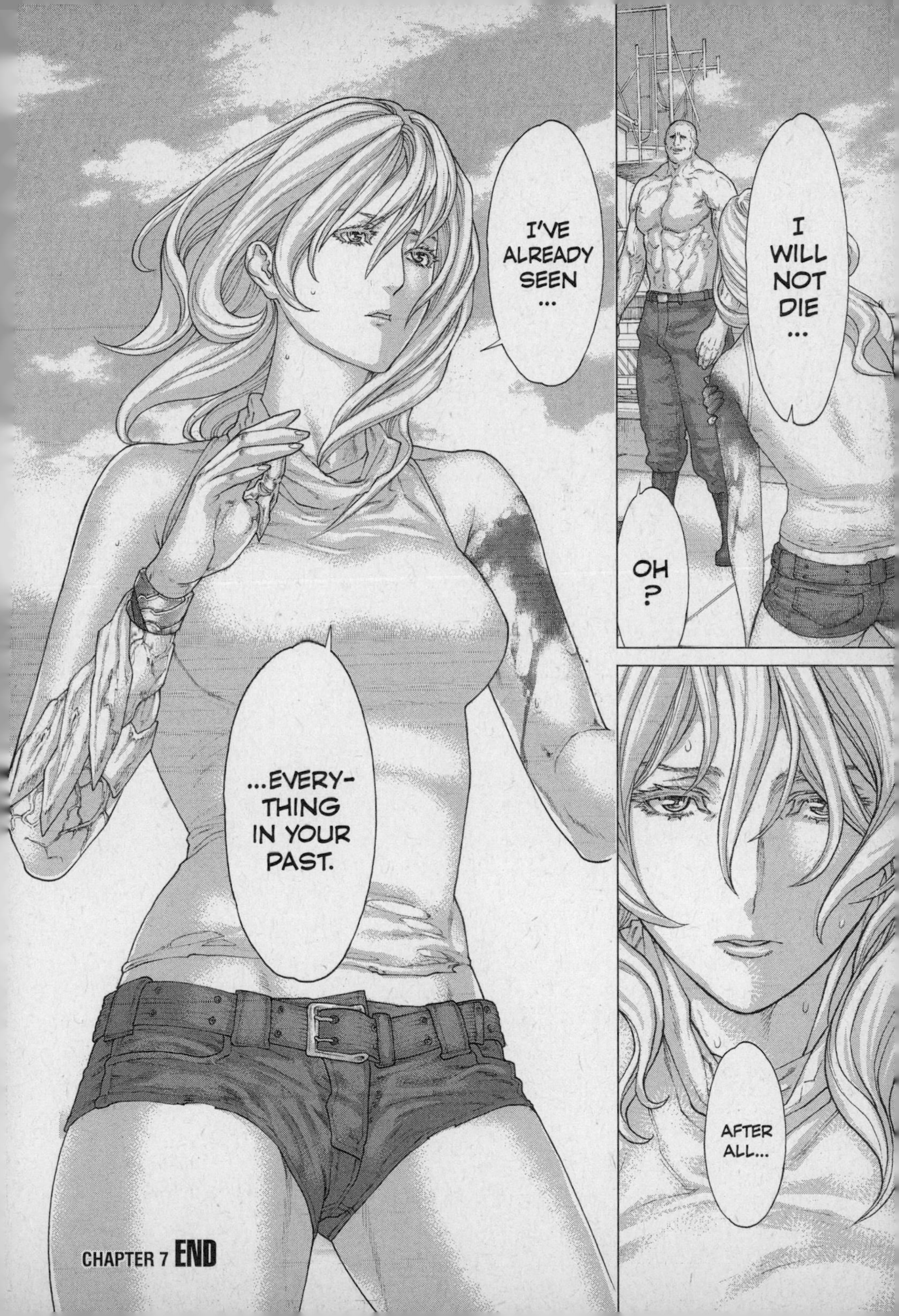
I WILL NOT DIE ...
OH ?
AFTER ALL...
I'VE ALREADY SEEN ...
...EVERY-THING IN YOUR PAST.
CHAPTER 7 END

GOLOSSEUM

CHAPTER 8
RUSSIANS TAKE CARE OF RUSSIANS

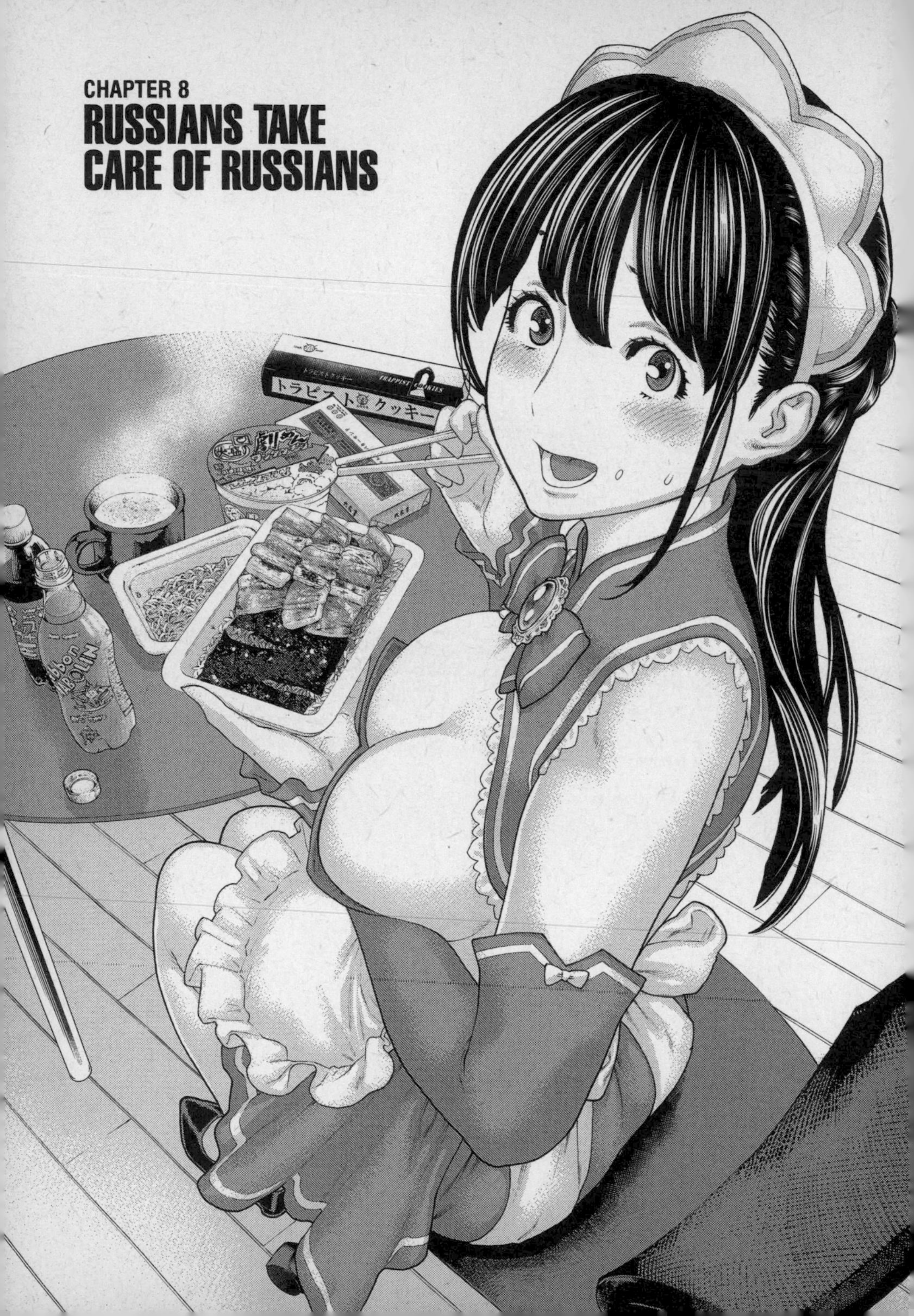
トラピストクッキー
TRAPPIST COOKIES

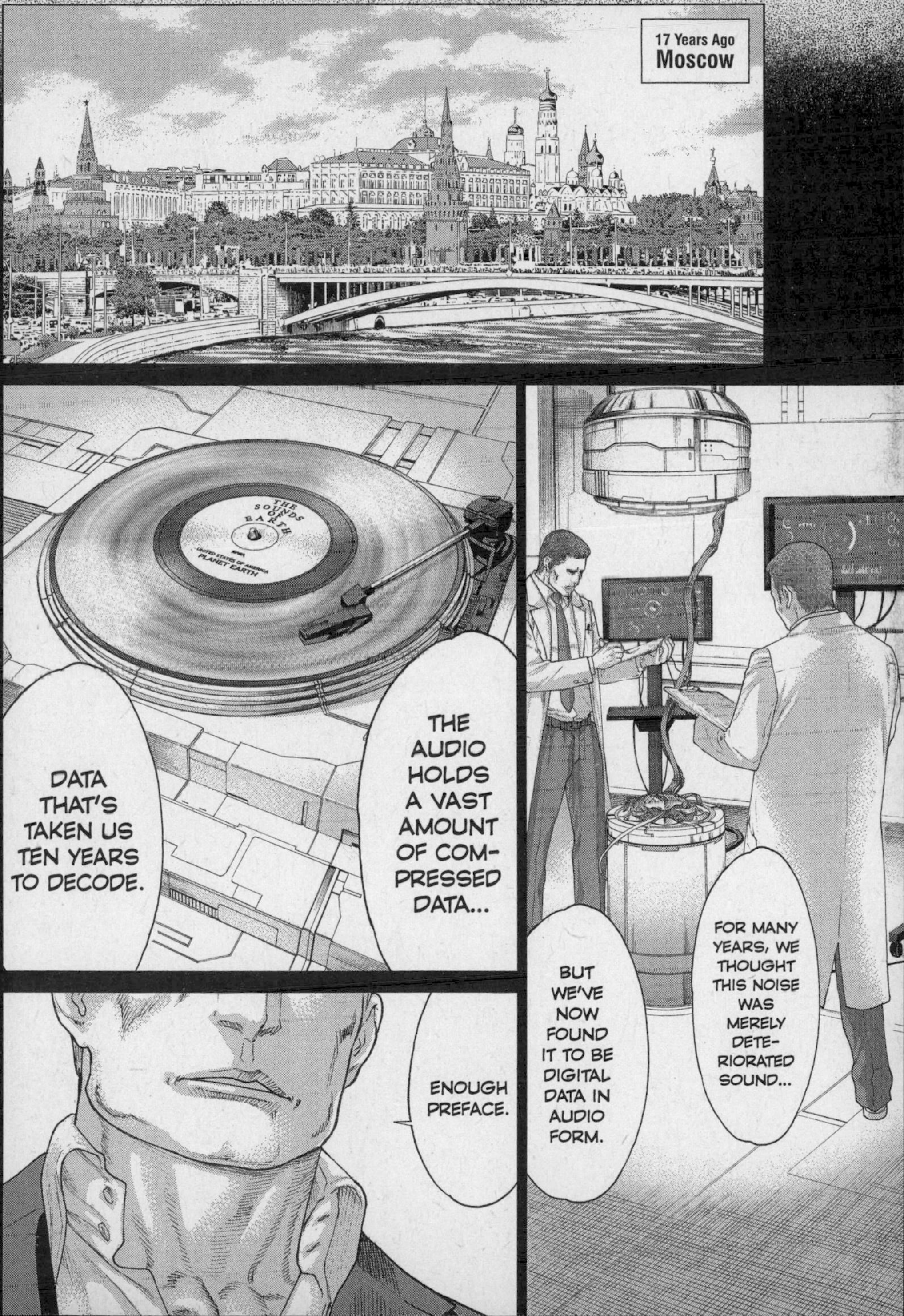
17 Years Ago
Moscow
FOR MANY YEARS, WE THOUGHT THIS NOISE WAS MERELY DETE-RIORATED SOUND...
BUT WE'VE NOW FOUND IT TO BE DIGITAL DATA IN AUDIO FORM.
THE SOUNDS OF EARTH
UNITED STATES OF AMERICA
PLANET EARTH
THE AUDIO HOLDS A VAST AMOUNT OF COM-PRESSED DATA...
DATA THAT'S TAKEN US TEN YEARS TO DECODE.
ENOUGH PREFACE.

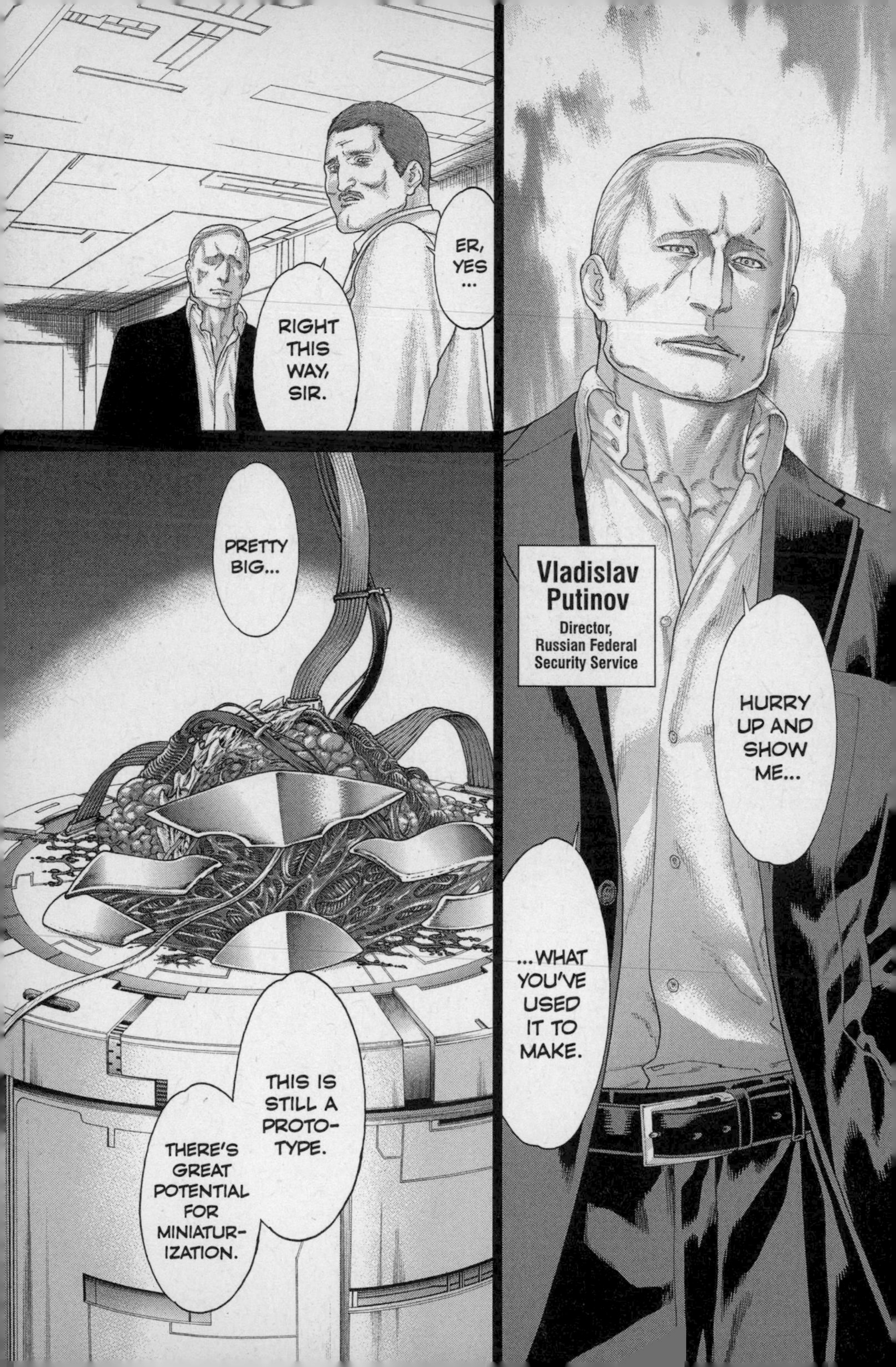
Vladislav Putinov Director, Russian Federal Security Service
HURRY UP AND SHOW ME...
...WHAT YOU'VE USED IT TO MAKE.
ER, YES ...
RIGHT THIS WAY, SIR.
PRETTY BIG...
THIS IS STILL A PROTOTYPE.
THERE'S GREAT POTENTIAL FOR MINIATURIZATION.

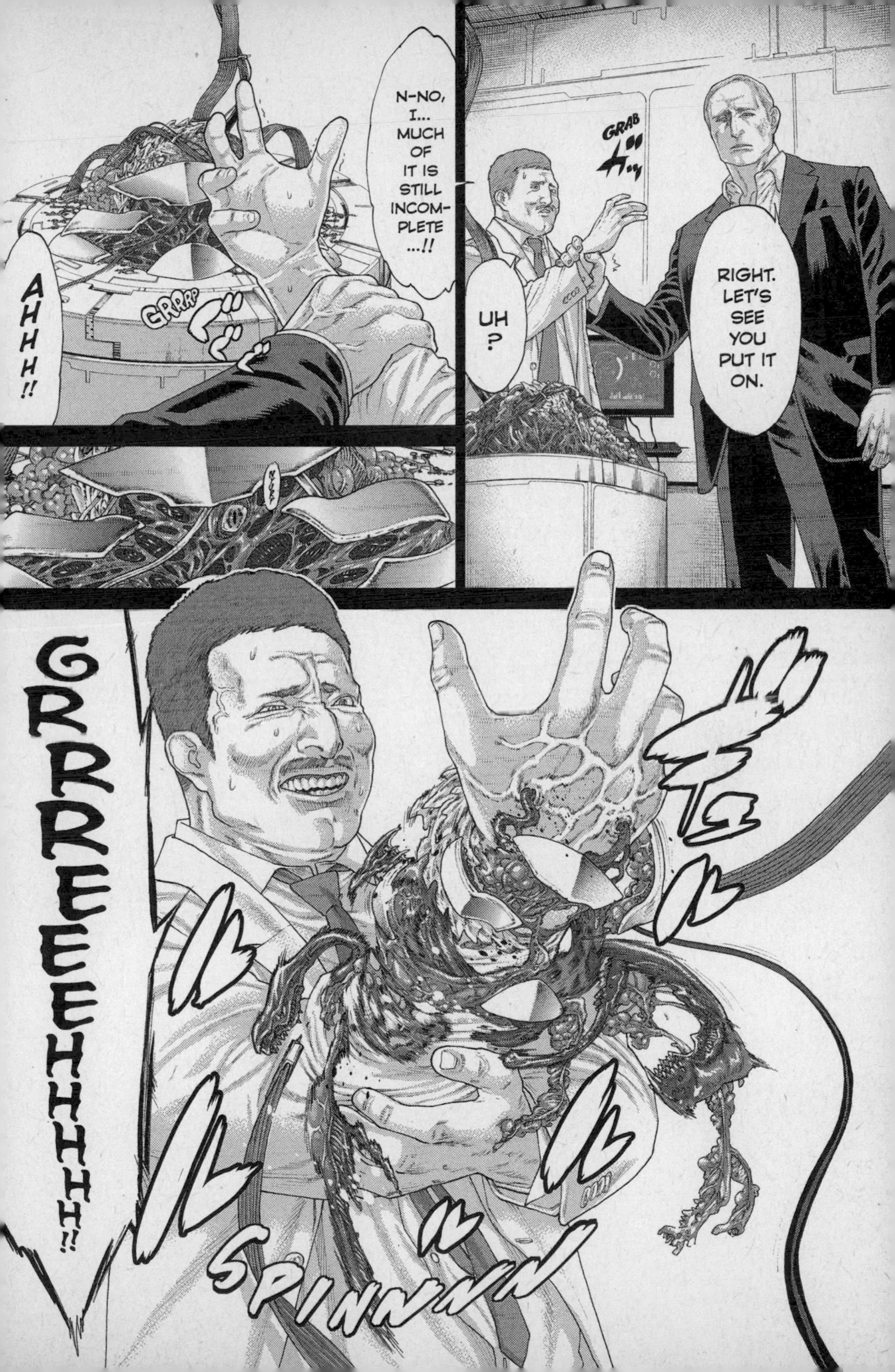
RIGHT. LET'S SEE YOU PUT IT ON.
GRAB
UH?
N-NO, I... MUCH OF IT IS STILL INCOMPLETE ...!!
GRRRP
AHHHH!!
GRRREEEHHHHH!!
SPINNNN

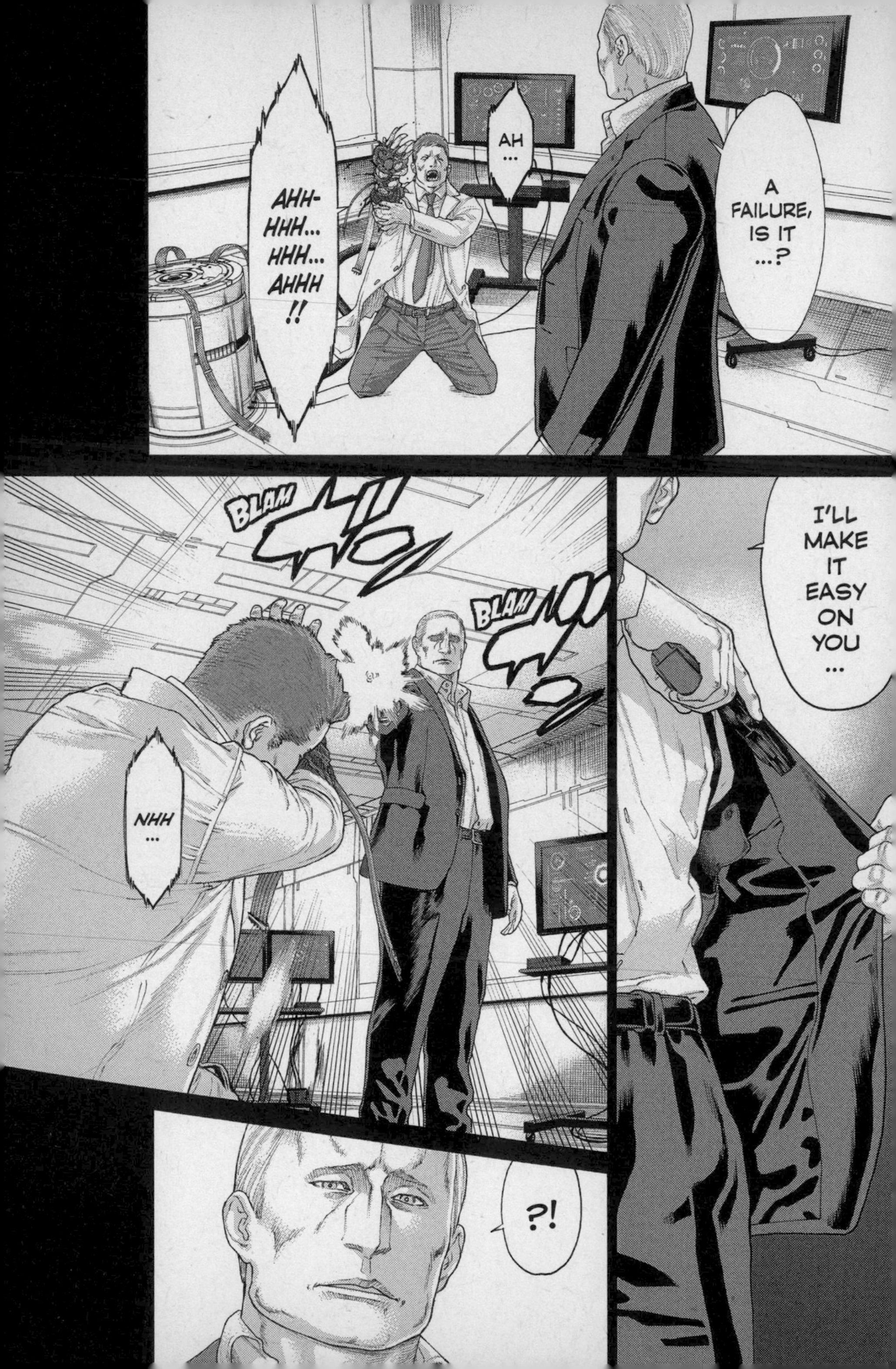
A FAILURE, IS IT ...?
AH ...
AHH-HHH... HHH... AHHH !!
I'LL MAKE IT EASY ON YOU ...
BLAM
BLAM
NHH ...
?!

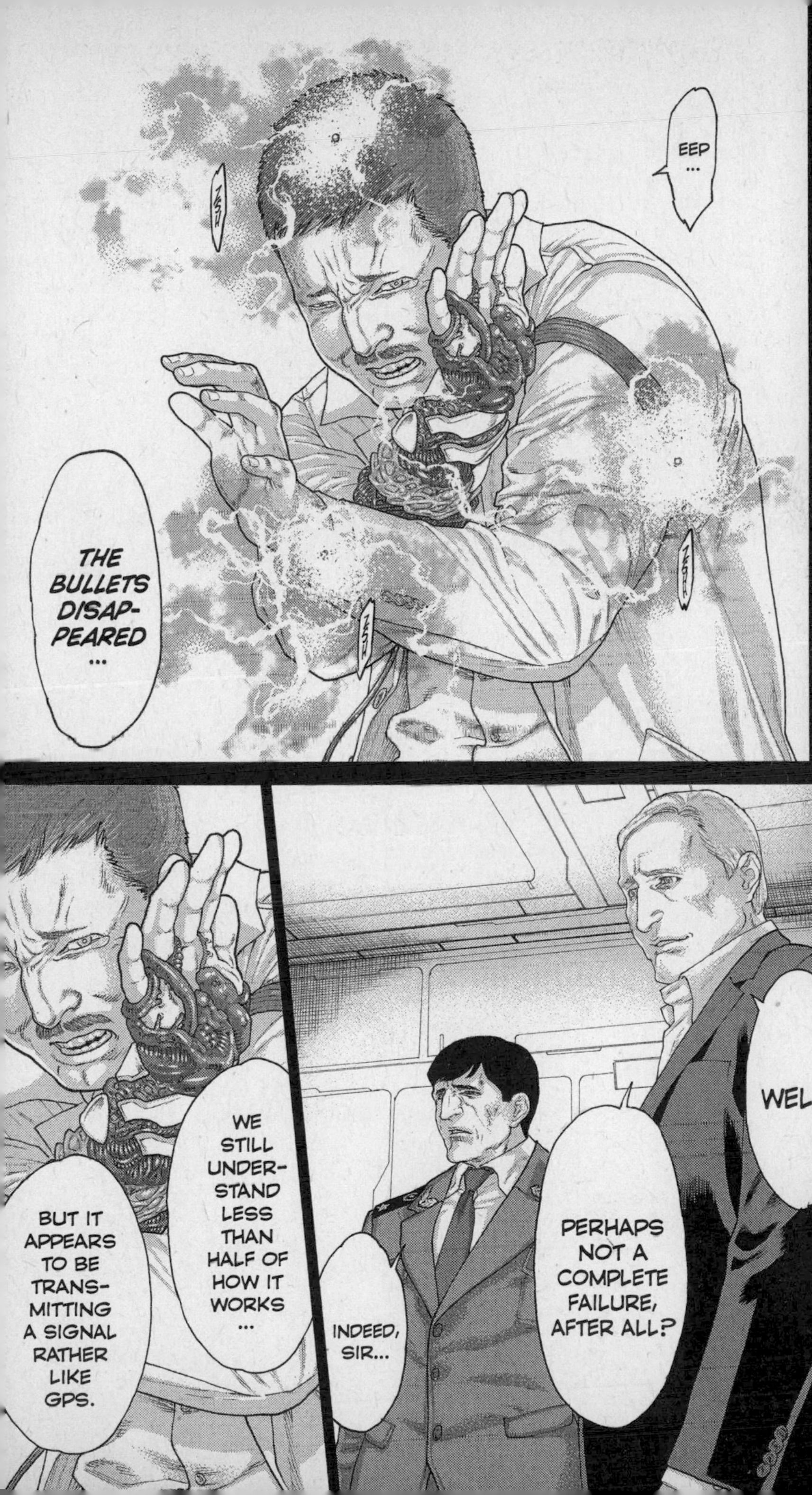
EEP ...
THE BULLETS DISAPPEARED ...
WELL!
PERHAPS NOT A COMPLETE FAILURE, AFTER ALL?
INDEED, SIR...
WE STILL UNDERSTAND LESS THAN HALF OF HOW IT WORKS ...
BUT IT APPEARS TO BE TRANSMITTING A SIGNAL RATHER LIKE GPS.

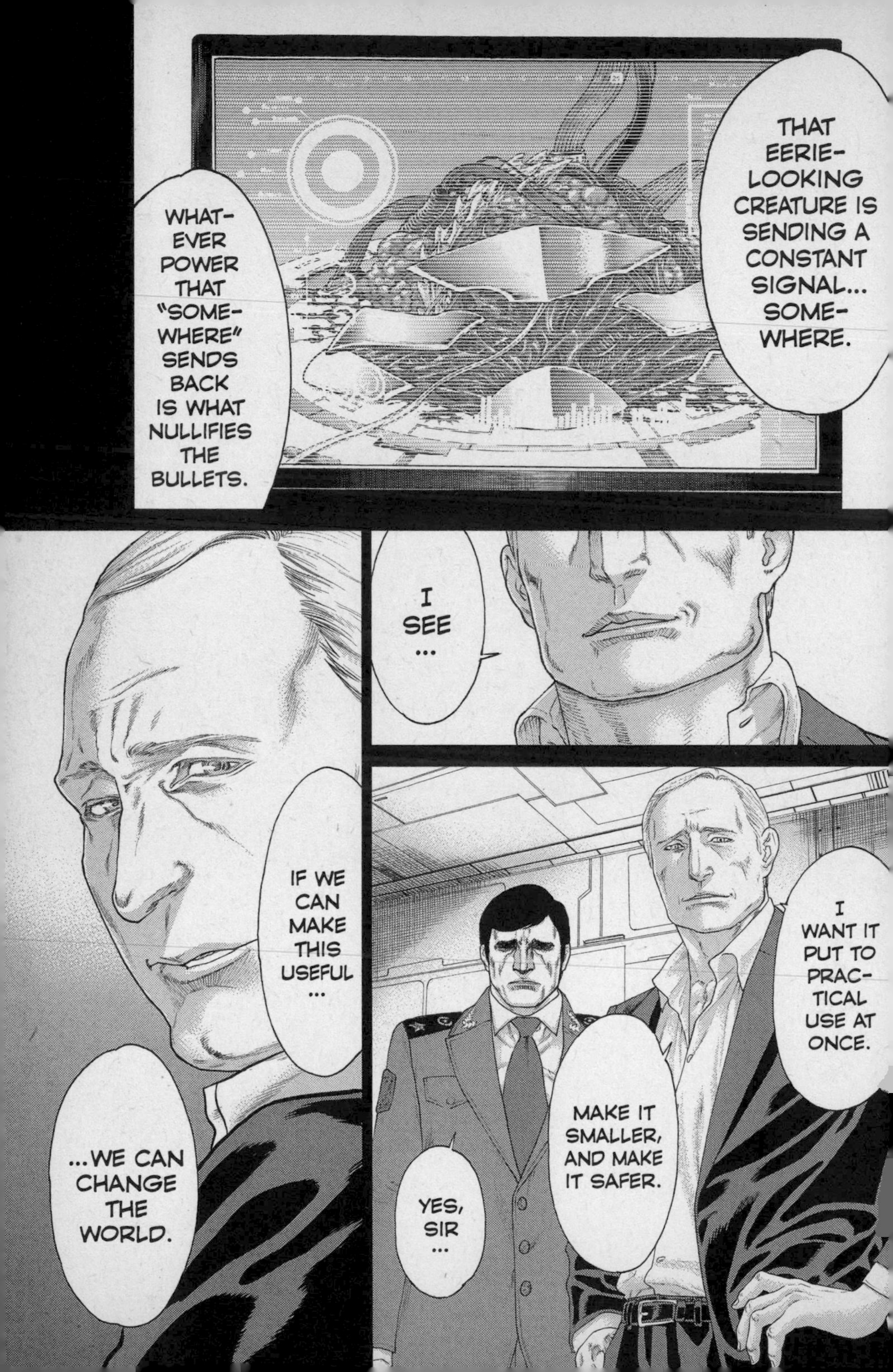
THAT EERIE-LOOKING CREATURE IS SENDING A CONSTANT SIGNAL... SOMEWHERE.
WHATEVER POWER THAT "SOMEWHERE" SENDS BACK IS WHAT NULLIFIES THE BULLETS.
I SEE...
I WANT IT PUT TO PRACTICAL USE AT ONCE.
MAKE IT SMALLER, AND MAKE IT SAFER.
YES, SIR...
IF WE CAN MAKE THIS USEFUL...
...WE CAN CHANGE THE WORLD.

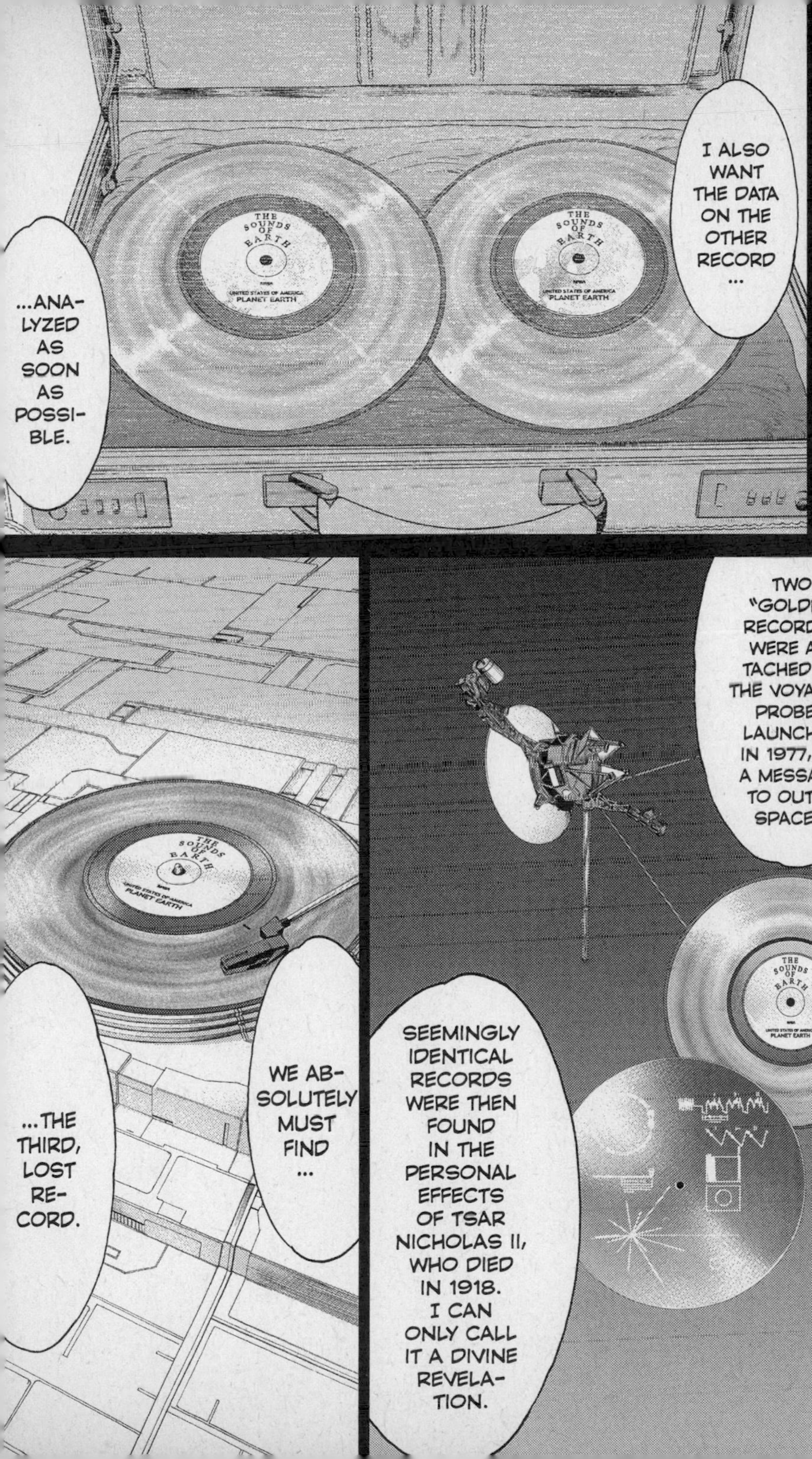
I ALSO WANT THE DATA ON THE OTHER RECORD ...
THE SOUNDS OF EARTH
UNITED STATES OF AMERICA
PLANET EARTH
...ANALYZED AS SOON AS POSSIBLE.
TWO "GOLDEN RECORDS" WERE ATTACHED TO THE VOYAGER PROBES LAUNCHED IN 1977, AS A MESSAGE TO OUTER SPACE...
THE SOUNDS OF EARTH
UNITED STATES OF AMERICA
PLANET EARTH
SEEMINGLY IDENTICAL RECORDS WERE THEN FOUND IN THE PERSONAL EFFECTS OF TSAR NICHOLAS II, WHO DIED IN 1918. I CAN ONLY CALL IT A DIVINE REVELATION.
THE SOUNDS OF EARTH
UNITED STATES OF AMERICA
PLANET EARTH
WE ABSOLUTELY MUST FIND ...
...THE THIRD, LOST RECORD.

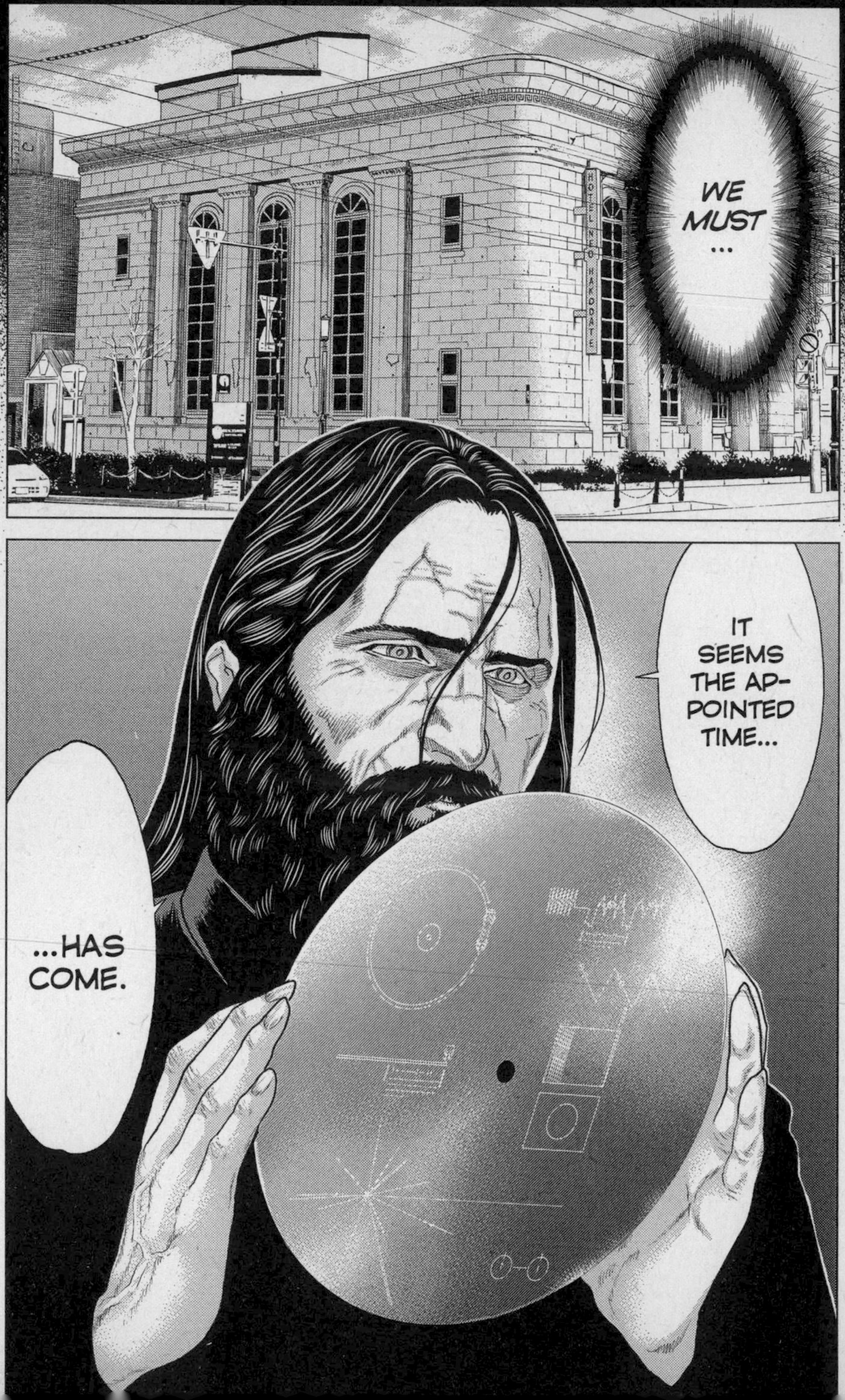
WE MUST ...
IT SEEMS THE AP-POINTED TIME...
...HAS COME.

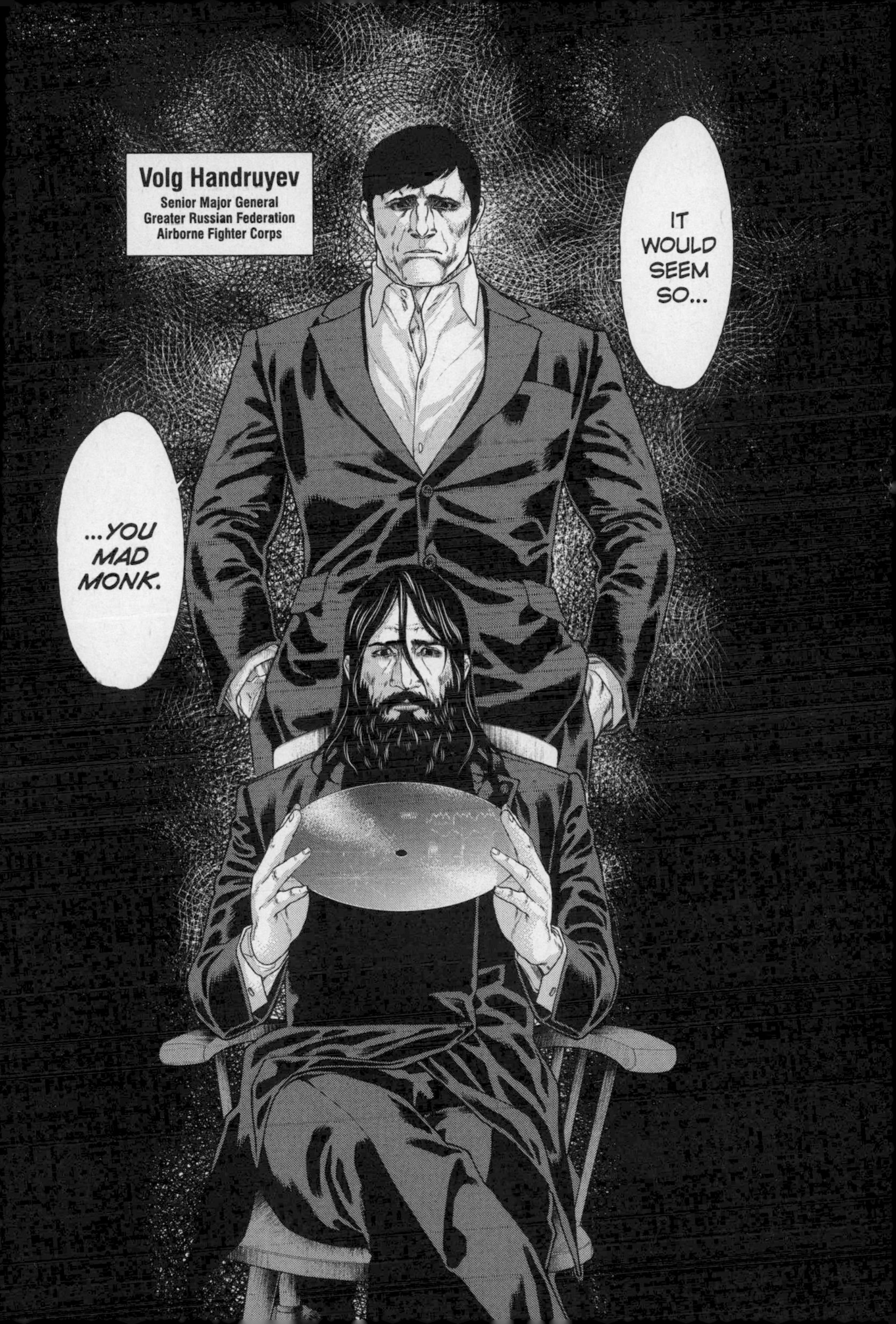
IT WOULD SEEM SO...
Volg Handruyev
Senior Major General
Greater Russian Federation
Airborne Fighter Corps
...YOU MAD MONK.

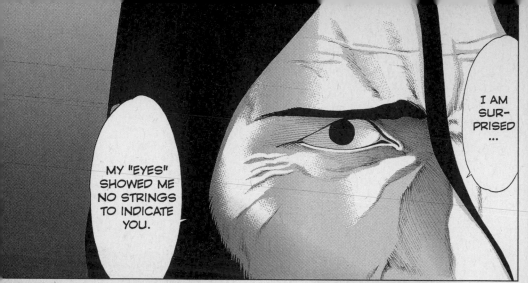

I AM SURPRISED...

MY "EYES" SHOWED ME NO STRINGS TO INDICATE YOU.

OF COURSE NOT...

I WAS PULLING THEM IN SO YOU *COULDN'T.*

...YOU POSSESS THE SAME "EYE" THAT I HAVE ...?

AH, SO THEN...

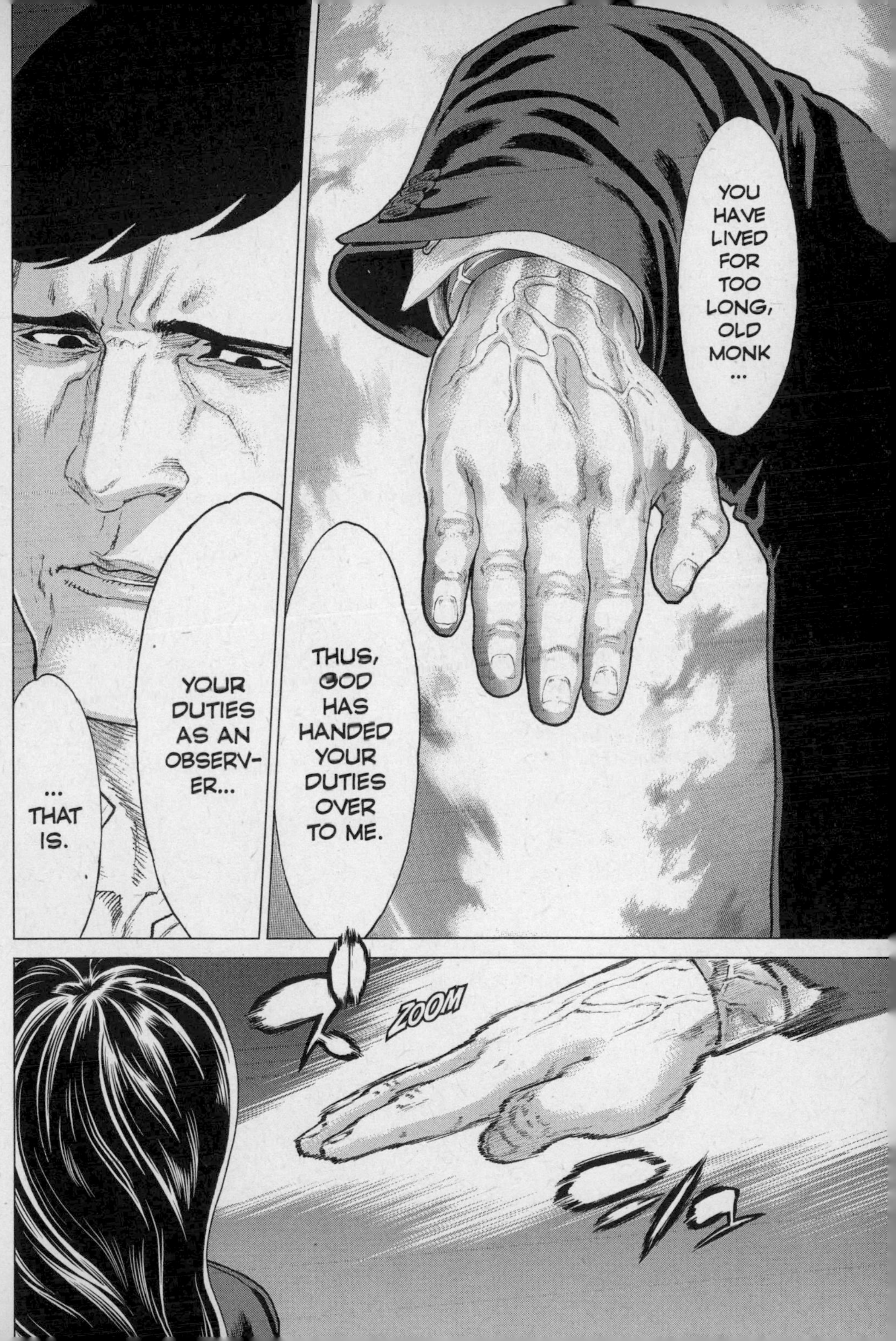
YOU HAVE LIVED FOR TOO LONG, OLD MONK ...
THUS, GOD HAS HANDED YOUR DUTIES OVER TO ME.
YOUR DUTIES AS AN OBSERVER-ER...
... THAT IS.
ZOOM

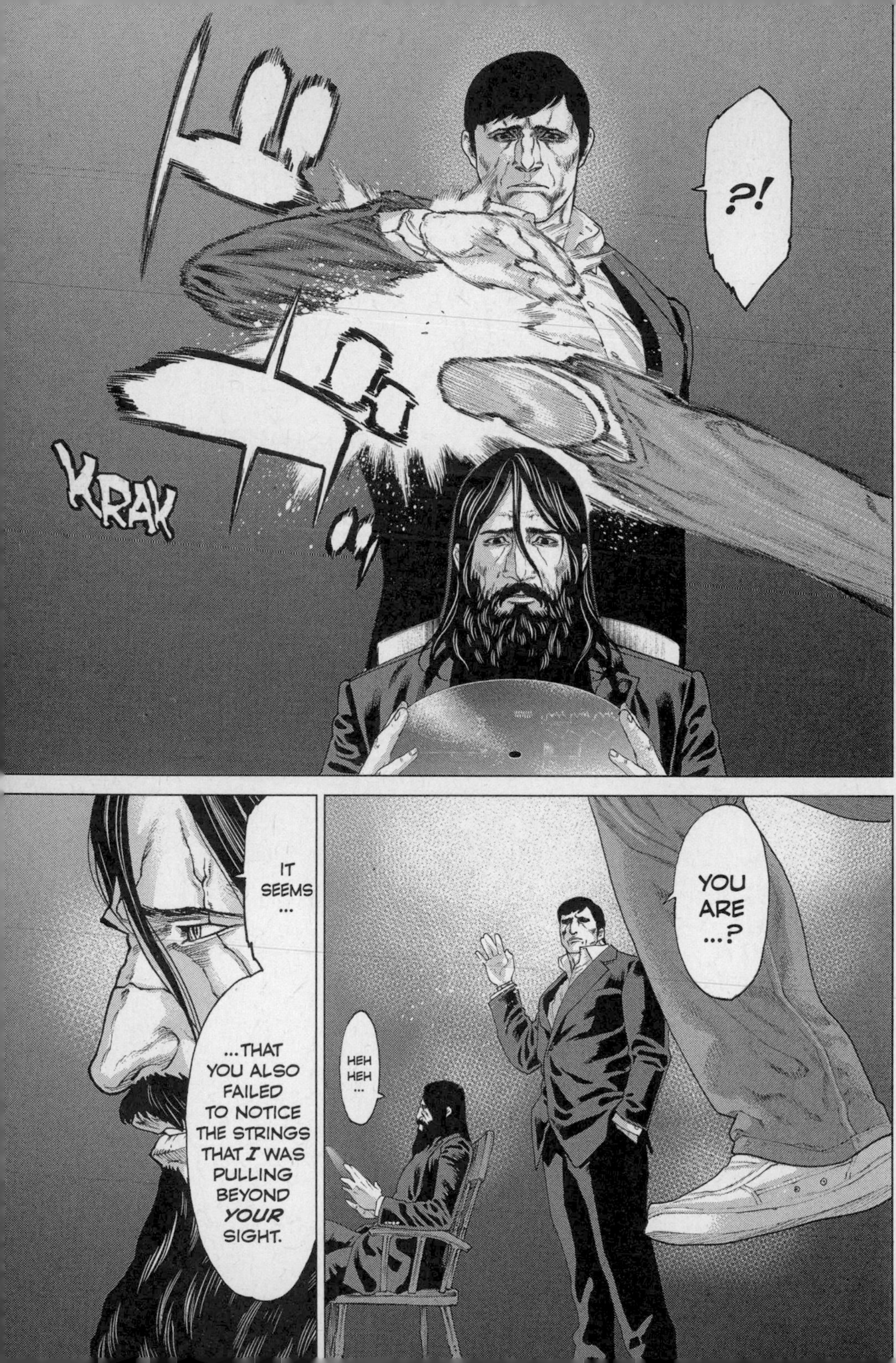
?!
KRAK
YOU ARE ...?
HEH HEH ...
IT SEEMS ...
...THAT YOU ALSO FAILED TO NOTICE THE STRINGS THAT I WAS PULLING BEYOND YOUR SIGHT.

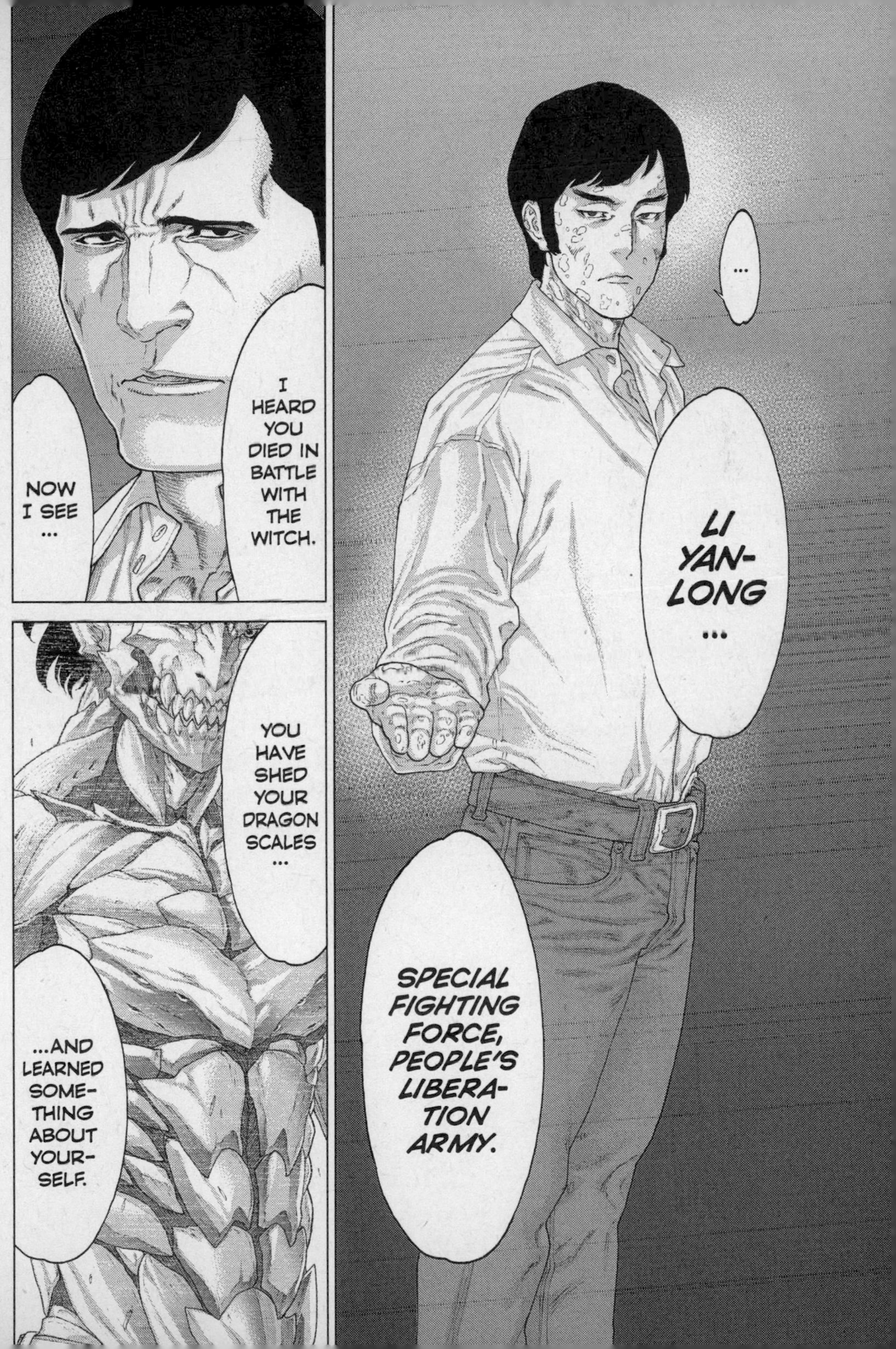
...
LI YAN-LONG ...
SPECIAL FIGHTING FORCE, PEOPLE'S LIBERATION ARMY.
I HEARD YOU DIED IN BATTLE WITH THE WITCH.
NOW I SEE ...
YOU HAVE SHED YOUR DRAGON SCALES ...
...AND LEARNED SOMETHING ABOUT YOURSELF.

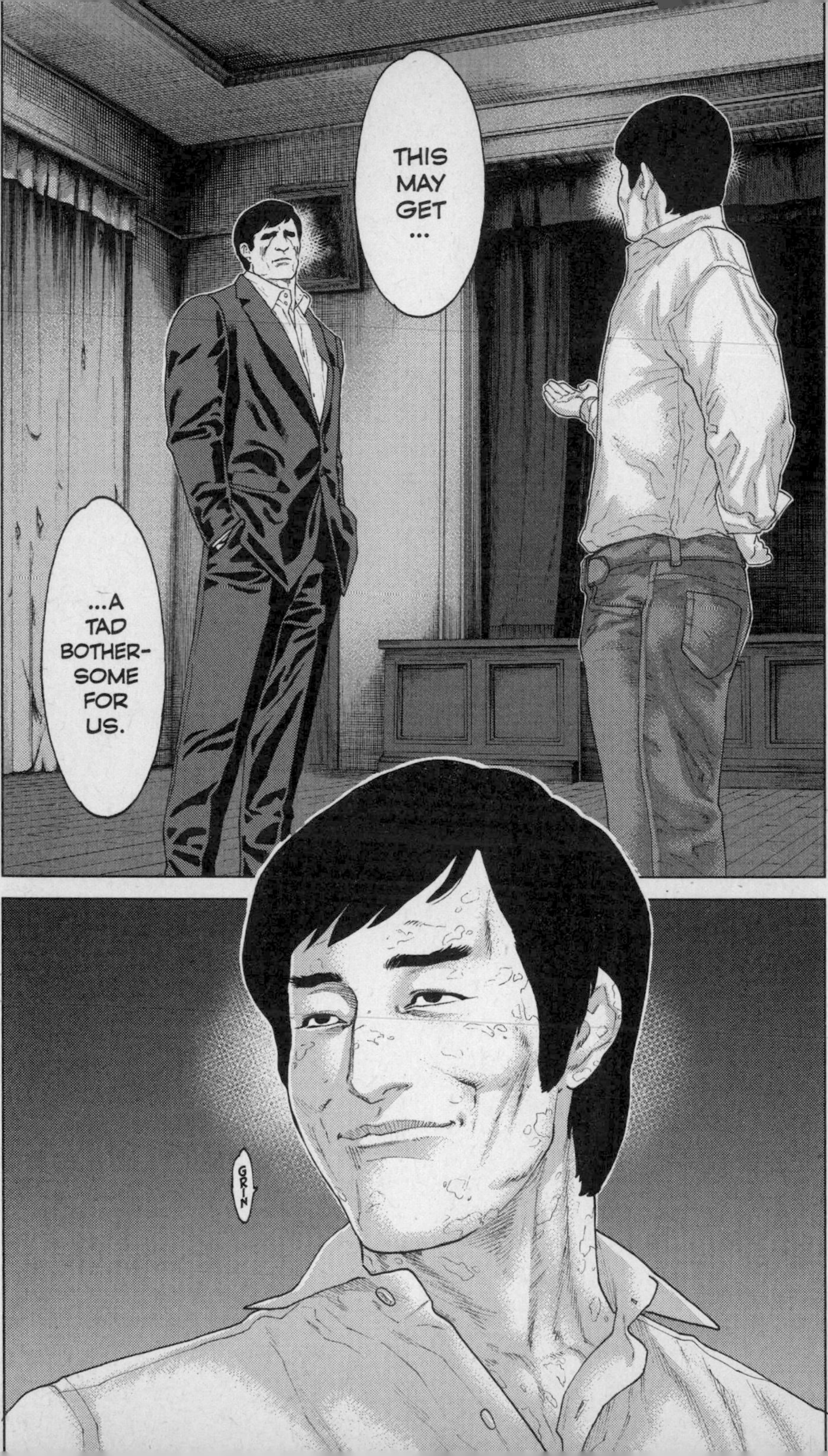
THIS MAY GET ...
...A TAD BOTHER-SOME FOR US.
GRIN

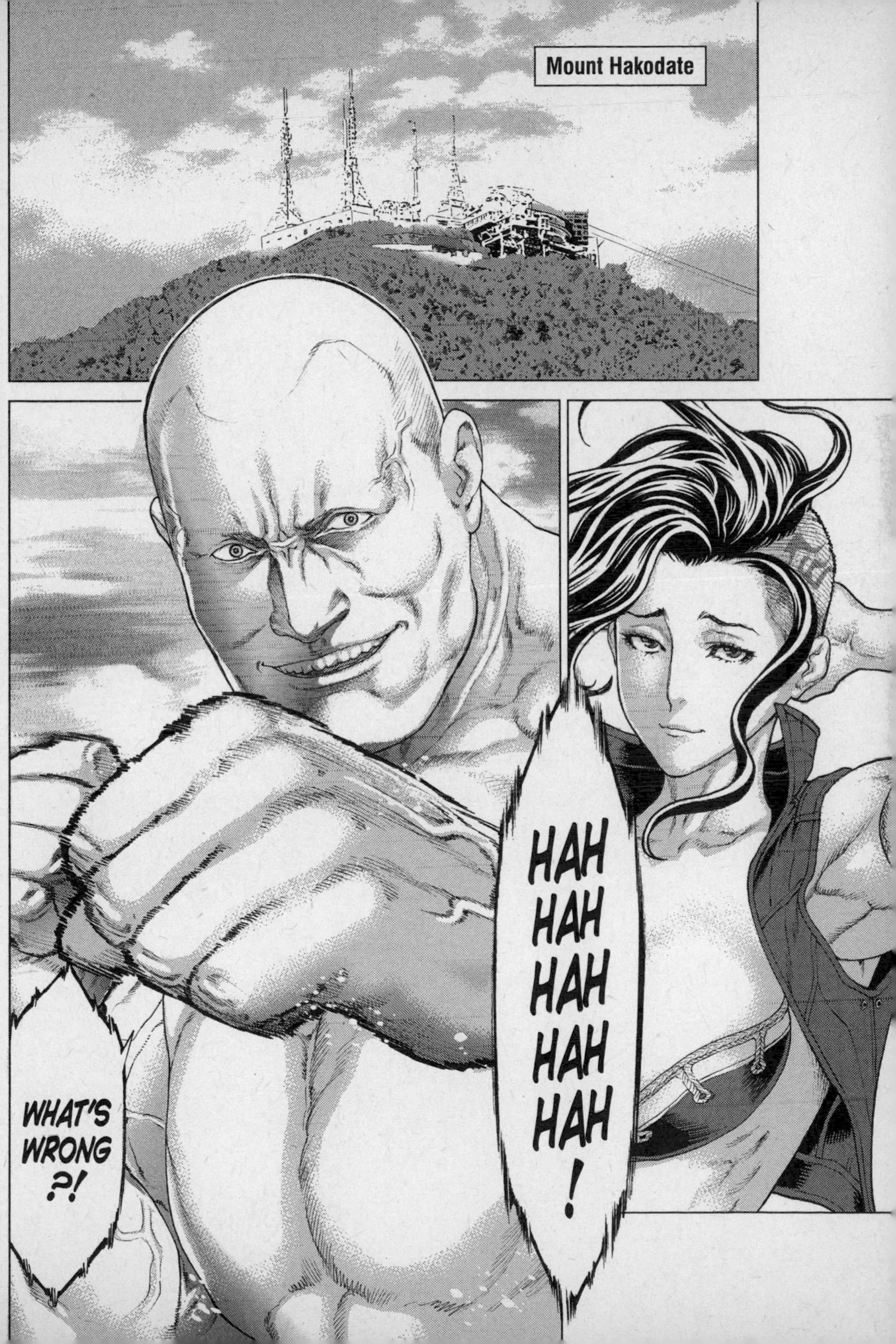
Mount Hakodate
HAH HAH HAH HAH HAH HAH!
WHAT'S WRONG?!

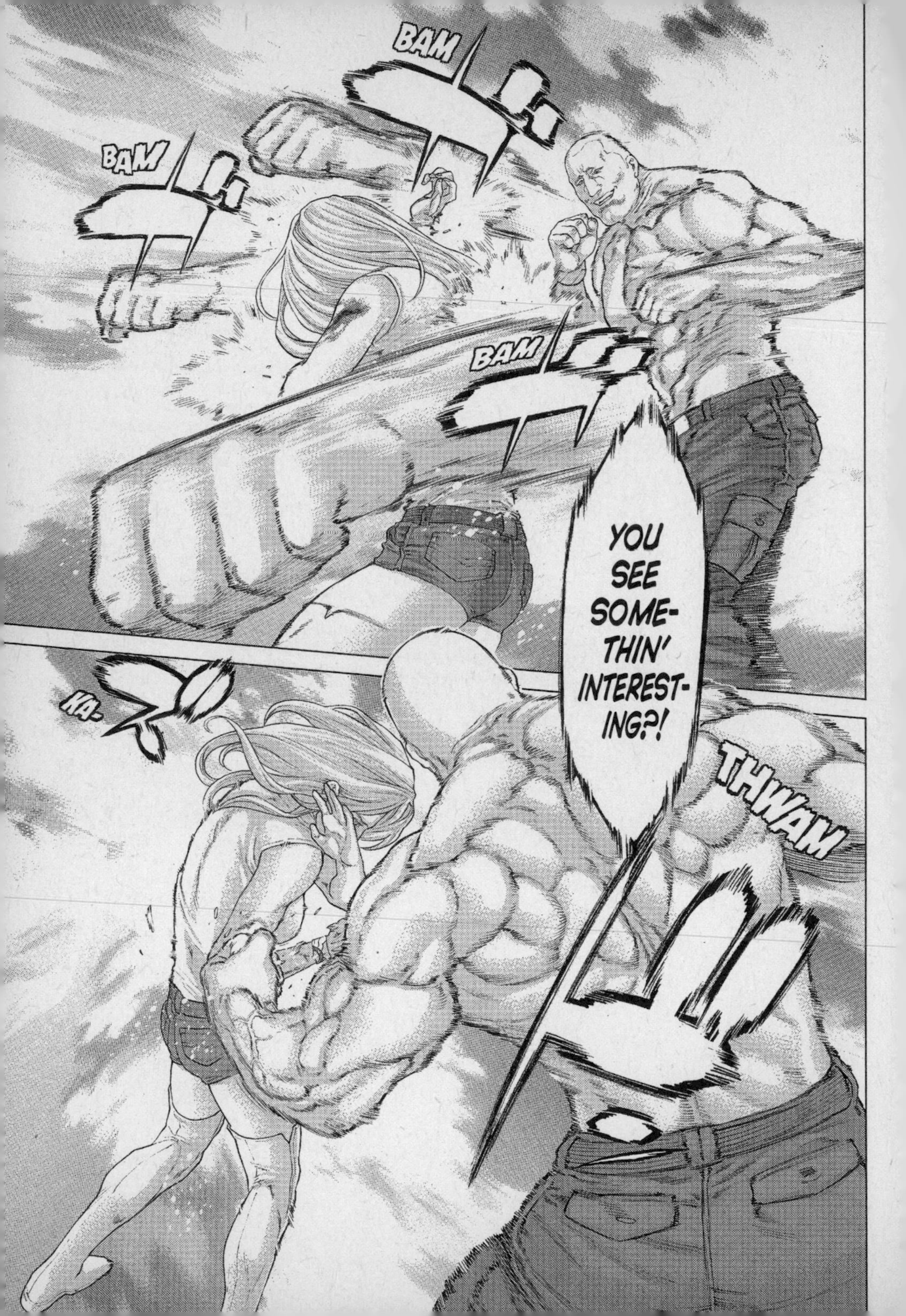
BAM
BAM
BAM
YOU SEE SOMETHIN' INTERESTING?!
THWAM
KA-

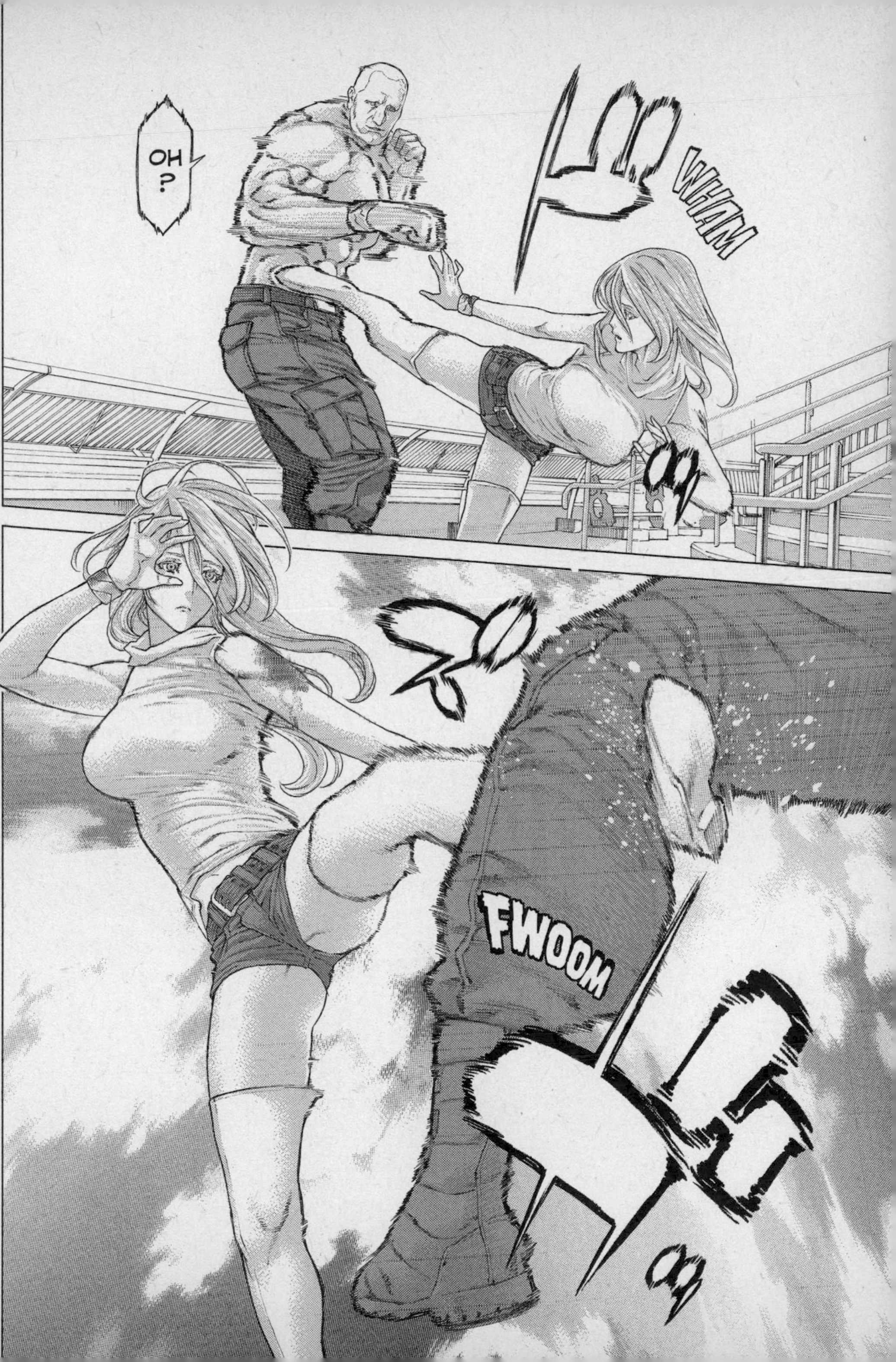
WHAM
OH?
FWOOM

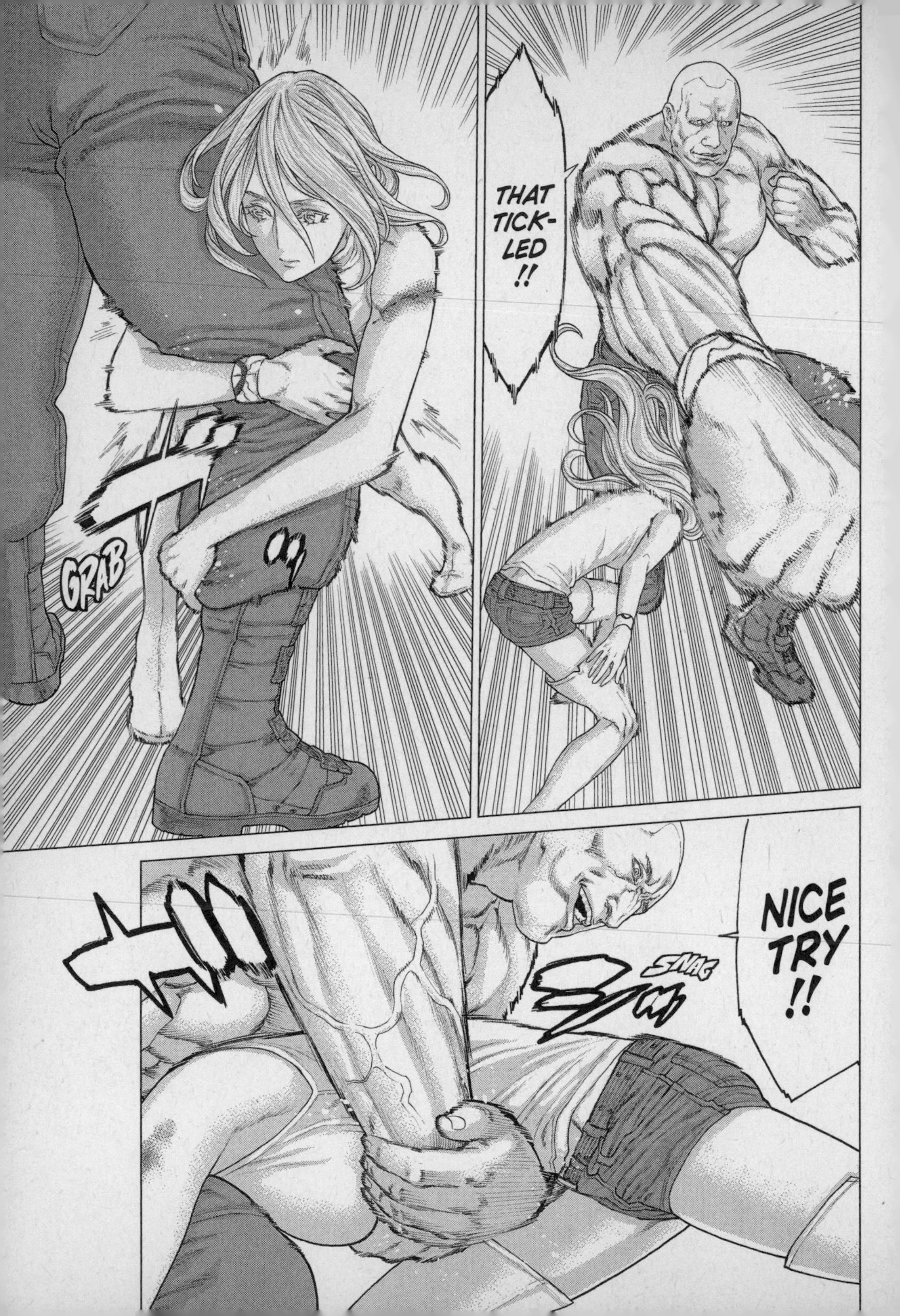
THAT TICK-LED !!
GRAB
NICE TRY !!
SNAG

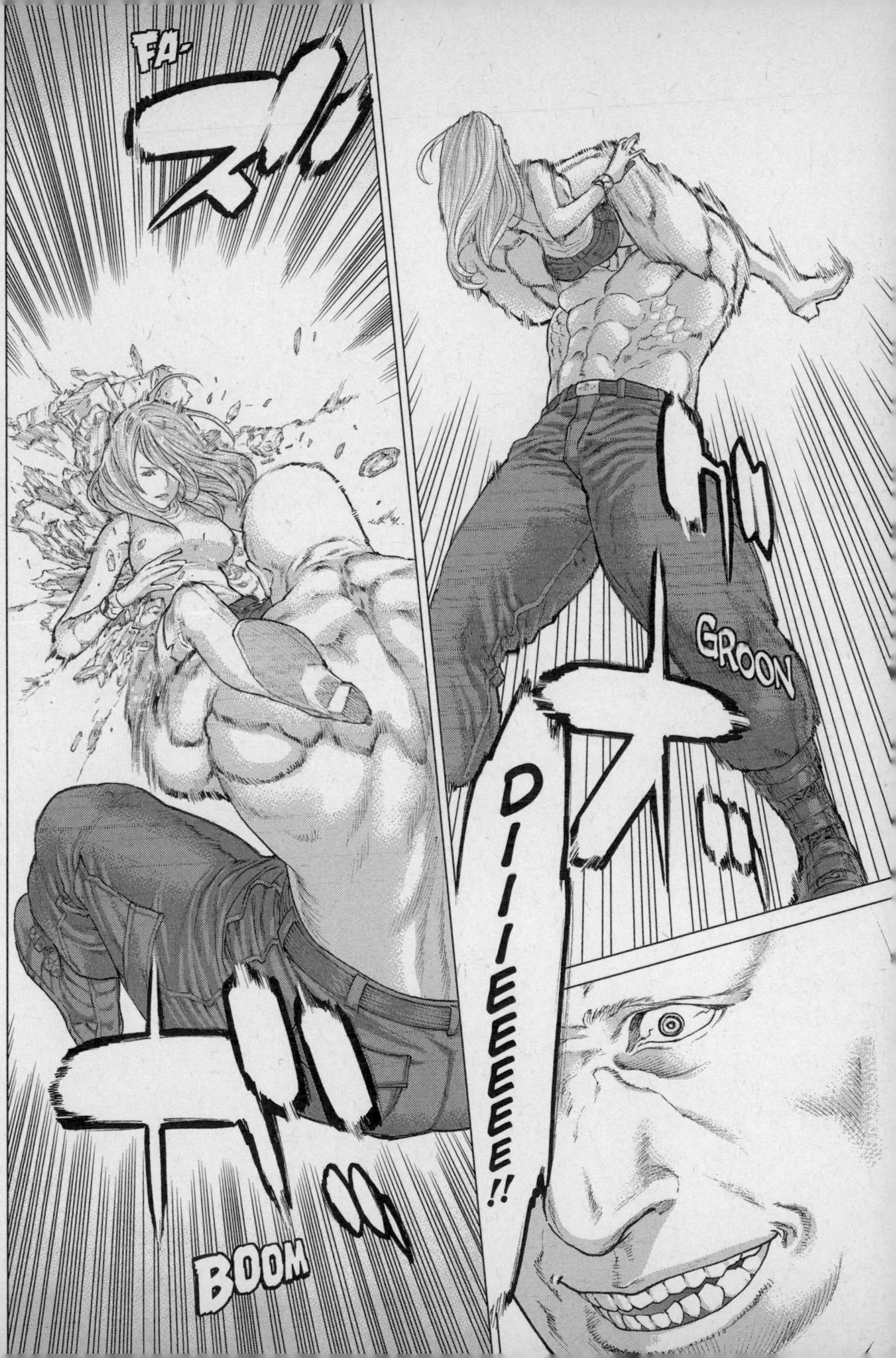
GROON
DIIIEEEEEE!!
FA-
BOOM

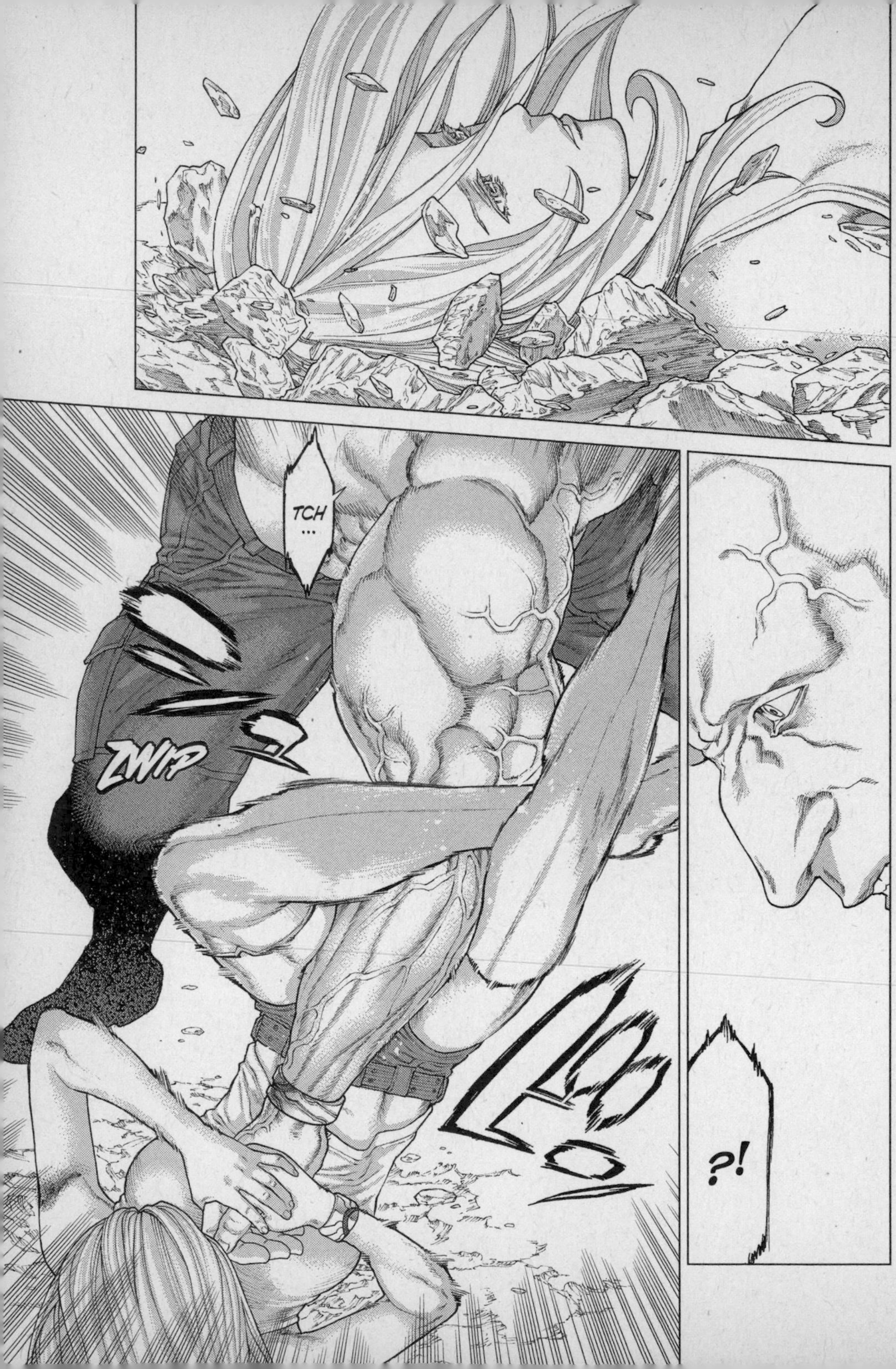
?!
TCH ...
ZWIP

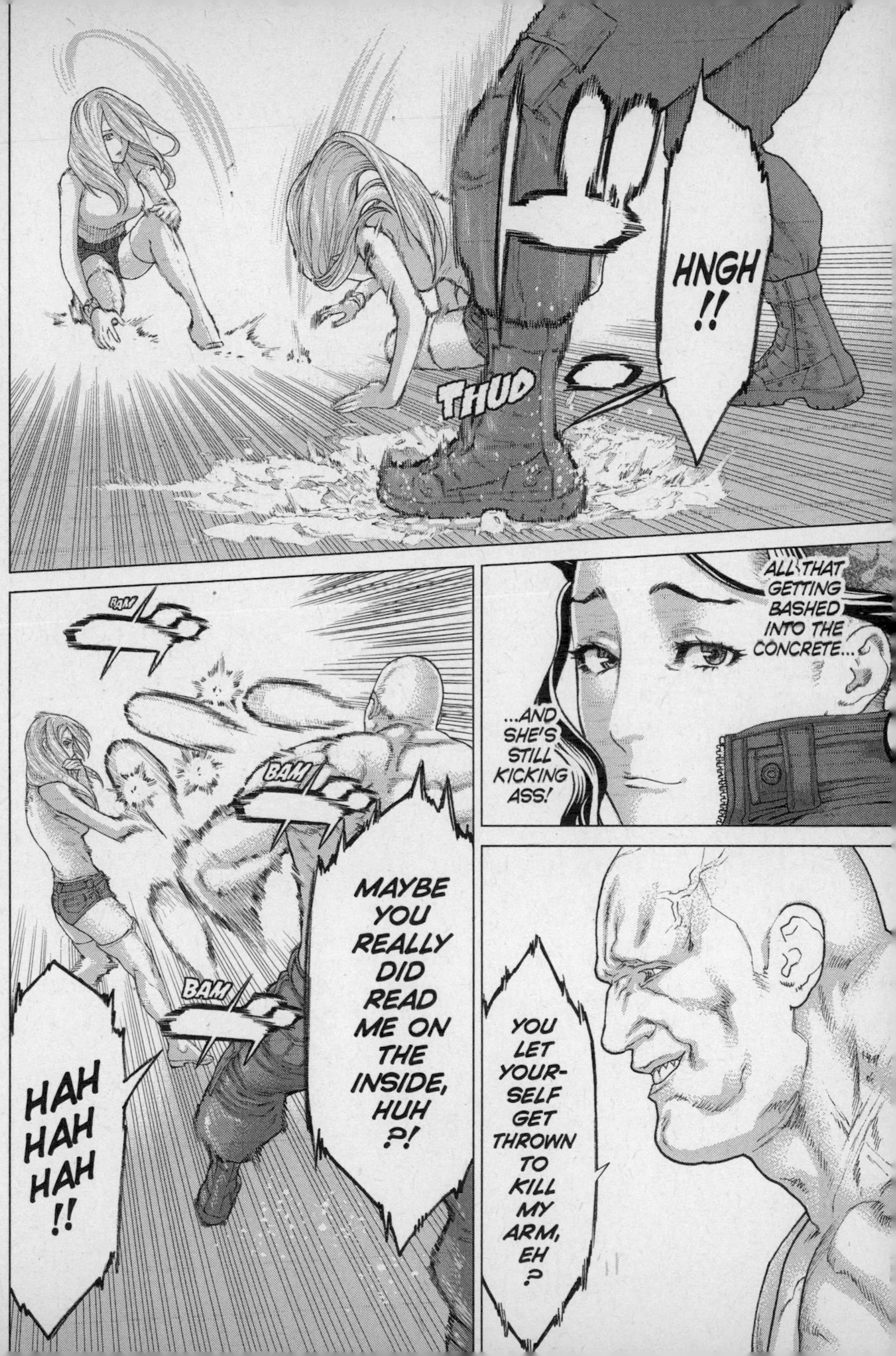
HNGH!!
THUD
ALL THAT GETTING BASHED INTO THE CONCRETE...
...AND SHE'S STILL KICKING ASS!
YOU LET YOURSELF GET THROWN TO KILL MY ARM, EH?
BAM
BAM
BAM
MAYBE YOU REALLY DID READ ME ON THE INSIDE, HUH?!
HAH HAH HAH!!

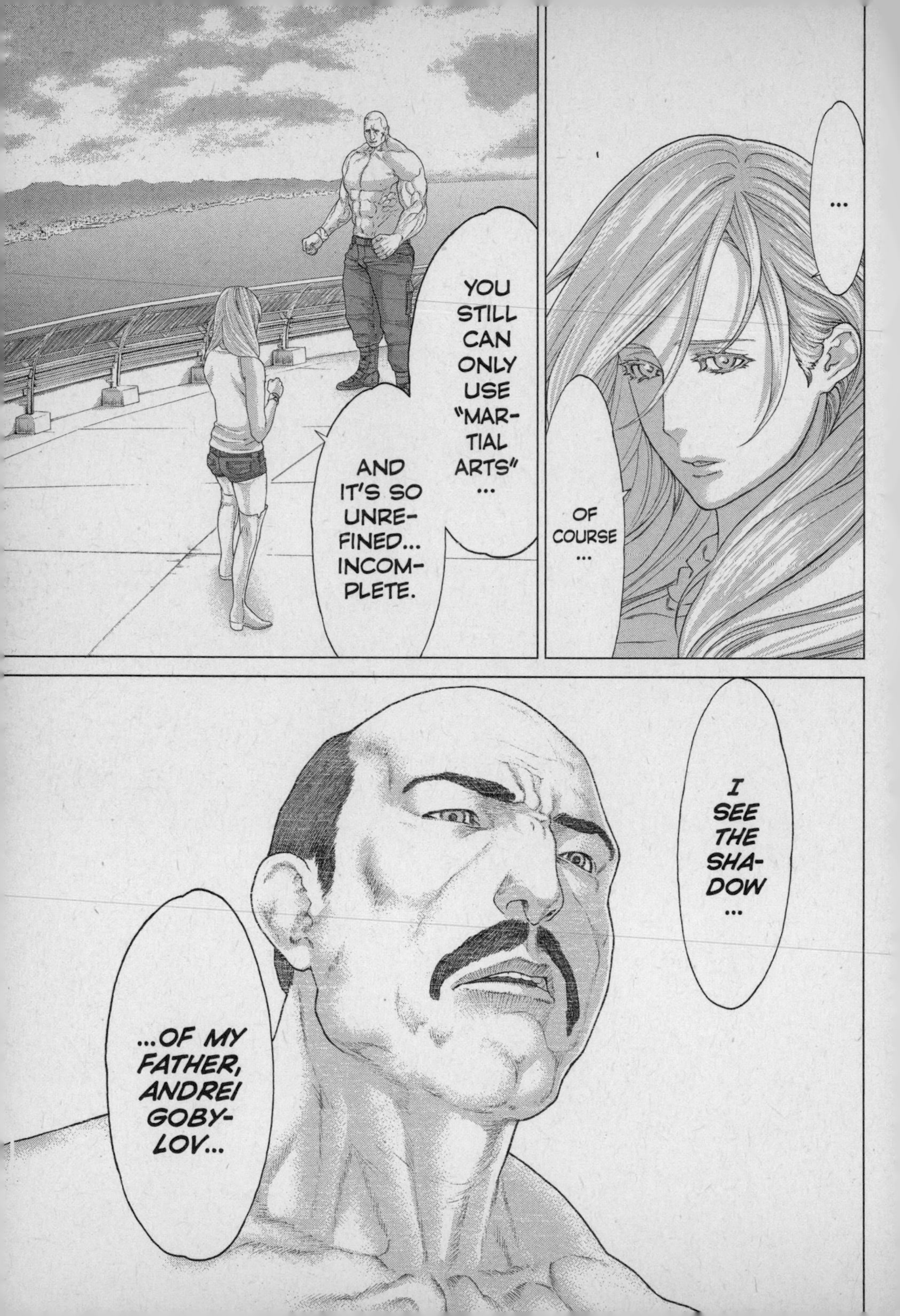
...
OF COURSE...
YOU STILL CAN ONLY USE "MARTIAL ARTS"...
AND IT'S SO UNREFINED... INCOMPLETE.
I SEE THE SHADOW...
...OF MY FATHER, ANDREI GOBYLOV...

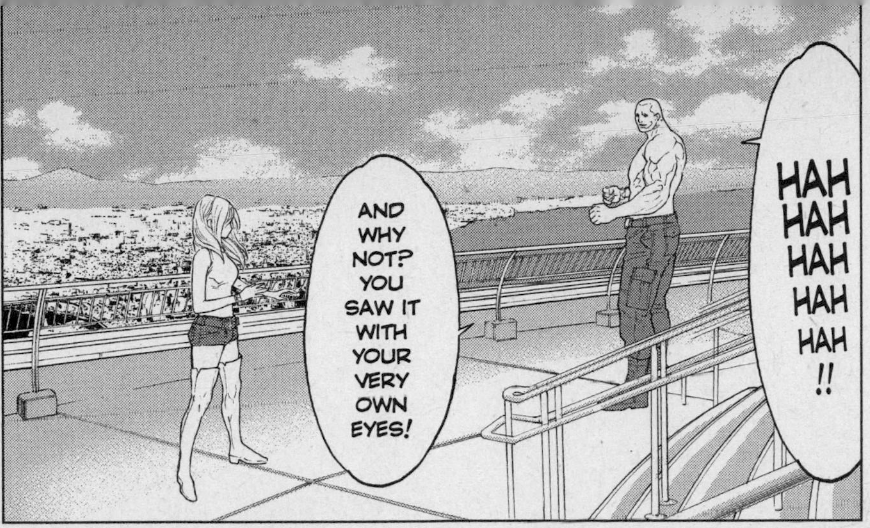
HAH HAH HAH HAH HAH !!
AND WHY NOT? YOU SAW IT WITH YOUR VERY OWN EYES!

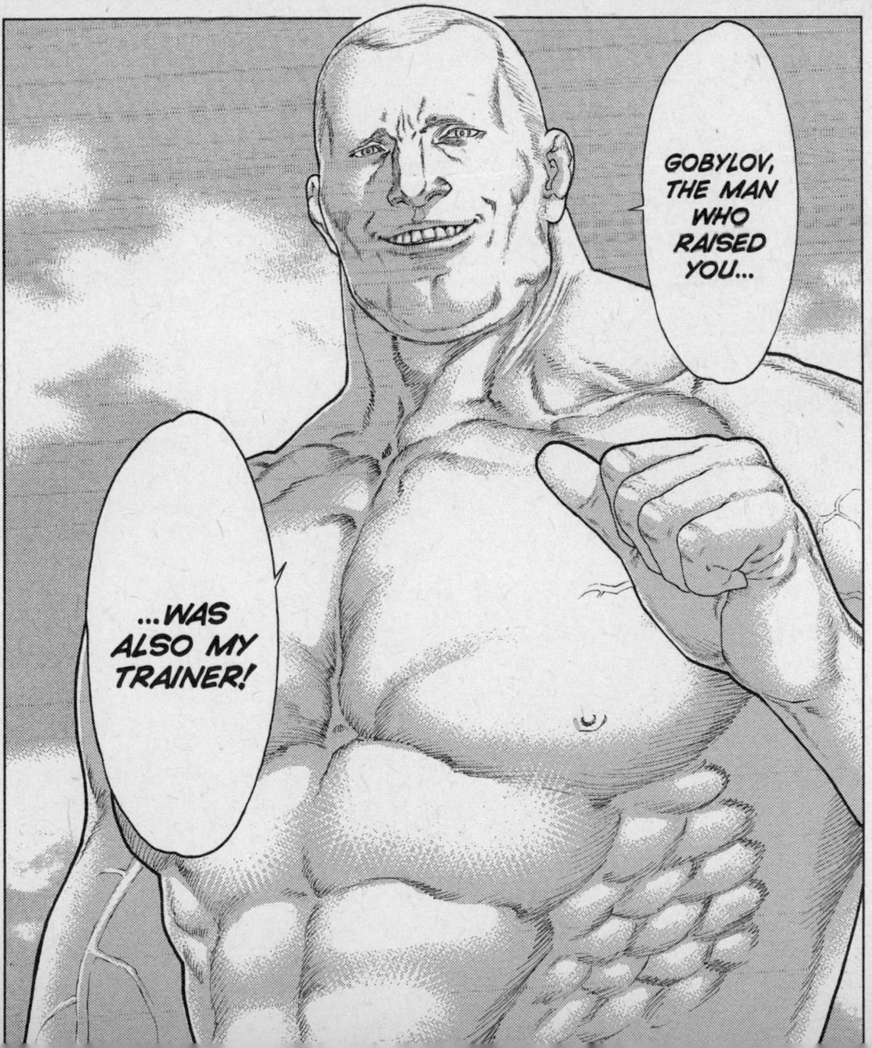
GOBYLOV, THE MAN WHO RAISED YOU...
...WAS ALSO MY TRAINER!

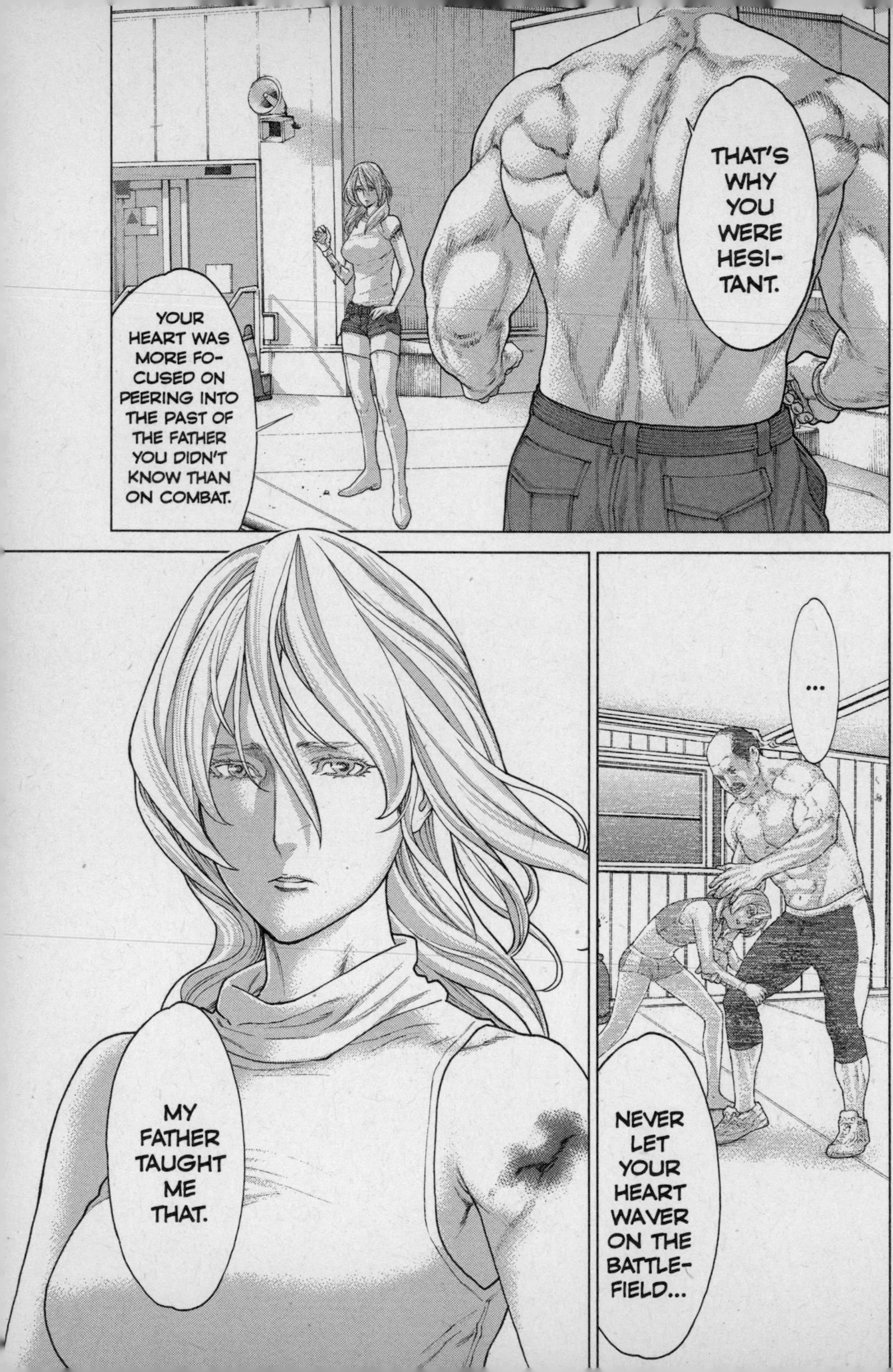
THAT'S WHY YOU WERE HESI-TANT.
YOUR HEART WAS MORE FO-CUSED ON PEERING INTO THE PAST OF THE FATHER YOU DIDN'T KNOW THAN ON COMBAT.
...
NEVER LET YOUR HEART WAVER ON THE BATTLE-FIELD...
MY FATHER TAUGHT ME THAT.

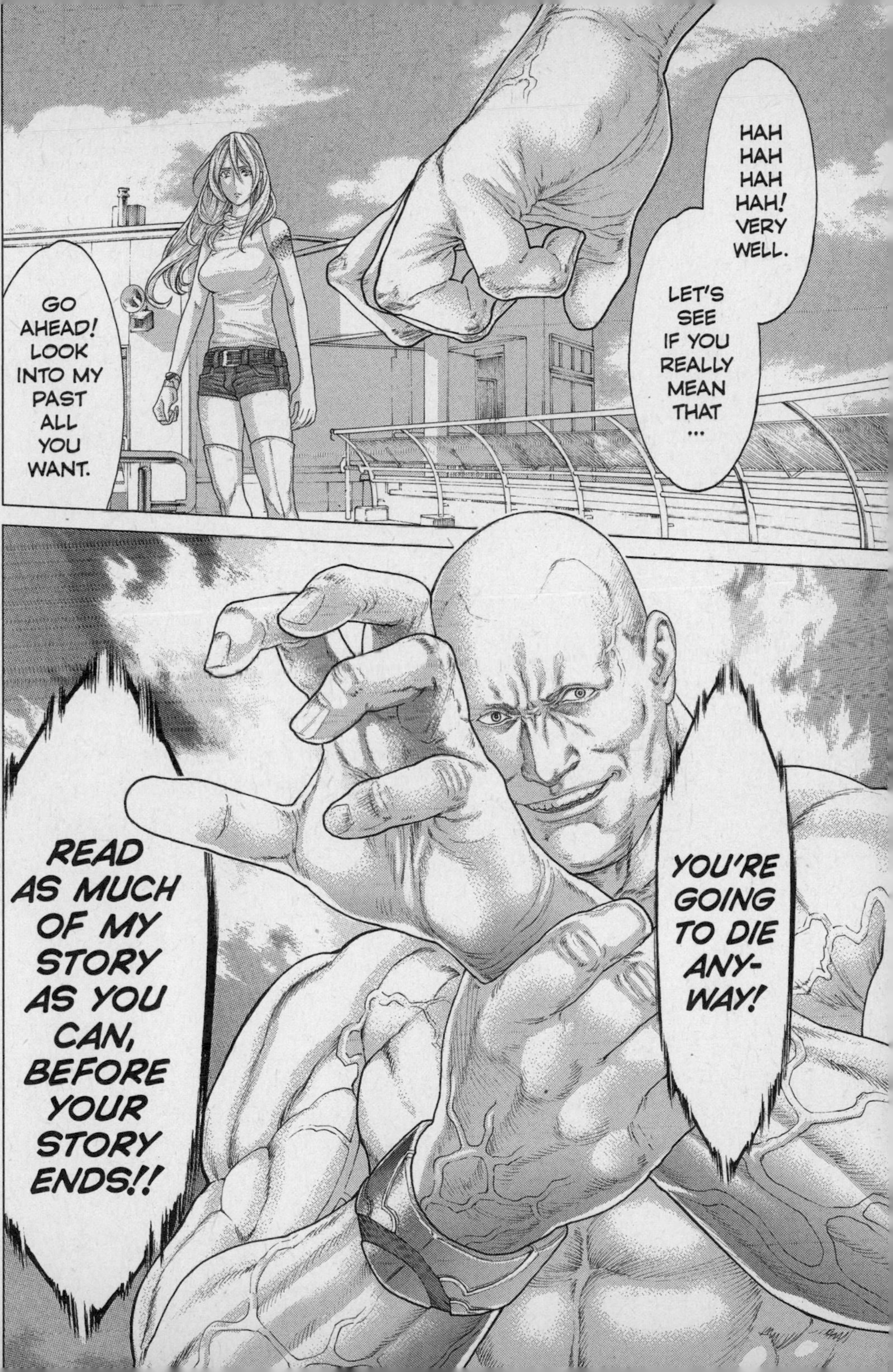
HAH HAH HAH HAH! VERY WELL.
LET'S SEE IF YOU REALLY MEAN THAT ...
GO AHEAD! LOOK INTO MY PAST ALL YOU WANT.
YOU'RE GOING TO DIE ANY-WAY!
READ AS MUCH OF MY STORY AS YOU CAN, BEFORE YOUR STORY ENDS!!

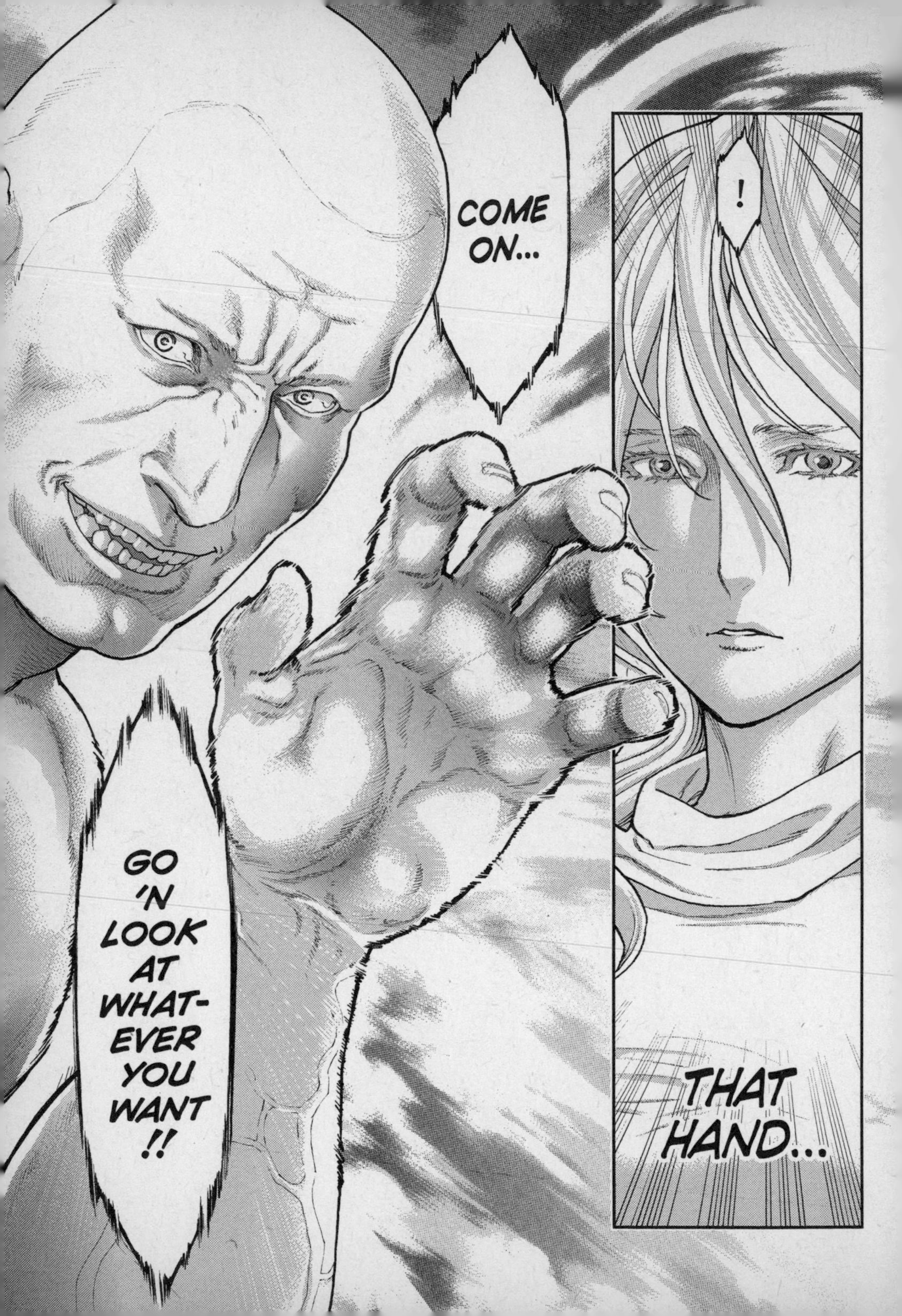
!
THAT HAND...
COME ON...
GO 'N LOOK AT WHATEVER YOU WANT!!

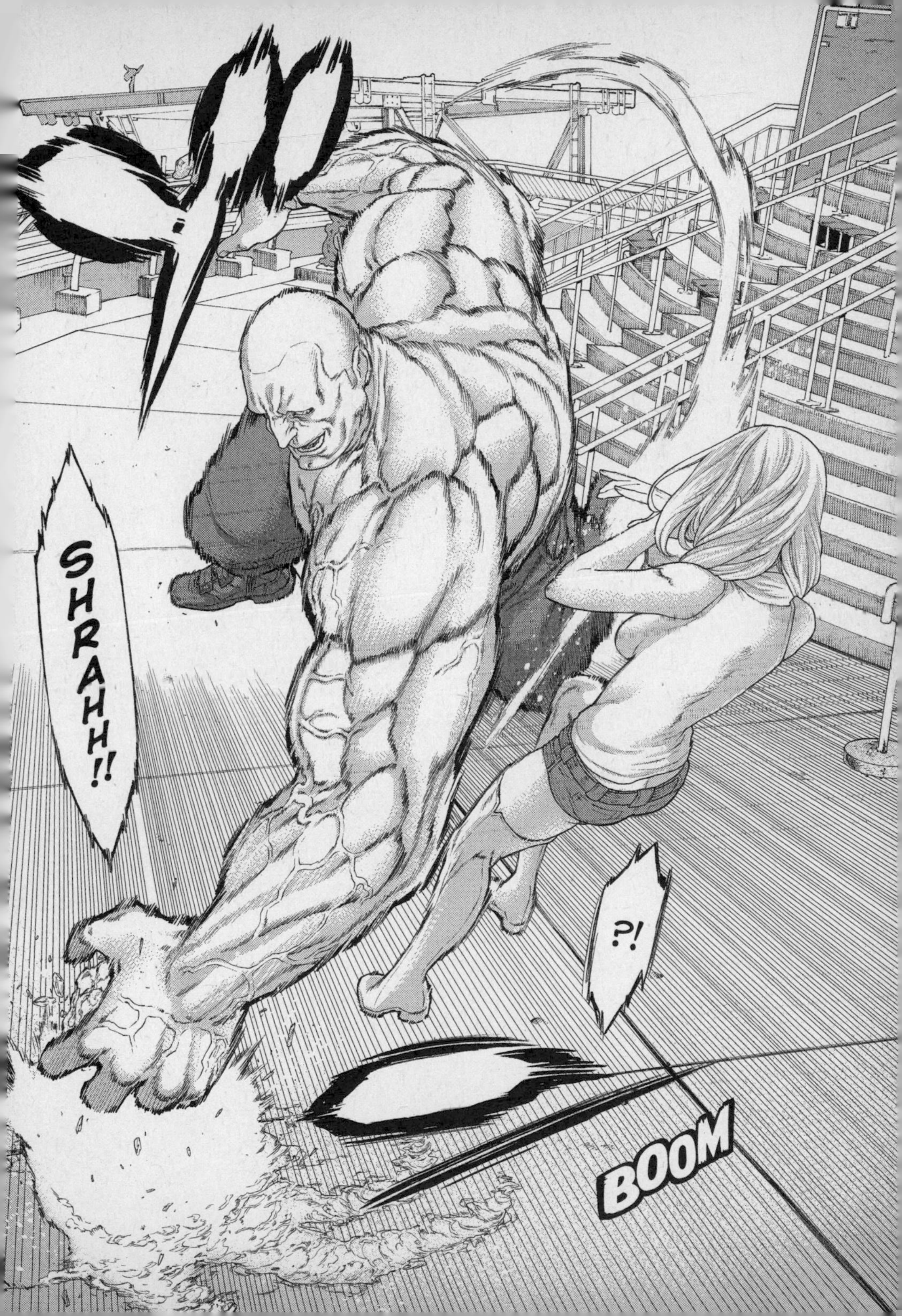
SHRAHH!!
?!
BOOM

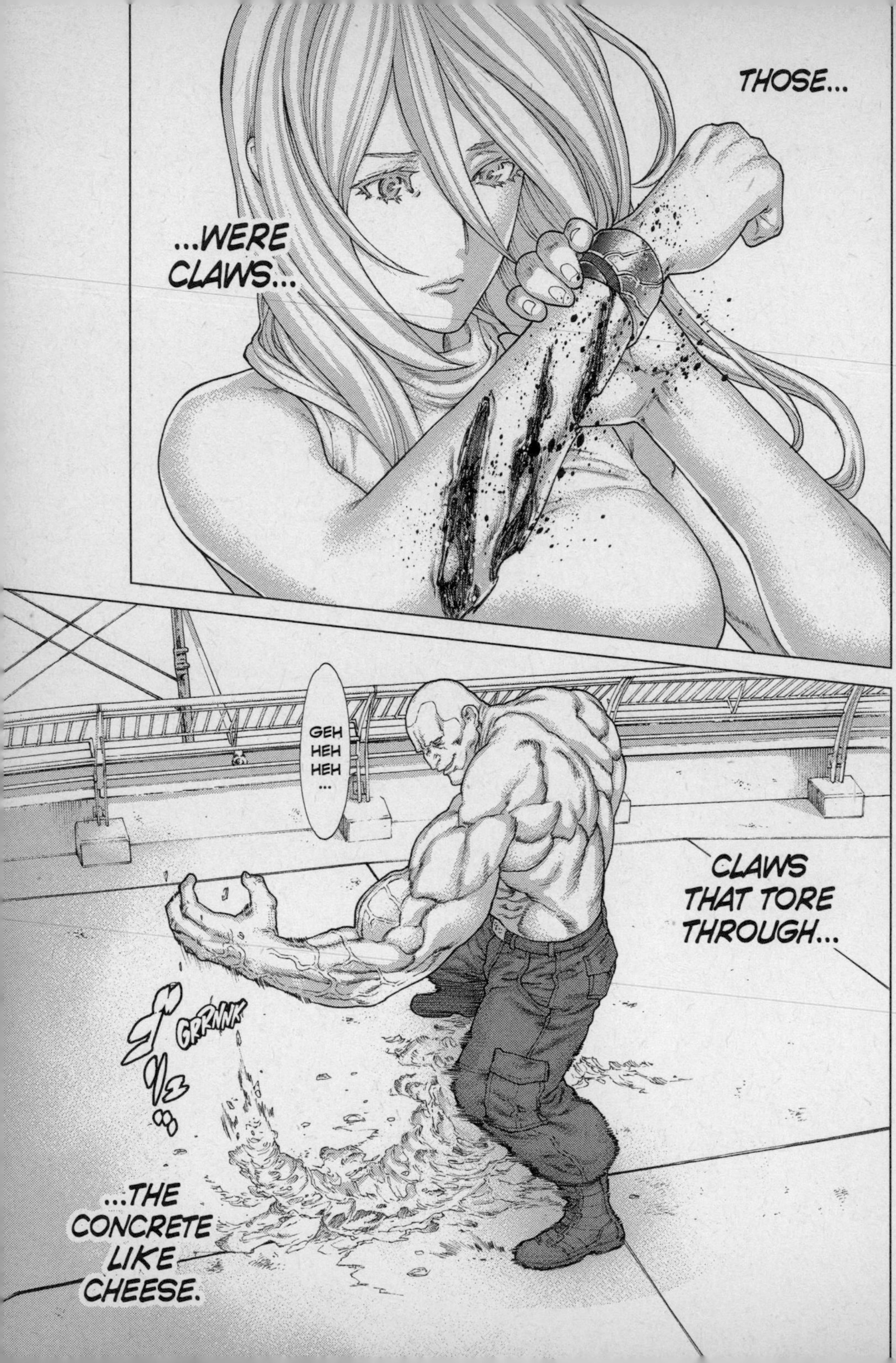
THOSE...
...WERE CLAWS...
GEH HEH HEH ...
CLAWS THAT TORE THROUGH...
GRRNNK
...THE CONCRETE LIKE CHEESE.

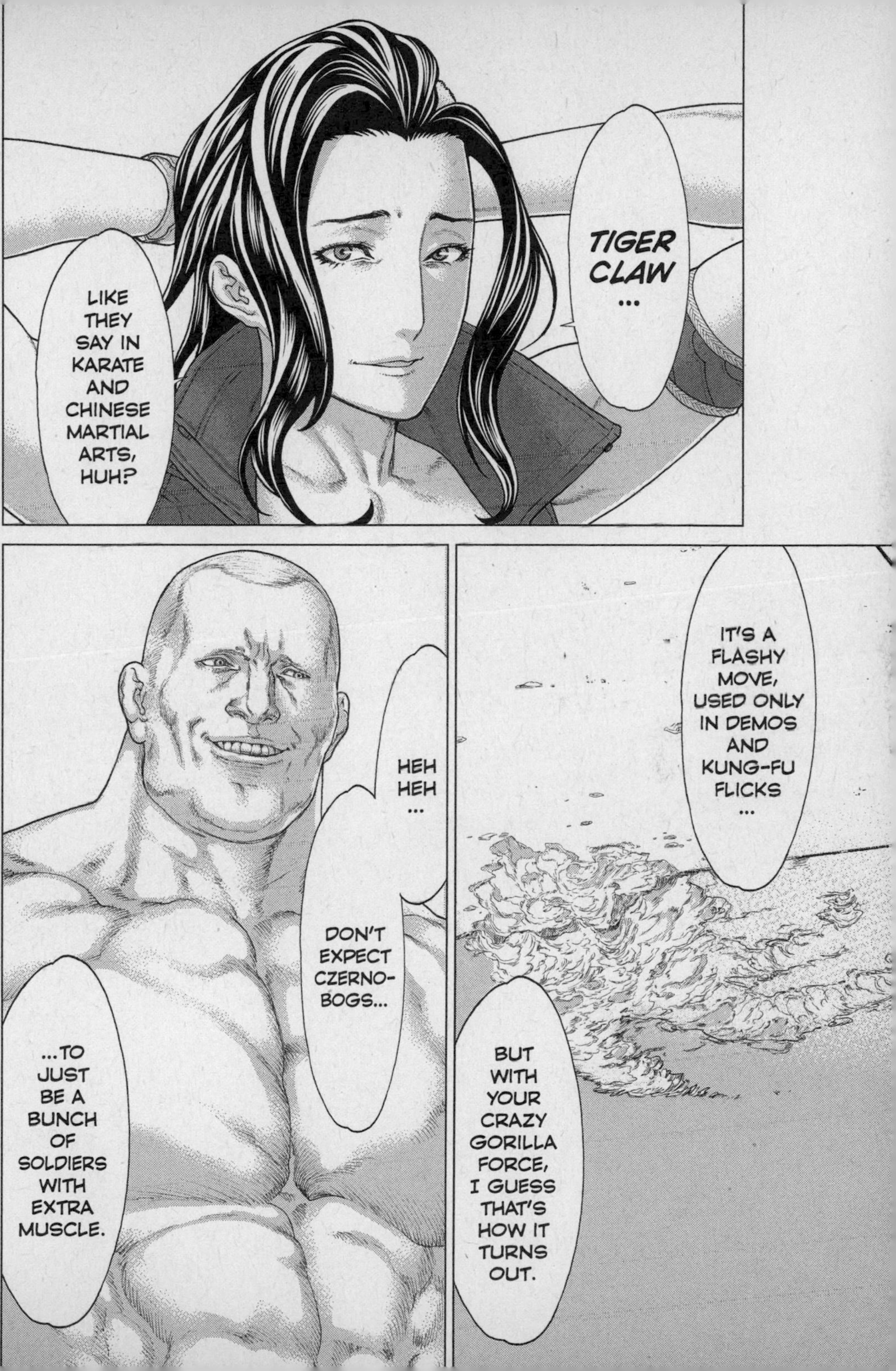
TIGER CLAW ...
LIKE THEY SAY IN KARATE AND CHINESE MARTIAL ARTS, HUH?
IT'S A FLASHY MOVE, USED ONLY IN DEMOS AND KUNG-FU FLICKS ...
BUT WITH YOUR CRAZY GORILLA FORCE, I GUESS THAT'S HOW IT TURNS OUT.
HEH HEH ...
DON'T EXPECT CZERNO-BOGS...
...TO JUST BE A BUNCH OF SOLDIERS WITH EXTRA MUSCLE.

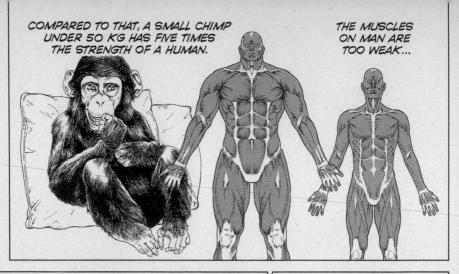

THE MUSCLES ON MAN ARE TOO WEAK...
COMPARED TO THAT, A SMALL CHIMP UNDER 50 KG HAS FIVE TIMES THE STRENGTH OF A HUMAN.
IF YOU EXPAND A MAN'S MUSCULAR CAPACITY IN SIZE...
YOU'D NEED TO BE 200-300 KG TO FINALLY REACH A GORILLA'S STRENGTH.
MEANWHILE, WE CZERNOBOGS HAVE 15 TIMES THE POWER OF A MAN THE SAME SIZE.
IN TERMS OF QUALITY STRENGTH, IT'S ENOUGH TO OUTCLASS A GORILLA*, STRONGEST OF THE PRIMATES.
*GORILLA: 12 times human strength

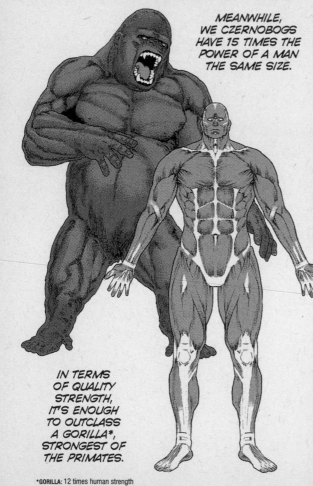

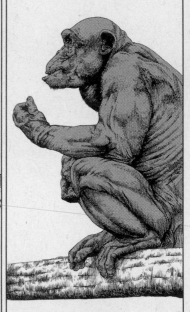

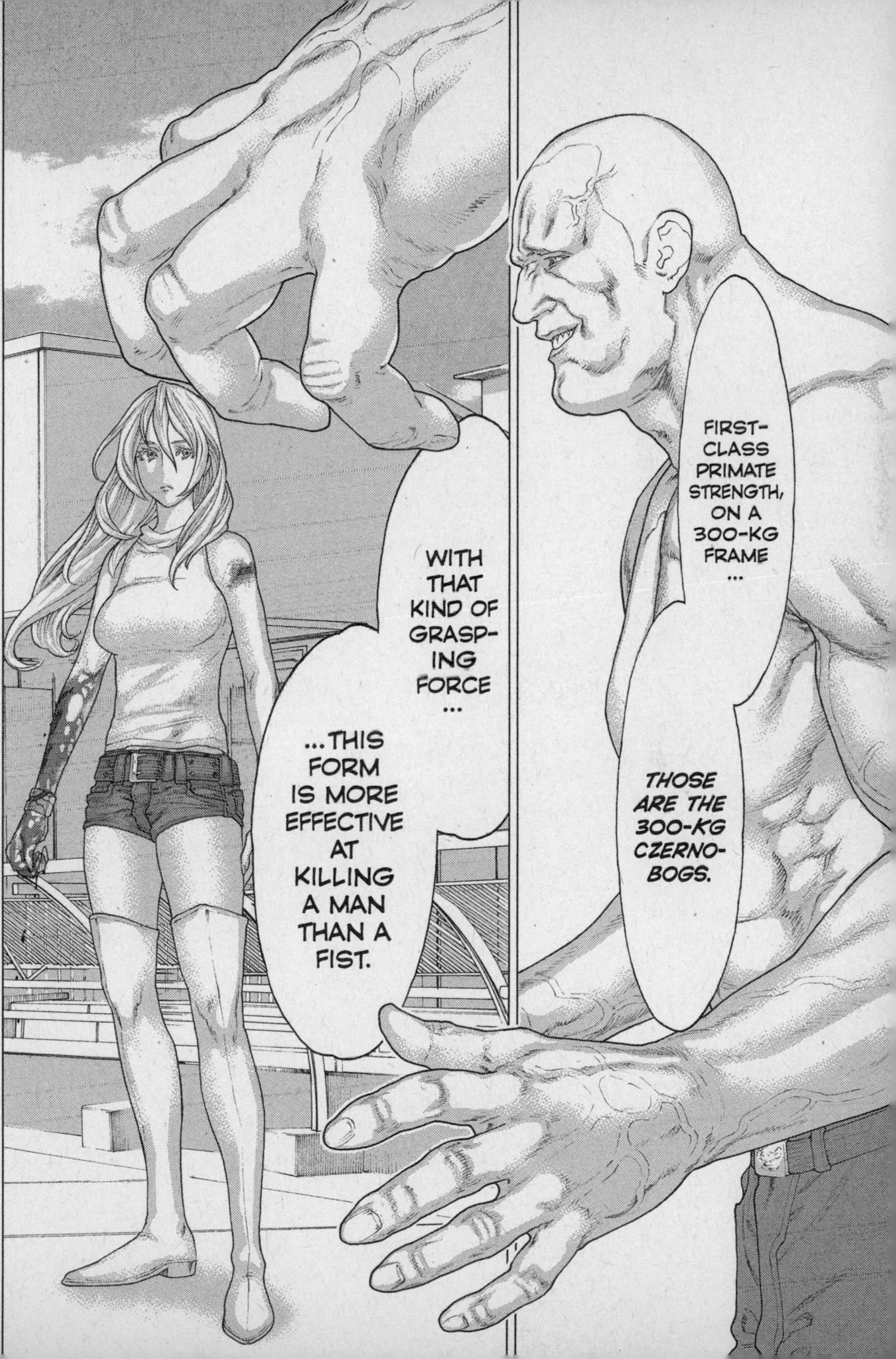
FIRST-CLASS PRIMATE STRENGTH, ON A 300-KG FRAME...
THOSE ARE THE 300-KG CZERNOBOGS.
WITH THAT KIND OF GRASPING FORCE...
...THIS FORM IS MORE EFFECTIVE AT KILLING A MAN THAN A FIST.

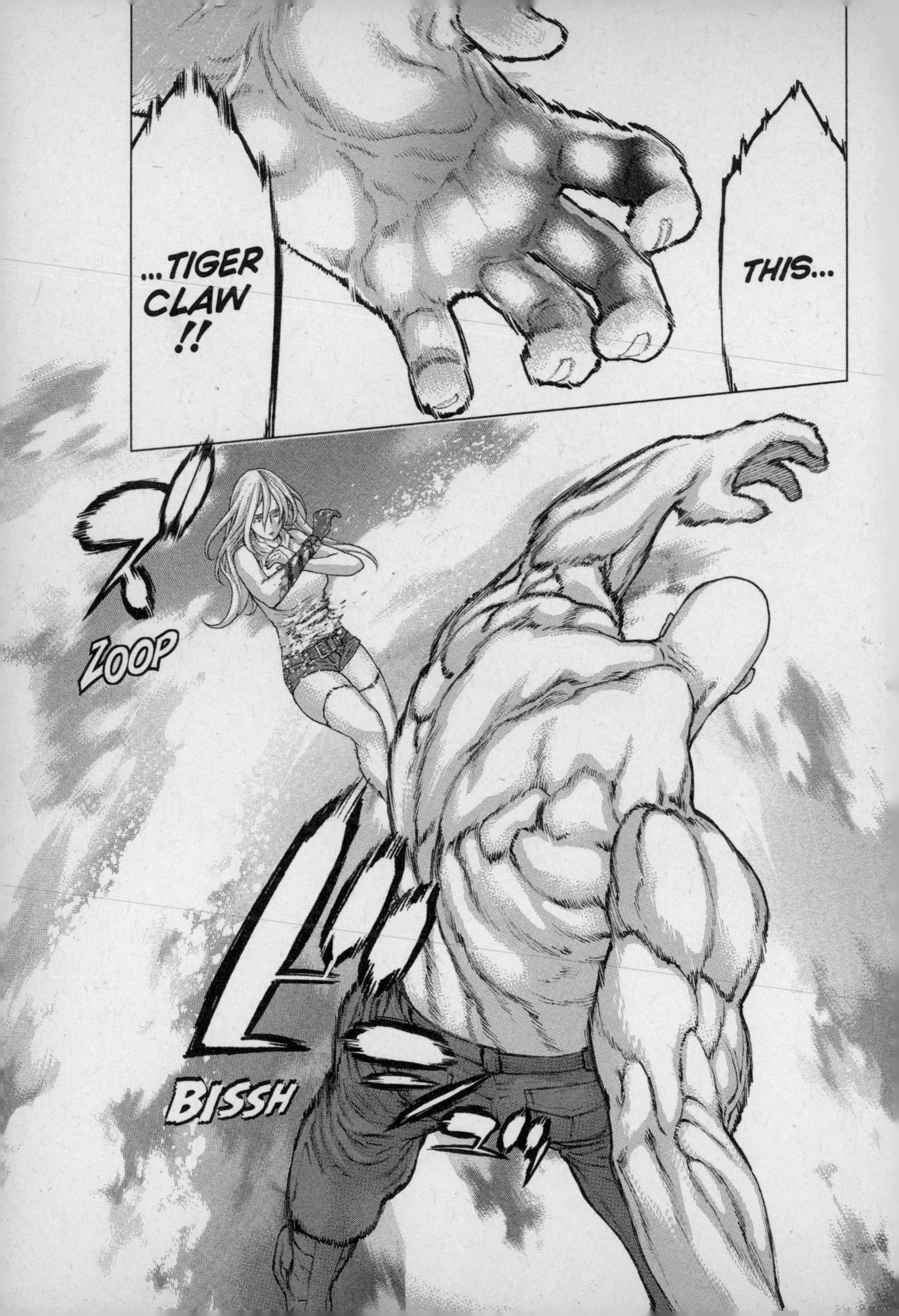
THIS...
...TIGER CLAW !!
ZOOP
BISSH

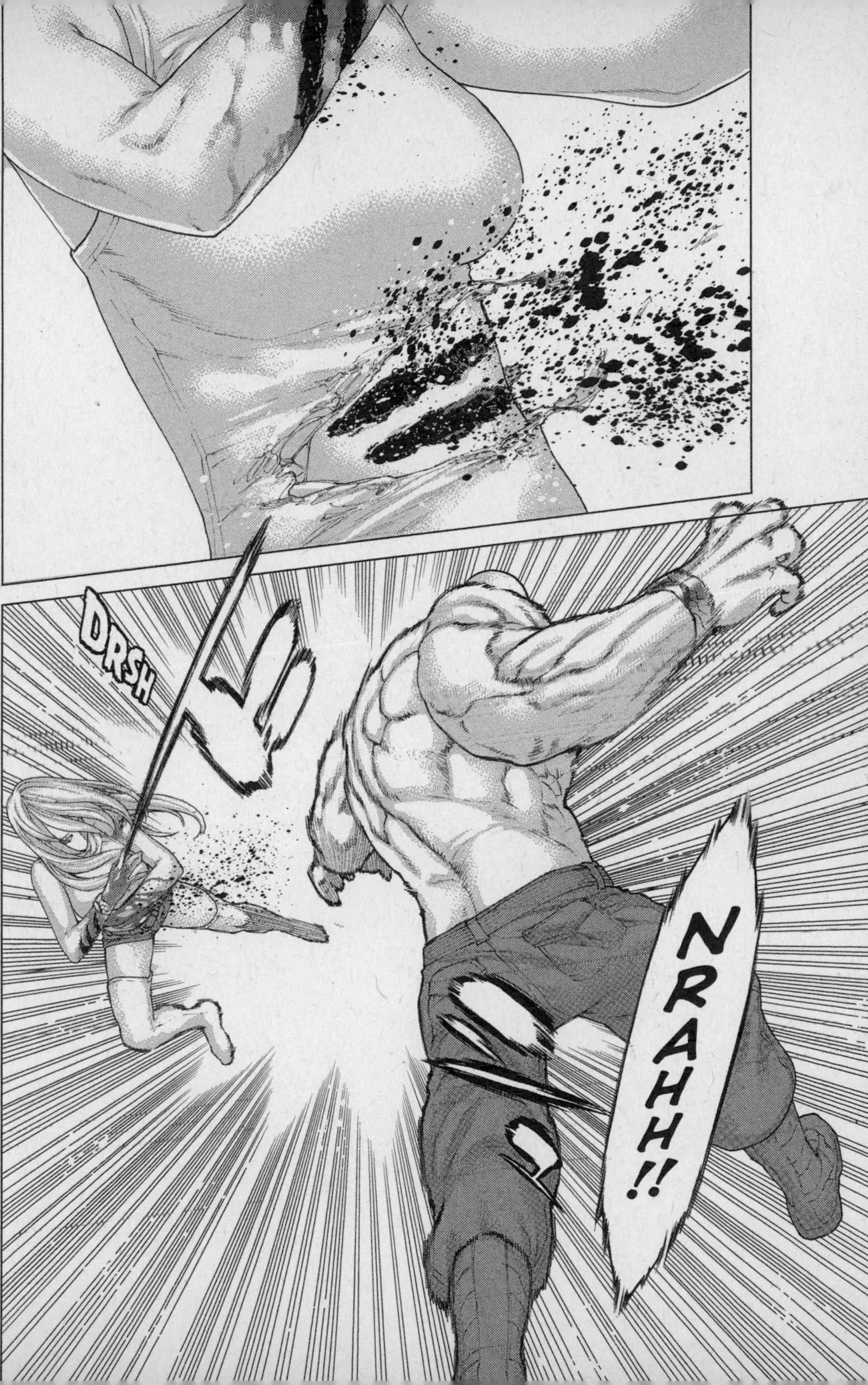
DRSH
NRAHH!!

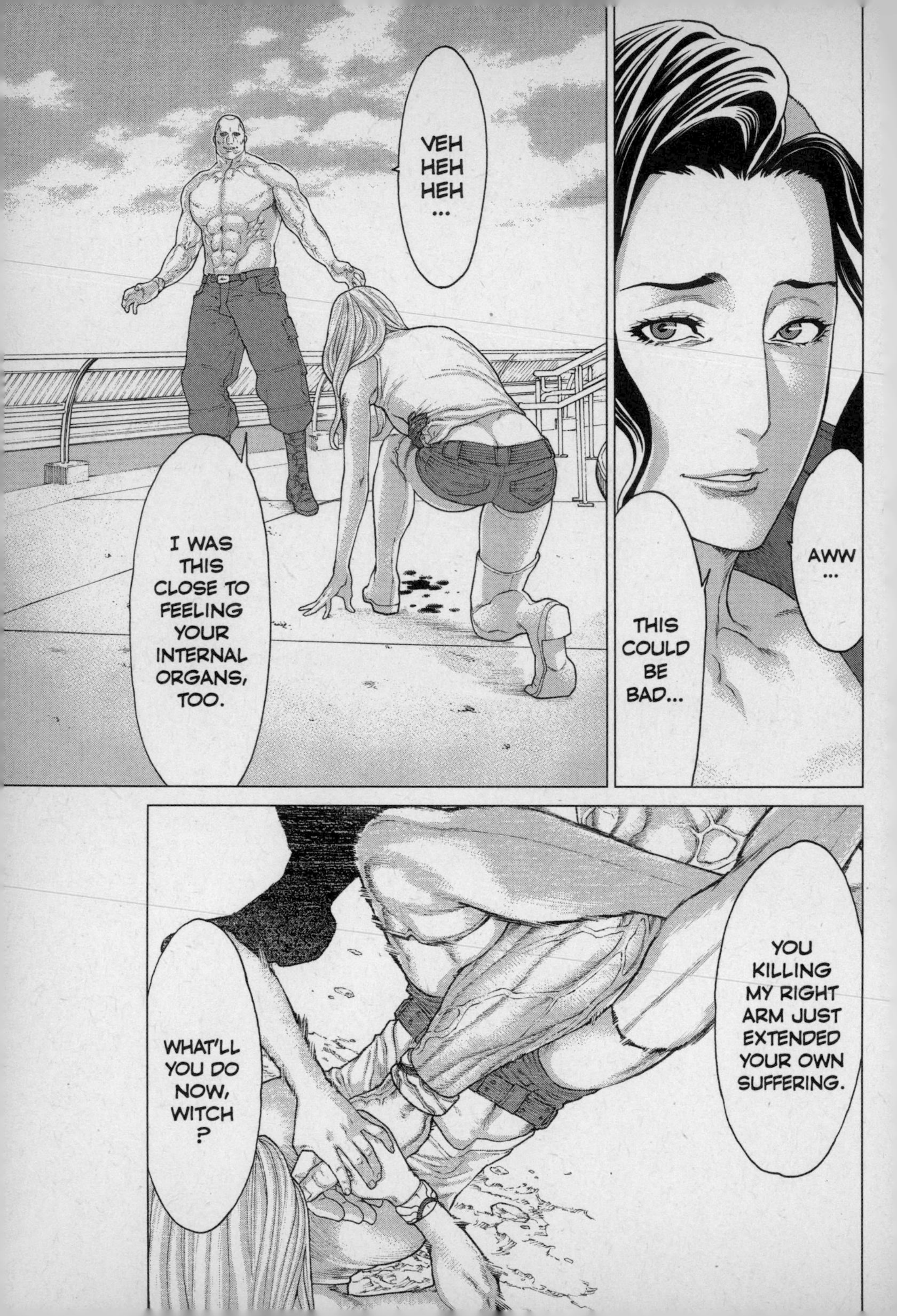
AWW ...
THIS COULD BE BAD...
VEH HEH HEH ...
I WAS THIS CLOSE TO FEELING YOUR INTERNAL ORGANS, TOO.
YOU KILLING MY RIGHT ARM JUST EXTENDED YOUR OWN SUFFERING.
WHAT'LL YOU DO NOW, WITCH ?

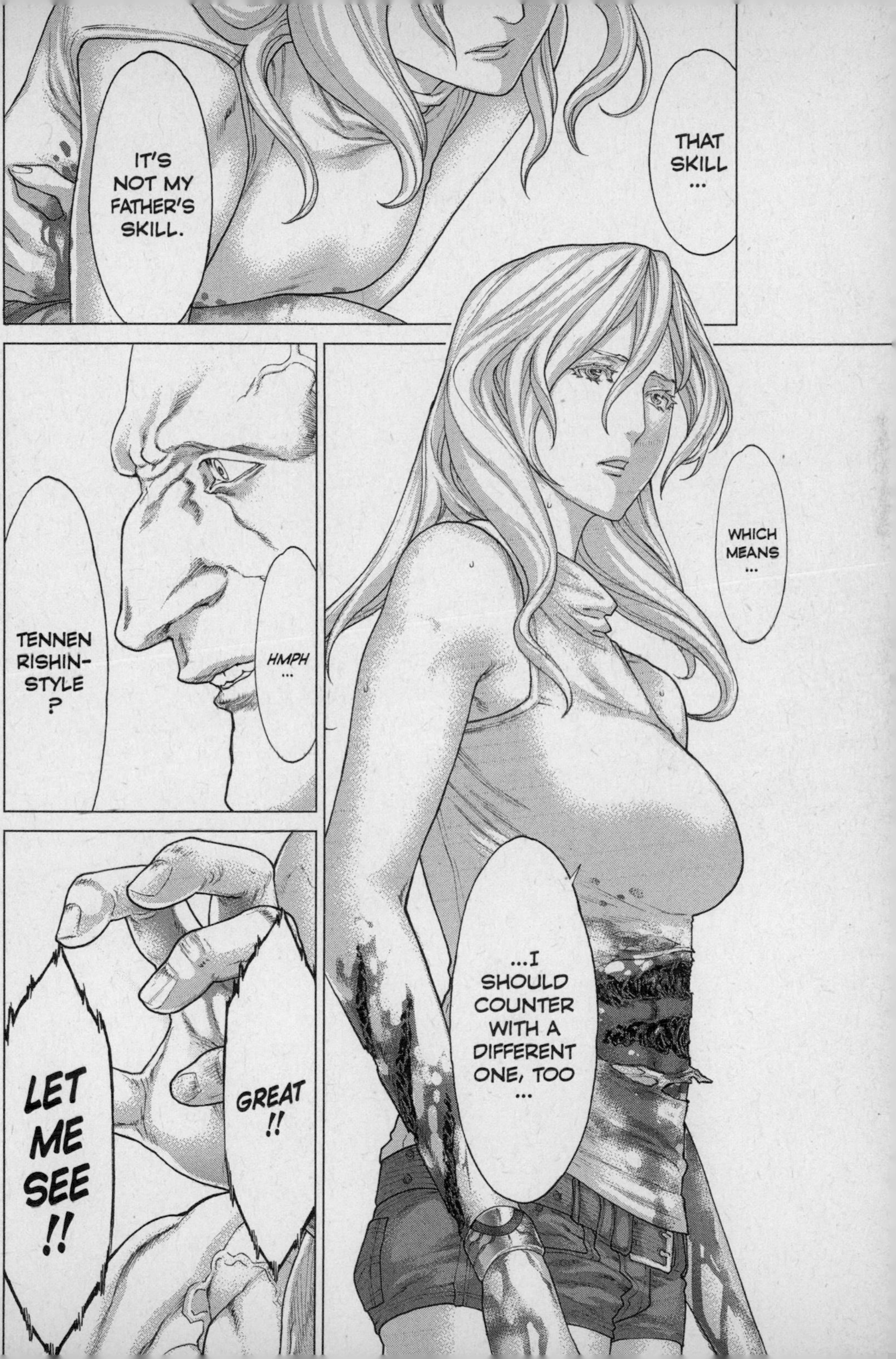
THAT SKILL ...
IT'S NOT MY FATHER'S SKILL.
WHICH MEANS ...
...I SHOULD COUNTER WITH A DIFFERENT ONE, TOO ...
HMPH ...
TENNEN RISHIN-STYLE ?
GREAT !!
LET ME SEE !!

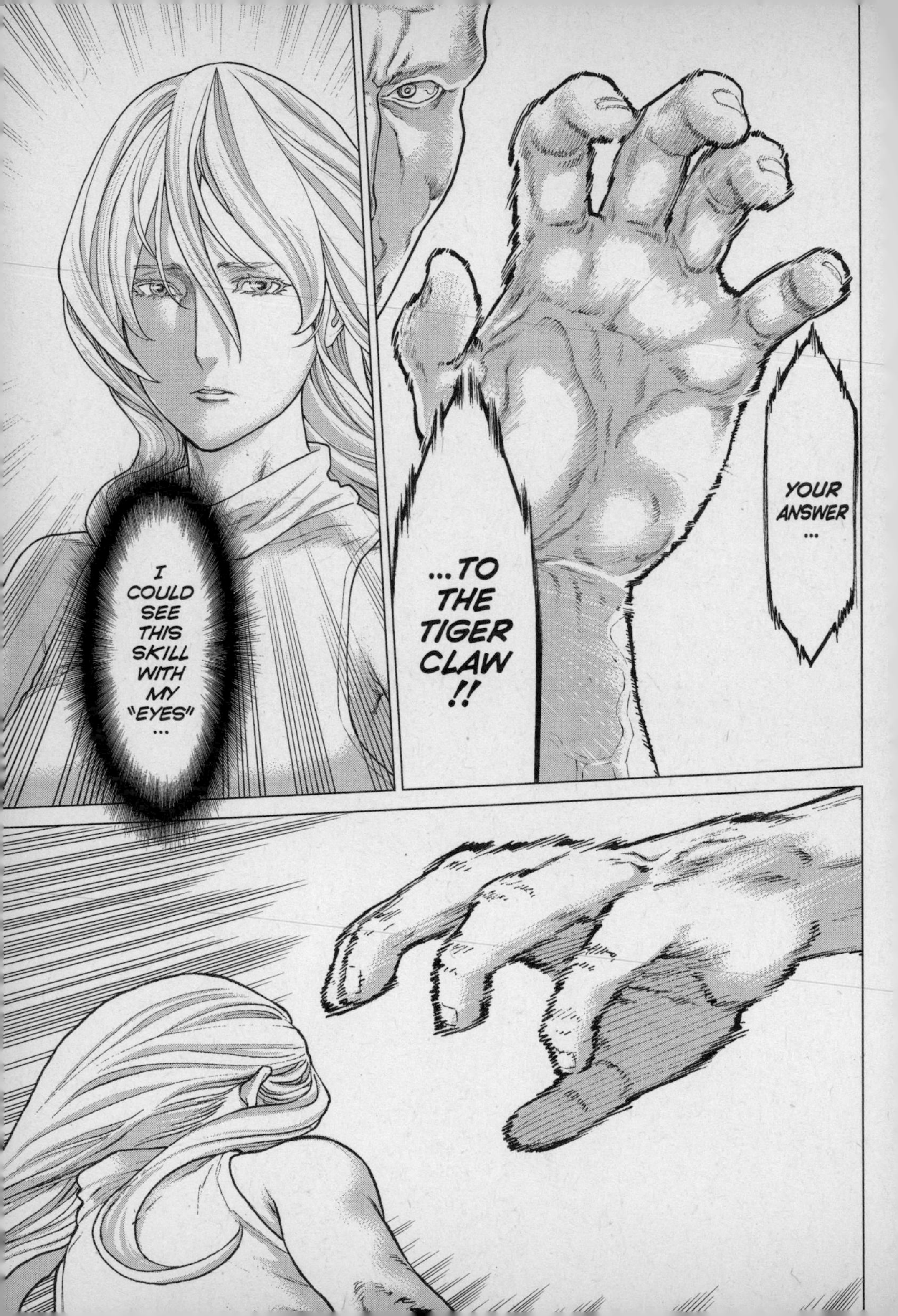
YOUR ANSWER...
...TO THE TIGER CLAW!!
I COULD SEE THIS SKILL WITH MY "EYES"...

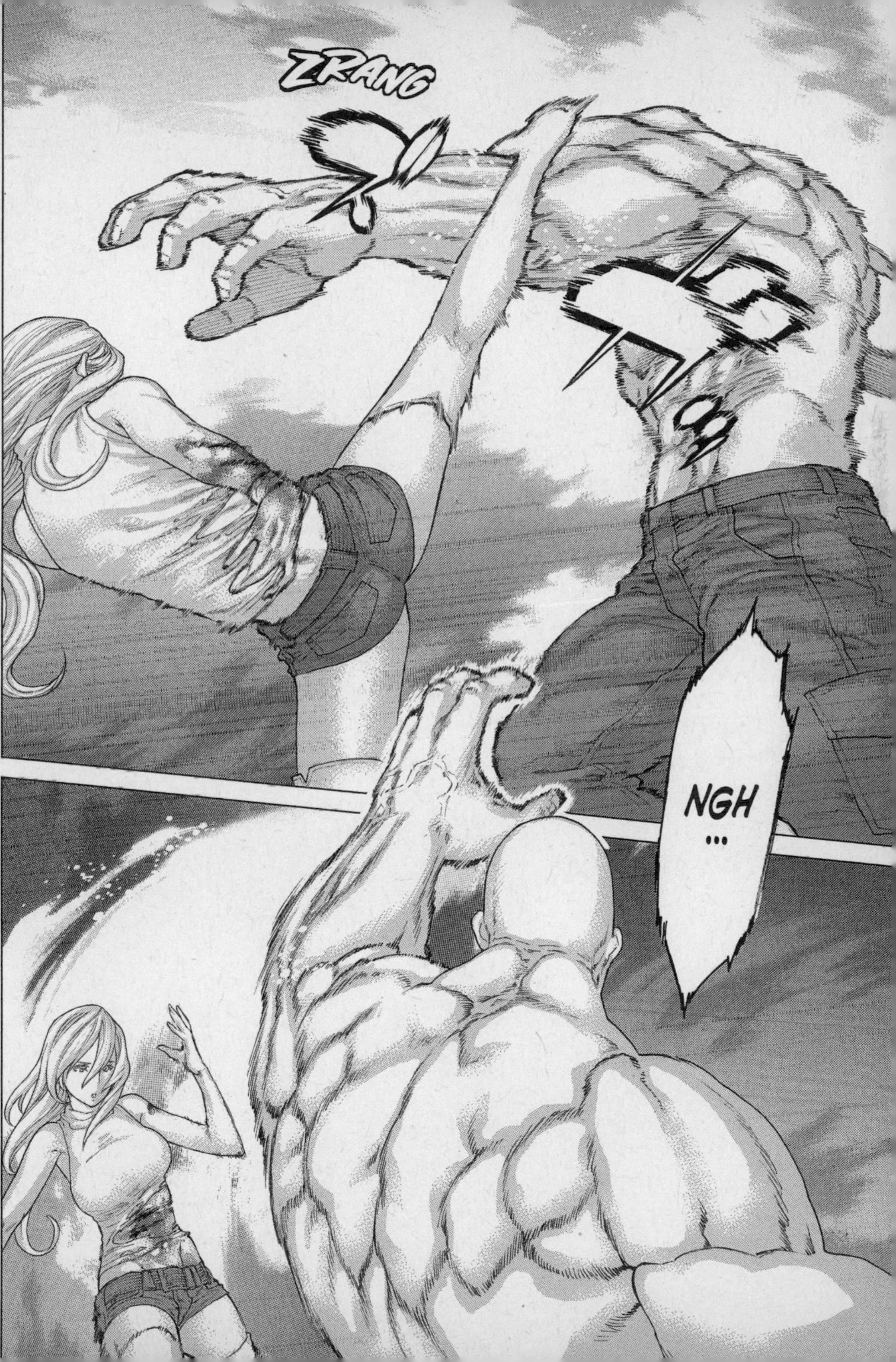
ZRANG
NGH
...

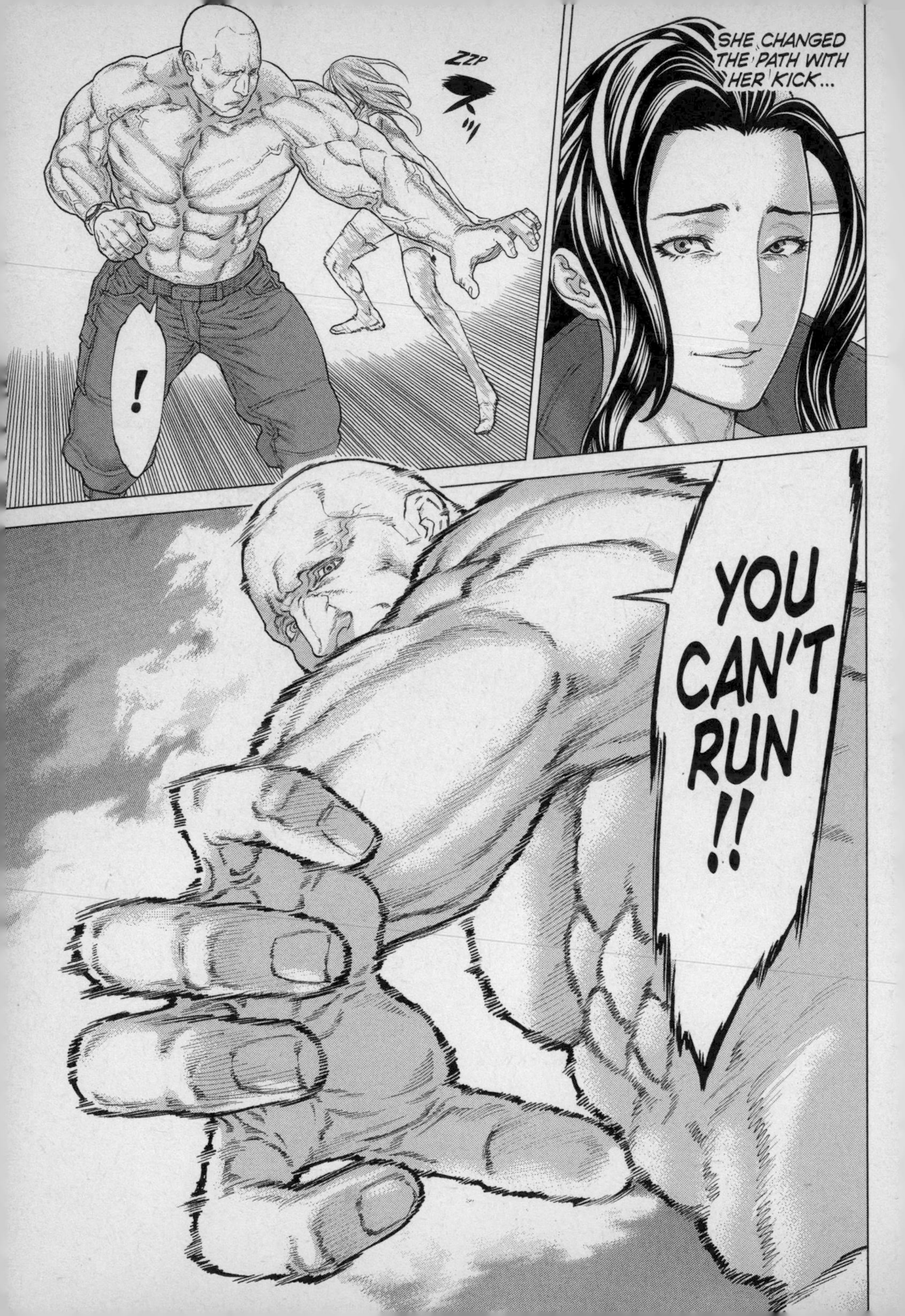
SHE CHANGED THE PATH WITH HER KICK...
ZZP
!
YOU CAN'T RUN!!

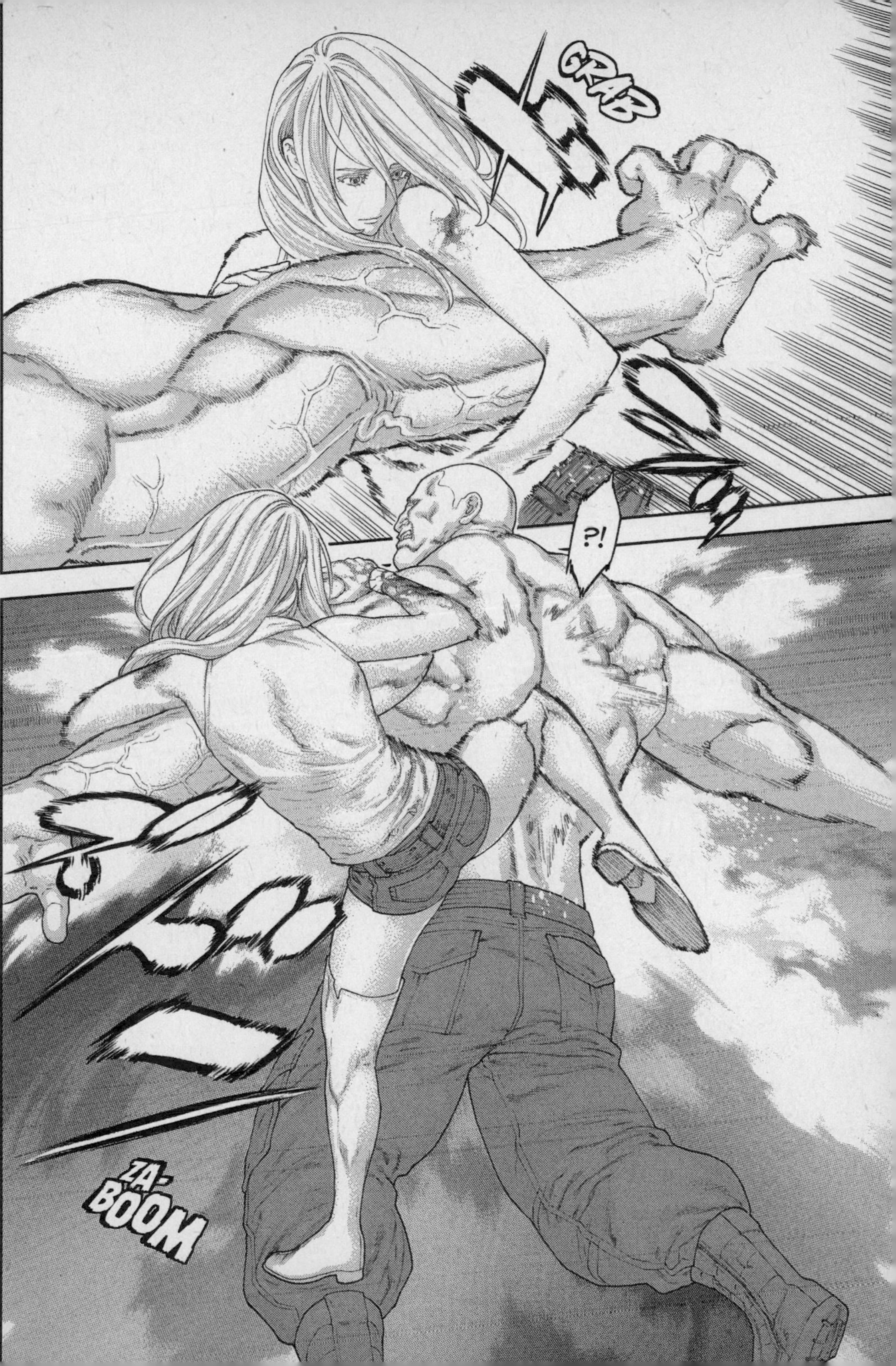
GRAB
?!
ZA-
BOOM

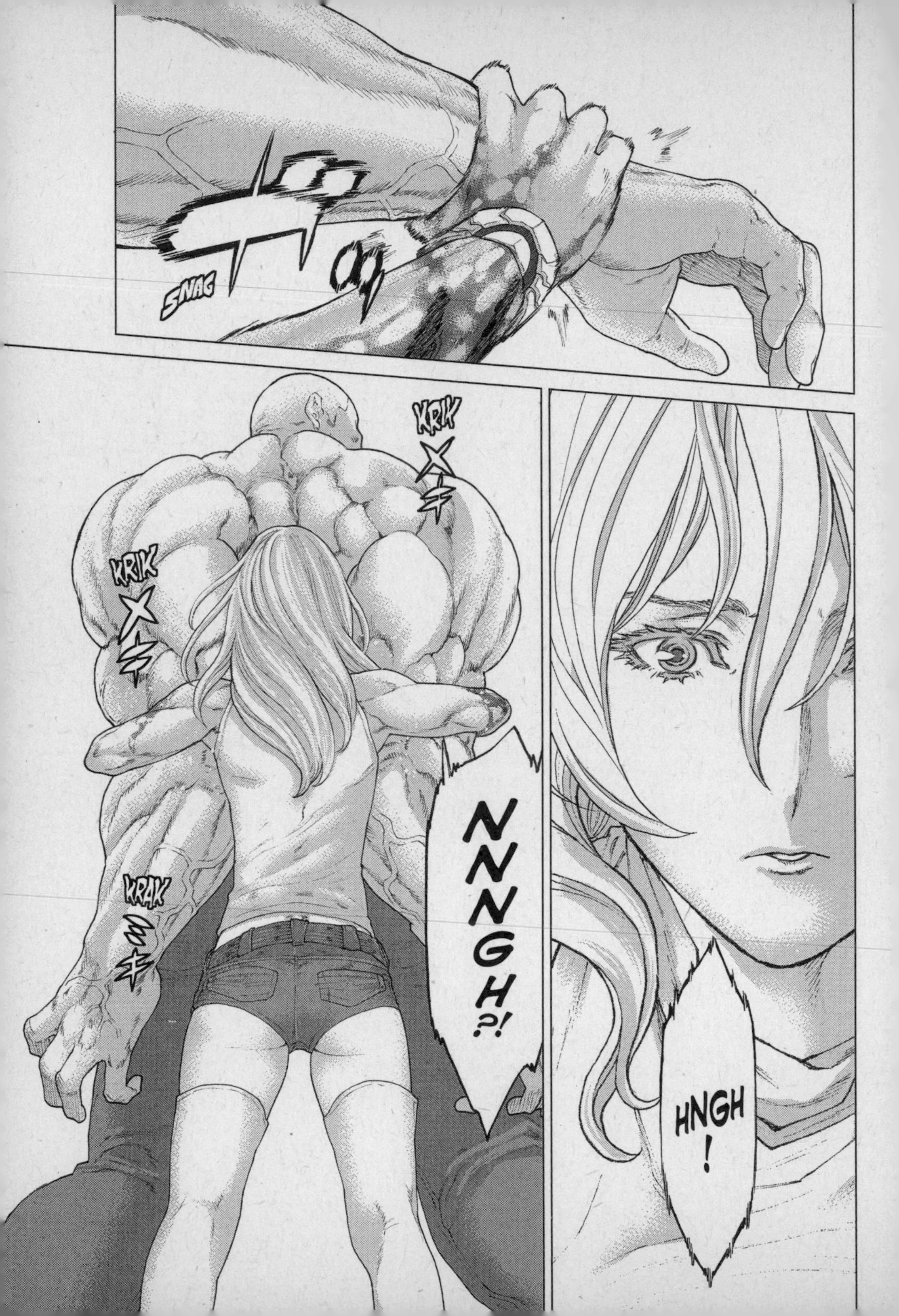
SNAG
HNGH!
KRIK
KRIK
NNNGH?!
KRAK

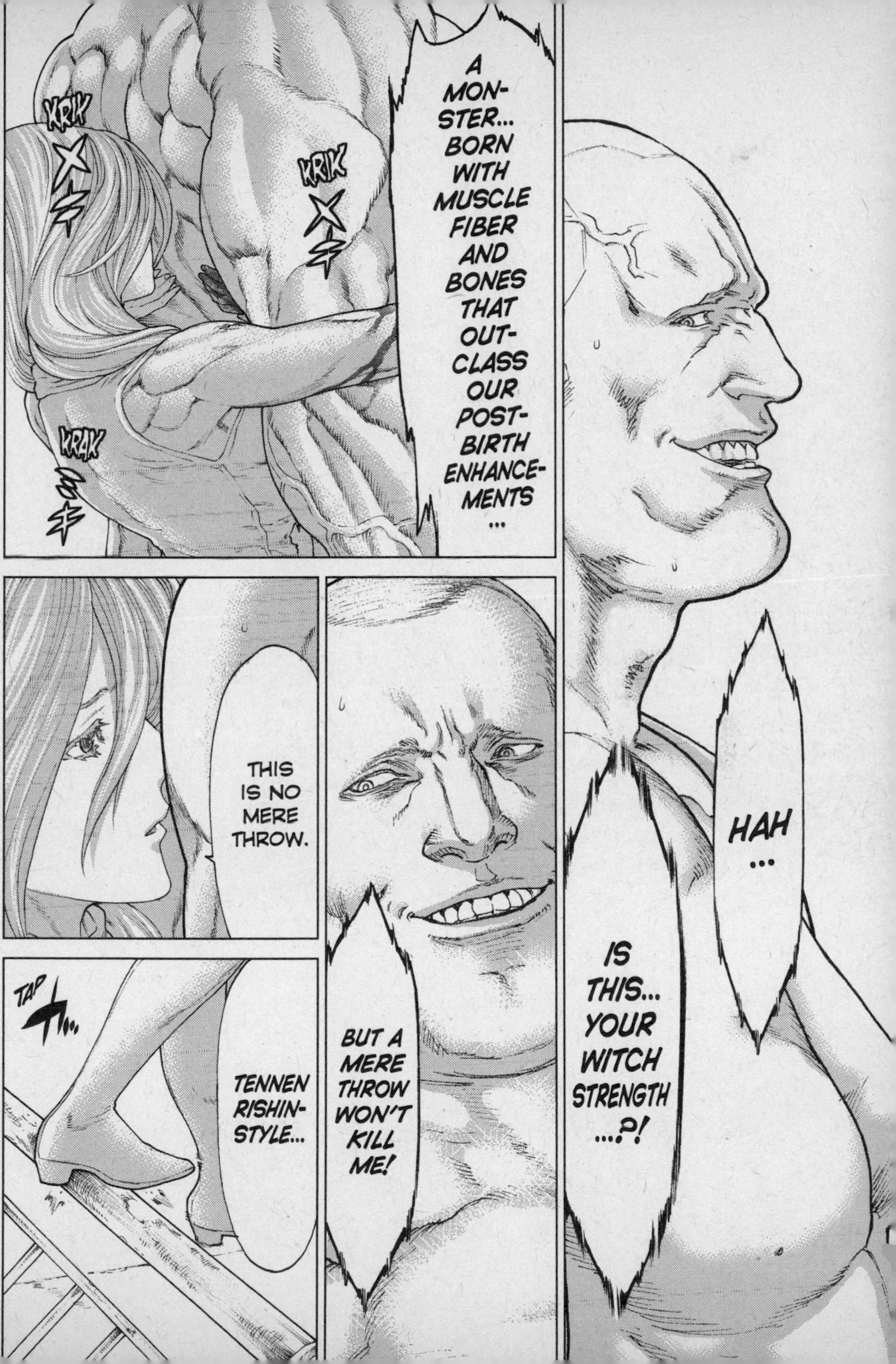
HAH...
IS THIS... YOUR WITCH STRENGTH...?!
A MONSTER... BORN WITH MUSCLE FIBER AND BONES THAT OUTCLASS OUR POST-BIRTH ENHANCEMENTS...
KRIK
KRIK
KRAK
BUT A MERE THROW WON'T KILL ME!
THIS IS NO MERE THROW.
TAP
TENNEN RISHIN-STYLE...

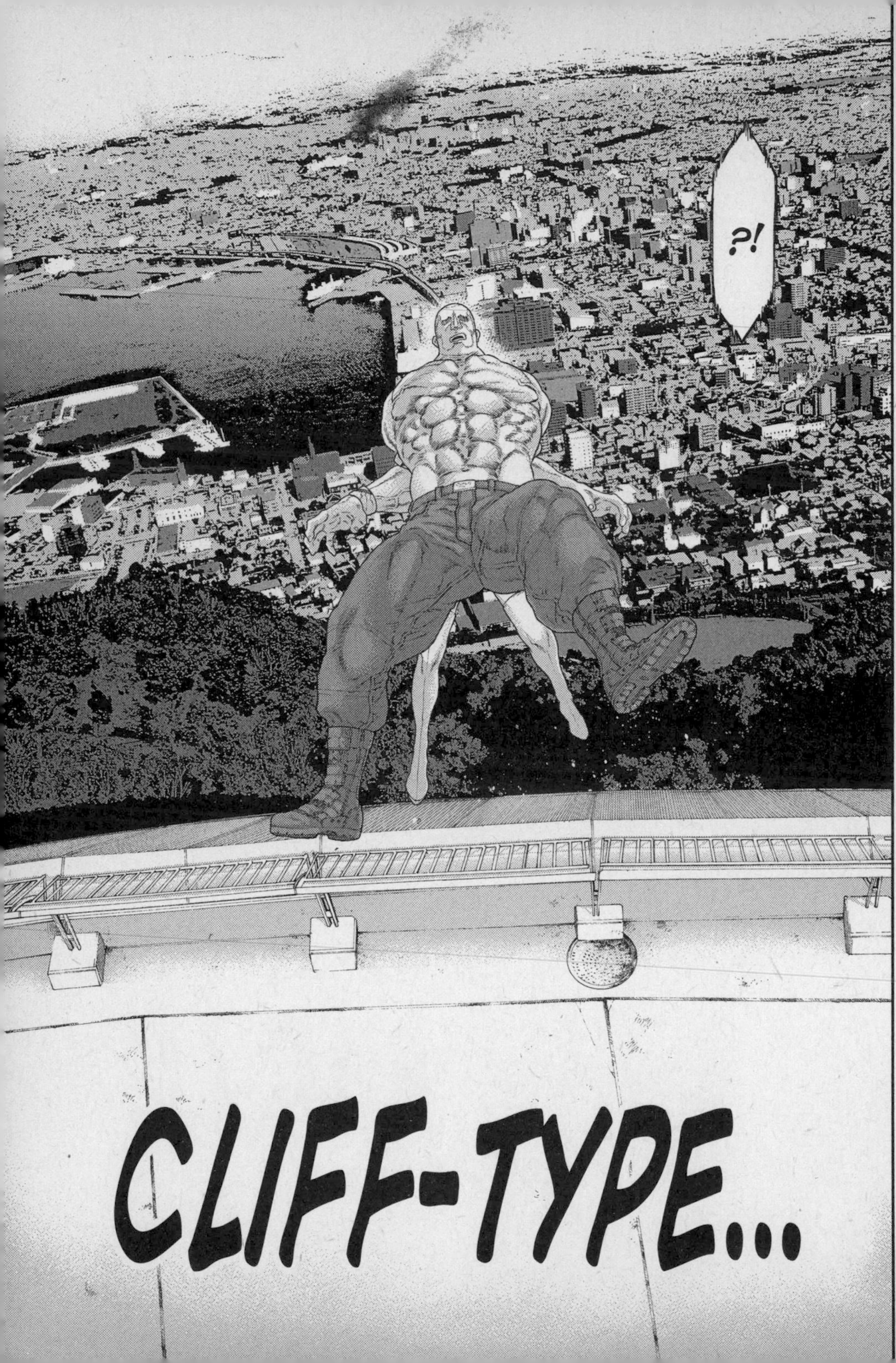
?!
CLIFF-TYPE...

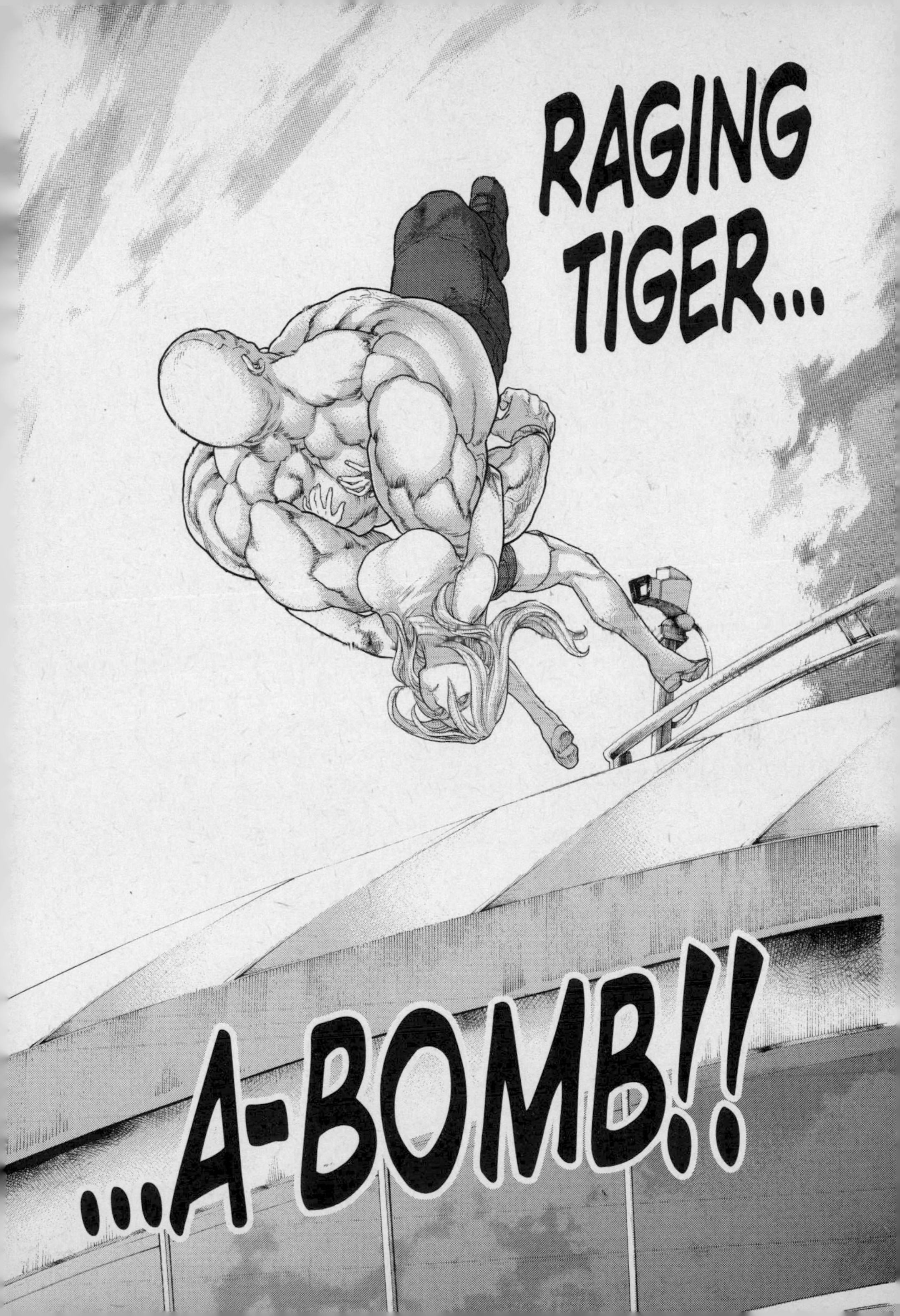
RAGING TIGER...
...A-BOMB!!

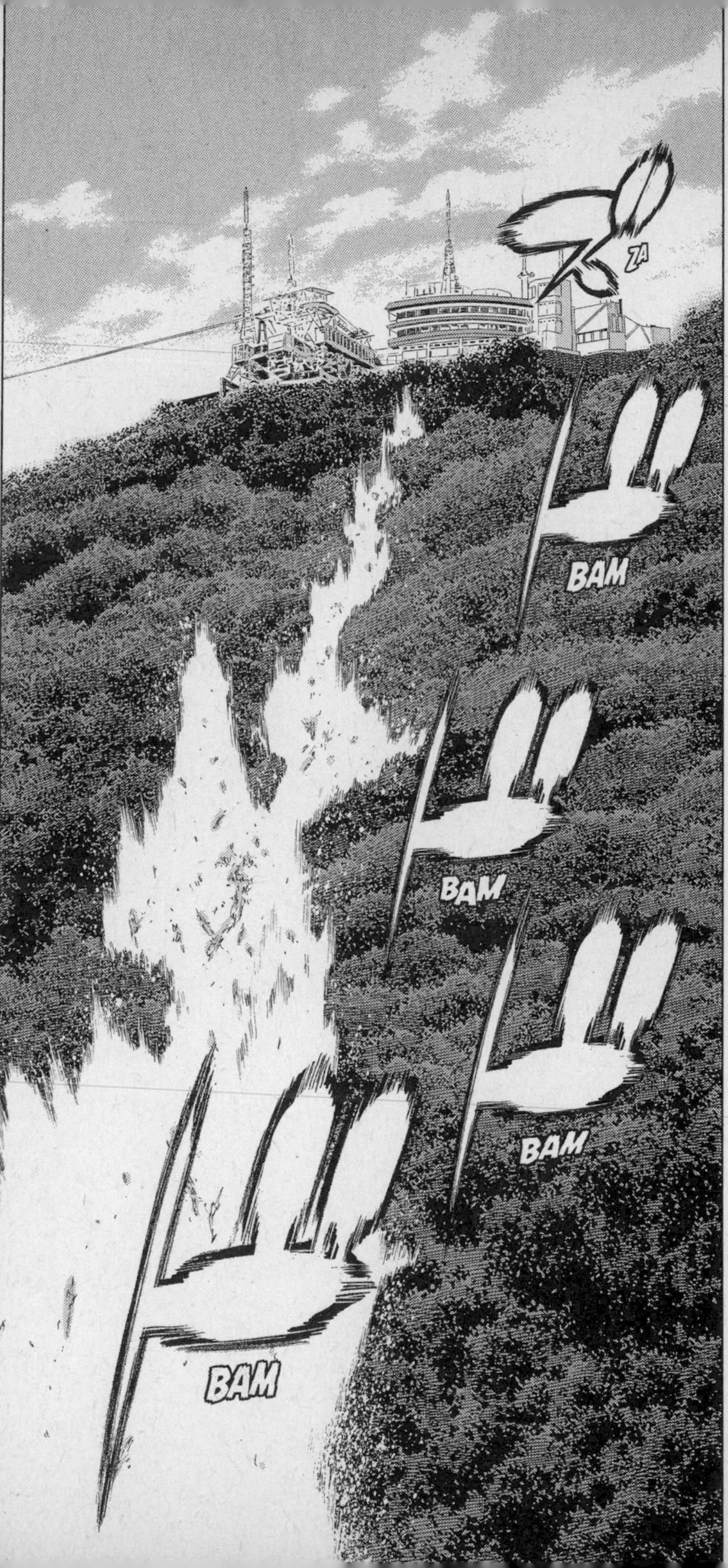
ZA
BAM
BAM
BAM
BAM
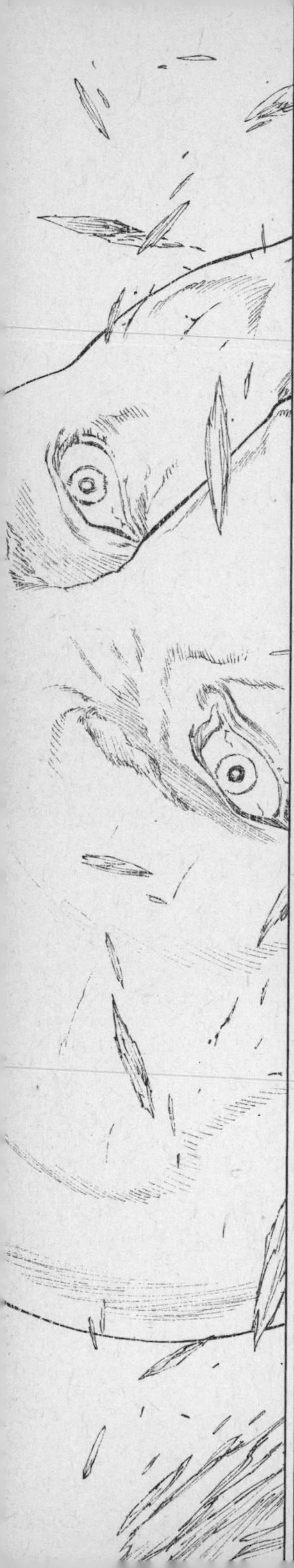

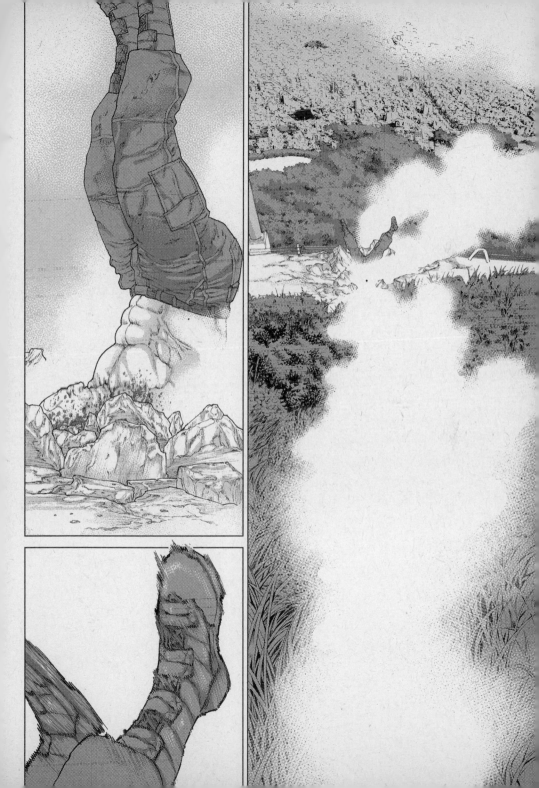

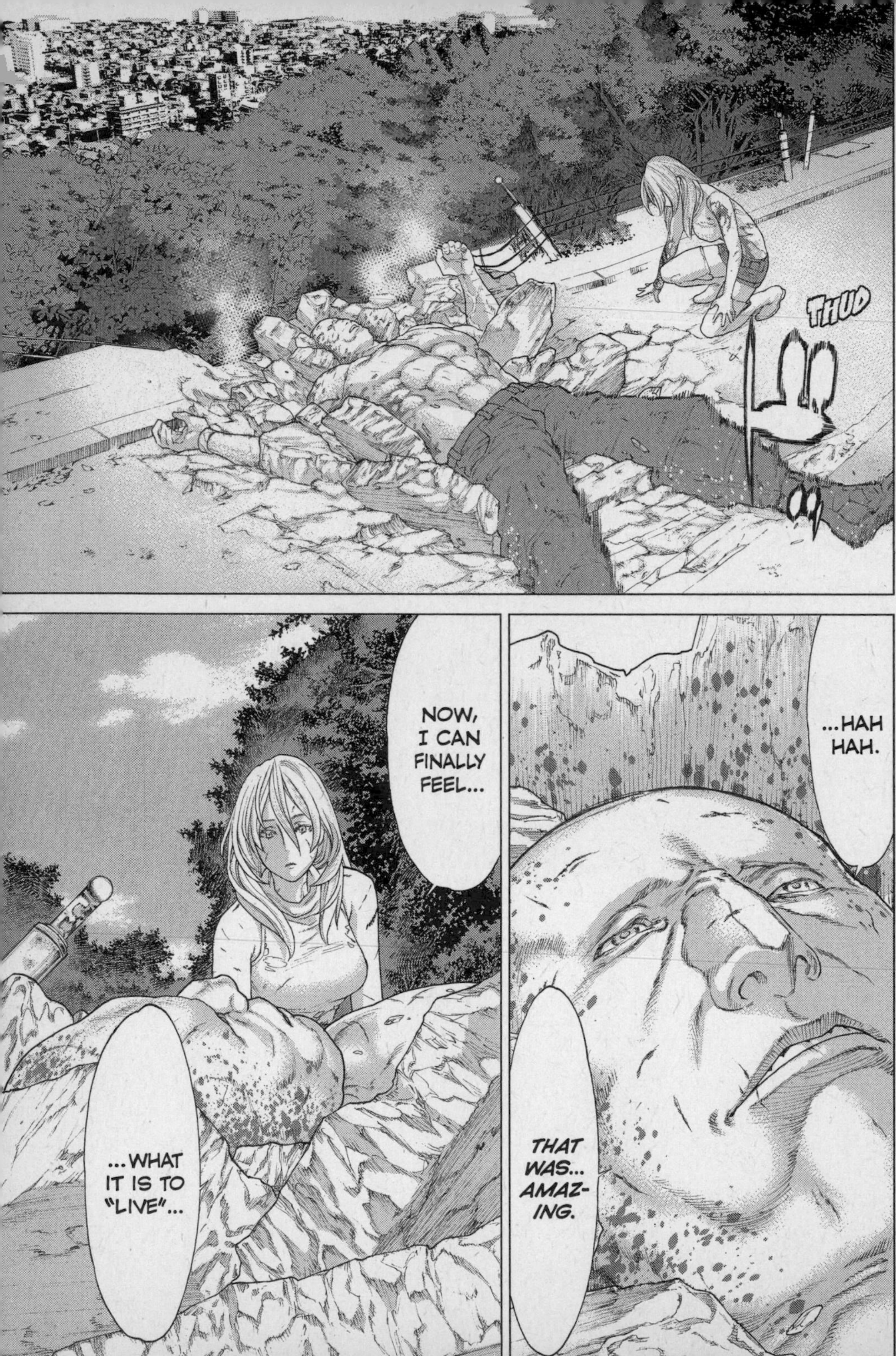
THUD
...HAH HAH.
THAT WAS... AMAZ-ING.
NOW, I CAN FINALLY FEEL...
...WHAT IT IS TO "LIVE"...

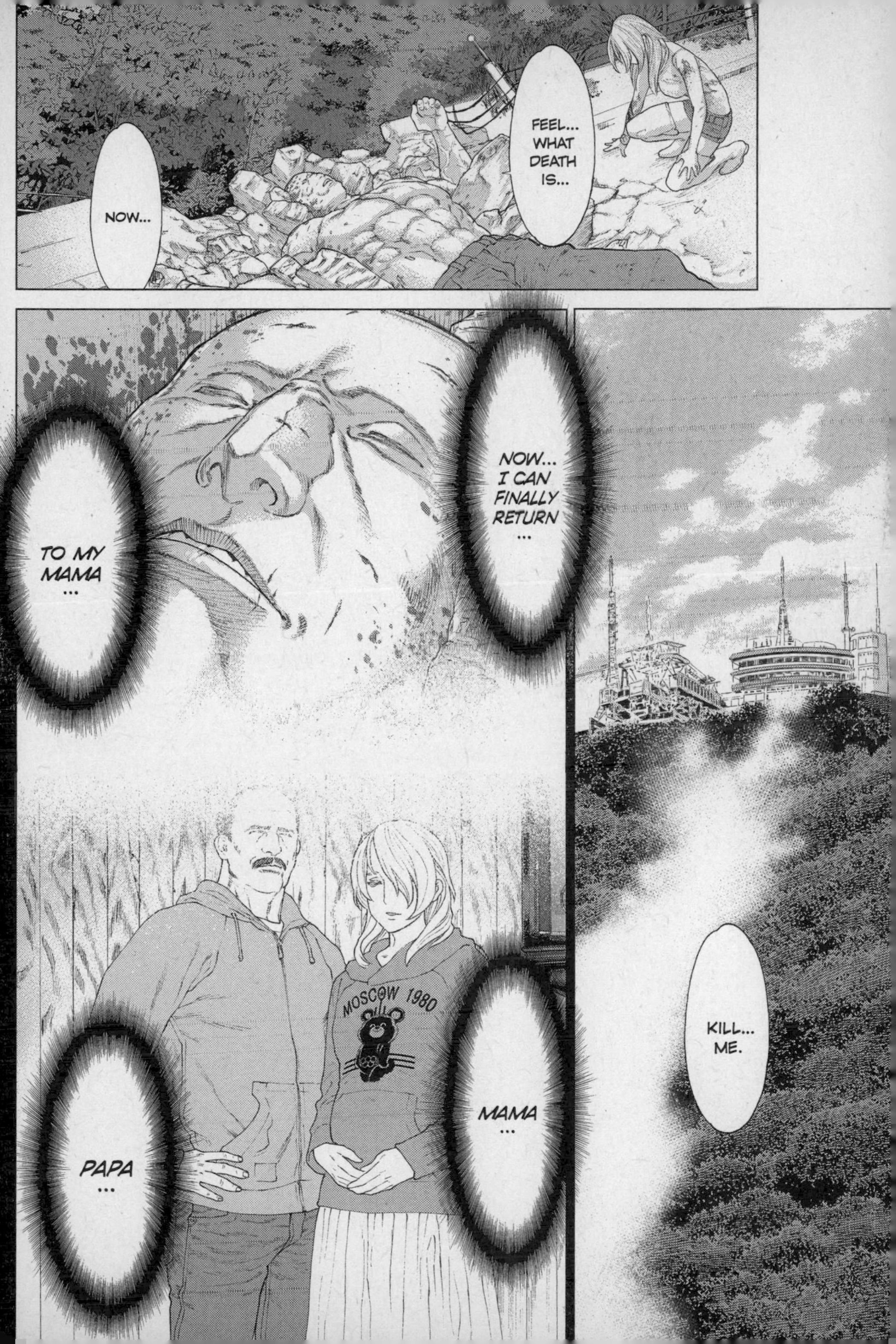
FEEL... WHAT DEATH IS...
NOW...
KILL... ME.
NOW... I CAN FINALLY RETURN ...
TO MY MAMA ...
MAMA ...
PAPA ...
MOSCOW 1980

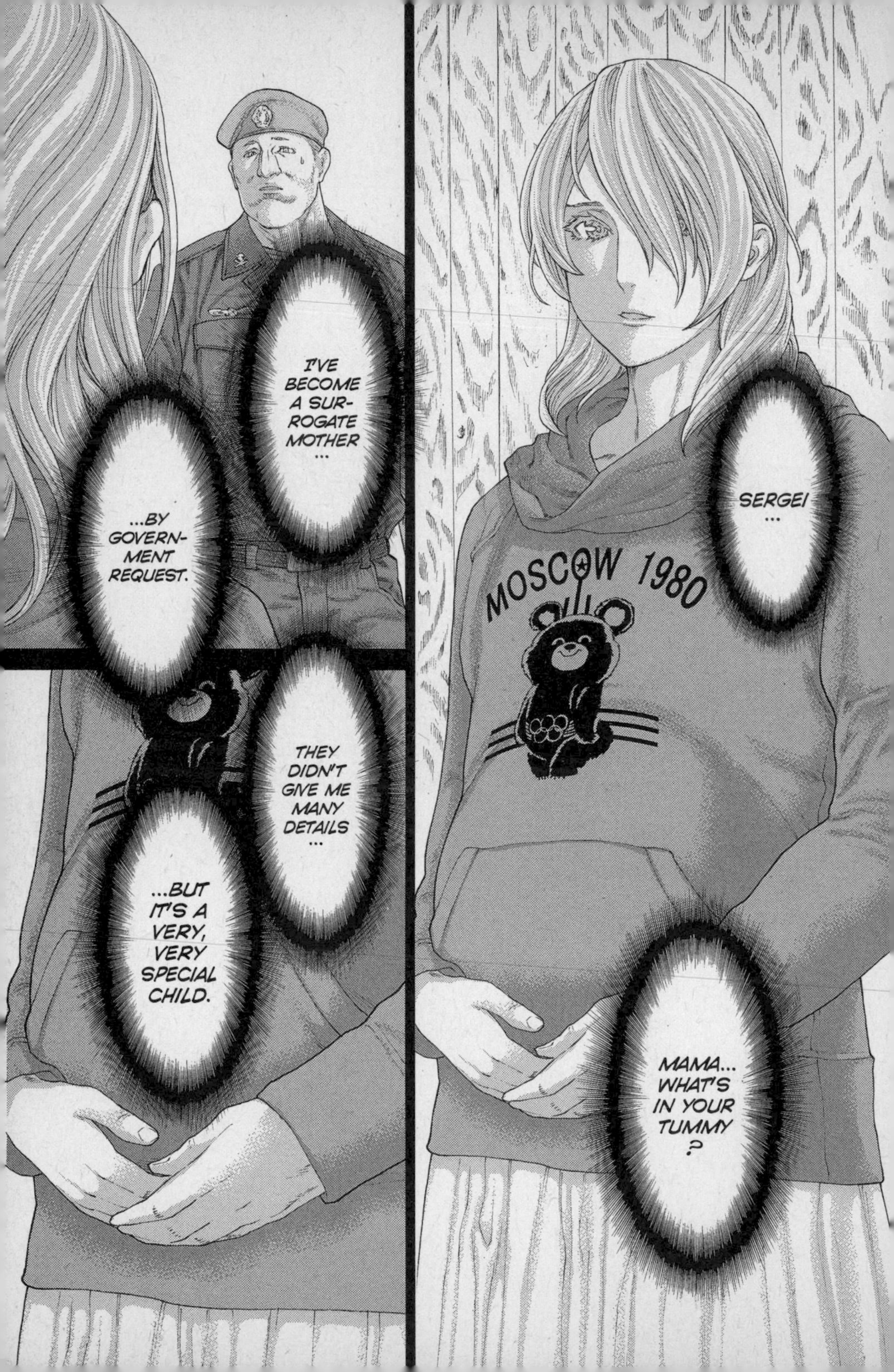
SERGEI...
MOSCOW 1980
MAMA... WHAT'S IN YOUR TUMMY?
I'VE BECOME A SUR-ROGATE MOTHER...
...BY GOVERN-MENT REQUEST.
THEY DIDN'T GIVE ME MANY DETAILS...
...BUT IT'S A VERY, VERY SPECIAL CHILD.

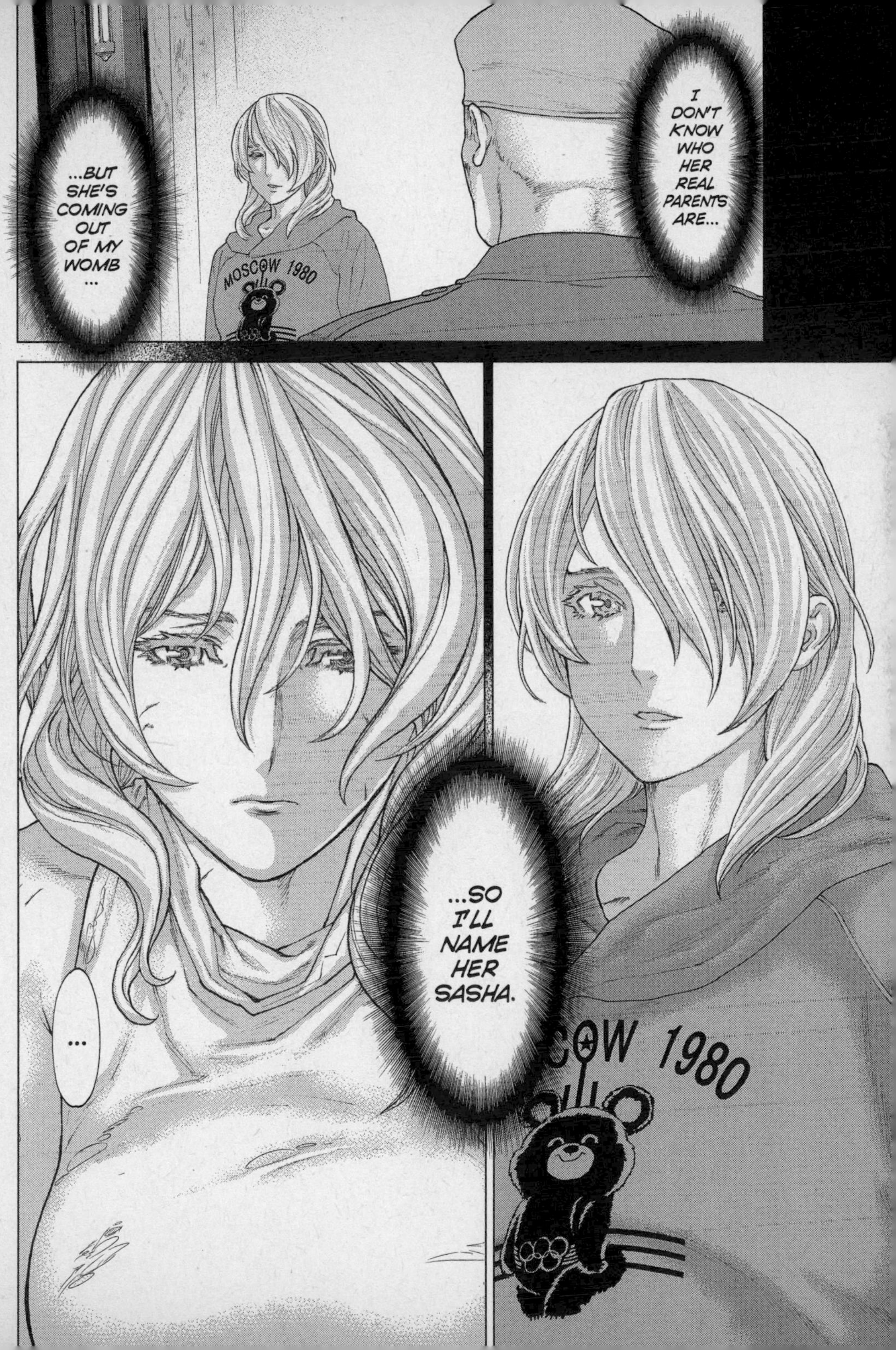
I DON'T KNOW WHO HER REAL PARENTS ARE...
...BUT SHE'S COMING OUT OF MY WOMB ...
MOSCOW 1980
...SO I'LL NAME HER SASHA.
COW 1980
...

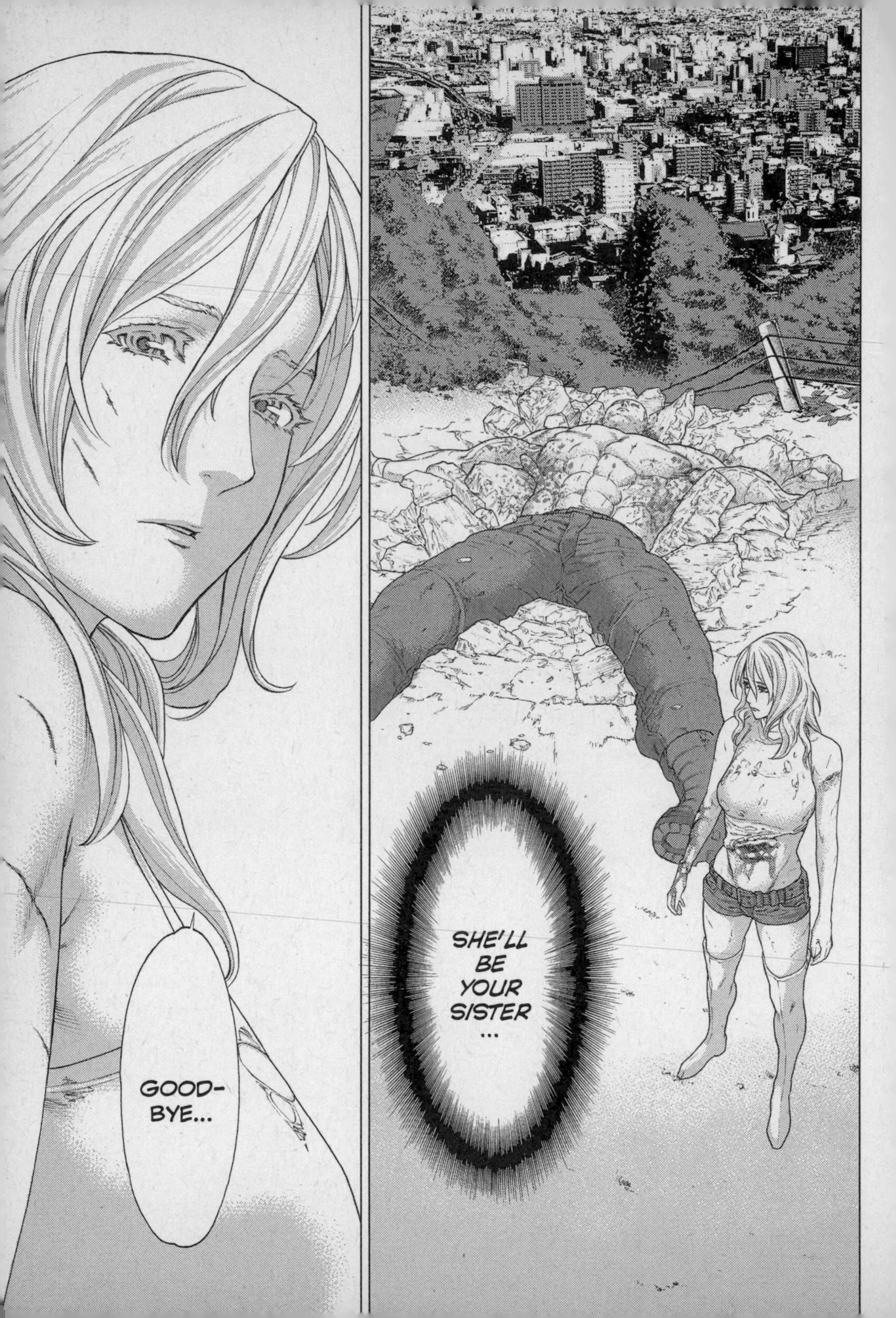
SHE'LL BE YOUR SISTER ...
GOOD-BYE...

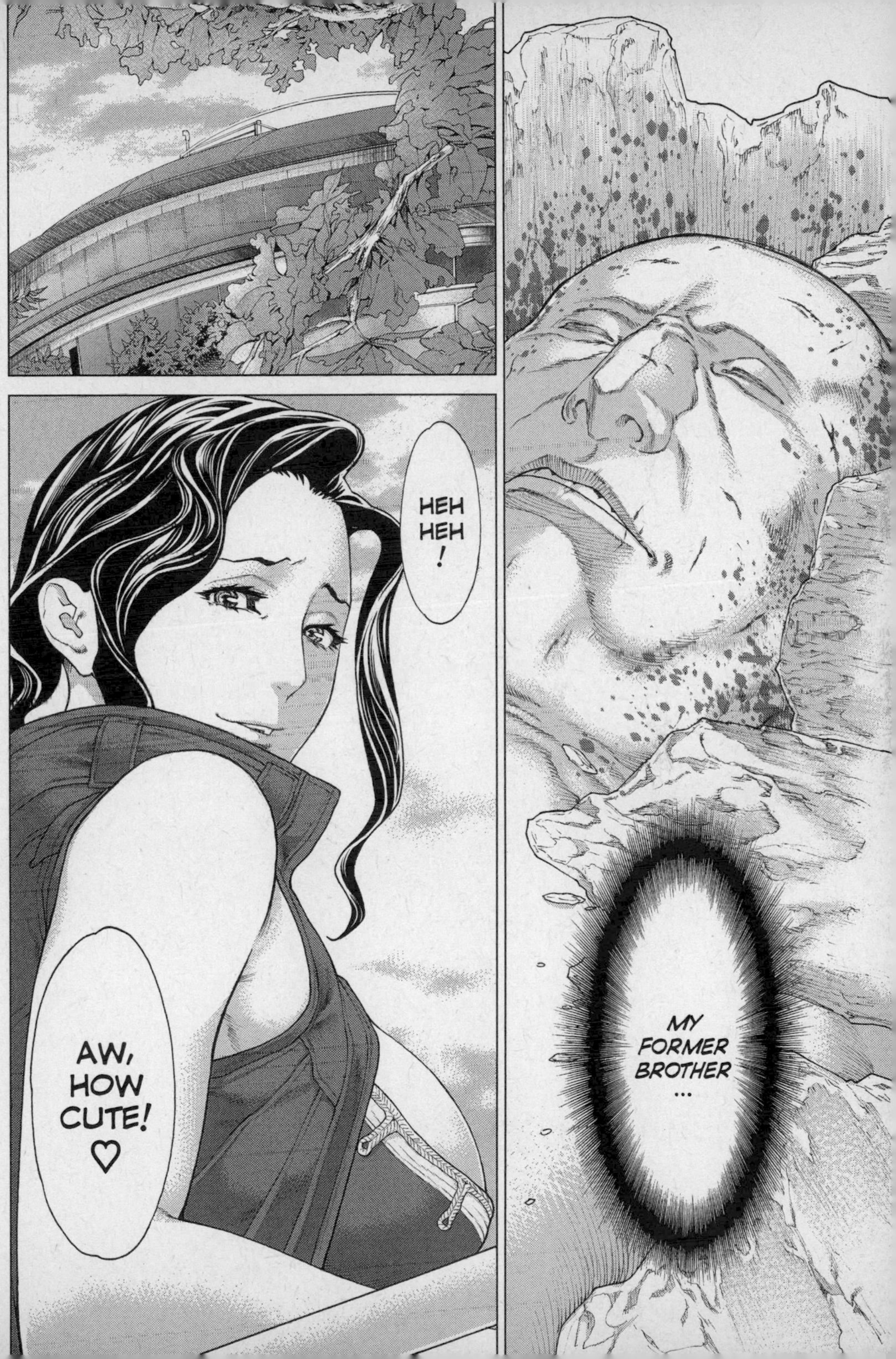
MY FORMER BROTHER ...
HEH HEH!
AW, HOW CUTE! ♡

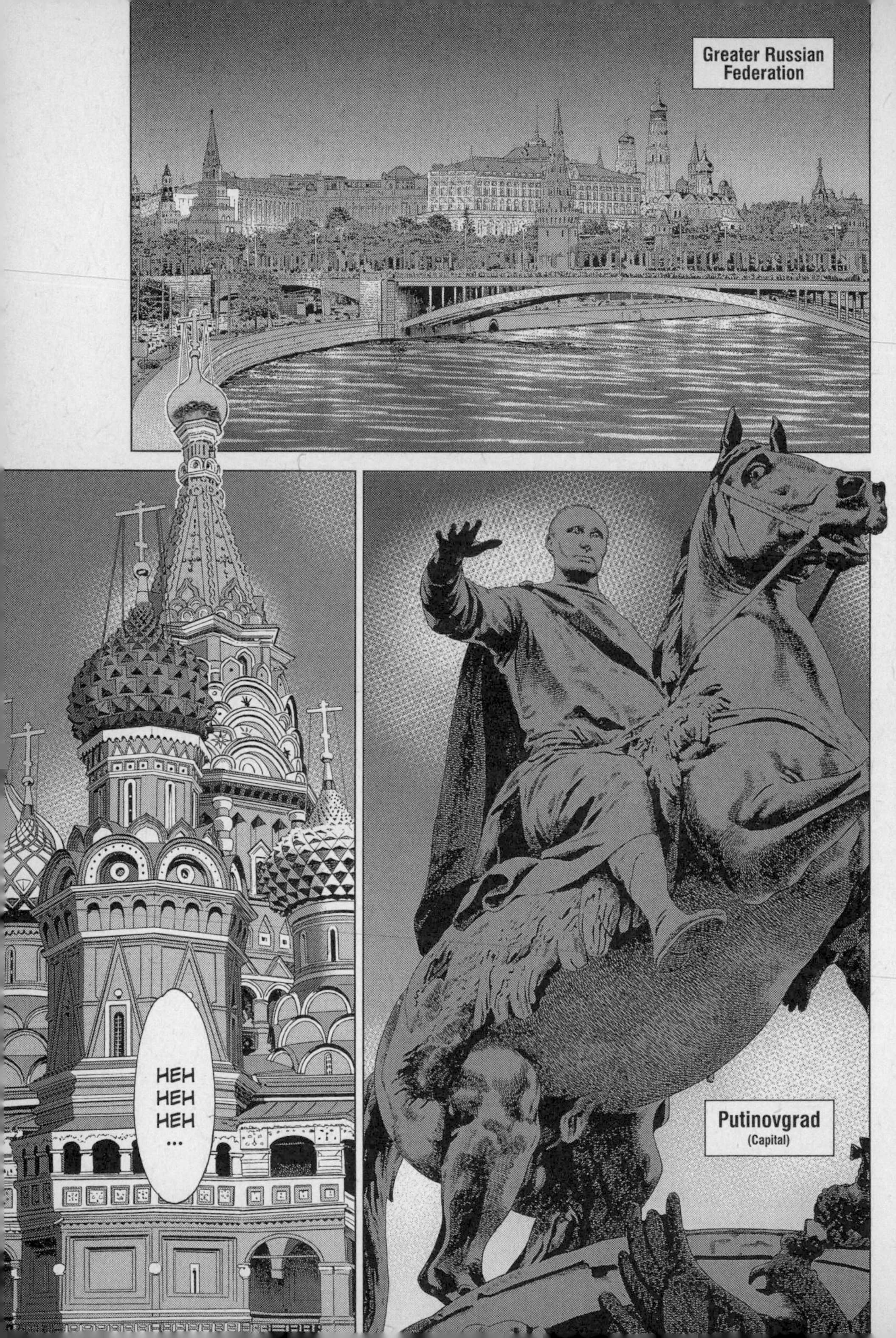
Greater Russian Federation
Putinovgrad (Capital)
HEH HEH HEH ...

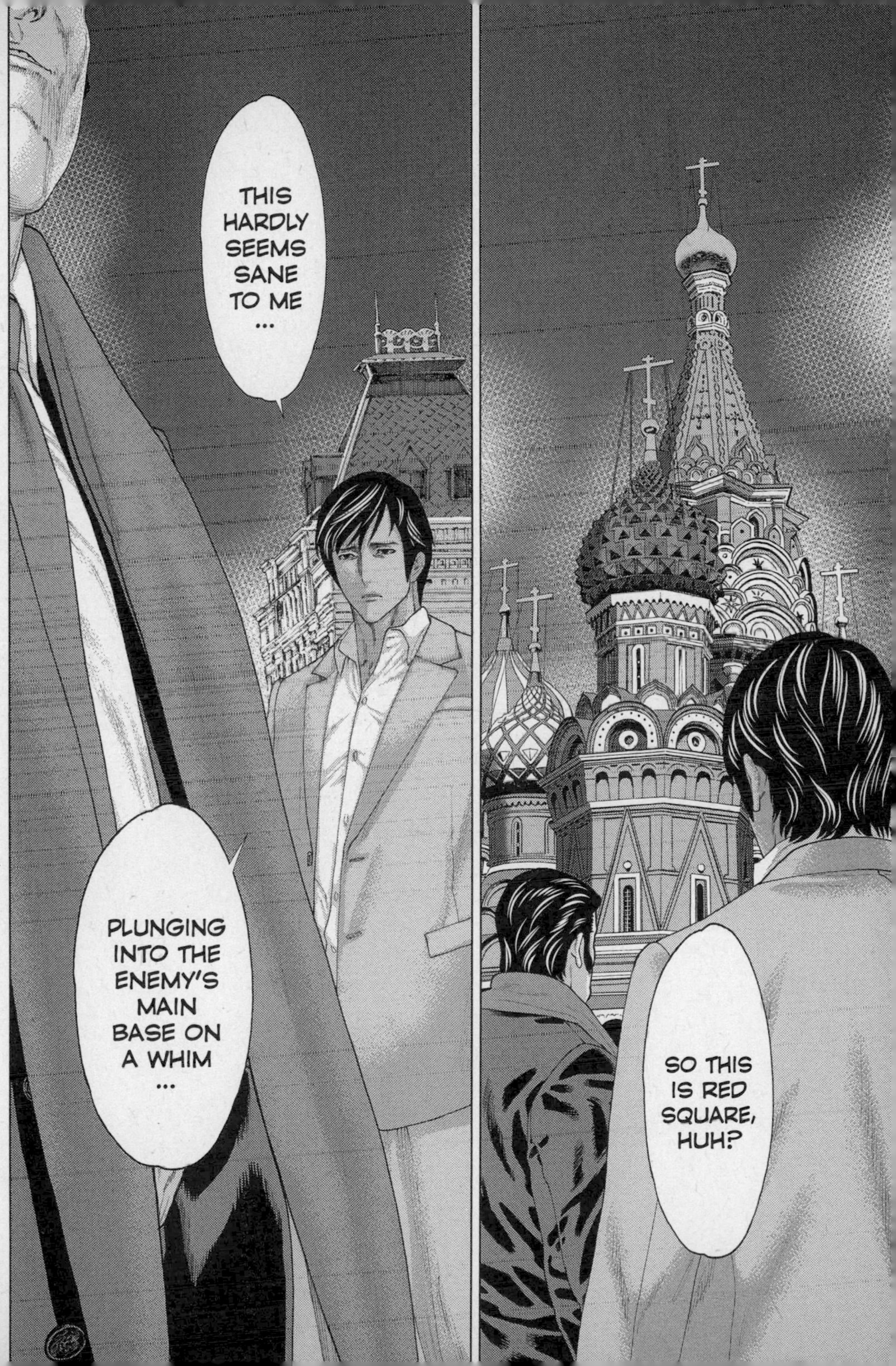
SO THIS IS RED SQUARE, HUH?
THIS HARDLY SEEMS SANE TO ME ...
PLUNGING INTO THE ENEMY'S MAIN BASE ON A WHIM ...

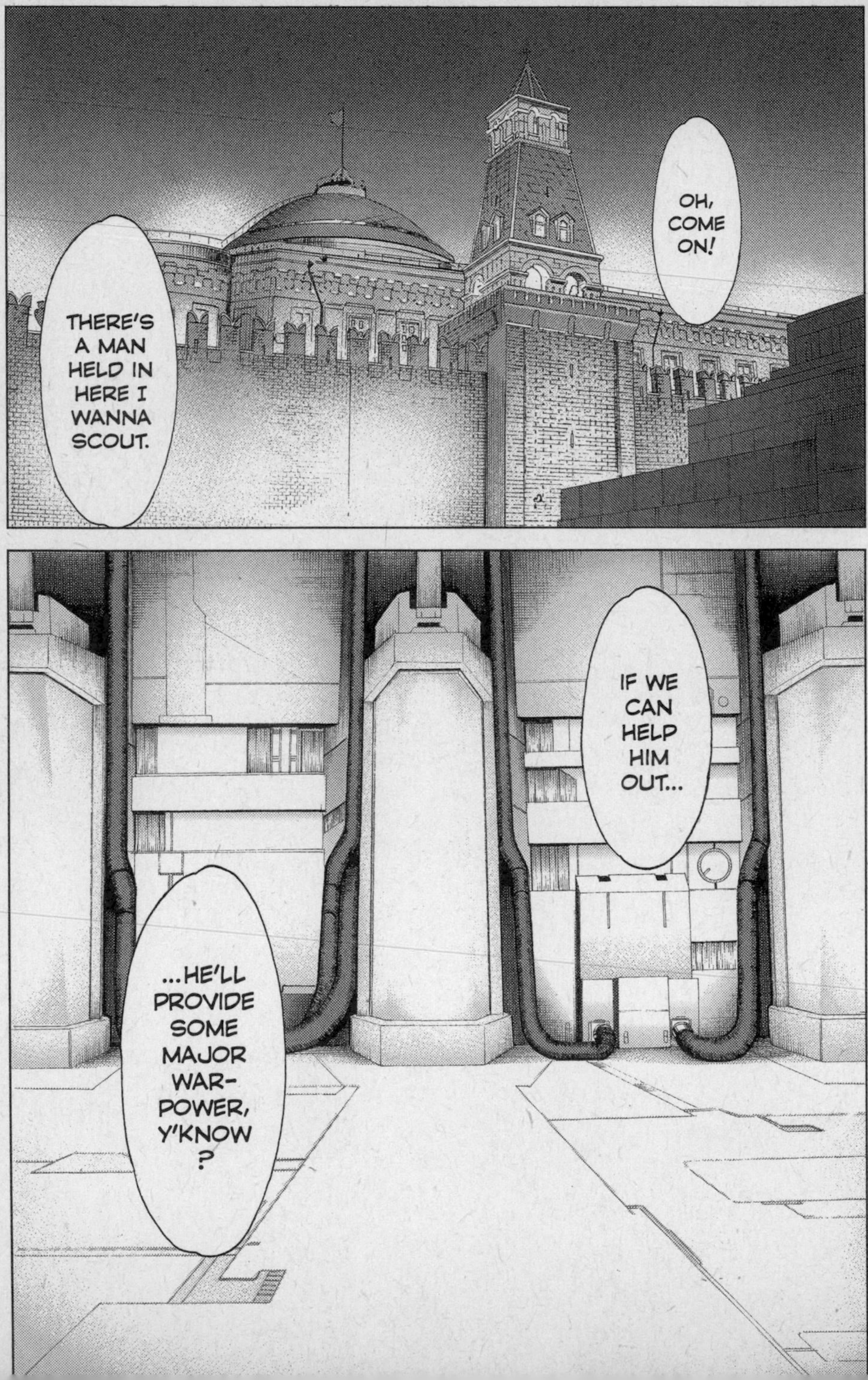
OH, COME ON!
THERE'S A MAN HELD IN HERE I WANNA SCOUT.
IF WE CAN HELP HIM OUT...
...HE'LL PROVIDE SOME MAJOR WAR-POWER, Y'KNOW?

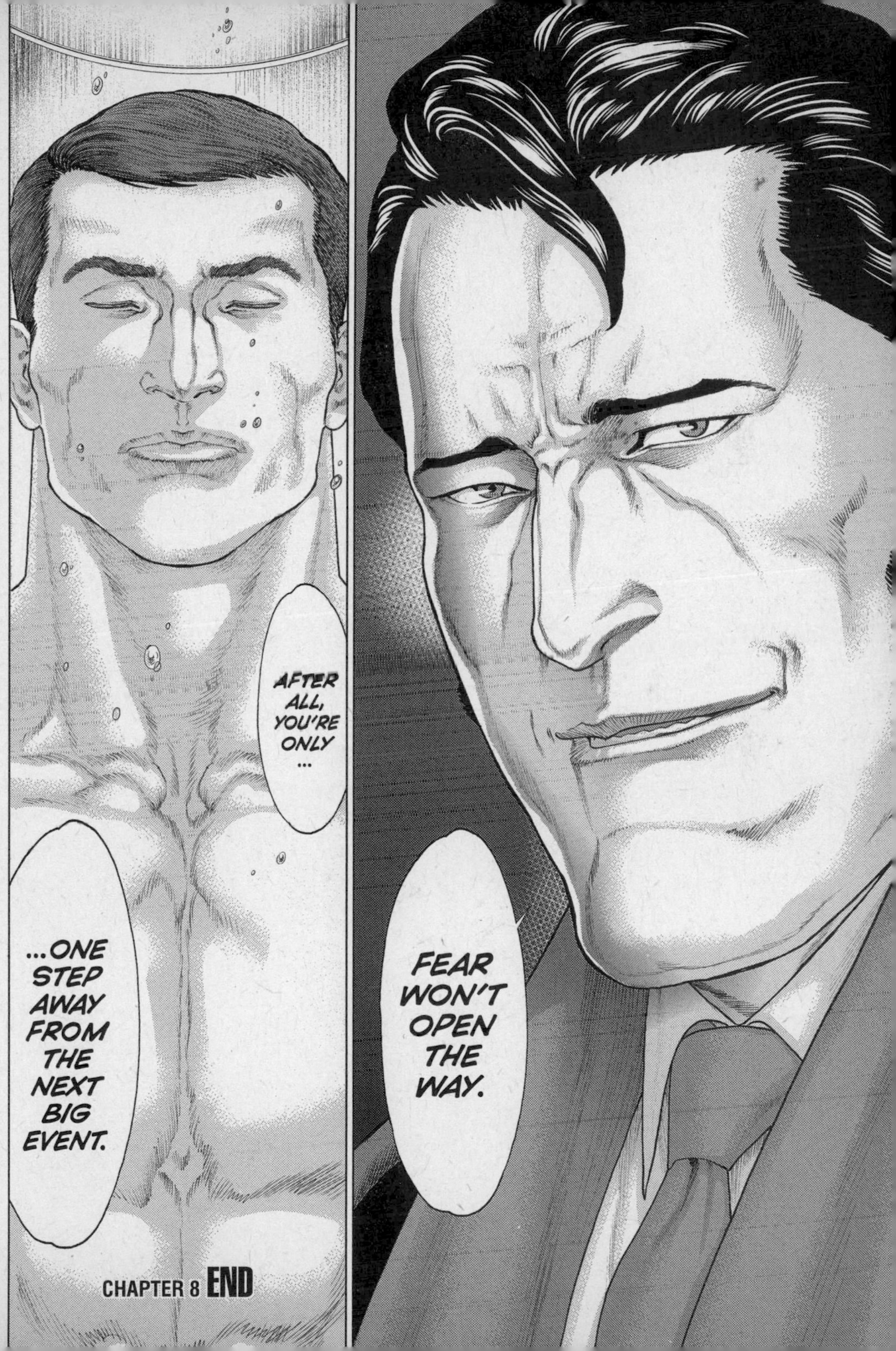
FEAR WON'T OPEN THE WAY.
AFTER ALL, YOU'RE ONLY ...
...ONE STEP AWAY FROM THE NEXT BIG EVENT.
CHAPTER 8 END

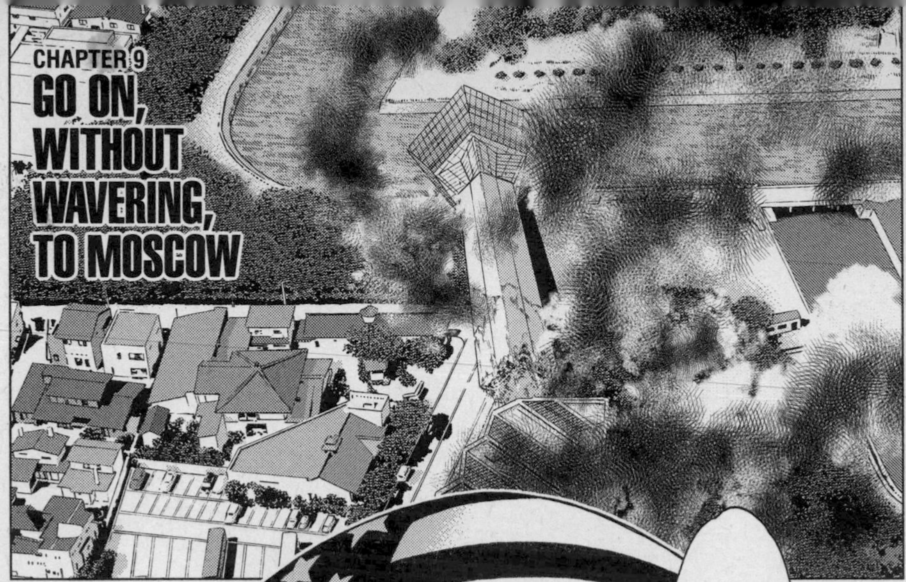
CHAPTER 9
GO ON, WITHOUT WAVERING, TO MOSCOW

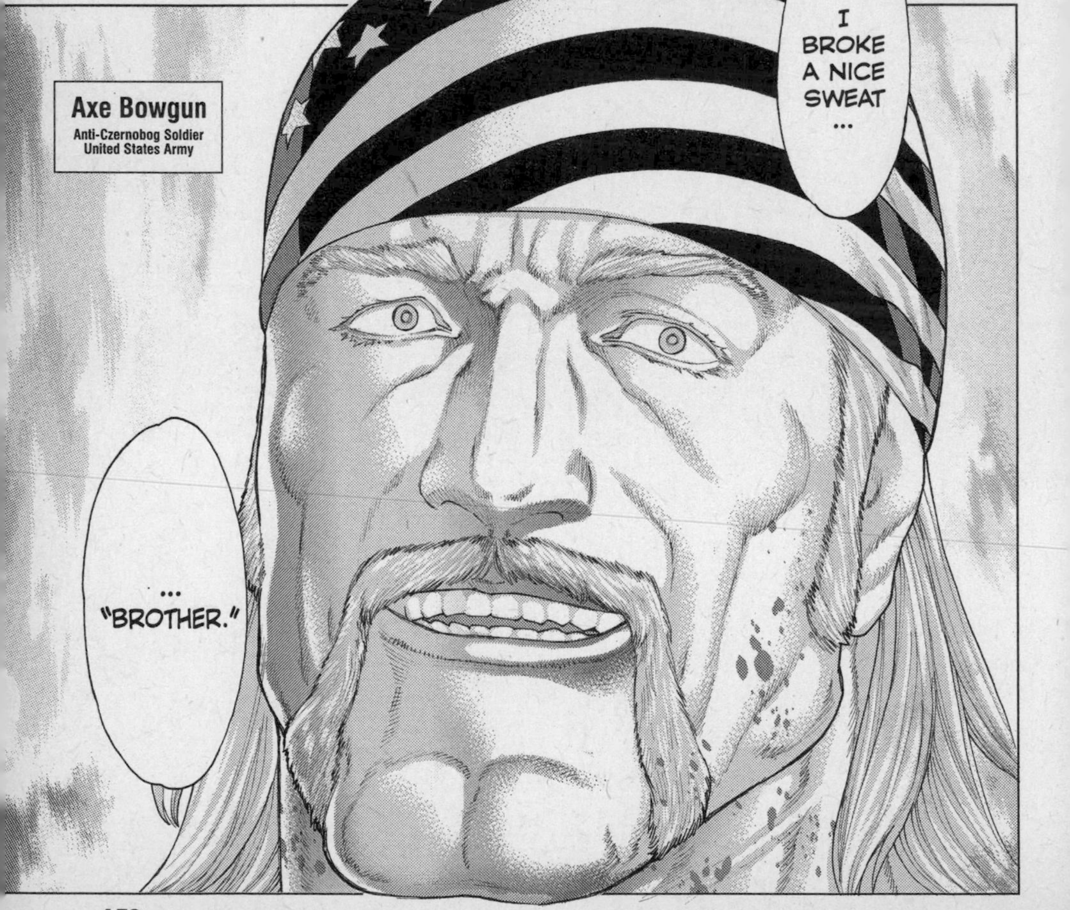
I BROKE A NICE SWEAT ...
Axe Bowgun
Anti-Czernobog Soldier
United States Army
... "BROTHER."

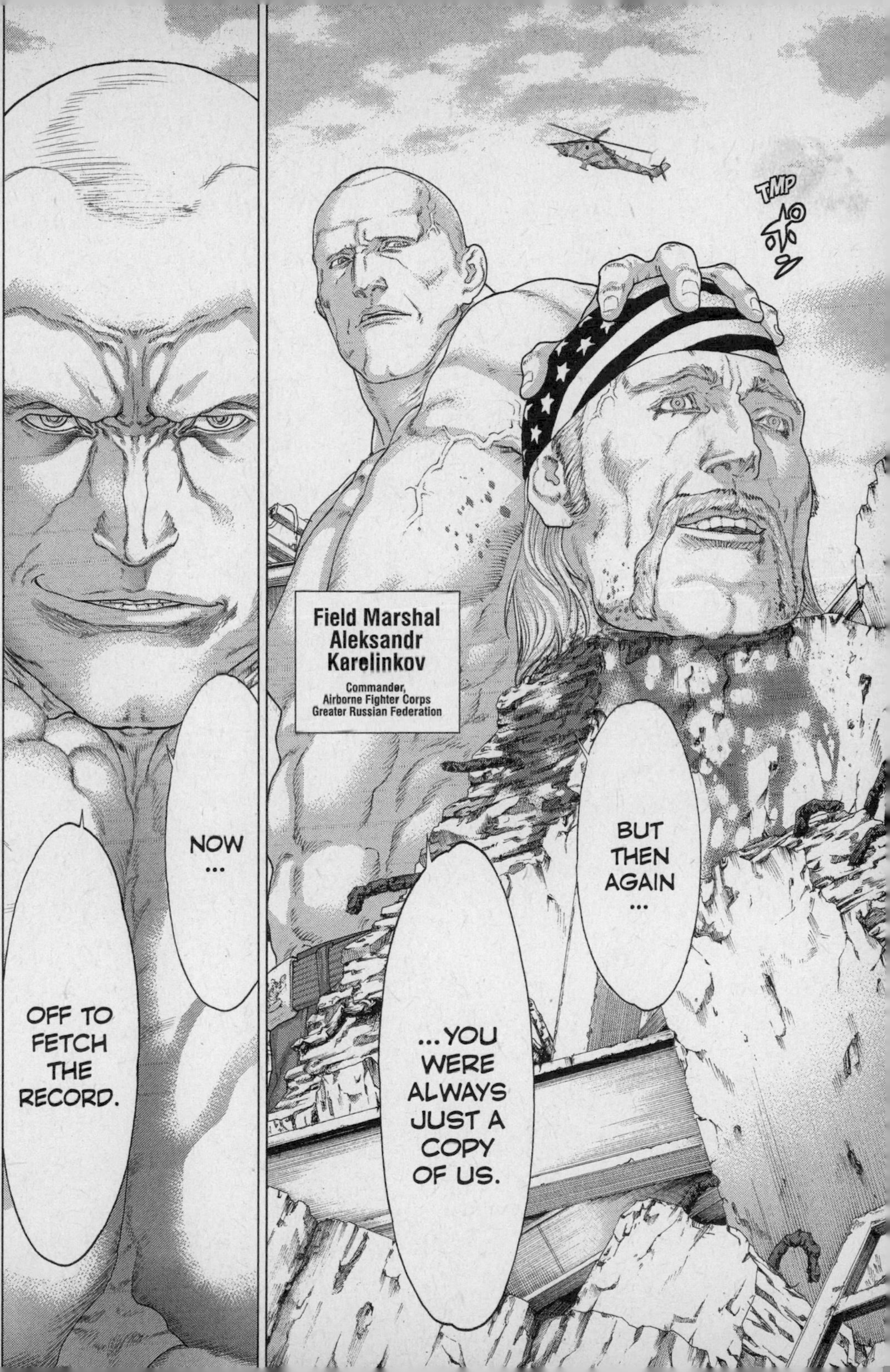
TMP
Field Marshal Aleksandr Karelinkov
Commander, Airborne Fighter Corps Greater Russian Federation
BUT THEN AGAIN ...
...YOU WERE ALWAYS JUST A COPY OF US.
NOW ...
OFF TO FETCH THE RECORD.

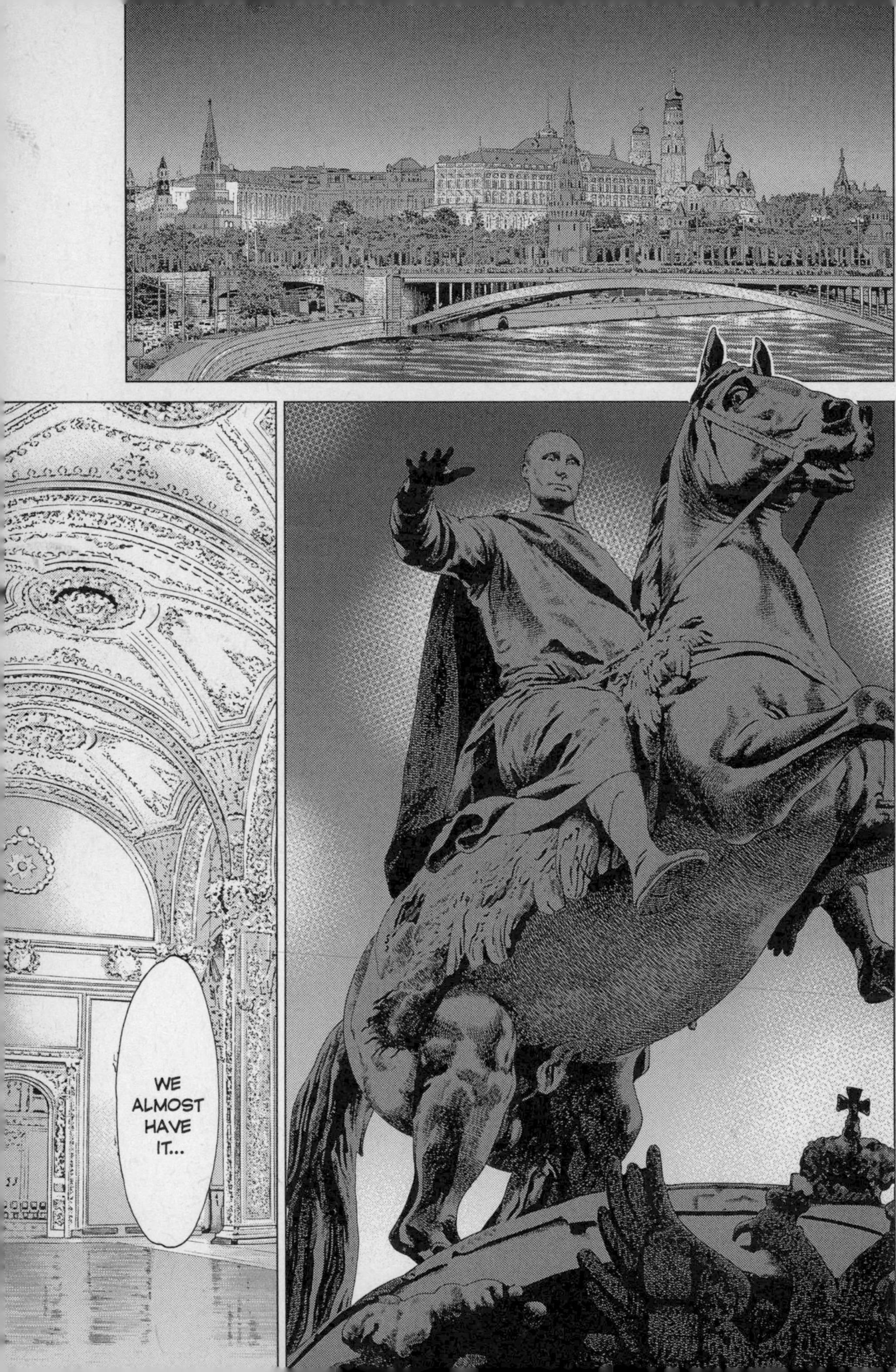
WE ALMOST HAVE IT...

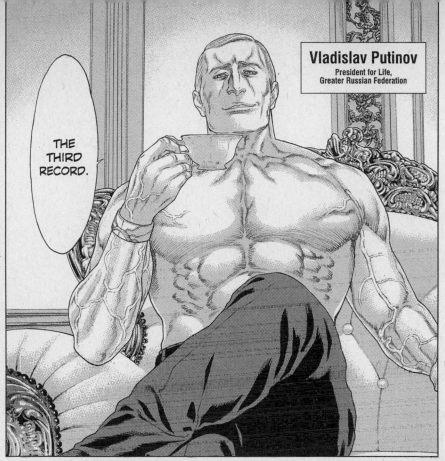

Vladislav Putinov
President for Life,
Greater Russian Federation
THE THIRD RECORD.
THE FIRST RECORD...
...CONTAINED THE PLANS FOR THE PEACEMAKER.
THE SECOND...
EVOLVED, ARTIFICIAL HUMANS.

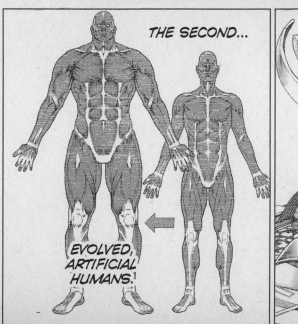

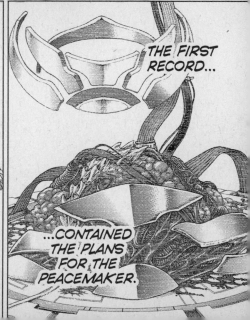

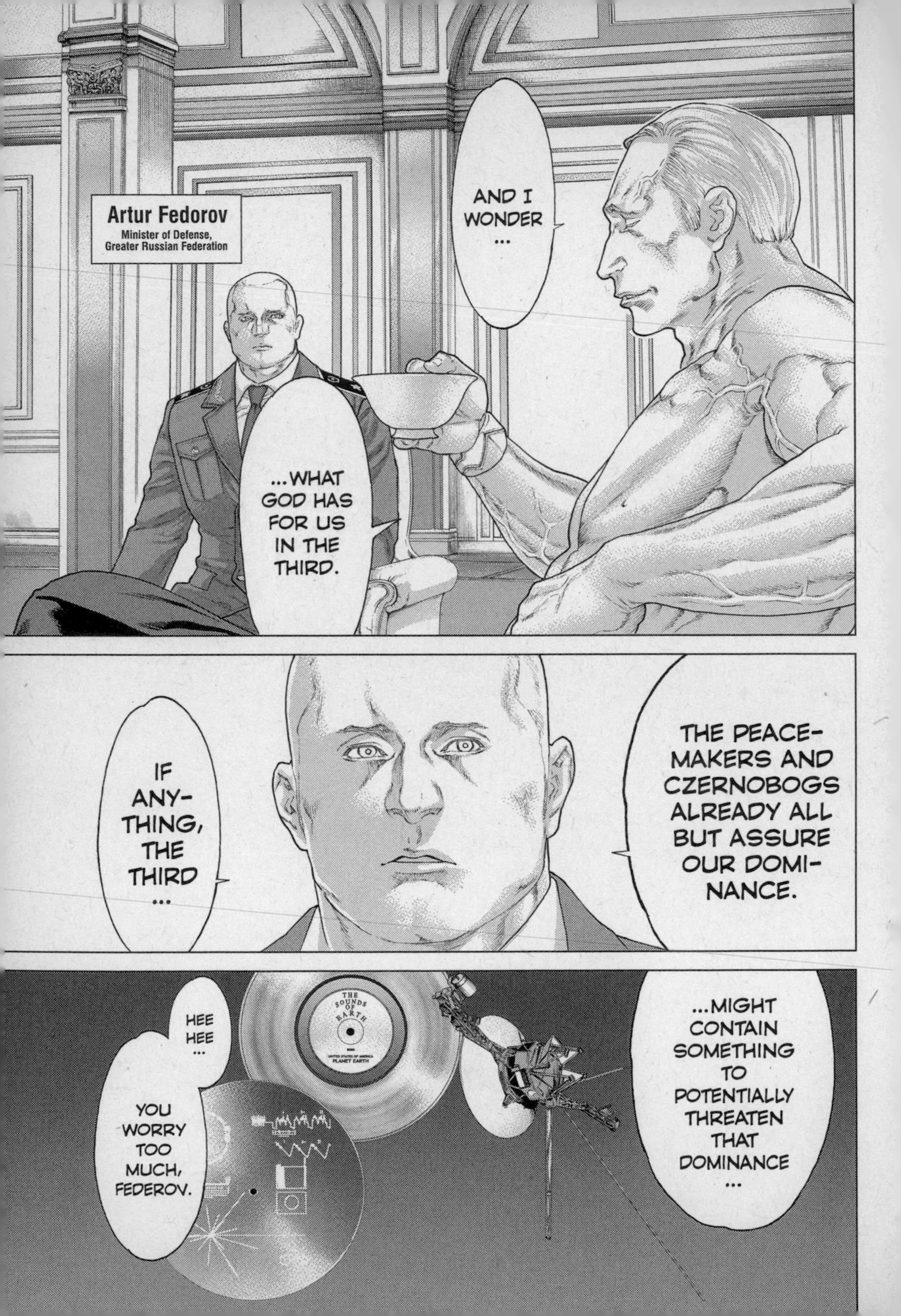
AND I WONDER ...
Artur Fedorov
Minister of Defense, Greater Russian Federation
...WHAT GOD HAS FOR US IN THE THIRD.
THE PEACE-MAKERS AND CZERNOBOGS ALREADY ALL BUT ASSURE OUR DOMI-NANCE.
IF ANY-THING, THE THIRD ...
...MIGHT CONTAIN SOMETHING TO POTENTIALLY THREATEN THAT DOMINANCE ...
THE SOUNDS OF EARTH
PLANET EARTH
HEE HEE ...
YOU WORRY TOO MUCH, FEDEROV.

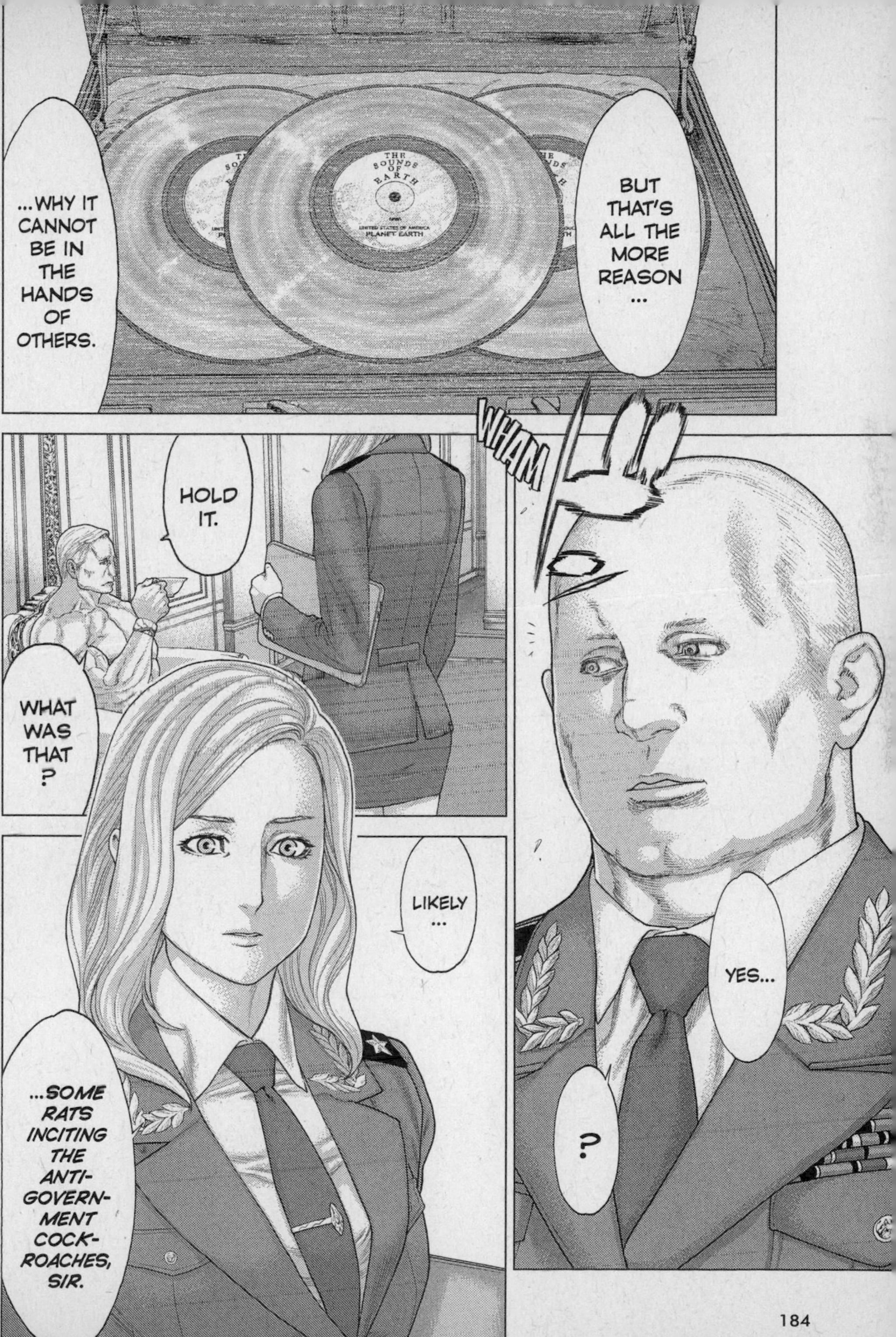
THE SOUNDS OF EARTH
UNITED STATES OF AMERICA
PLANET EARTH
BUT THAT'S ALL THE MORE REASON ...
...WHY IT CANNOT BE IN THE HANDS OF OTHERS.
WHAM
YES...
?
HOLD IT.
WHAT WAS THAT ?
LIKELY ...
...SOME RATS INCITING THE ANTI-GOVERNMENT COCKROACHES, SIR.

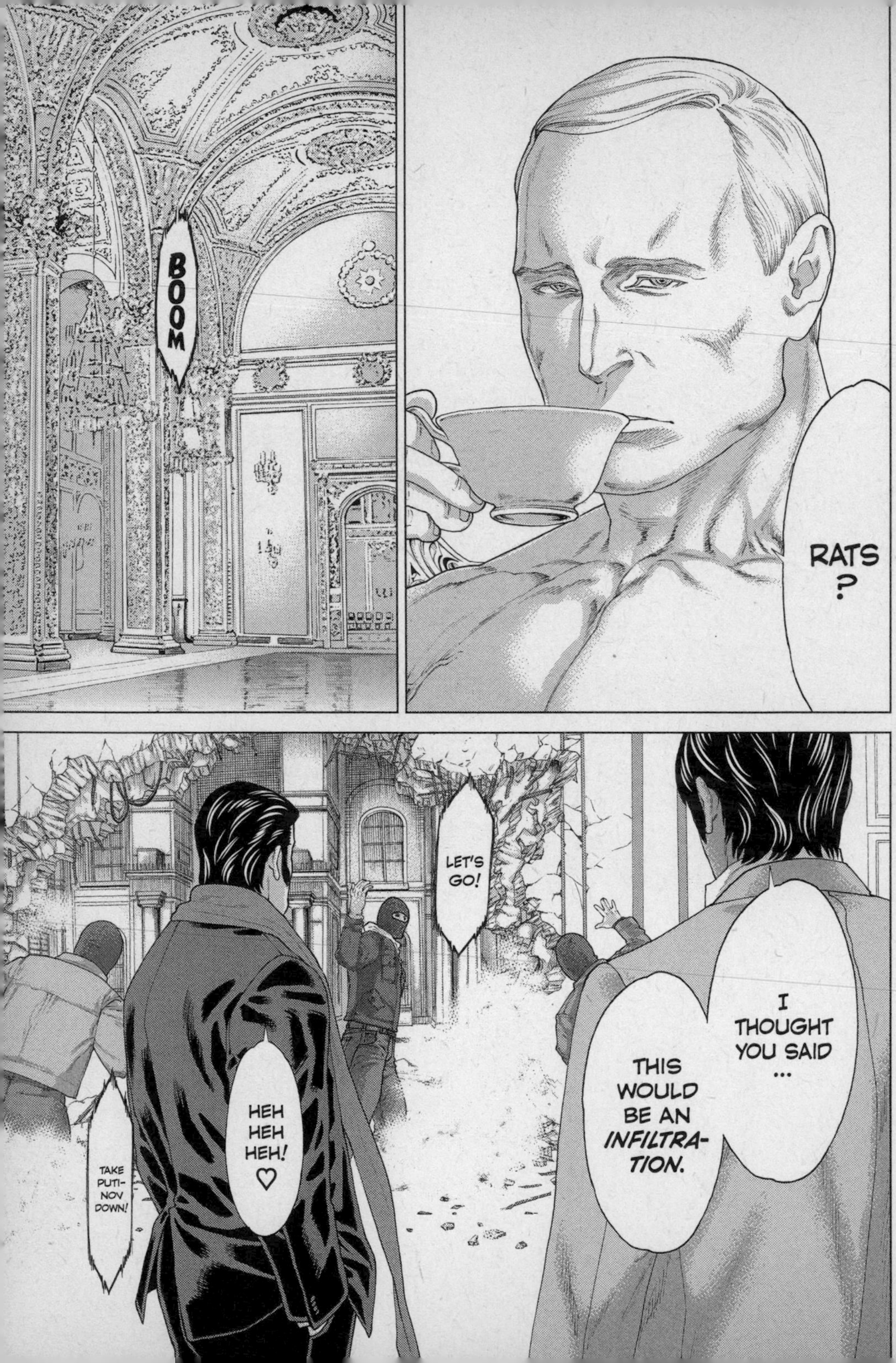
RATS ?
BOOM
I THOUGHT YOU SAID ...
THIS WOULD BE AN *INFILTRATION.*
LET'S GO!
HEH HEH HEH! ♡
TAKE PUTI-NOV DOWN!

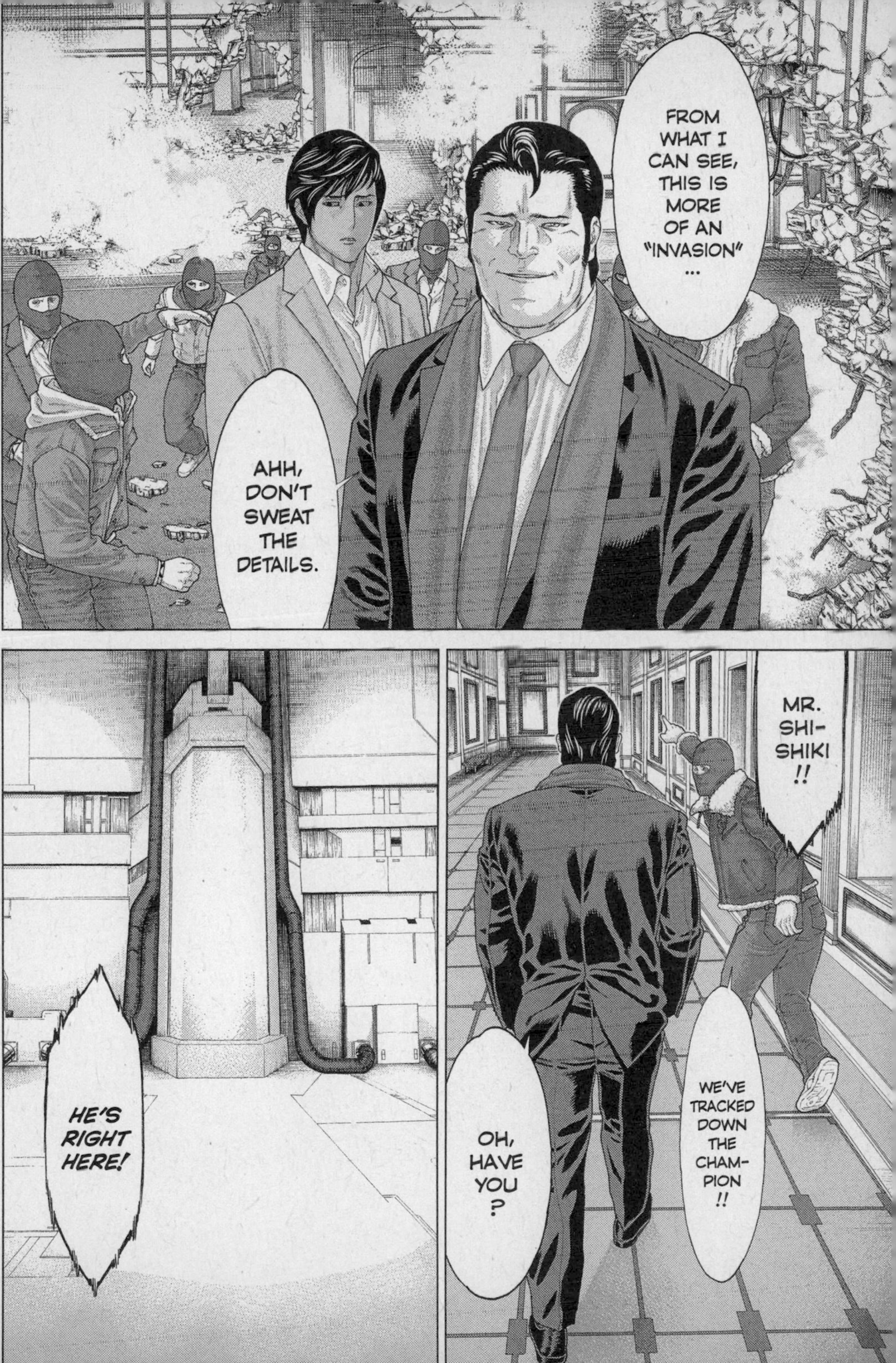
FROM WHAT I CAN SEE, THIS IS MORE OF AN "INVASION"...
AHH, DON'T SWEAT THE DETAILS.
MR. SHI-SHIKI!!
WE'VE TRACKED DOWN THE CHAMPION!!
OH, HAVE YOU?
HE'S RIGHT HERE!

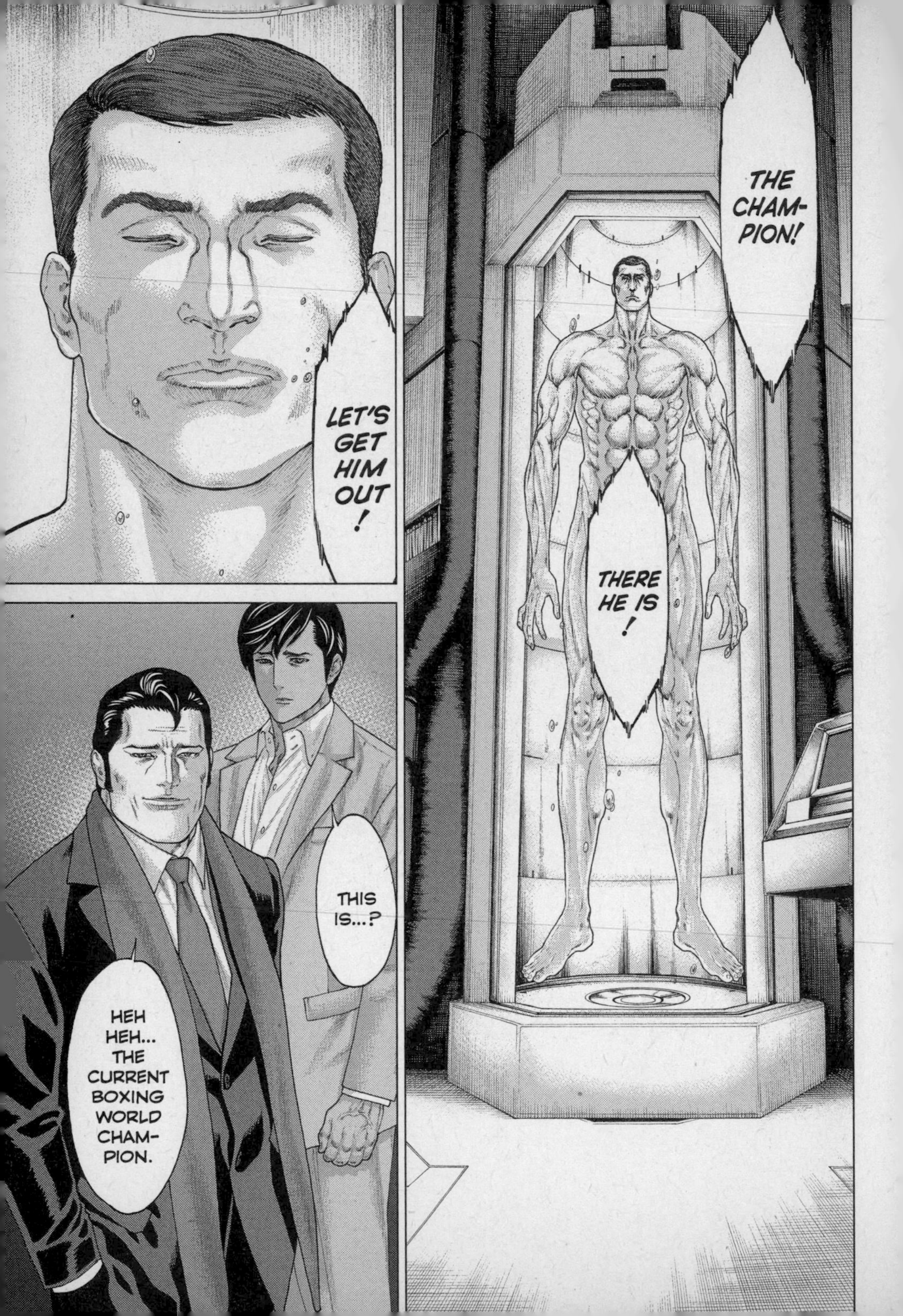
THE CHAMPION!
THERE HE IS!
LET'S GET HIM OUT!
THIS IS...?
HEH HEH... THE CURRENT BOXING WORLD CHAMPION.

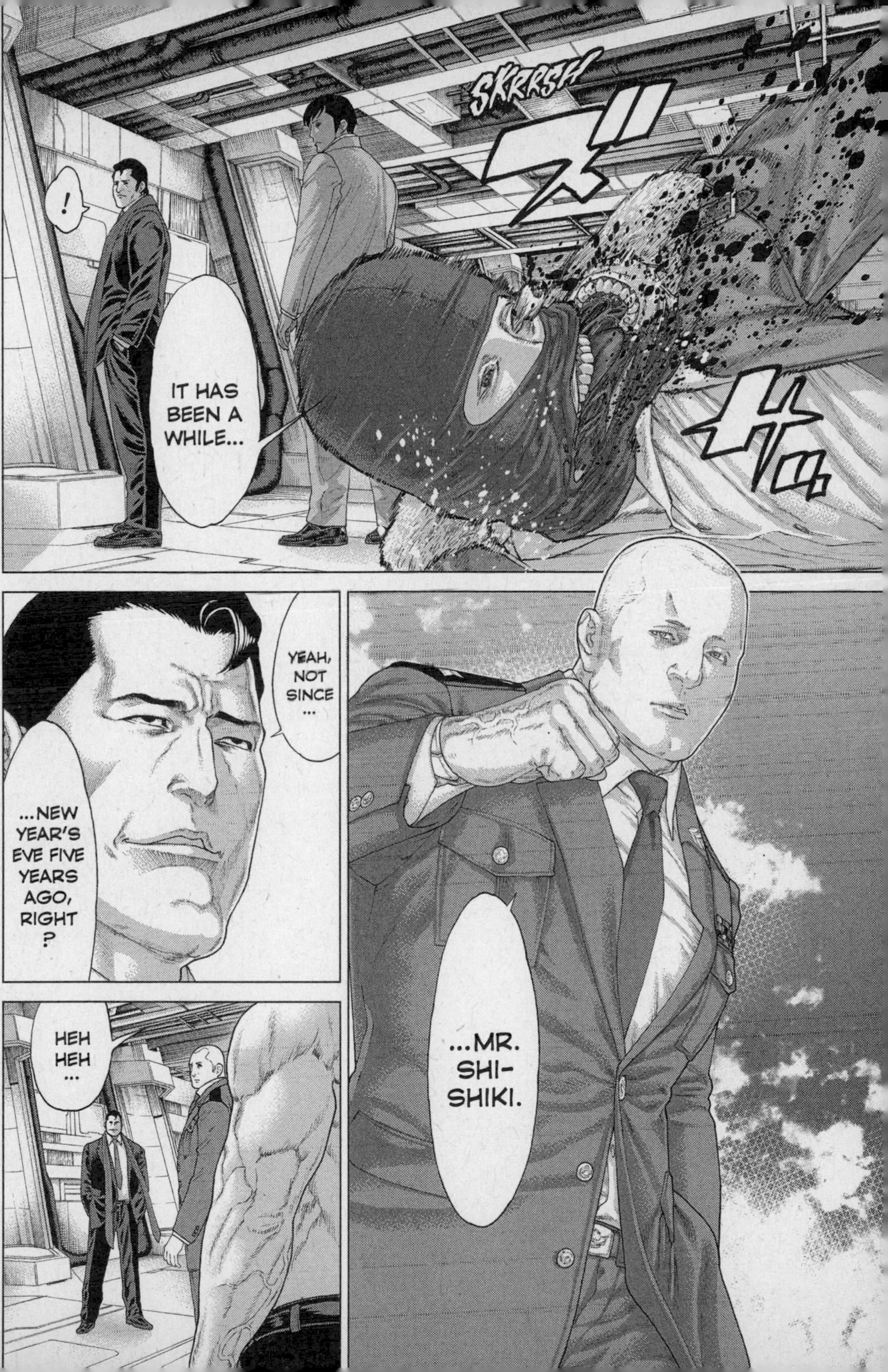
SKRRSH
!
IT HAS BEEN A WHILE...
...MR. SHI-SHIKI.
YEAH, NOT SINCE ...
...NEW YEAR'S EVE FIVE YEARS AGO, RIGHT?
HEH HEH ...

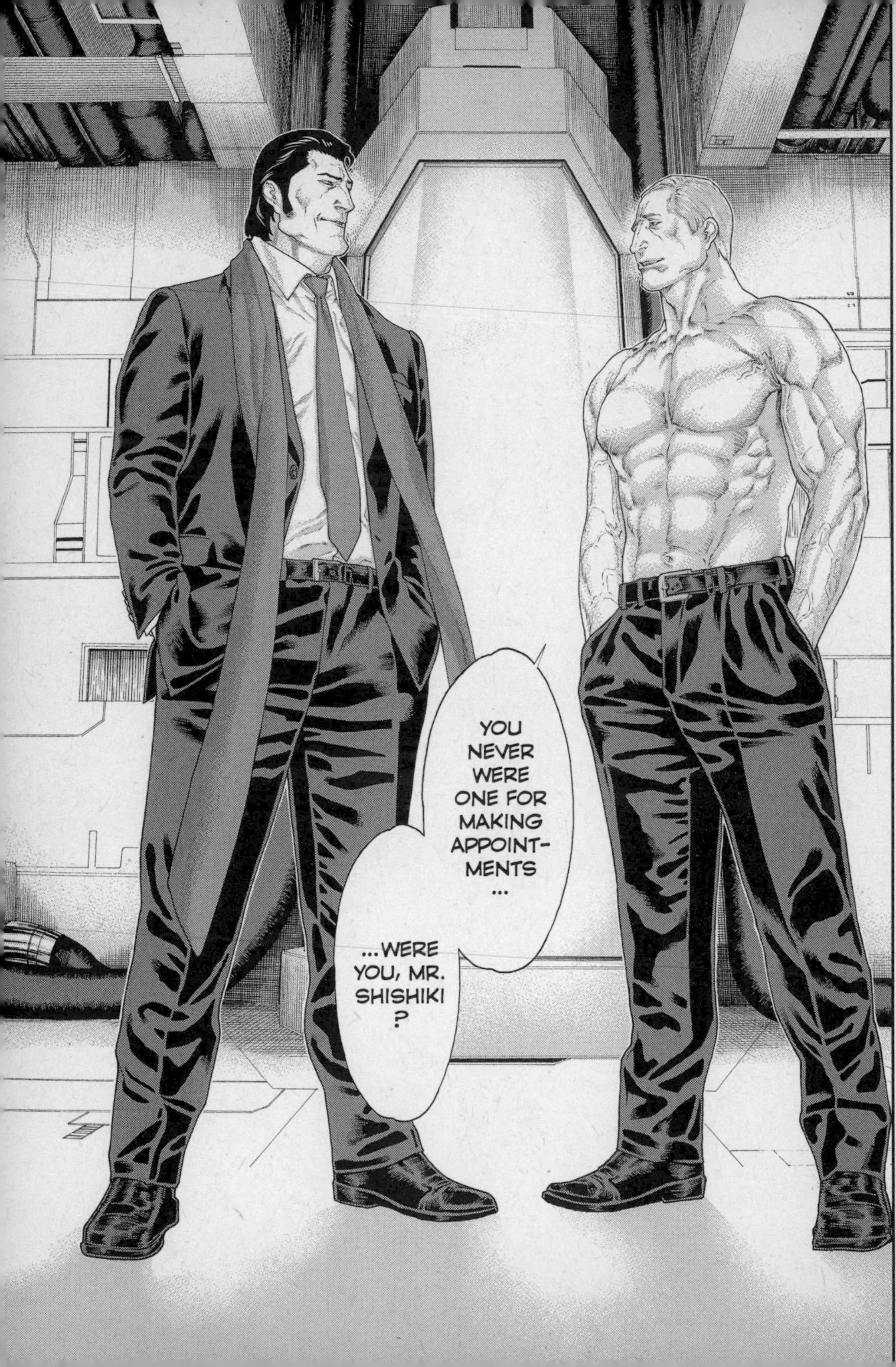
YOU NEVER WERE ONE FOR MAKING APPOINTMENTS ...
...WERE YOU, MR. SHISHIKI ?

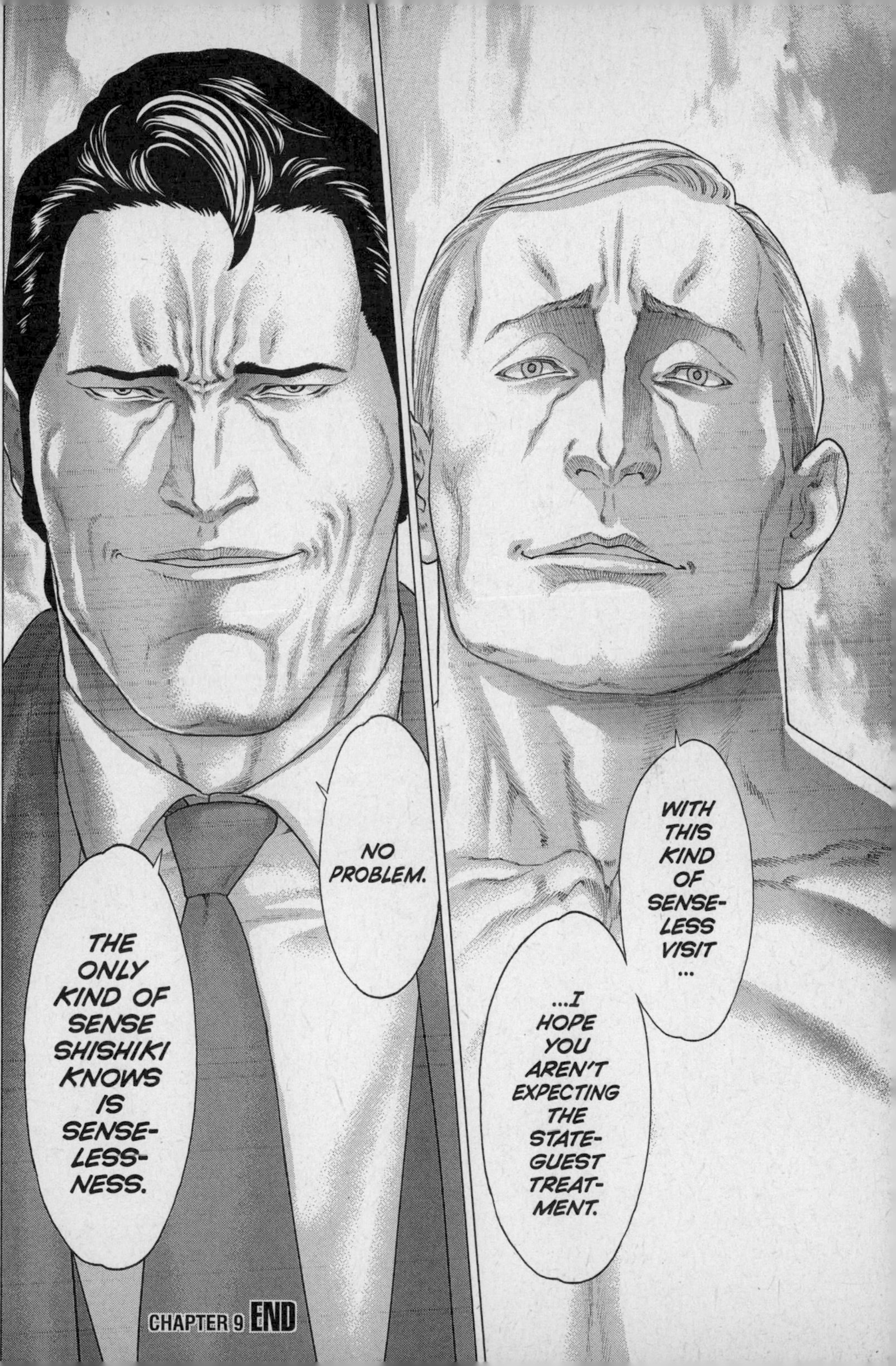
WITH THIS KIND OF SENSELESS VISIT...
...I HOPE YOU AREN'T EXPECTING THE STATE-GUEST TREATMENT.
NO PROBLEM.
THE ONLY KIND OF SENSE SHISHIKI KNOWS IS SENSELESSNESS.
CHAPTER 9 END

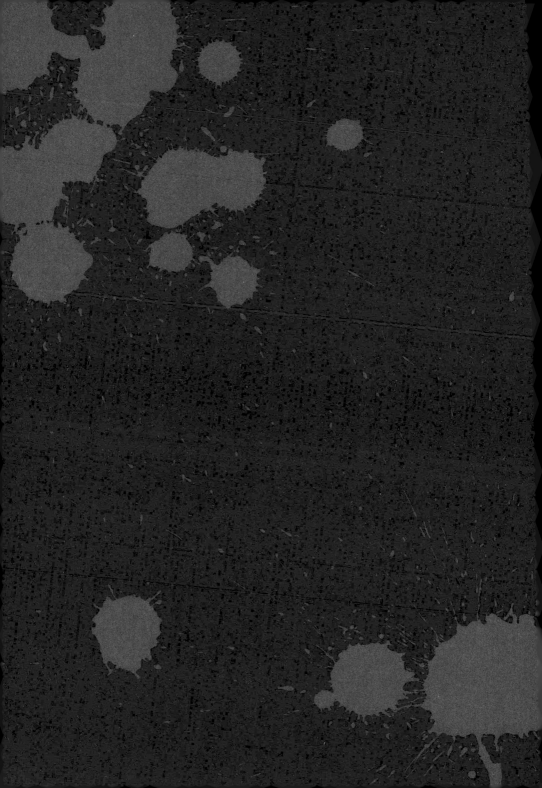

GOLOSSEUM

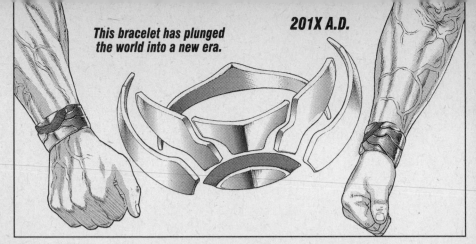

201X A.D.
This bracelet has plunged the world into a new era.
This "PEACE-MAKER" bracelet, allegedly developed by the Greater Russian Republic ...
...has the power to NEUTRALIZE ALL NON-PEACEFUL ATTACKS, from bullets and knives to missiles, nuclear bombs, poison gas, and bio-weapons.
The only attacks left to mankind are bare-handed MARTIAL ARTS.
In order to become the emperor of this new era...
...one man has embarked on a PEACEFUL INVASION.

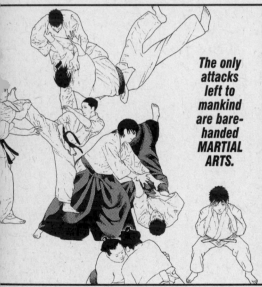

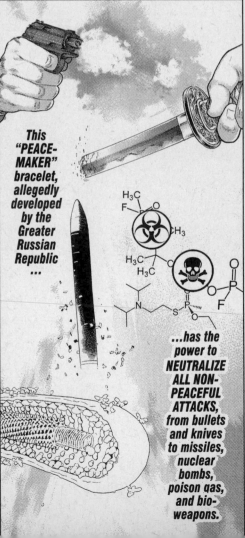

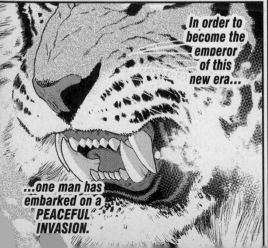

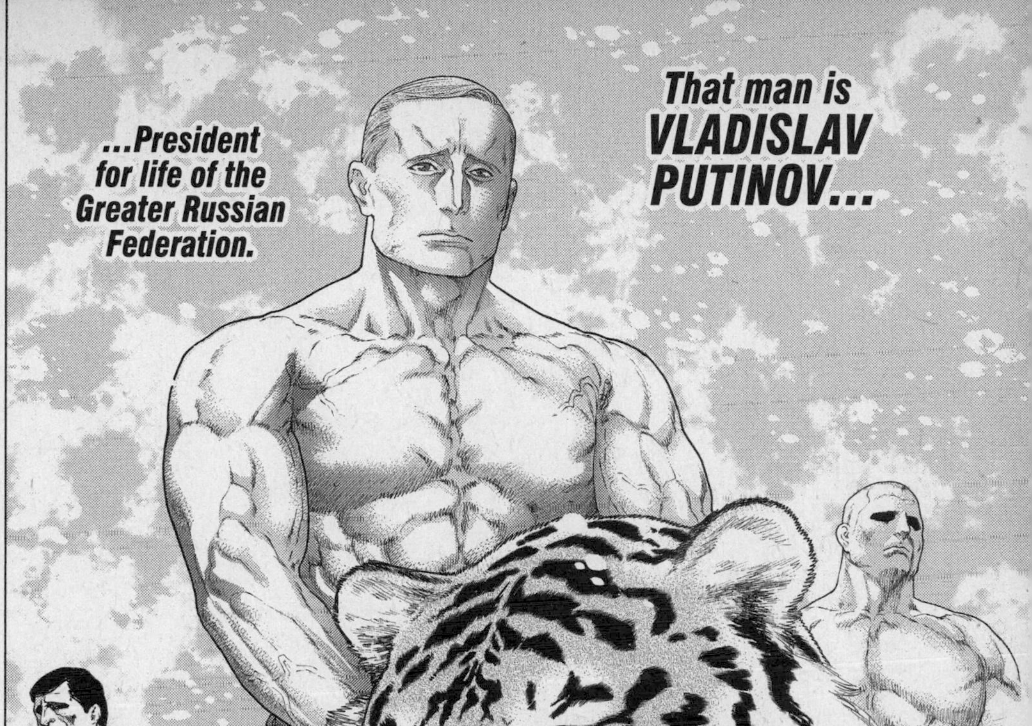
That man is VLADISLAV PUTINOV...
...President for life of the Greater Russian Federation.
EXTRA CHAPTER:
THE MOUNTING GAMES

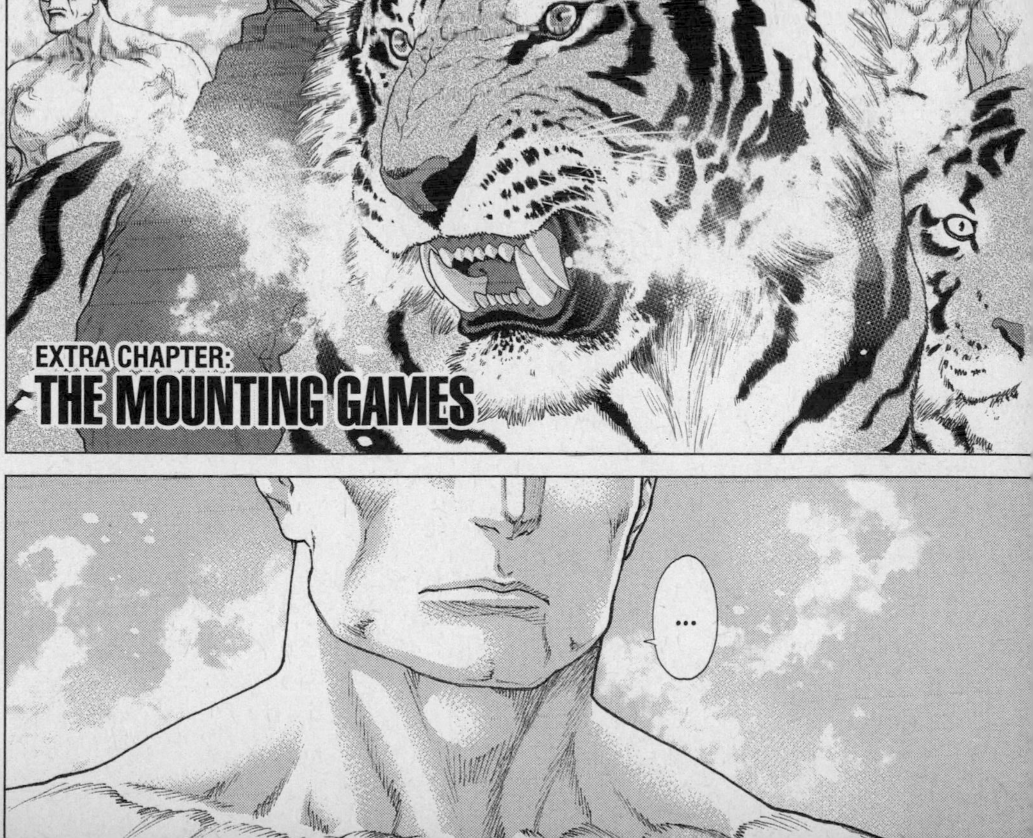
...

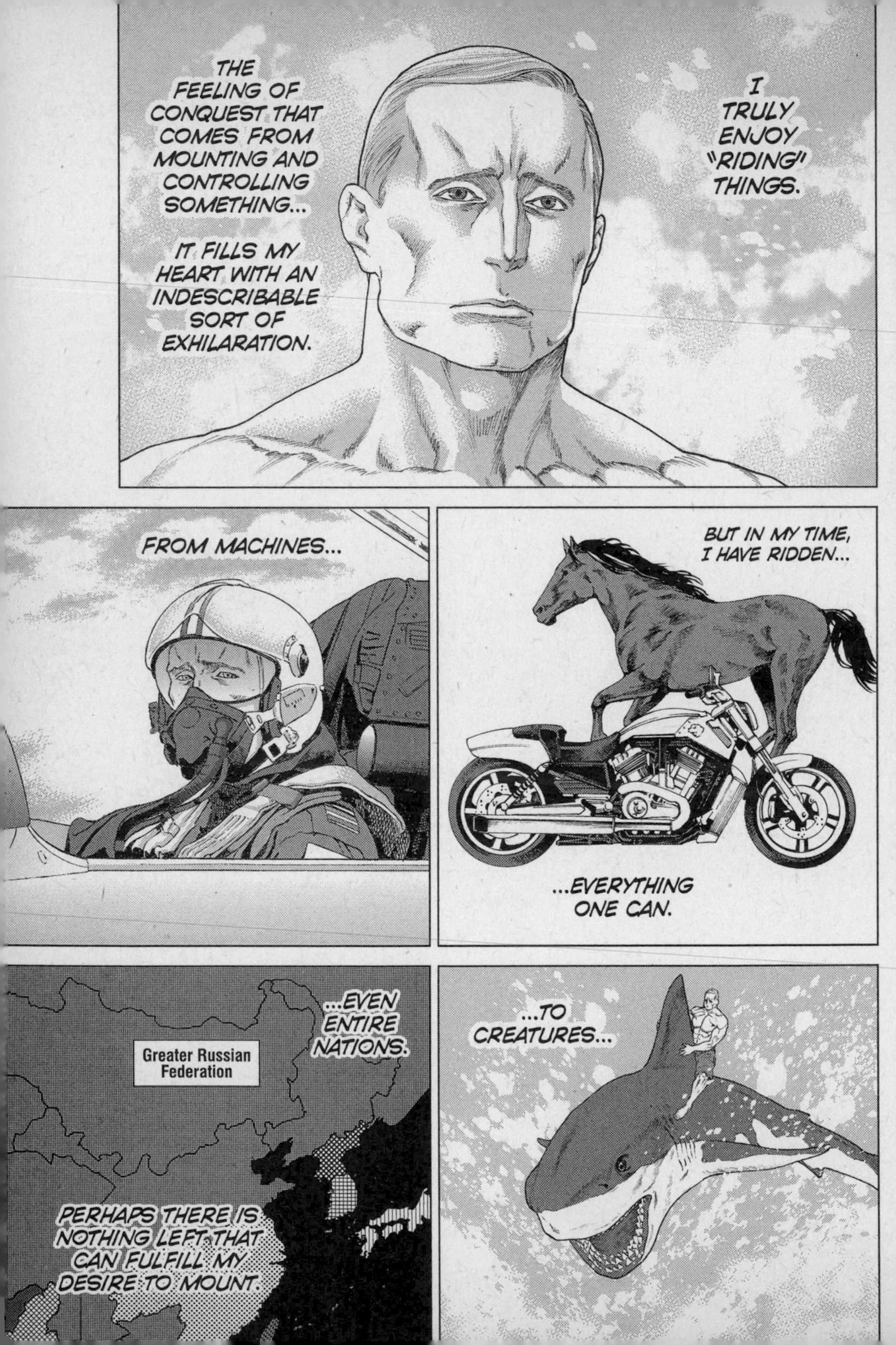
I TRULY ENJOY "RIDING" THINGS.
THE FEELING OF CONQUEST THAT COMES FROM MOUNTING AND CONTROLLING SOMETHING...
IT FILLS MY HEART WITH AN INDESCRIBABLE SORT OF EXHILARATION.
BUT IN MY TIME, I HAVE RIDDEN...
...EVERYTHING ONE CAN.
FROM MACHINES...
...TO CREATURES...
...EVEN ENTIRE NATIONS.
Greater Russian Federation
PERHAPS THERE IS NOTHING LEFT THAT CAN FULFILL MY DESIRE TO MOUNT.

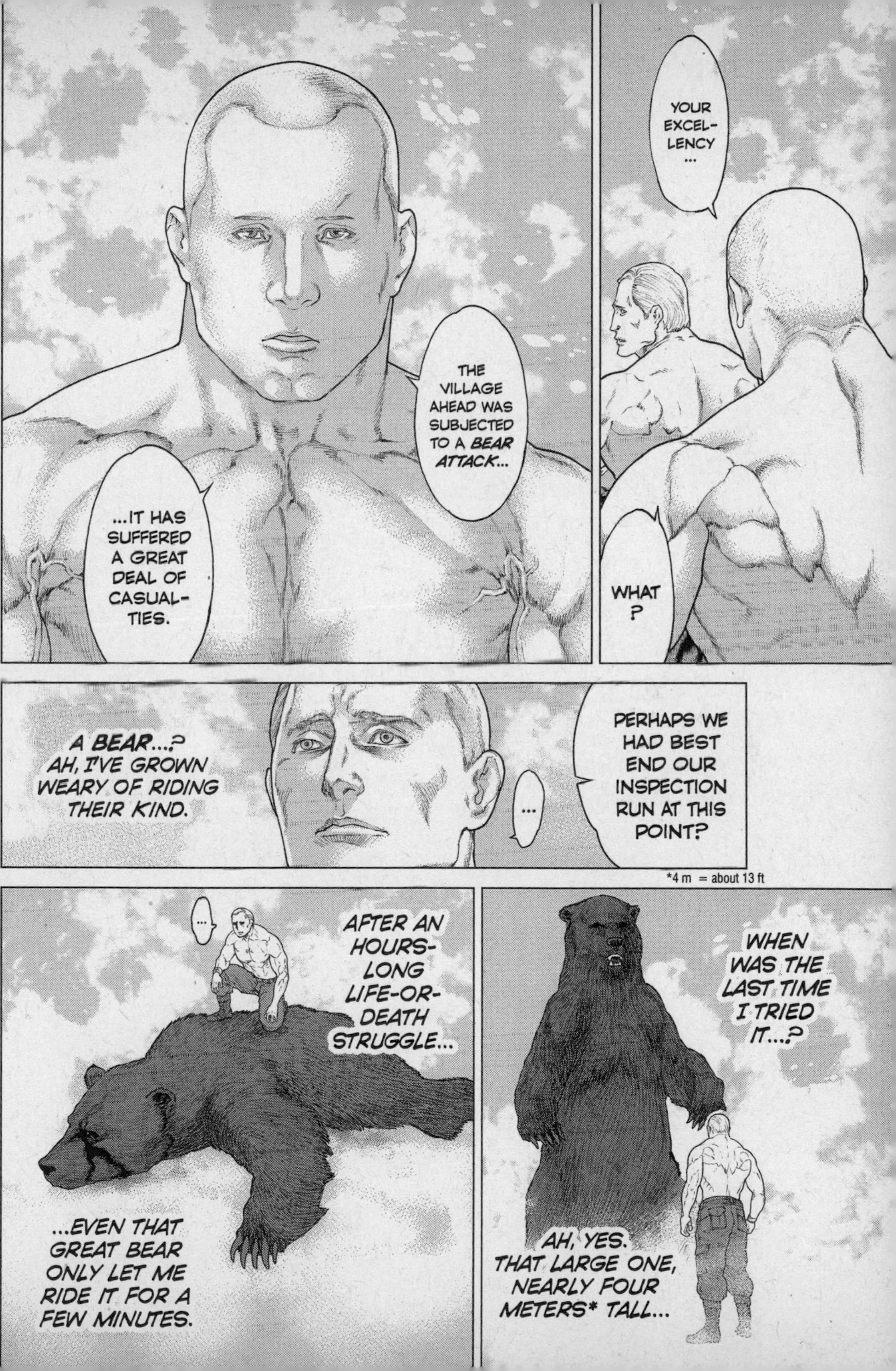
YOUR EXCELLENCY ...
WHAT?
THE VILLAGE AHEAD WAS SUBJECTED TO A *BEAR ATTACK*...
...IT HAS SUFFERED A GREAT DEAL OF CASUALTIES.
PERHAPS WE HAD BEST END OUR INSPECTION RUN AT THIS POINT?
...
A *BEAR*...? AH, I'VE GROWN WEARY OF RIDING THEIR KIND.
WHEN WAS THE LAST TIME I TRIED IT...?
AH, YES. THAT LARGE ONE, NEARLY FOUR METERS* TALL...
AFTER AN HOURS-LONG LIFE-OR-DEATH STRUGGLE...
...
...EVEN THAT GREAT BEAR ONLY LET ME RIDE IT FOR A FEW MINUTES.

*4 m = about 13 ft

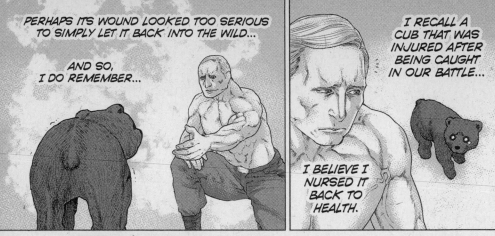

I RECALL A CUB THAT WAS INJURED AFTER BEING CAUGHT IN OUR BATTLE...
I BELIEVE I NURSED IT BACK TO HEALTH.
PERHAPS ITS WOUND LOOKED TOO SERIOUS TO SIMPLY LET IT BACK INTO THE WILD...
AND SO, I DO REMEMBER...
...PLACING A PEACEMAKER BRACELET...
...UPON THAT BEAR'S PAW.
* Peacemakers can heal wounds, too!
IF IT REMAINS ALIVE...
...I CAN ONLY HOPE IT IS A LARGE, GRAND SPECIMEN.
WE ALSO HAVE UN-CONFIRMED REPORTS...
...THAT BULLETS HAVE NO EFFECT UPON THE OFFEND-ING BEAR.
WE BELIEVE IT MAY BE EQUIPPED WITH A PEACE-MAKER.
...

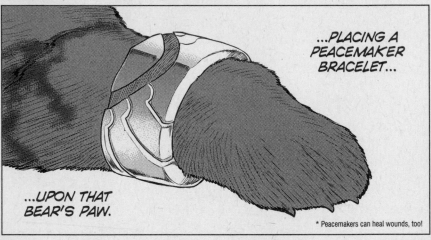

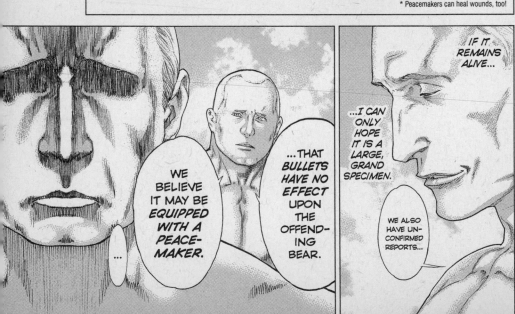

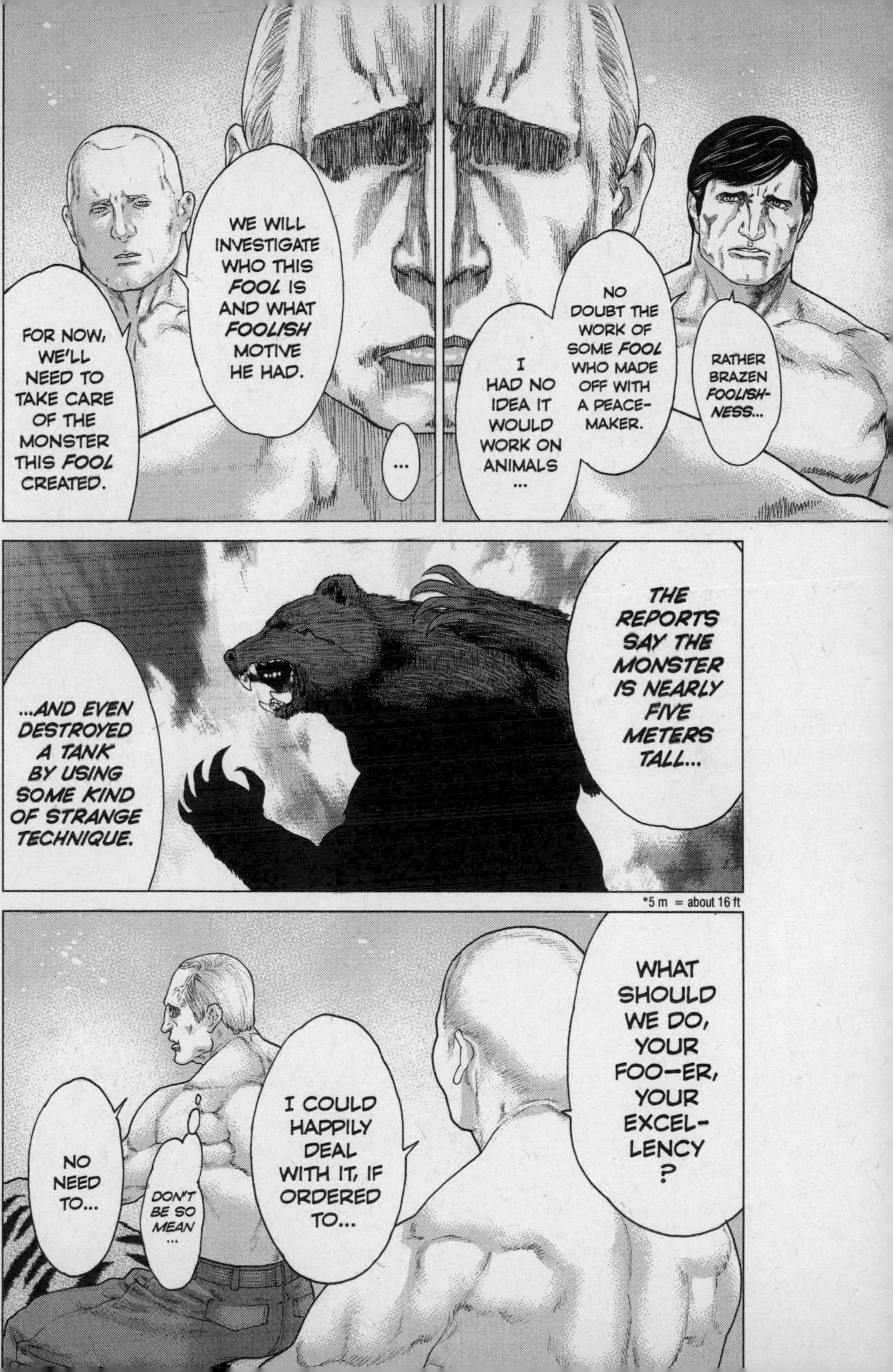
RATHER BRAZEN FOOLISHNESS...
NO DOUBT THE WORK OF SOME FOOL WHO MADE OFF WITH A PEACEMAKER.
I HAD NO IDEA IT WOULD WORK ON ANIMALS ...
...
WE WILL INVESTIGATE WHO THIS FOOL IS AND WHAT FOOLISH MOTIVE HE HAD.
FOR NOW, WE'LL NEED TO TAKE CARE OF THE MONSTER THIS FOOL CREATED.
THE REPORTS SAY THE MONSTER IS NEARLY FIVE METERS TALL...
...AND EVEN DESTROYED A TANK BY USING SOME KIND OF STRANGE TECHNIQUE.
*5 m = about 16 ft
WHAT SHOULD WE DO, YOUR FOO—ER, YOUR EXCELLENCY?
I COULD HAPPILY DEAL WITH IT, IF ORDERED TO...
DON'T BE SO MEAN ...
NO NEED TO...

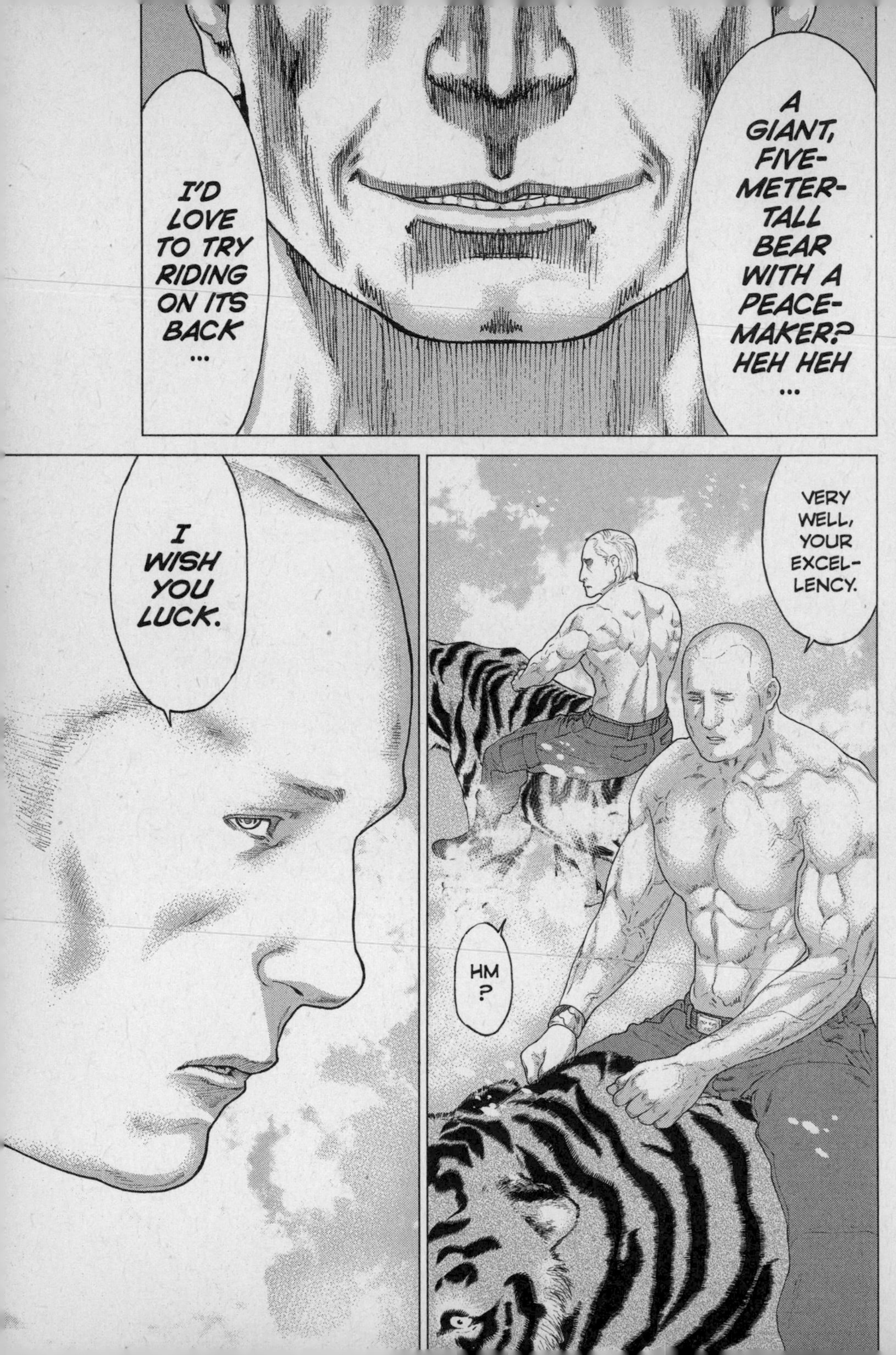
A GIANT, FIVE-METER-TALL BEAR WITH A PEACE-MAKER? HEH HEH ...
I'D LOVE TO TRY RIDING ON ITS BACK ...
VERY WELL, YOUR EXCEL-LENCY.
HM ?
I WISH YOU LUCK.

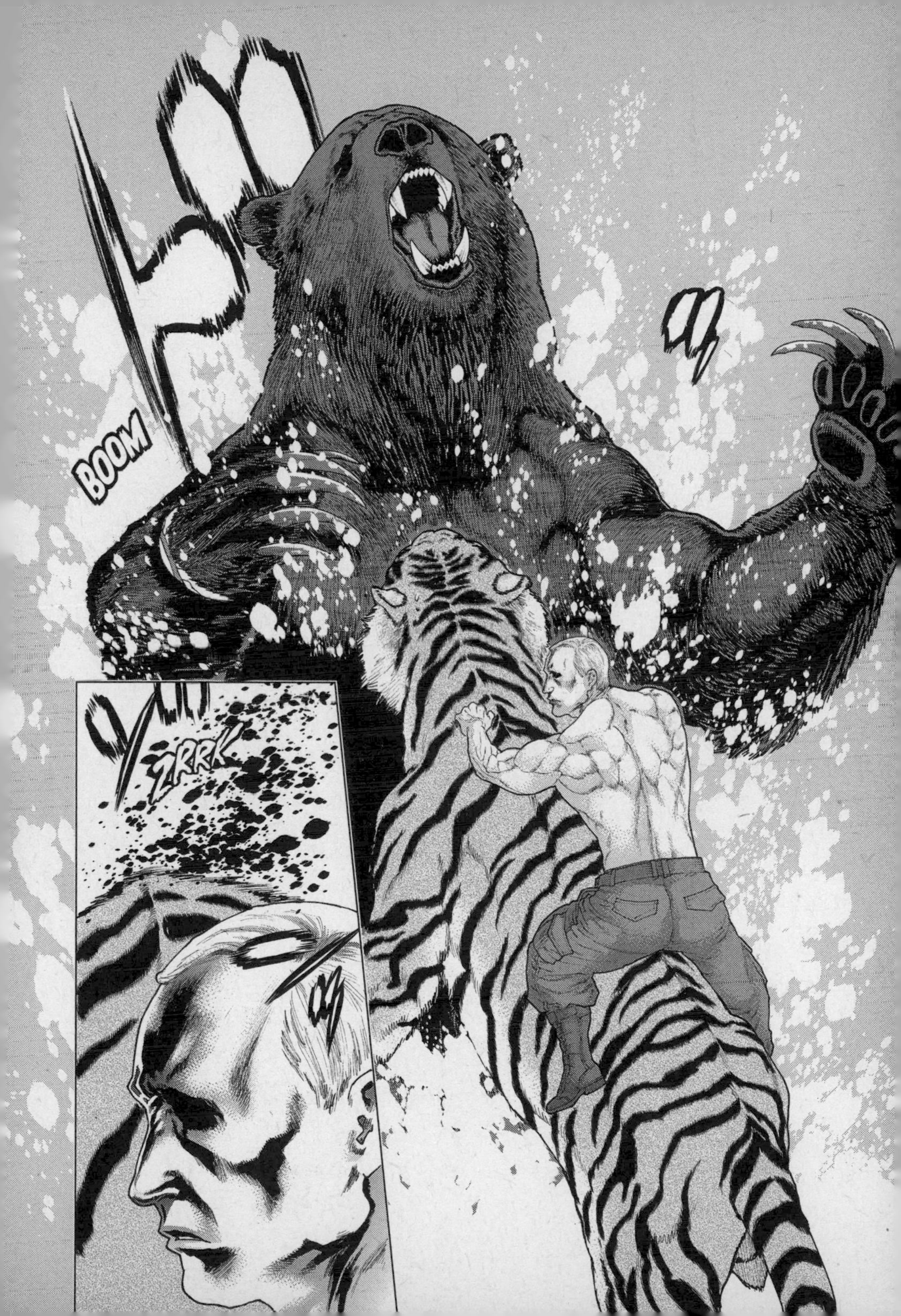
BOOM
ZRRK

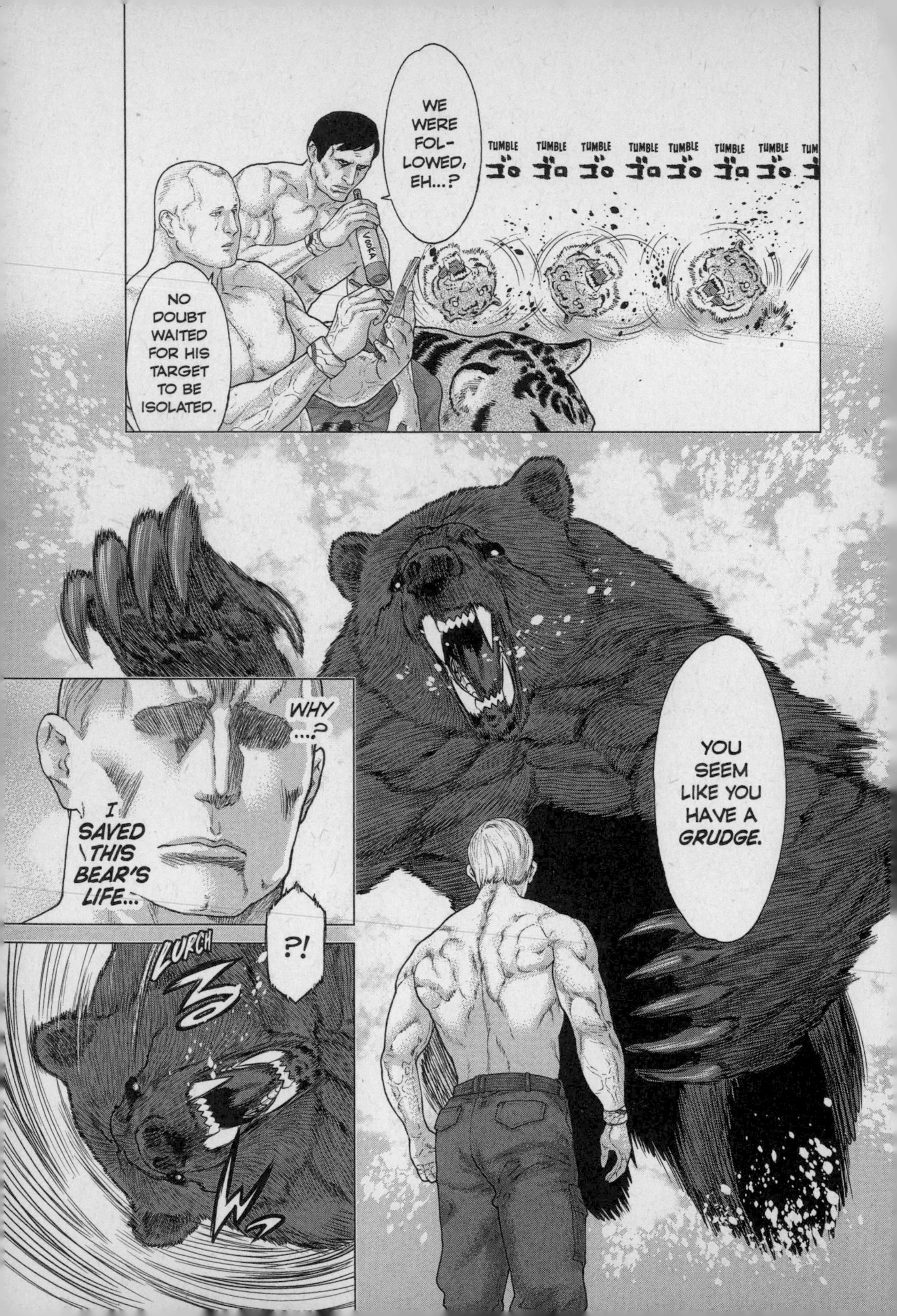
TUMBLE TUMBLE TUMBLE TUMBLE TUMBLE TUMBLE TUMBLE TUM
ゴロゴロゴロゴロゴロゴロゴロゴ
WE WERE FOL-LOWED, EH...?
VODKA
NO DOUBT WAITED FOR HIS TARGET TO BE ISOLATED.
YOU SEEM LIKE YOU HAVE A GRUDGE.
WHY ...?
I SAVED THIS BEAR'S LIFE...
?!
LURCH

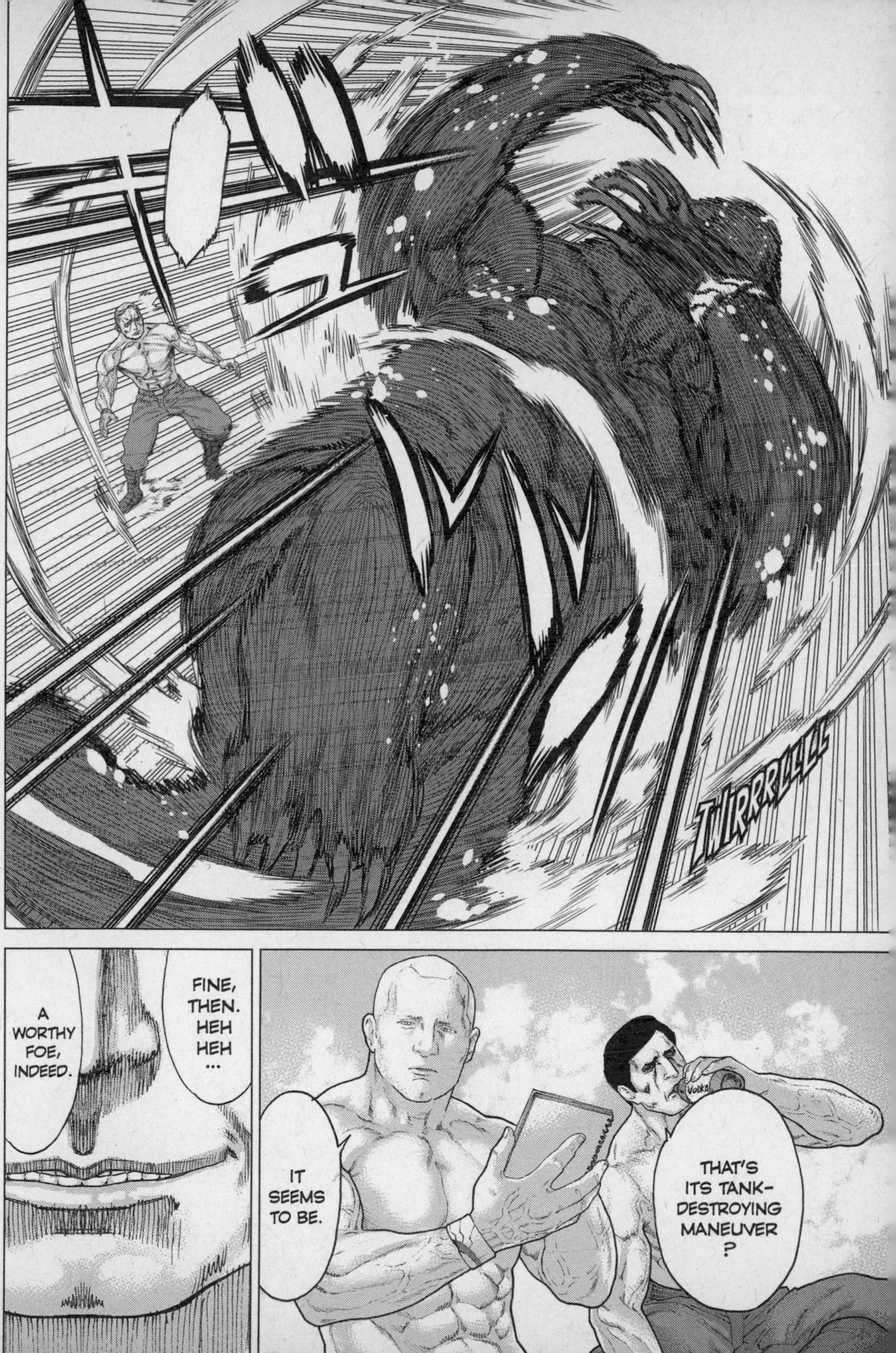
TWIRRRLLLL
THAT'S ITS TANK-DESTROYING MANEUVER?
IT SEEMS TO BE.
FINE, THEN. HEH HEH ...
A WORTHY FOE, INDEED.

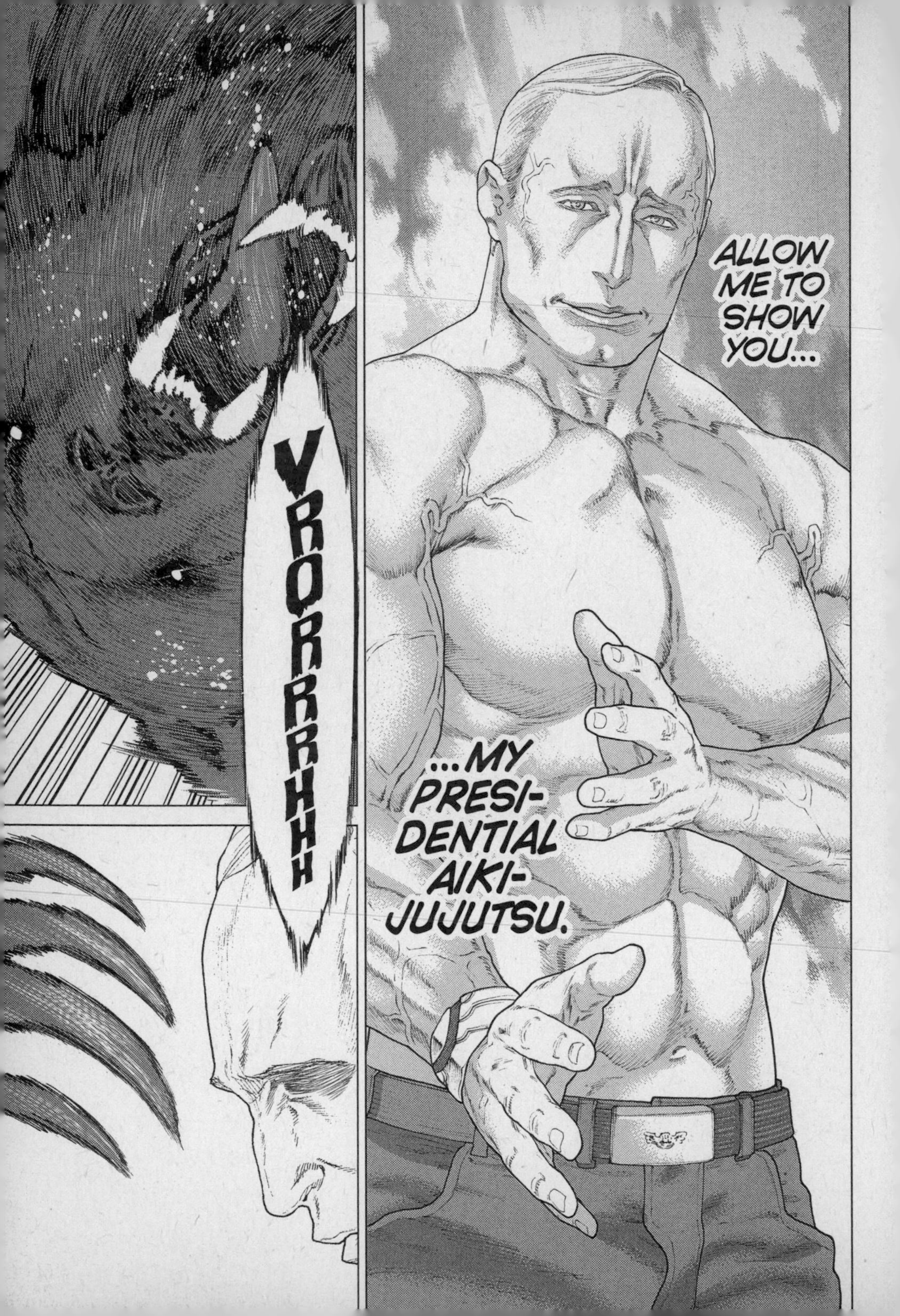
ALLOW ME TO SHOW YOU...
...MY PRESI-DENTIAL AIKI-JUJUTSU.
VRORRRHHH

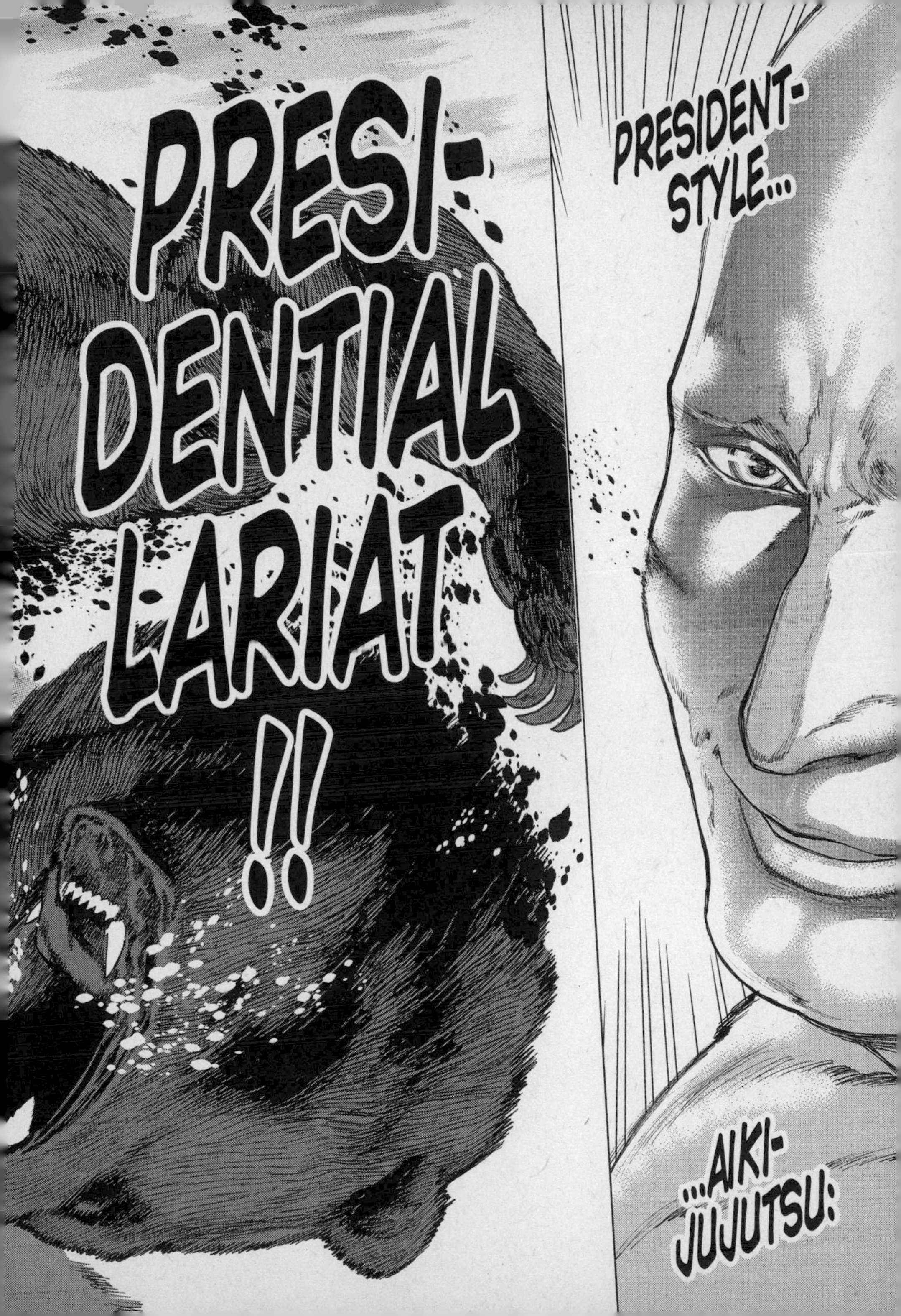
PRESIDENT-STYLE...
...AIKI-JUJUTSU:
PRESI-DENTIAL LARIAT!!

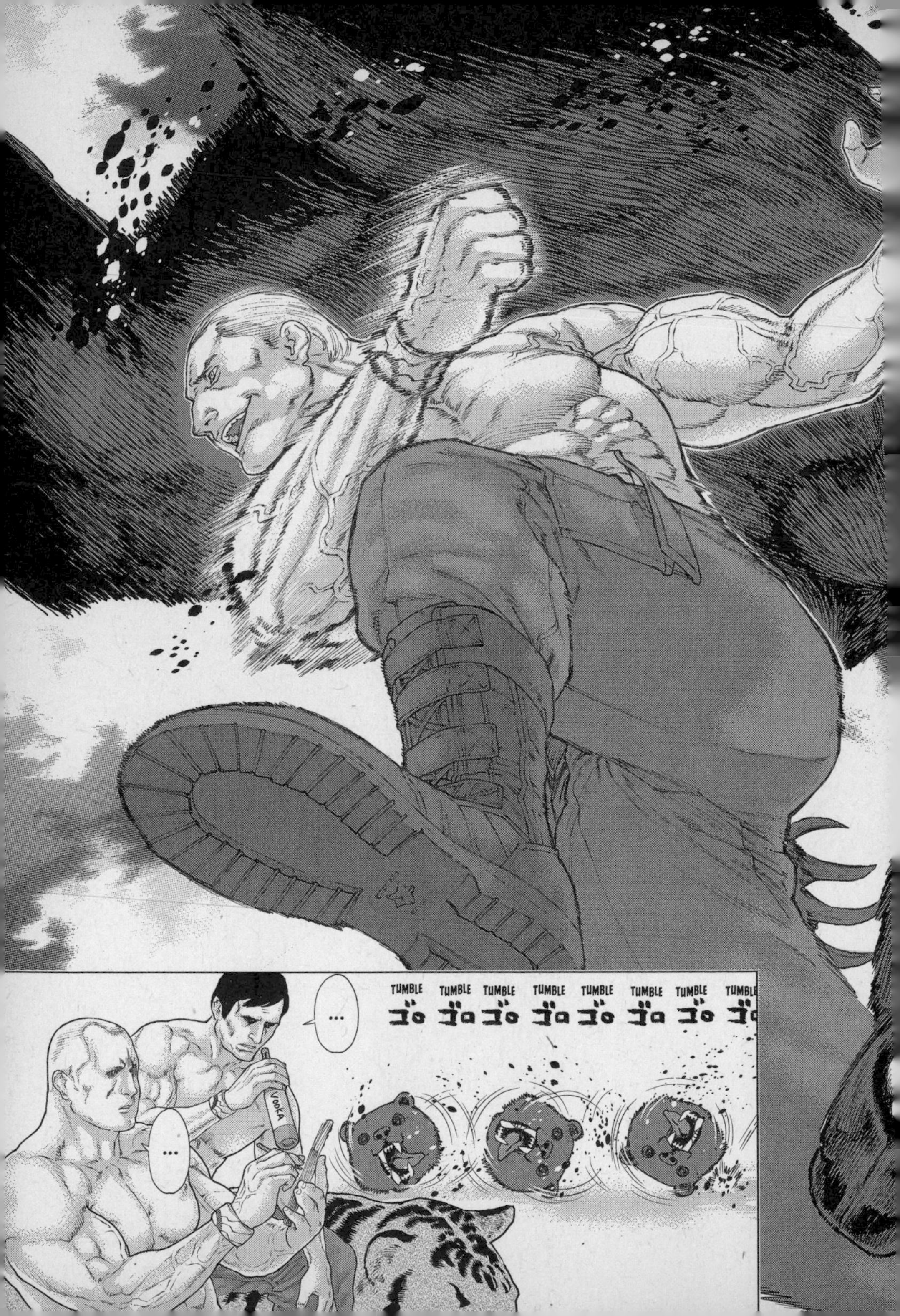

TUMBLE TUMBLE TUMBLE TUMBLE TUMBLE TUMBLE TUMBLE TUMBLE
ゴロゴロゴロゴロゴロゴロゴロゴロ
...
VODKA
...

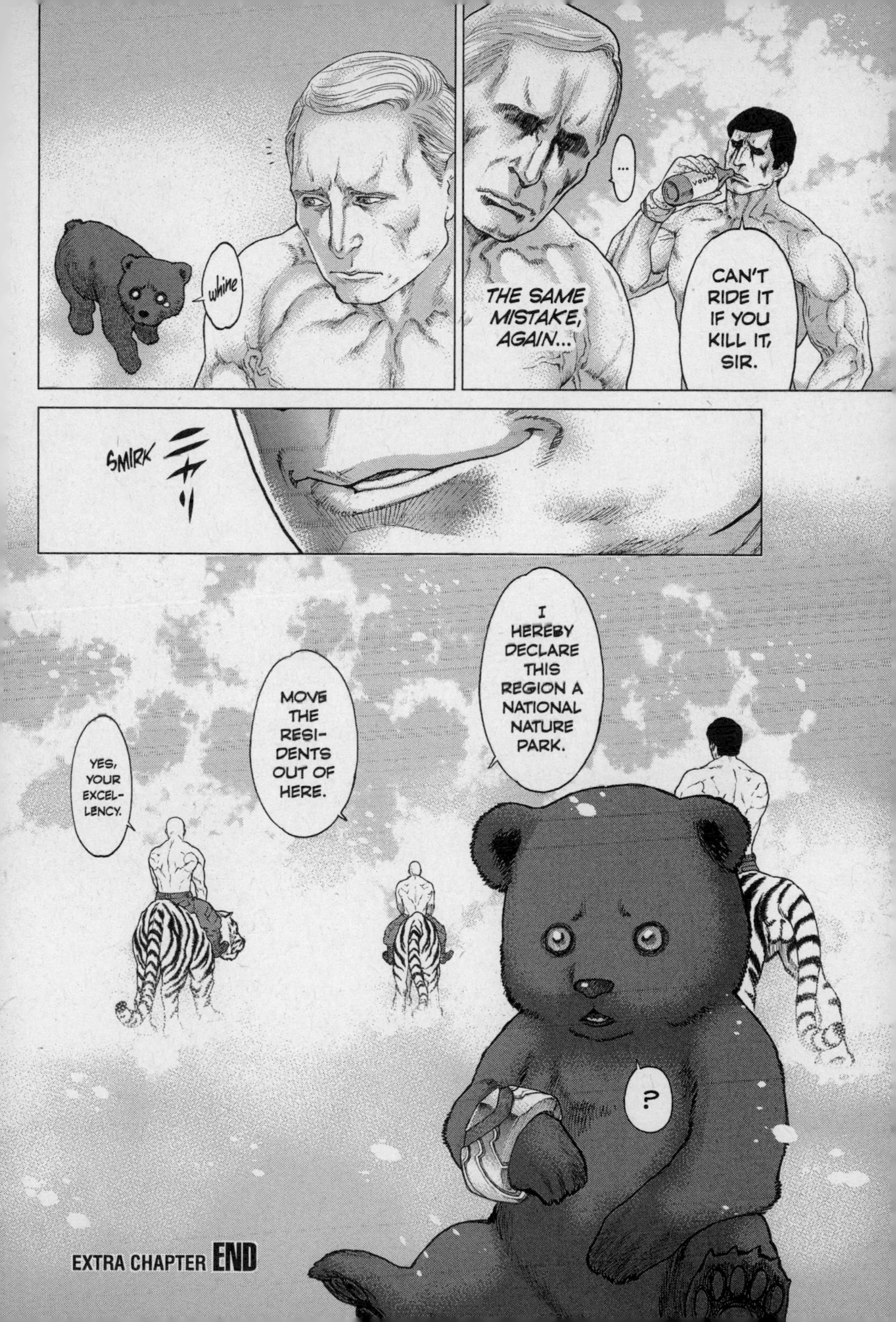
...
CAN'T RIDE IT IF YOU KILL IT, SIR.
THE SAME MISTAKE, AGAIN...
whine
SMIRK
I HEREBY DECLARE THIS REGION A NATIONAL NATURE PARK.
MOVE THE RESI- DENTS OUT OF HERE.
YES, YOUR EXCEL- LENCY.
?
EXTRA CHAPTER END

Golosseum Volume 2 END
Calligraphy: Natsuki Takazuka   Research assistance: Patisserie Swallowtail (Ikebukuro)

CZERNOBOGS

Human beings that have been "enhanced" by injections of gene-altering viruses that adjust their human-genome data after birth. Their muscle fibers are stronger than an average person's by a measure of several to several dozen orders of magnitude, giving them roughly the strength to fight—or even dominate—a similarly sized gorilla. Bone-extending operations and alloy-metal replacements also provide the chance of enhancing the body's inherent bone structure. Czernobogs are placed into "classes" between 100 kg and 300 kg, with Field Marshal Aleksandr Karelinkov, strongest of the Greater Russian forces, comprising the only member of the so-called "400 kg" class.

100-KG-CLASS CZERNOBOGS

Talented martial artists or bare-handed combatants in the 100-kg weight range are injected with gene-altering viruses to enhance their bodies; no further operations are performed upon them. This class comprises 90 percent of all Czernobogs. Their Peacemaker-enhanced natural healing functions automatically restore their genetic data to normal, so they must undergo further viral injections on a regular basis. Since they are largely indistinguishable from the general public, they are deployed in a wide variety of infiltration ops.

200-KG-CLASS CZERNOBOGS

Enhanced fighters selected from the 100-kg-class forces. The 200-kg-class possess bodies that are impervious to the gene restoration performed by their Peacemaker's natural healing functions. It is believed that the Peacemaker "allows" for genetic alteration on bodies that, through some natural quirk or talent, continue to grow and strengthen through training until old age sets in. Their skeletal structures have been enhanced and enlarged by "extension" operations that harness the Peacemaker's rapid healing capabilities. The 200-kg class encompasses approximately 10 percent of all Czernobogs. Their role is often compared to the one taken by tanks in the era of pre-Peacemaker armies.

300-KG-CLASS CZERNOBOGS

The highest echelon of Czernobogs, selected from the 200-kg-class forces. These giants have been further enhanced through bone extensions and full skeletal replacements using metal-alloy bones. In the current "peaceful" era, their tactical strength is said to be equivalent to the atomic bombs or ICBMs of the pre-Peacemaker years. Unconfirmed intelligence states that the United States has also successfully developed fighters in this class. They comprise less than 0.0001 percent of all Czernobogs.

WARHEAD-SPECIFIC CZERNOBOGS

Fighters enhanced to serve as human rockets. Originally from the ranks of gymnasts and the lighter weight classes of strike-oriented martial arts. Launched by a rocket, they are tasked with destroying aircraft or ground facilities. Selected among soldiers who do not reach the expected enhancements after being injected with gene-altering viruses. Although equipped with a Peacemaker and parachute, approximately 30 percent of soldiers die after launch due to a failed landing, since Peacemakers provide no protection against ground impacts.

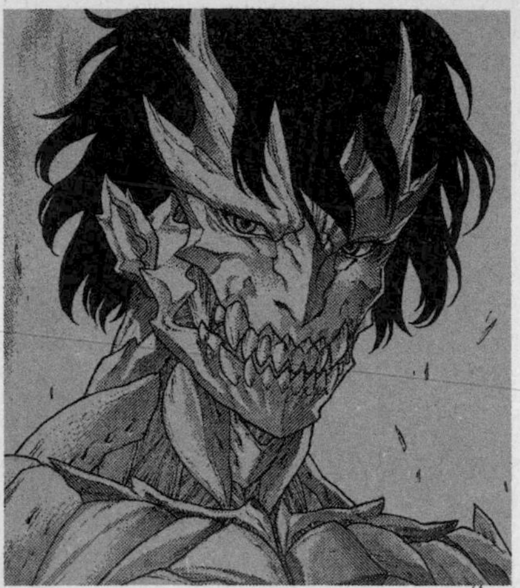

NATURAL-BORN CZERNOBOGS
Unconfirmed intelligence suggests the existence of Czernobogs born from genetic alteration performed on the sperm and egg prior to conception, with no need for gene-altering viruses after birth.

COUNTERMEASURES
Peacekeeping martial-arts forces have few effective measures available. Rapid procurement and research of gene-altering viruses is required. Other nations have hatched plans to equip gorillas, chimpanzees, bears, and other bipeds with Peacemakers to serve as fighters, but the difficulty of controlling the behavior of such animals makes the prospects of practical applications dim. Intelligence speaks of a "dragon soldier" project carried out in the past by the People's Liberation Army, but its potential applications (if any) remain unknown.

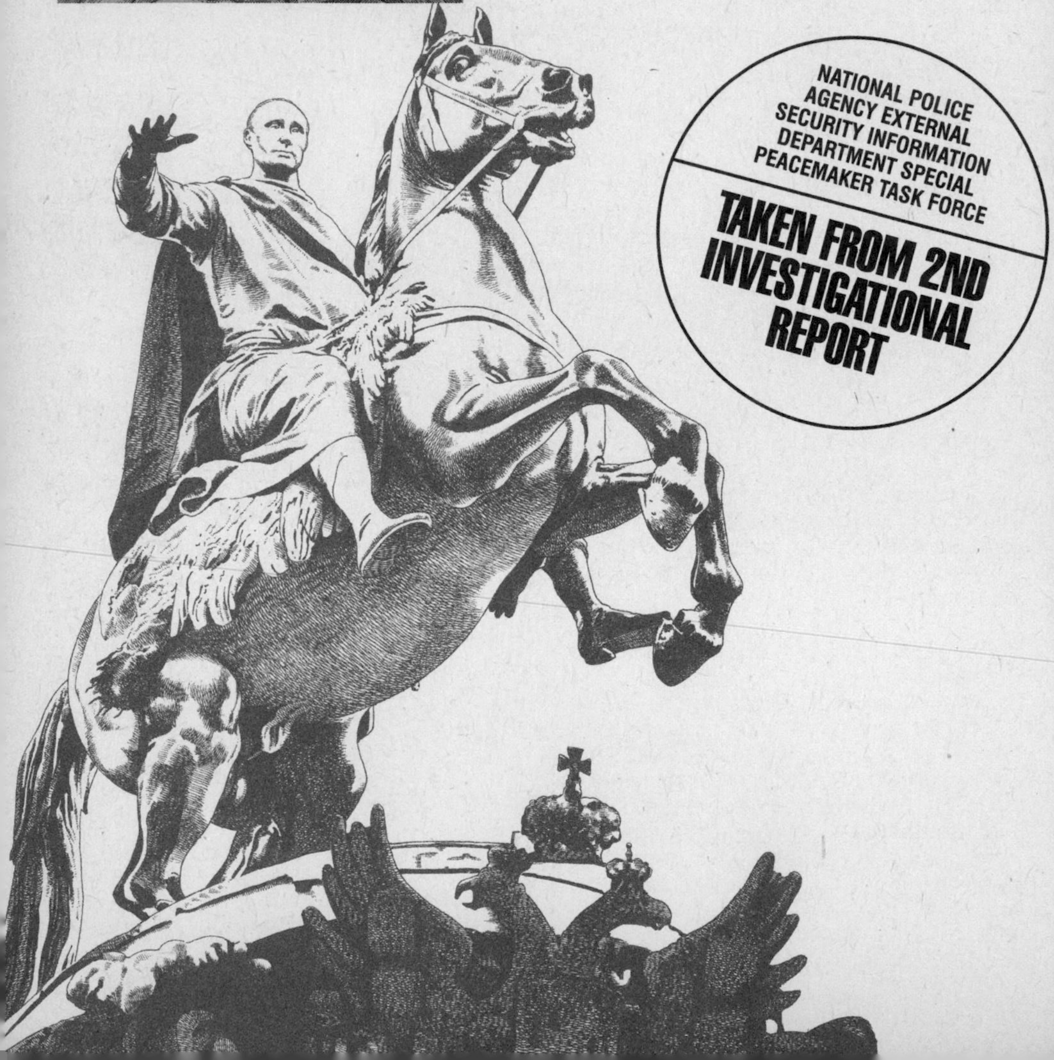

NATIONAL POLICE AGENCY EXTERNAL SECURITY INFORMATION DEPARTMENT SPECIAL PEACEMAKER TASK FORCE

TAKEN FROM 2ND INVESTIGATIONAL REPORT

TRANSLATION NOTES

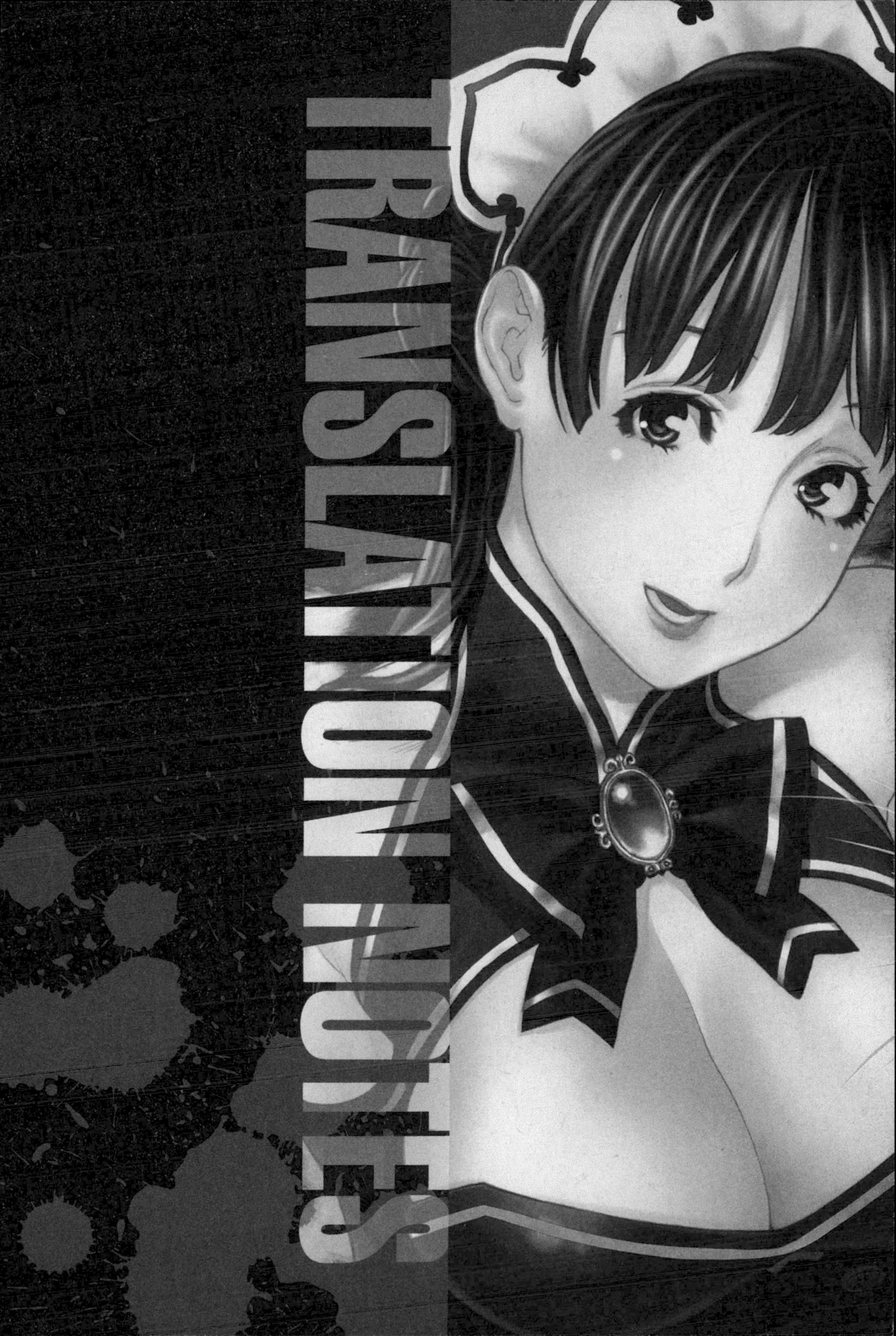

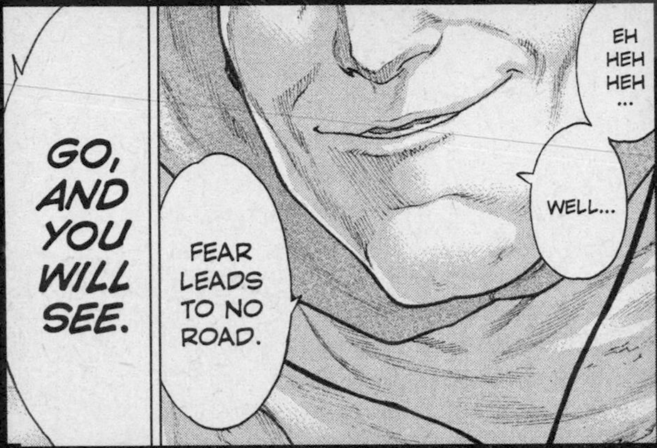
GO, AND YOU WILL SEE.
FEAR LEADS TO NO ROAD.
EH HEH HEH ...
WELL...

"FEAR LEADS TO NO ROAD. GO, AND YOU WILL SEE."

Shishiki is quoting lines from "The Road," a poem written by 20th-century philosopher Tetsuo Kiyozawa. It was popularized by Antonio Inoki, a world-famous Japanese pro wrestler who provided the direct inspiration for Shishiki's looks.

The full poem reads as follows:

What awaits when crossing this road?
Do not have fear
Fear leads to no road
Take a step, and it becomes a road
And that step becomes a road
Go on, without wavering
Go, and you will see

The title of Chapter 9 is also a pun in Japanese on the final two lines of the poem.

MOUNT HAKODATE

Mount Hakodate is a 1,096-foot mountain about ten minutes away by bus from central Hakodate. It can be climbed on foot, by car or bus, or via a cable car. The peak offers stunning views of the city and peninsula below, making it a popular tourist site.

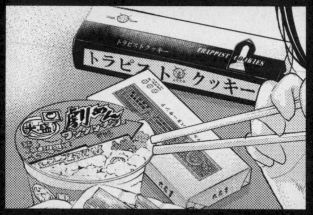

HOKKAIDO SNACKS

The opening page for Chapter 8 features a spread of specialty foods and snacks from Hokkaido. "Trappist Cookies" are made by the Tobetsu Trappist Monastery located outside of Hakodate (one of seven in Japan and twenty across Asia) and sold in Japan. "Gekimen Wonton-men" is a brand of instant ramen with dried dumplings that originated in Hokkaido in 1978. The bottle of "Ribbon Nabolin" is Ribbon Napolin in real life, a kind of orange soda made in northern Japan since 1911. Like a lot of other things depicted in this manga, all are well-known pieces of Hokkaido culture and popular souvenirs to take home from a visit.

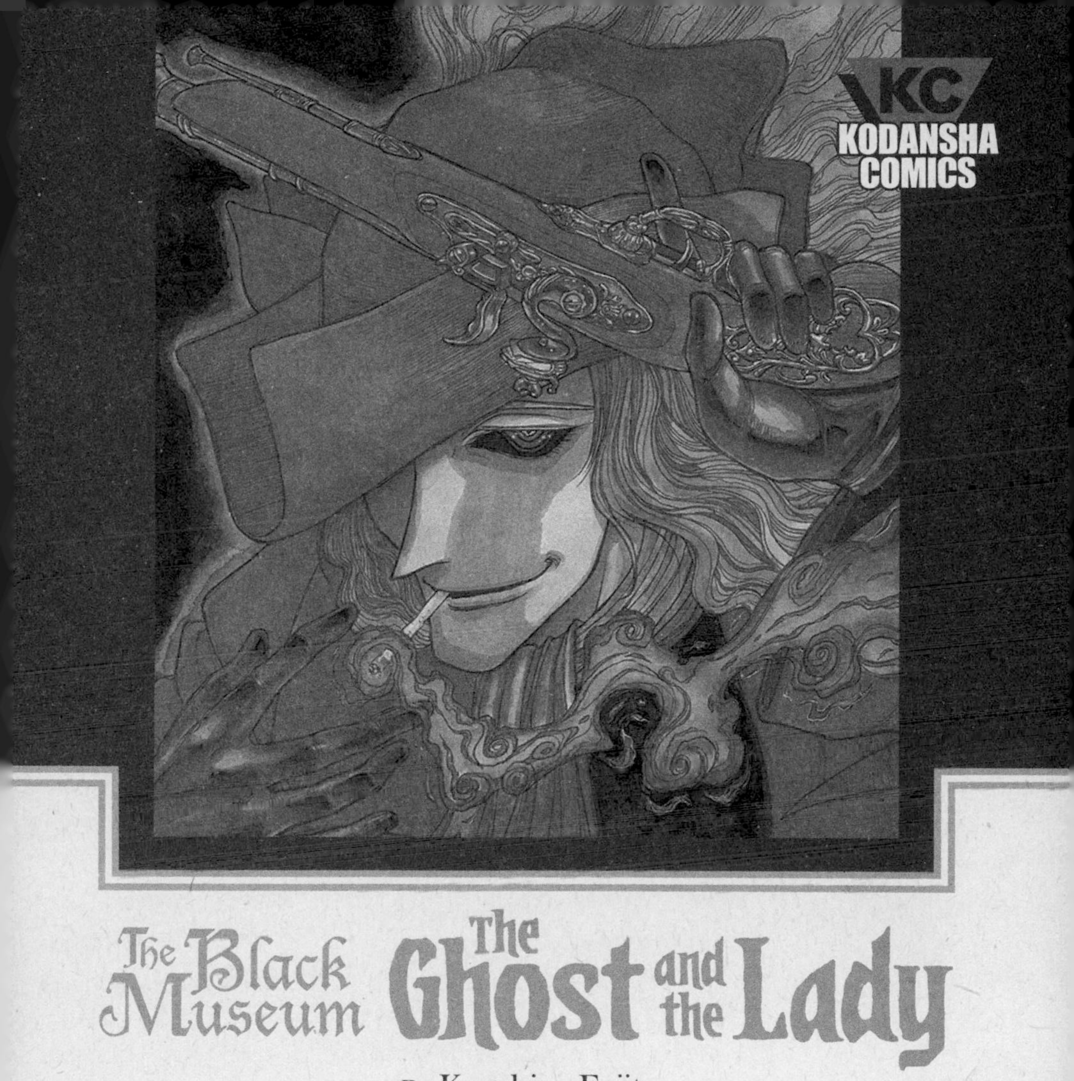
KC
KODANSHA
COMICS

The Black Museum: The Ghost and the Lady

By Kazuhiro Fujita

Deep in Scotland Yard in London sits an evidence room dedicated to the greatest mysteries of British history. In this "Black Museum" sits a misshapen hunk of lead—two bullets fused together—the key to a wartime encounter between Florence Nightingale, the mother of modern nursing, and a supernatural Man in Grey. This story is unknown to most scholars of history, but a special guest of the museum will tell the tale of The Ghost and the Lady...

Praise for Kazuhiro Fujita's *Ushio and Tora*

"A charming revival that combines a classic look with modern depth and pacing... **Essential viewing both for curmudgeons and new fans alike.**" — Anime News Network

"**GREAT!** The first episode of Ushio and Tora captures the essence of '90s anime." — IGN

KC
KODANSHA
COMICS

Japan's most powerful spirit medium delves into the ghost world's greatest mysteries!

Story by Kyo Shirodaira, famed author of mystery fiction and creator of *Spiral*, *Blast of Tempest*, and *The Record of a Fallen Vampire*.

Both touched by spirits called yôkai, Kotoko and Kurô have gained unique superhuman powers. But to gain her powers Kotoko has given up an eye and a leg, and Kurô's personal life is in shambles. So when Kotoko suggests they team up to deal with renegades from the spirit world, Kurô doesn't have many other choices, but Kotoko might just have a few ulterior motives...

IN/SPECTRE

STORY BY KYO SHIRODAIRA
ART BY CHASHIBA KATASE

KC KODANSHA COMICS

> *New action series from Hiroyuki Takei, creator of the classic shonen franchise Shaman King!*

In medieval Japan, a bell hanging on the collar is a sign that a cat has a master. Norachiyo's bell hangs from his katana sheath, but he is nonetheless a stray — a ronin. This one-eyed cat samurai travels across a dishonest world, cutting through pretense and deception with his blade.

STRAY CAT SAMURAI

By
Hiroyuki Takei

THE HEROIC LEGEND OF
A R S L A N

READ THE NEW SERIES FROM THE CREATOR OF FULLMETAL ALCHEMIST, HIROMU ARAKAWA! NOW A HIT TV SERIES!

"Arakawa proves to be more than up to the task of adapting Tanaka's fantasy novels and fans of historical or epic fantasy will be quite pleased with the resulting book."
-Anime News Network

ECBATANA IS BURNING!

Arslan is the young and curious prince of Pars who, despite his best efforts doesn't seem to have what it takes to be a proper king like his father. At the age of 14, Arslan goes to his first battle and loses everything as the blood-soaked mist of war gives way to scorching flames, bringing him to face the demise of his once glorious kingdom. However, it is Arslan's destiny to be a ruler, and despite the trials that face him, he must now embark on a journey to reclaim his fallen kingdom.

INUYASHIKI

A superhero like none you've ever seen, from the creator of "Gantz"!

Ichiro Inuyashiki is down on his luck. He looks much older than his 58 years, his children despise him, and his wife thinks he's a useless coward. So when he's diagnosed with stomach cancer and given three months to live, it seems the only one who'll miss him is his dog.

Then a blinding light fills the sky, and the old man is killed... only to wake up later in a body he almost recognizes as his own. Can it be that Ichiro Inuyashiki is no longer human?

Comes in extra-large editions with color pages!

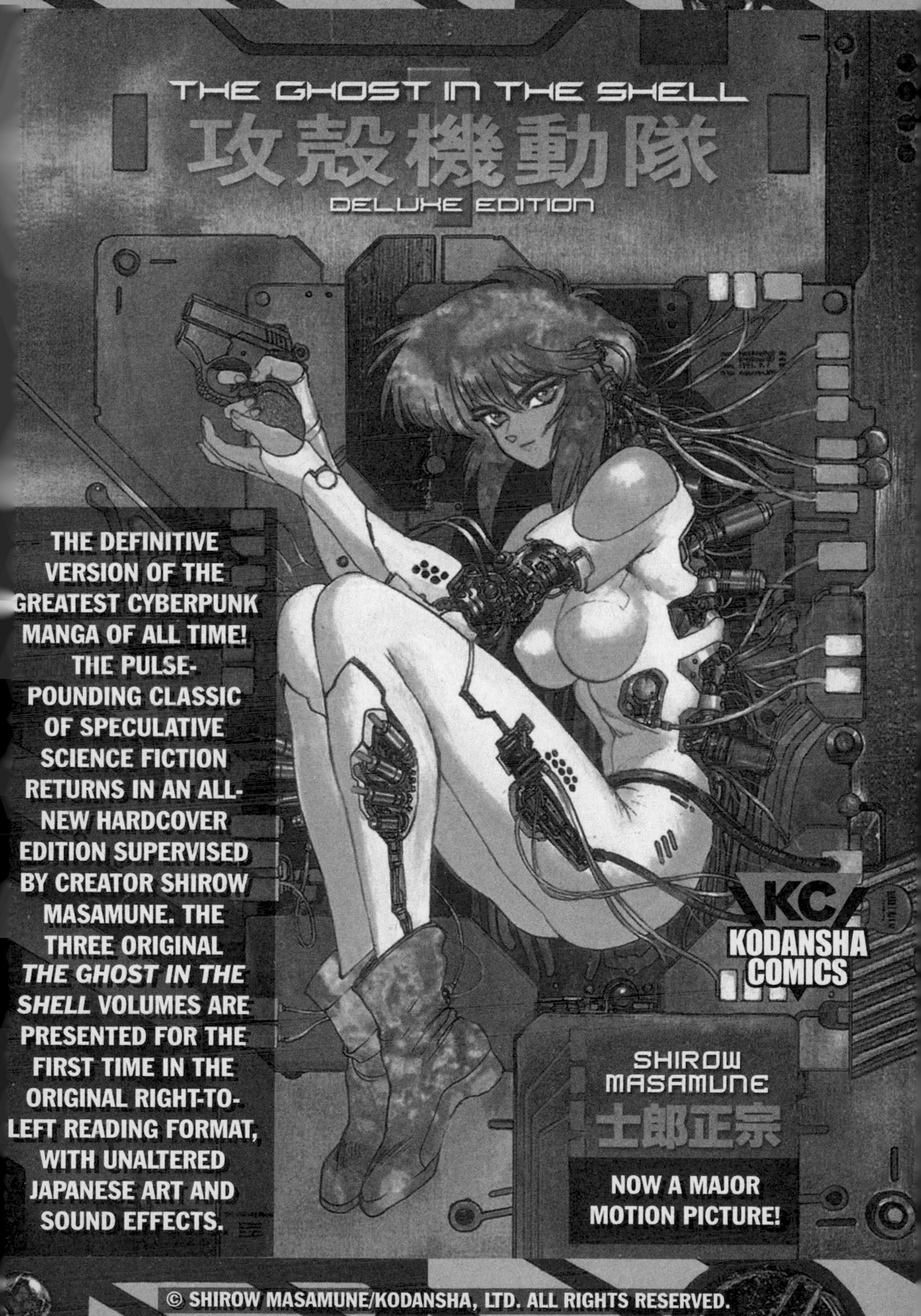

OTOMO
大友克洋

A GLOBAL TRIBUTE TO THE MIND BEHIND AKIRA

A celebration of manga legend Katsuhiro Otomo from more than 80 world-renowned fine artists and comics legends
With contributions from:
- Stan Sakai
- Tomer and Asaf Hanuka
- Sara Pichelli
- Range Murata
- Aleksi Briclot
And more!
168 pages of stunning, full-color art

DELUXE EDITION

BATTLE ANGEL ALITA

After more than a decade out of print, the original cyberpunk action classic returns in glorious 400-page hardcover deluxe editions, featuring an all-new translation, color pages, and new cover designs!

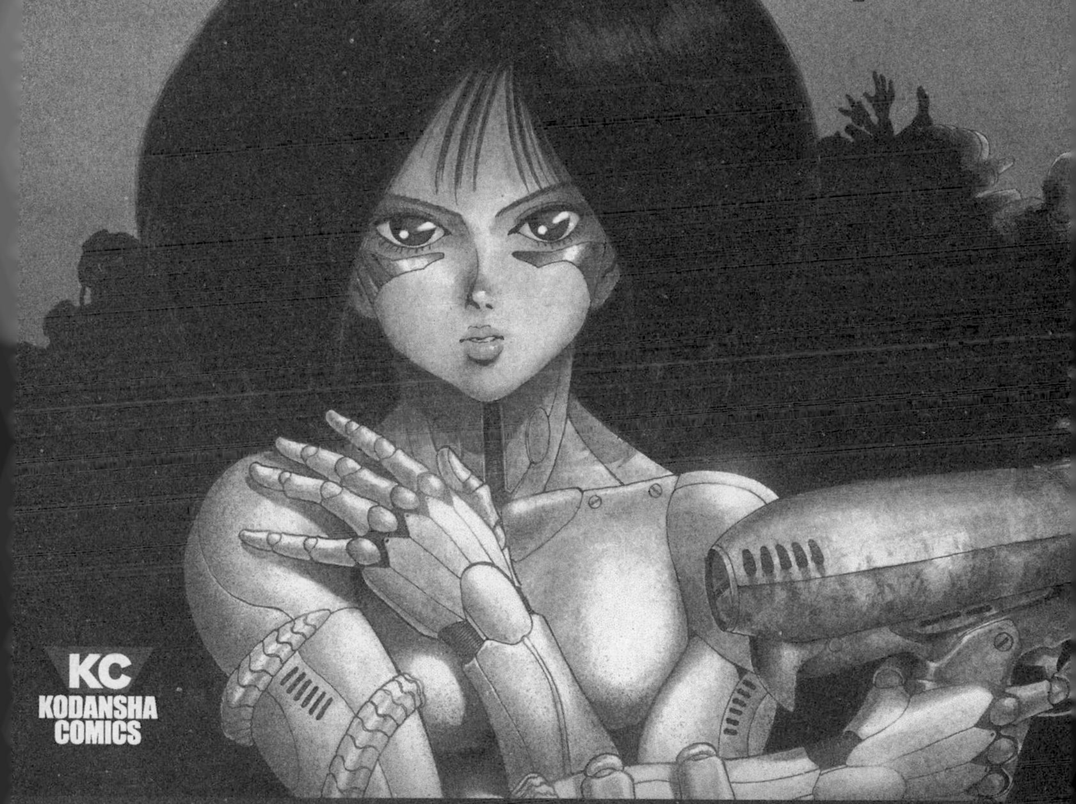
KC
KODANSHA COMICS

Far beneath the shimmering space-city of Zalem lie the trash-heaps of The Scrapyard... Here, cyber-doctor and bounty hunter Daisuke Ido finds the head and torso of an amnesiac cyborg girl. He names her Alita and vows to fill her life with beauty, but in a moment of desperation, a fragment of Alita's mysterious past awakens in her. She discovers that she possesses uncanny prowess in the legendary martial art known as panzerkunst. With her newfound skills, Alita decides to become a hunter-warrior - tracking down and taking out those who prey on the weak. But can she hold onto her humanity in the dark and gritty world of The Scrapyard?